Sixth Grade Math
with Confidence
Student Workbook
Part B

Sixth Grade Math with Confidence

Student Workbook

Part B

KATE SNOW

WELL-TRAINED MIND PRESS

Names: Snow, Kate (Teacher), author.
Title: Sixth grade math with confidence. Student workbook part B / Kate Snow.
Other titles: Student workbook part B
Description: [Charles City, Virginia] : Well-Trained Mind Press, [2026] | Series: Snow, Kate (Teacher). Math with confidence. | Interest grade level: 6. | Summary: Learn Sixth Grade Math with confidence! Use Workbooks Part A and Part B to teach and reinforce the lessons in the Sixth Grade Math with Confidence Instructor Guide. These colorful pages offer clear, step-by-step examples, varied practice with new concepts, and systematic review of previously-learned skills. Lesson activity pages include visual aids, real-world applications, and game boards to simplify your teaching. Practice pages provide written practice with new concepts. Review pages ensure students retain what what they've learned and master essential skills. Unit Wrap-Ups at the end of each unit provide review and assessment. You'll use Workbook Part A for Units 1-8, and Workbook Part B for Units 9-16.--Publisher.
Identifiers: ISBN: 9781944481940 (paperback)
Subjects: LCSH: Mathematics--Study and teaching (Elementary) | CYAC: Mathematics. | LCGFT: Problems and exercises. | BISAC: JUVENILE NONFICTION / Mathematics / Algebra. | JUVENILE NONFICTION / Mathematics / Fractions.
Classification: LCC: QA107.2 .S666 2026 | DDC: 372.7--dc23

1 2 3 4 5 6 7 8 9   Versa   31 30 29 28 27 26

Table of Contents

Author's Note

You'll need three books to teach *Sixth Grade Math with Confidence*. All three books are essential for the program.

- The Instructor Guide contains the scripted lesson plans for the entire year.
- Student Workbook Part A contains the workbook pages for the first half of the year (Units 1–8).
- Student Workbook Part B contains the workbook pages for the second half of the year (Units 9–16).

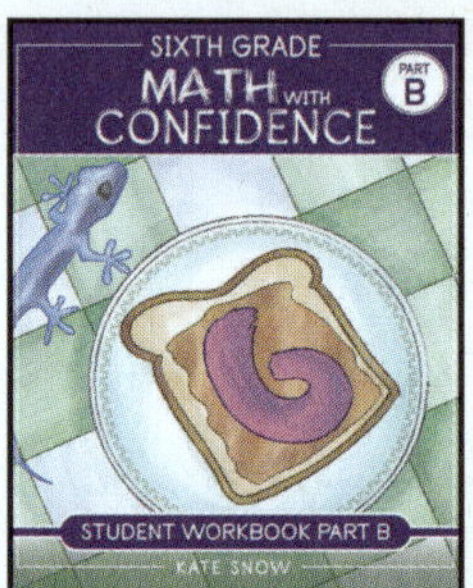

The Student Workbooks are not meant to be used as stand-alone workbooks. The hands-on teaching activities in the Instructor Guide are an essential part of the program. You'll need the directions in the Instructor Guide to guide your child through the Lesson Activities pages. The icon with two heads means that your child should complete these pages with you, and that she is not expected to complete these pages on her own.

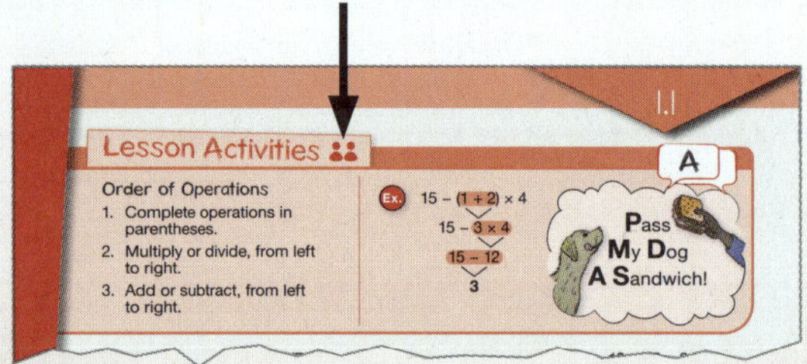

The Practice and Review pages give your child practice with new concepts and review previously-learned skills. The icon with one head means that your child may complete these pages on his own. Most sixth-graders will be able to complete these pages independently, and it's fine if your child sometimes needs a little extra support or coaching.

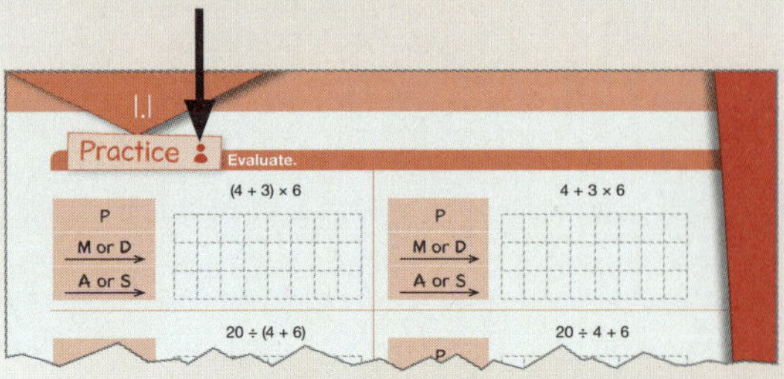

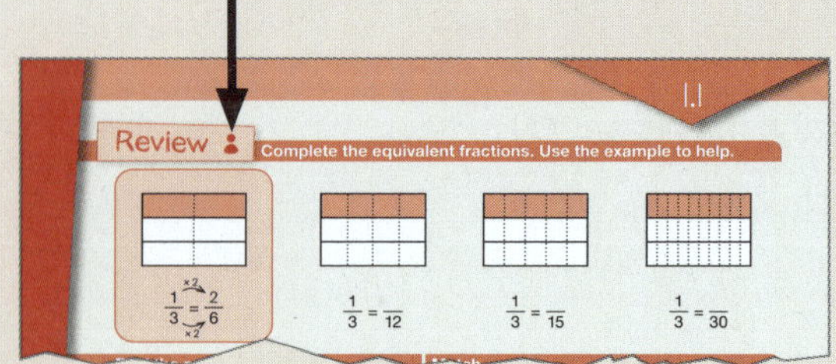

Lesson Activities

Equation Expression Inequality	$3 + 2 < 9$	$7 \times 5 + 6$	$8 = 10 - 2$

Variables and Expressions

A **variable** is a letter that stands for a number. We use variables to represent numbers that can vary or change.

An **expression** is part of a number sentence without an equals sign. When we write an expression with a variable, the expression tells what to do to the variable.

To write an expression with a variable, use words to describe what to do to the variable. Then, translate the words into mathematical symbols.

Ex. The hexagon has 6 equal sides. Write an expression that tells the perimeter of the hexagon. Use s to stand for the length of each side.

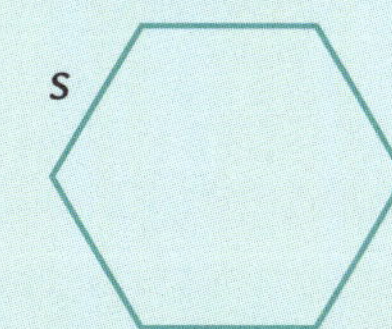

Ex. Evaluate the expression for $s = 10$. If each side is 10 cm long, what is the hexagon's perimeter?

$6 \cdot s$

$6 \cdot 10 = \textbf{60 cm}$

Describe in words how to use Caleb's age to find Veronica's age.

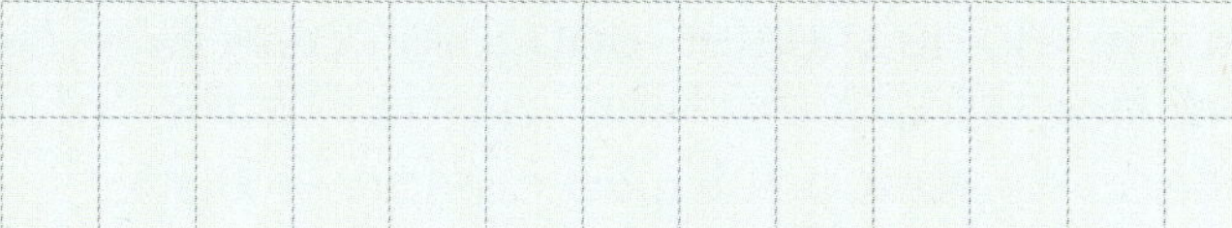

Describe in words how to find the cost to rent a bike for a certain number of hours.

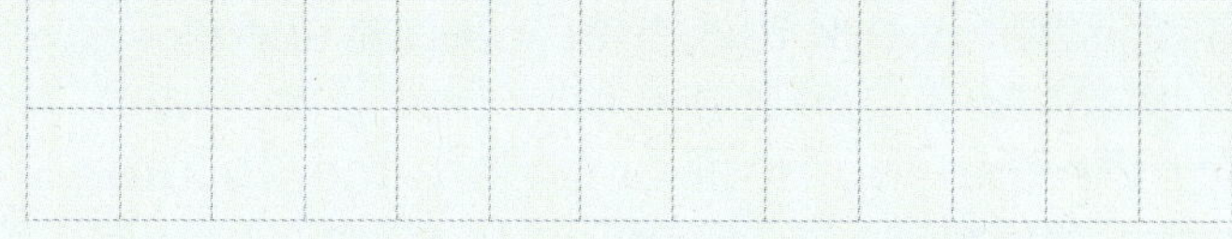

Write an expression that tells Veronica's age. Use c to stand for Caleb's age.

Write an expression that tells the total cost of renting a bike. Use h to stand for the number of hours the bike is rented.

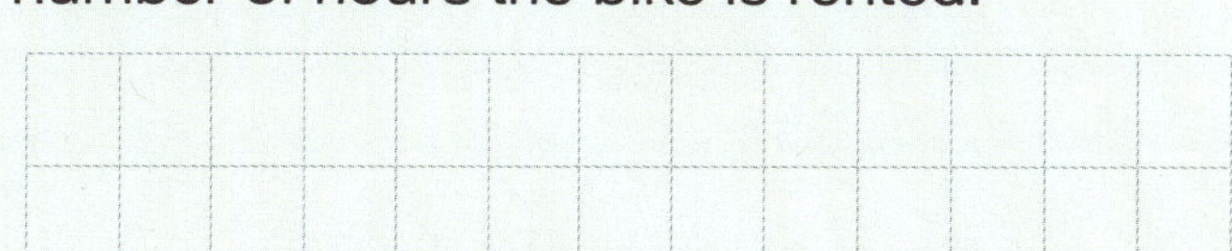

Evaluate the expression for $c = 13$. If Caleb is 13, how old is Veronica?

Evaluate the expression for $h = 4$. How much does it cost to rent a bike for 4 hours?

Practice

Write an expression to match the words. Use n to stand for the unknown number.

The sum of the number and 8	4 divided by the number	The product of 7 and the number
______________	______________	______________
The number squared	15 minus the number	The number increased by 5
______________	______________	______________
3 less than the number	The number divided by 20	10 times the number
______________	______________	______________

Complete the charts.

e	$e + 6$
1	7
2	
3	
4	

f	$3 \cdot f$
1	3
2	
3	
4	

g	g^2
1	1
2	
3	
4	

Answer the questions.

3 children work together to earn some money and split it equally. Use d to stand for the total number of dollars the children earn. Write an expression that tells how many dollars each child gets.

Evaluate the expression for $d = 60$. If the children earn $60 in all, how many dollars does each child get?

At the movie theater, popcorn costs $7 per box. Use p to stand for the number of boxes of popcorn that a customer buys. Write an expression that tells the total cost of the popcorn.

Evaluate the expression for $p = 4$. How much does it cost to buy 4 boxes of popcorn?

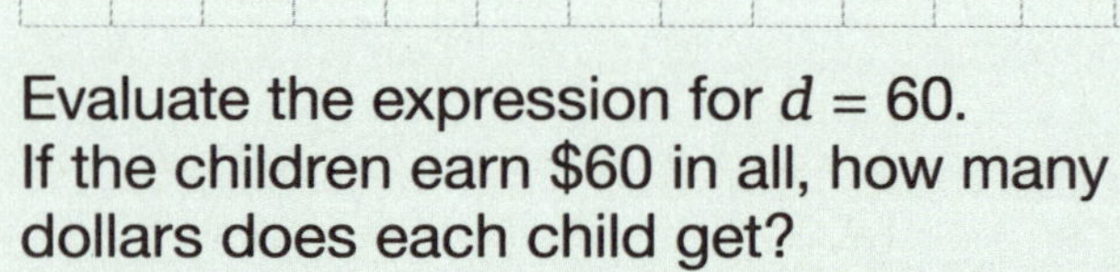

Review

Evaluate. Use cancelling where possible.

$6 \cdot 2 + 15 \div 3$

$7 \cdot (6 + 4) - 2^3$

$\dfrac{5 + 15}{5 - 3}$

Move the decimal point to find the product or quotient.

$0.298 \times 10 =$ _____________

$32.1 \times 100 =$ _____________

$4.5 \times 1,000 =$ _____________

$0.298 \div 10 =$ _____________

$32.1 \div 100 =$ _____________

$4.5 \div 1,000 =$ _____________

Find the LCM. Then, use the LCM to evaluate the expressions. Write your answers in simplest form.

LCM of 4, 5, and 2: _______

$\dfrac{3}{4} - \dfrac{3}{5} + \dfrac{1}{2}$

$\dfrac{5}{4} - \dfrac{1}{5} - \dfrac{1}{2}$

Solve. Write the equations you use.

Levi has 8 packs of candy. He shares the candy equally with his brother. If there are 23 pieces of candy in each pack, how many pieces of candy does each brother get?

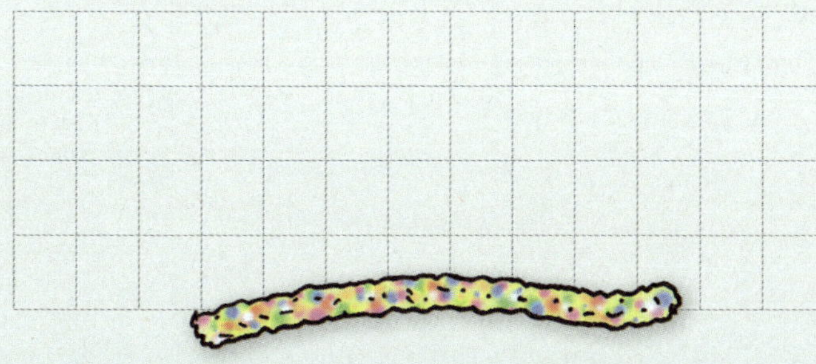

What is the area of the rectangle?

8 in.

20 in.   6 in.

Lesson Activities

$2 \cdot d$

Evaluate for $d = 15$.

$2 \cdot e + 4$

Evaluate for $e = 8$.

$3 \cdot f$

Evaluate for $f = 4$.

Coefficients

When we multiply a number by a variable, the number is called the variable's coefficient.

We don't usually use the times sign (×) when we write coefficients, because it might get confused with the letter x. Instead, we use the multiplication dot or write the coefficient directly in front of the variable. All of these expressions mean "5 times g."

$$5 \times g \qquad 5 \cdot g \qquad 5g$$

Ex. What is the coefficient of h in this expression?

$$4h + 1$$

coefficient   variable

Ex. Evaluate the expression for $h = 6$.

$$4h + 1$$
$$4 \cdot 6 + 1$$
$$24 + 1$$
$$\mathbf{25}$$

Variable Roll (2-Player Game)

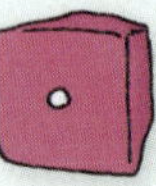

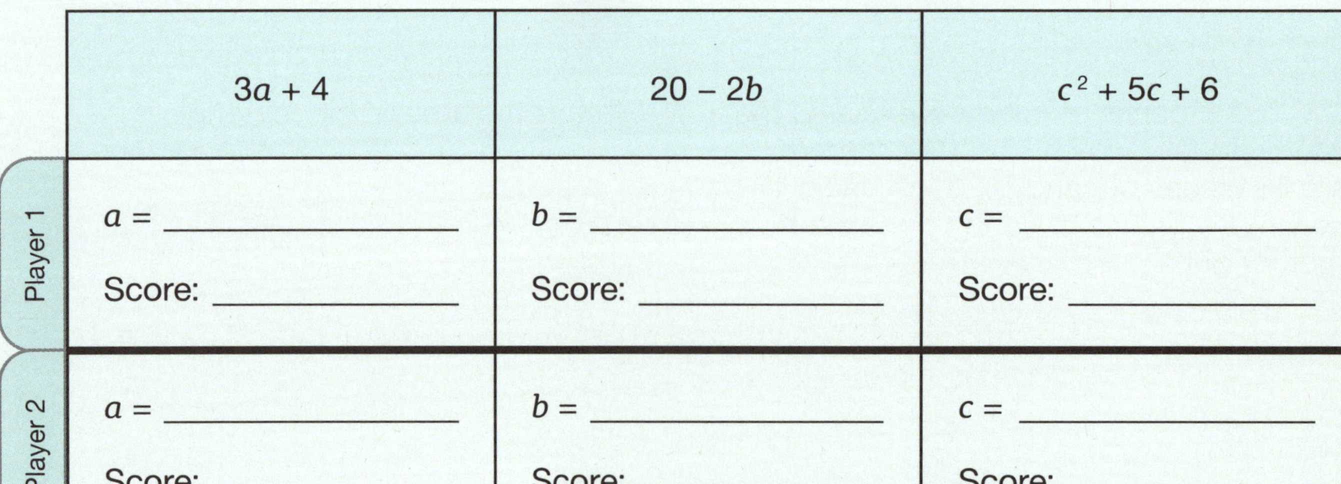

	$3a + 4$	$20 - 2b$	$c^2 + 5c + 6$
Player 1	$a =$ _________ Score: _________	$b =$ _________ Score: _________	$c =$ _________ Score: _________
Player 2	$a =$ _________ Score: _________	$b =$ _________ Score: _________	$c =$ _________ Score: _________

Practice

Complete the charts.

m	2m	2m + 1
1	2	3
2		
3		
4		
5		

n	4n	4n − 3
1	4	1
2		
3		
4		
5		

Evaluate each expression for $z = 5$. Use the order of operations.

$4z + 1$

$8z - 9$

$z^2 + 4z + 4$

$5z - 4z$

$3z + z$

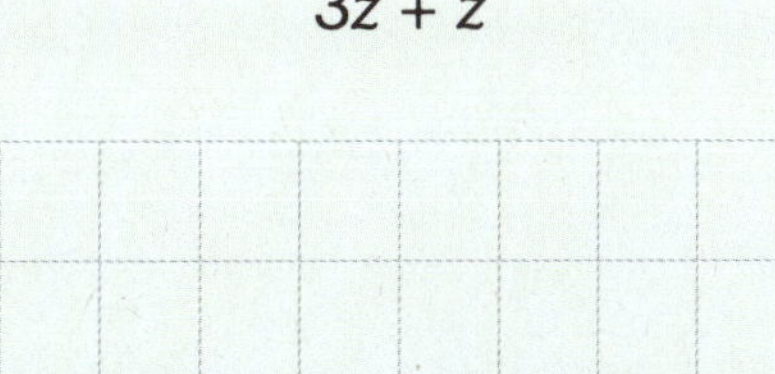

$7z + 3z + 2$

Answer the questions.

Use y to stand for the rectangle's length. Write an expression that tells the area of the rectangle.

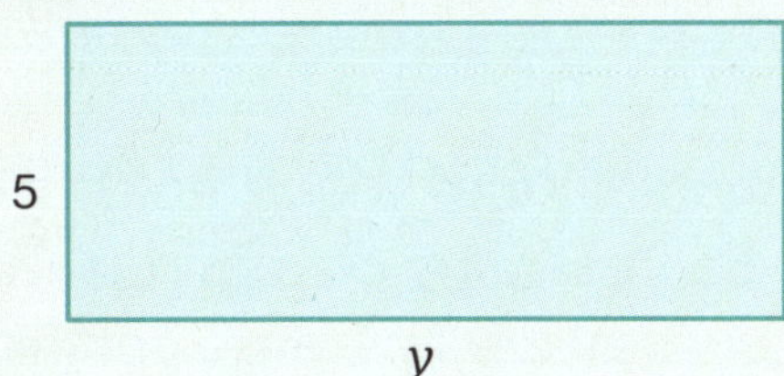

Expression: _______________________

Evaluate your expression for $y = 8$.

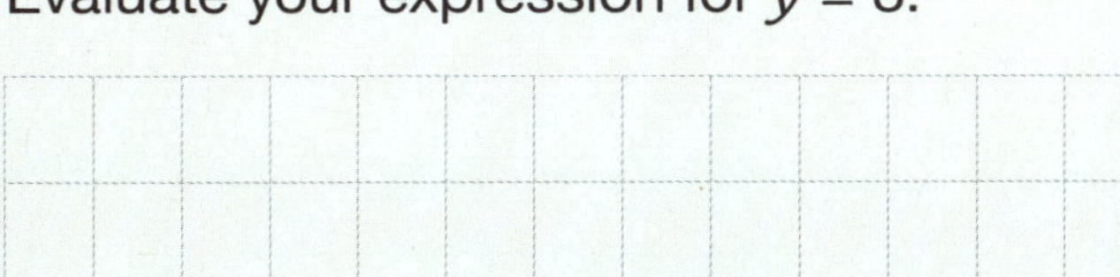

Use h to stand for the parallelogram's height. Write an expression that tells the area of the parallelogram.

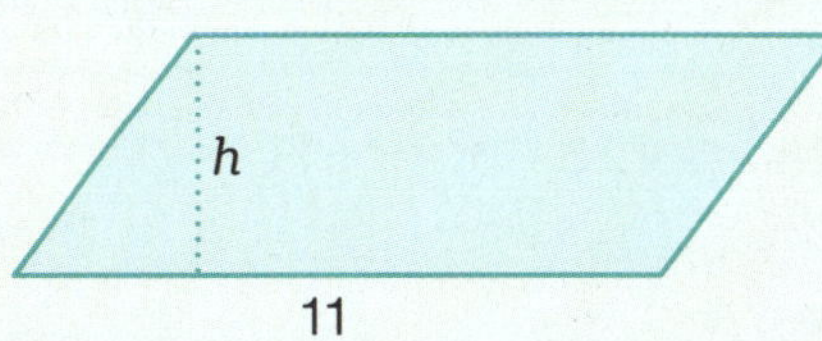

Expression: _______________________

Evaluate your expression for $h = 5$.

Review 

Evaluate.

$5 \cdot 13 \cdot 2$

$6 \cdot (30 + 1)$

$\dfrac{16 \cdot 3}{4}$

Find the products.

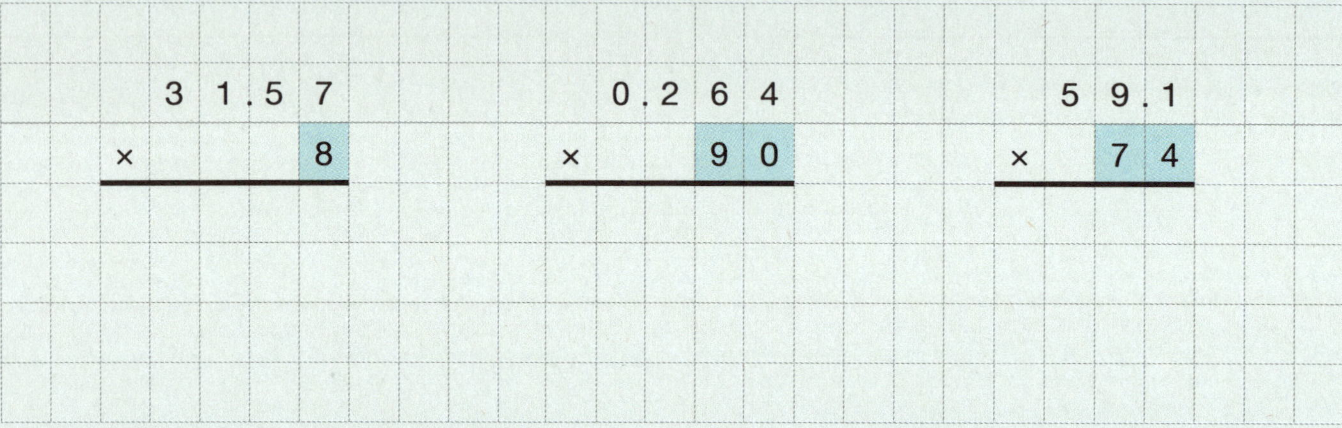

$$3\ 1\ .\ 5\ 7 \times 8$$

$$0\ .\ 2\ 6\ 4 \times 9\ 0$$

$$5\ 9\ .\ 1 \times 7\ 4$$

Rewrite each division problem as a multiplication problem and solve. Write your answers in simplest form. Convert improper fractions to mixed numbers.

$\dfrac{1}{2} \div \dfrac{1}{8} =$

$\dfrac{1}{2} \div \dfrac{3}{8} =$

$\dfrac{1}{2} \div \dfrac{7}{8} =$

Solve. Write the equations you use.

Each small container holds $\dfrac{3}{4}$ c. of yogurt. How many cups of yogurt are in 6 small containers?

A large container of yogurt holds 4 c. of yogurt. Each serving of yogurt is $\dfrac{3}{4}$ c. How many servings are in a large container?

Lesson Activities 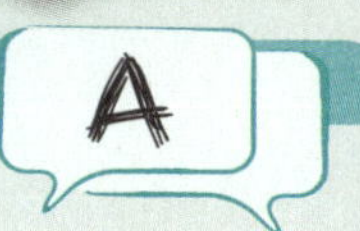

$$2m + 3 + m + 1$$

A

Evaluate the expression for $m = 20$.

B

Terms and Constants

The **terms** of an expression are the parts that are added or subtracted together.

Terms without variables are called **constants**, because they stay constant and don't change.

Like terms are terms that are like each other.

- Terms with the same variable are like terms.
- Constants are like terms.

Ex. How many terms are in this expression? How many constants?

$$2m + 3 + m + 1 \qquad 2m + 3 + m + 1$$

4 terms   2 constants

Ex. Identify the like terms in this expression.

$$2m + 3 + m + 1$$

2m and m both have the same variable, so they are like terms.

3 and 1 are both constants, so they are like terms.

Combine Like Terms

To simplify expressions, combine the like terms.

If two terms have the same variable, add or subtract their coefficients. (If a variable doesn't have a coefficient, we think of its coefficient as 1.)

If two terms are constants, add or subtract the constants.

Ex. Simplify the expression.

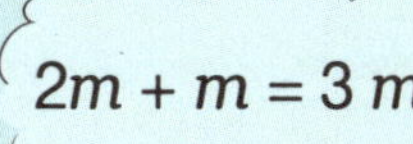
$$2m + 3 + m + 1$$
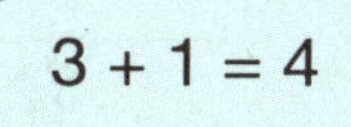

$2m + m = 3m$ $\qquad$ $3 + 1 = 4$

$$3m + 4$$

$$2m + 3m$$

$$4m - m$$

$$2 + m + 3$$

Four in a Row (2-Player Game)

$x + x + x$	$4x + 5$	$5x - 3x + 4$	$6x$
$x + 9$	$x + 6x$	$9x$	$2 + 3 + 4x$
$7x - 2x$	$8x$	$8x - 2x$	$2x + 4$
$7x$	$10x - x$	$2x + 1$	$x + 7 + 2$
$2x + 5 - 4$	$3x$	$x + 7x$	$5x$

Practice

Circle the expressions that are equivalent to the expression in the star.

$3a + 2a$	$8b - 5b$	$2y + 5 + 3$	$5d - 2d + 10$
$3 \cdot 2a$	$2b + 1$	$y + y + 3 + 3$	$3d + d + 10$
$5 + a$	$b + b + b + b$	$2 + y + 6$	$4d + 7 + 3$
$a + a + a + a + a$	$4b - b$	$3y - y + 6$	$2d + 5 + 2d + 5$

Answer the questions. Write your expressions in simplest form.

Quinn makes a rectangular banner. The banner is 20 cm wide and g cm long. Write an expression that tells the banner's perimeter.

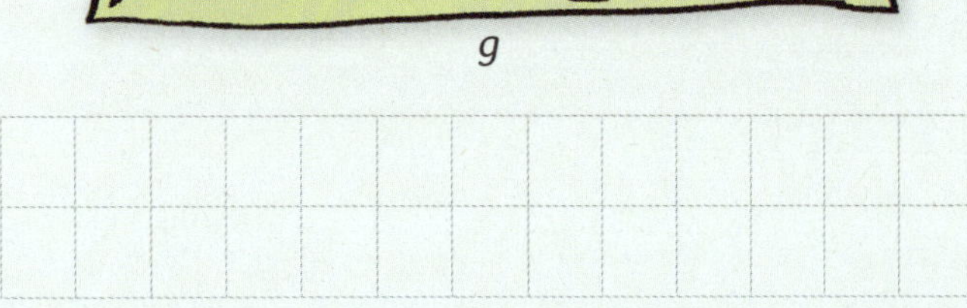

Greg glues together 3 identical wood panels. Each panel is m inches long. Then, he adds a 2-inch border on either end. Write an expression that tells the total length.

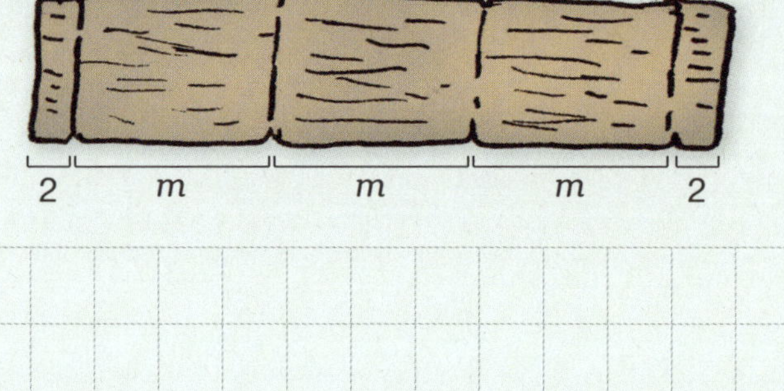

Review

Write the decimal equivalent for each fraction. Then, write <, >, or = in the circles.

$\frac{1}{2} =$ __________	$\frac{1}{5} =$ __________	$\frac{3}{5} =$ __________
$\frac{1}{4} =$ __________	$\frac{2}{5} =$ __________	$\frac{4}{5} =$ __________
$\frac{3}{4} =$ __________		

$1\frac{1}{2}$ ◯ 1.6	$2\frac{1}{4}$ ◯ 2.097	$4\frac{3}{4}$ ◯ 4.6
$3\frac{2}{5}$ ◯ 3.517	$5\frac{4}{5}$ ◯ 5.8	$7\frac{3}{5}$ ◯ 7.6001

Find the product. Write your answers in simplest form. Convert improper fractions to mixed numbers.

$\frac{3}{15} \times \frac{5}{6} =$	$\frac{8}{2} \times \frac{6}{10} =$	$\frac{9}{8} \times \frac{8}{7} =$

Solve. Write the equations you use in the work space.

Lucy's family picks 11.7 kg of blueberries. They want to divide the blueberries into 8 equal bags to freeze. How many kilograms of blueberries should they put in each bag? Write your answer with 2 decimal digits.

Ian received the following scores at the bowling tournament.

207   225
184   238

What is the sum of his scores?

What is the average of his scores? Write your answer with 1 decimal digit.

WORK SPACE

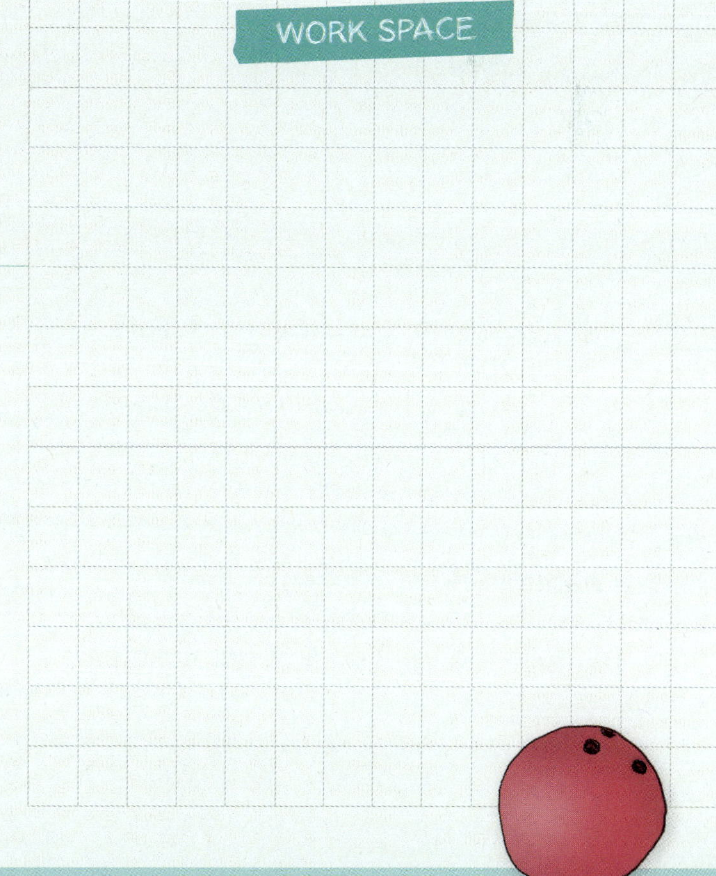

Lesson Activities 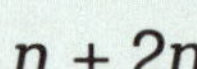

$n + 2n$	$n + 3 + 2$	$n + 4$	$3n - 2n$

Use Multiplication Properties to Simplify Expressions

When we multiply a number by an expression in parentheses, we sometimes write the number directly in front of the parentheses. To simplify an expression with parentheses, remove the parentheses and write it in the simplest way possible.

Ex. Use the distributive property to simplify $3(n + 4)$.

$3(n + 4)$

$3n + 3 \cdot 4$

$3n + 12$

Ex. Use the associative property to simplify $3(2z)$.

We can multiply in any order without changing the product. So, we can multiply $3 \cdot 2$ first.

$3(2z)$

$6z$

$6(n + 1)$	$6(2n)$	$6(2n + 1)$

Each ticket to the concert costs d dollars, plus an additional \$4 service fee. Write an expression that tells the cost of one ticket.

Selena wants to buy 5 tickets to the concert. Write an expression (in simplest form) that tells the total cost of her tickets.

Use your expression to complete the chart.

Ticket Type	Cost per Ticket	Selena's Total Cost
VIP	\$100	
Reserved	\$60	
General admission	\$30	

Practice 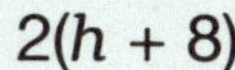 Simplify each expression.

2(h + 8)	3(h + 8)	4(h + 8)

2(3w + 1)	3(3w + 1)	4(3w + 1)

Circle the expressions that are equivalent to the expressions in the star.

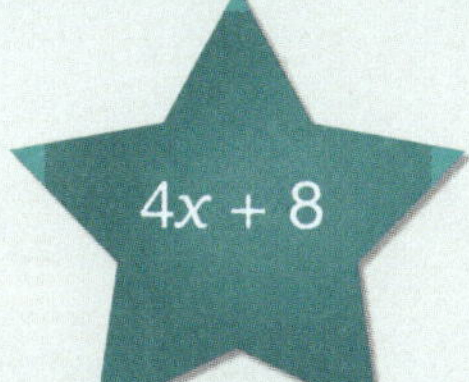 4x + 8	 10x + 15	 6x + 12
2(x + 4)	5(x + 3)	4(2x + 3)
2(2x + 2)	2(5x + 3)	2(3x + 6)
4(x + 2)	5(2x + 3)	3(2x + 4)
4(2x + 2)	3(5x + 5)	6(x + 2)

Answer the questions. Write your expressions in simplest form.

Mary Anne's family is planning a new garden bed that will have both flowers and vegetables. They haven't yet decided on the length of the flower bed.

6 ft. 

a 5 ft.

Use the diagram to write an expression that tells the total length of the garden.

Write an expression that tells the area of the whole garden.

Evaluate your expression for $a = 10$. If the flower bed is 10 ft. long, what is the total area of the garden?

Review 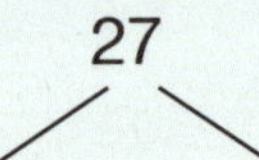

Use a factor tree to find the prime factorization for each number. (Write the prime factors in order from least to greatest.) Then, find the GCF.

27

81

Prime Factorizations

27 = ______________________

81 = ______________________

What is the GCF of 27 and 81?

Find the missing numbers in the equations.

______ = 90 + 6	______ = 85 − 2	______ = 9 × 7	______ = 64 ÷ 8
60 = 20 + ______	75 = 100 − ______	32 = ______ × 8	20 = ______ ÷ 5

Find the perimeter and area of the triangle.

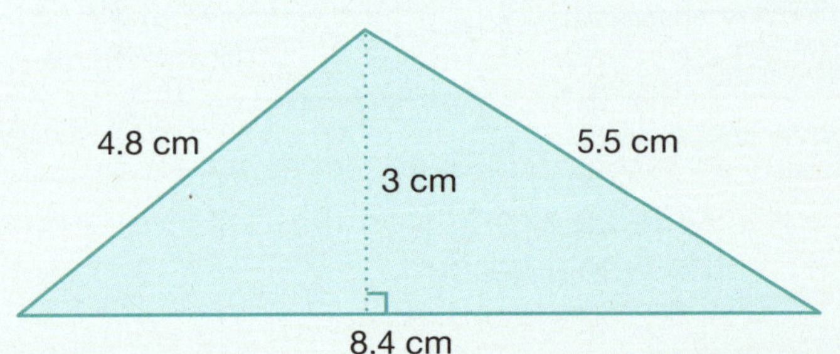

Perimeter: ________________   Area: ________________

Circle the numbers that are prime. X the numbers that are not prime.

1	2	3	4	5	6	7	8	9	10
11	12	13	14	15	16	17	18	19	20

Lesson Activities

3s + 2t
2t
3s

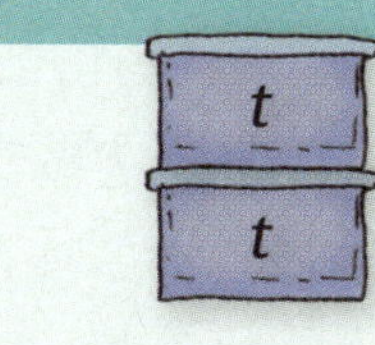 

Expressions with Two Variables

If there is more than one variable in an expression, we use a different letter for each variable.

Terms with the same variable are like terms. To simplify expressions with more than one variable, we combine like terms.

 **Ex.** Write an expression for the perimeter of a rectangle with length l and width w.

$$l + w + l + w$$
$$2l + 2w$$

w

l

$3a + 4b + a + 2b$

$4x - x + 2y + 3y$

$3 + 5r + 2s + 7 + 3r$

Write an expression (in simplest terms) for the perimeter of the pentagon.

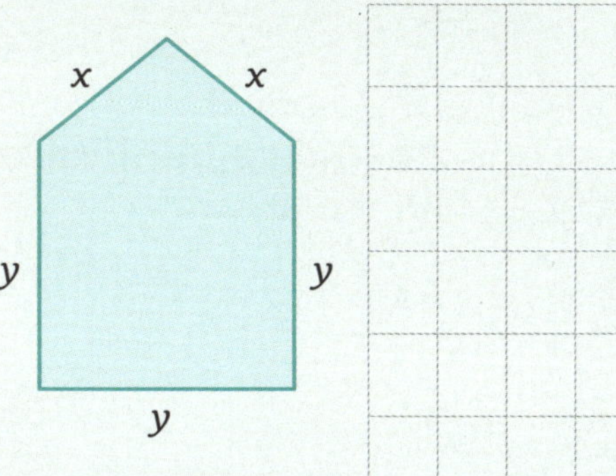

Cameron orders m T-shirts and n pairs of shorts. Each T-shirt costs \$15, and each pair of shorts costs \$20. He also pays a \$10 shipping fee. Write an expression that shows the total cost of his order.

What is the pentagon's perimeter if $x = 7$ and $y = 12$? Evaluate your expression to find the answer.

How much does Cameron pay if he buys 3 T-shirts and 2 pairs of shorts? Evaluate your expression to find the answer.

Practice

Simplify each expression.

$u + u + v + v + v$

$x + y + 3 + x + 8$

$5m + 3m + 6n - n$

$2p + 4 + 3r + p + 6$

$s + t + 6 - s$

★ $3(a + b) + 2a$

Complete the chart.

c	d	$c + d$	$5(c + d)$
1	5	6	30
0	6		
7	3		
8	2		
15	15		

e	f	$e \cdot f$	$e \cdot f + 1$
1	3	3	4
4	0		
3	4		
6	2		
10	10		

Use the menu to answer the questions.

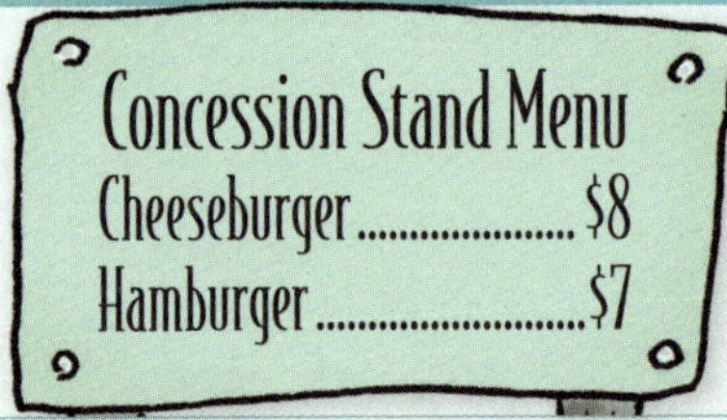

Write an expression that tells the total cost of an order from the concession stand. Use c to stand for the number of cheeseburgers and h to stand for the number of hamburgers in the order.

How much does it cost to buy 3 cheeseburgers and 2 hamburgers? Evaluate your expression to find the answer.

★ Ana's family paid $23 for their order. How many cheeseburgers and how many hamburgers did they buy?

Review   Match.

The sum of x, 3, and 8		$\dfrac{3x}{8}$
3 times x, plus 8		$3x + 8$
3 times x, divided by 8		$3(x + 8)$
3 times the quantity x plus 8		$x + 3 + 8$

Circle the fractions whose simplest form is the fraction in the star.

$\dfrac{1}{4}$ $\dfrac{2}{8}$ $\dfrac{4}{12}$ $\dfrac{4}{16}$ $\dfrac{6}{28}$ $\dfrac{20}{80}$ $\dfrac{25}{45}$

$\dfrac{1}{3}$ $\dfrac{3}{12}$ $\dfrac{3}{9}$ $\dfrac{5}{15}$ $\dfrac{3}{10}$ $\dfrac{33}{99}$ $\dfrac{25}{75}$

$\dfrac{2}{3}$ $\dfrac{6}{9}$ $\dfrac{8}{12}$ $\dfrac{9}{15}$ $\dfrac{4}{6}$ $\dfrac{15}{30}$ $\dfrac{30}{45}$

Solve. Write the equations you use in the work space.

Each bookshelf costs $139.83.
How much do 4 bookshelves cost?

WORK SPACE

What is the unit price for 1 box of cereal?
Write your answer with 2 decimal digits.

Unit Wrap-Up

Use the expression to answer the questions.

$4r + 5s + 8$	How many terms are in this expression?	What are the variables in this expression?
What is the constant in this expression?	What is the coefficient of r?	What is the coefficient of s?

Complete the charts.

m	$5m$	$5m + 4$
1		
2		
3		
4		
5		
6		

n	$n + 2$	$3(n + 2)$
1		
2		
3		
4		
5		
6		

Simplify each expression.

$a + 4 + 2a + a + 2$

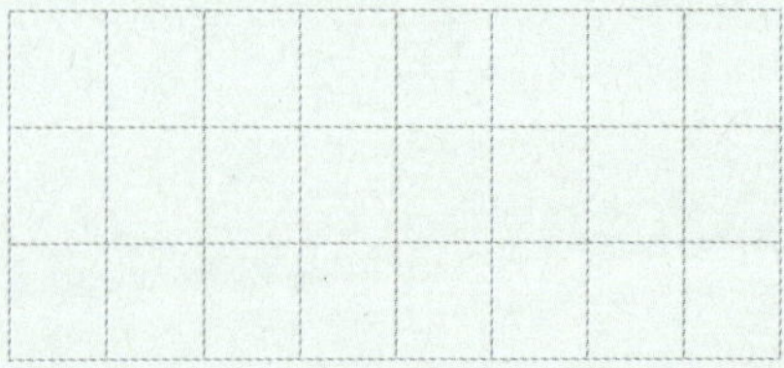

$7b - 2b + 6$

$x + y + 4 + y + 1$

$3(7w)$

$4(z + 5)$

$5(3c + 6)$

Unit Wrap-Up

Evaluate each expression for $t = 10$. Use the order of operations.

$3t - 4 \cdot 5$

$$\dfrac{34 + 6}{t}$$

$t^2 - 3t + 7$

Answer the questions. Write your expressions in simplest form.

Write an expression for the total length of the line.

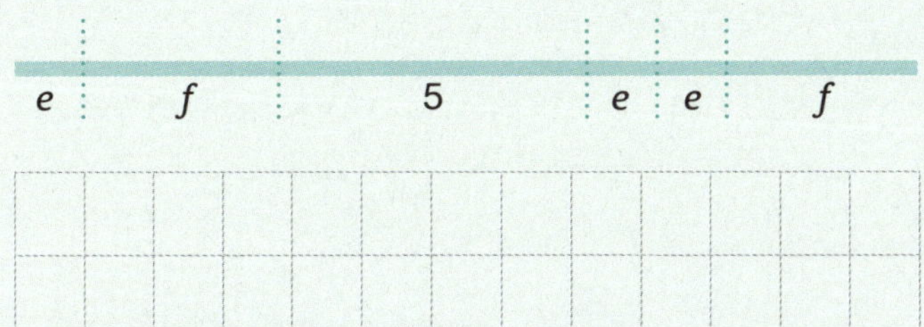

How long is the line if $e = 2$ and $f = 4$? Evaluate your expression to find the answer.

Write an expression that tells the total area of the rectangle.

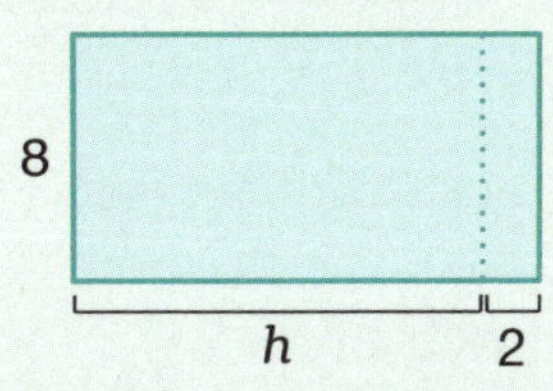

What is the area of the rectangle if $h = 10$?

What is the area of the rectangle if $h = 12$?

Eric earns $12 per hour for shoveling snow. Write an expression that tells how much he earns for t hours of shoveling.

Eric already has $20. Write an expression that tells the total amount of money he will have after he shovels snow for t hours.

How much money will Eric have after he shovels snow for 6 hours?

Grace's family buys 2 adult tickets and 3 child tickets for the concert. They also pay a $5 service fee. Write an expression that shows the total amount they pay. Use a for the cost of each adult ticket and c for the cost of each child ticket.

Adult tickets cost $25 and child tickets cost $20. Evaluate your expression to find the total amount that Grace's family pays.

Lesson Activities

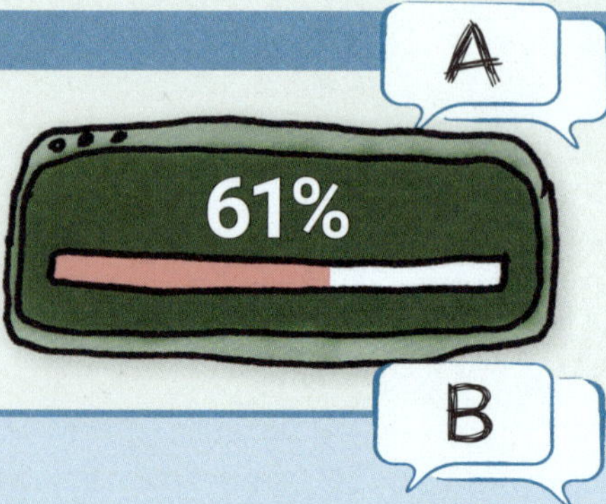

A

B

Percentages

Percent means "out of 100." We use a percentage to represent part of a whole, just like a fraction or decimal.

 **Ex.** Write 61% as a fraction.

Percent means "out of 100," so we write the percentage as the numerator and 100 as the denominator.

$$61\% = \frac{61}{100}$$

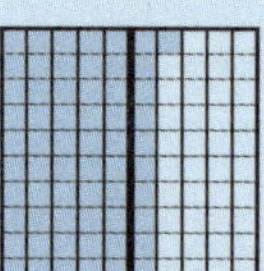

Ex. Write 25% as a decimal.

We use fractions as a bridge between percentages and decimals.

$$25\% = \frac{25}{100} = 0.25$$

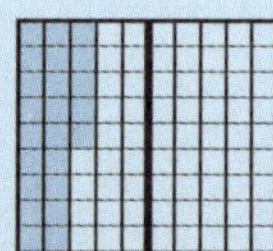

 **Ex.** Write $\frac{99}{100}$ as a percentage.

$$\frac{99}{100} = 99\%$$

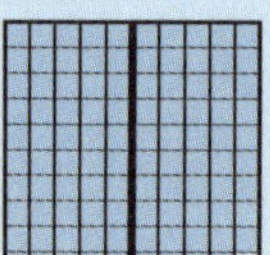

Ex. Write 0.03 as a percentage.

$$0.03 = \frac{3}{100} = 3\%$$

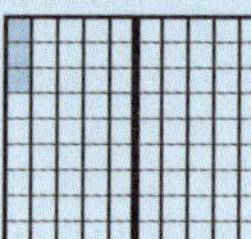

C

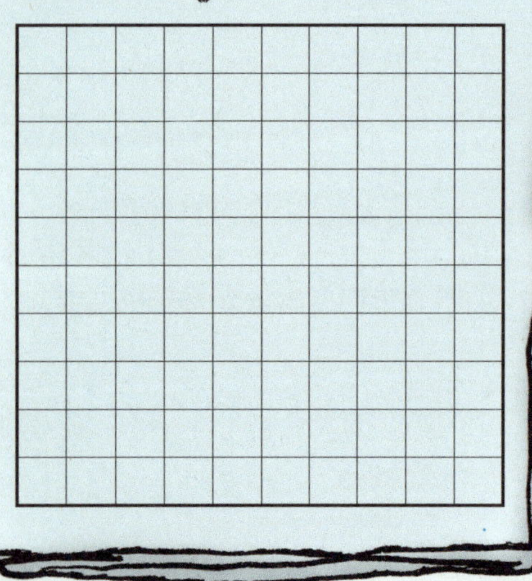

Flavor	Percent	Fraction	Decimal
Apple	32%		
Grape		$\frac{16}{100}$	
Orange		$\frac{28}{100}$	
Pineapple			0.14
Other			
Total	100%	$\frac{100}{100}$	1.00

Practice

Match.

0%	$\frac{50}{100}$	1.00
55%	$\frac{0}{100}$	0.50
100%	$\frac{100}{100}$	0.00
50%	$\frac{5}{100}$	0.05
5%	$\frac{55}{100}$	0.55

Complete the chart to match the pie graph.

What is your favorite season?

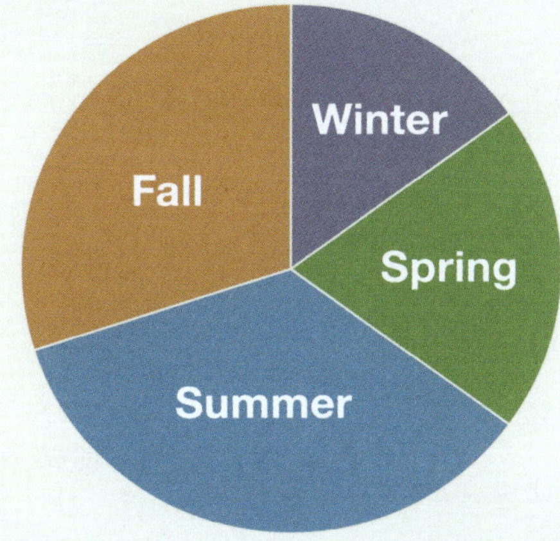

Season	Percent	Fraction	Decimal
Winter	15%		
Spring		$\frac{20}{100}$	
Summer			0.35
Fall		$\frac{30}{100}$	

Answer the questions.

Emma took a test with 100 questions. She answered 93 of the questions correctly. What fraction of the questions did she answer correctly?

What percentage of the questions did she answer correctly?

What percentage of the questions did she answer incorrectly?

Hudson is completing a training class online. The progress bar says that he has completed 79% of the class so far. What fraction of the class has he completed?

What fraction of the class does he have left to complete?

What percentage of the class does he have left to complete?

Review

Rewrite each "of" statement as a multiplication problem. Then, solve.

$\frac{9}{10}$ of 60

$\frac{7}{8}$ of 56

$\frac{4}{9}$ of 72

Rewrite each division problem as a multiplication problem and solve. Write your answers in simplest form. Convert improper fractions to mixed numbers.

$3\frac{3}{4} \div \frac{7}{8} =$

$5\frac{1}{4} \div 1\frac{1}{6} =$

$4 \div \frac{2}{3} =$

Write the word that matches each definition.

coefficient

term

variable

constant

A letter that stands for a number	A number multiplied by a variable
Part of an expression that is added or subtracted	Term with only a number and no variable part

Answer the questions.

Eli saves and spends his money in a 3:2 ratio. What fraction of his money does he save?

Layla mixes 1 part dish soap with 3 parts water to make homemade bubble solution. What fraction of the total amount is water?

Lesson Activities

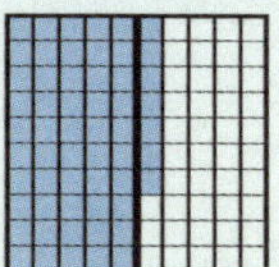 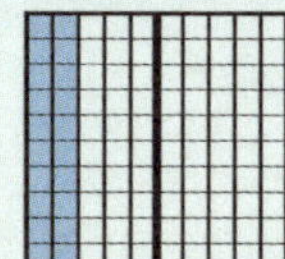 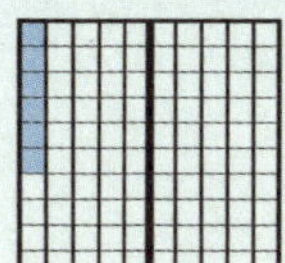 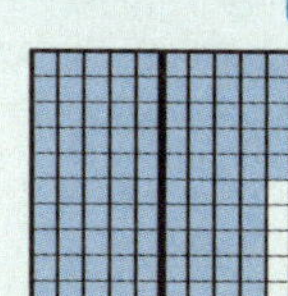

A

$57\% = \dfrac{57}{100}$ $20\% = \dfrac{}{100}$ $6\% = \dfrac{}{100}$ $95\% = \dfrac{}{100}$

$57\% = \underline{0.57}$ $20\% = \underline{}$ $6\% = \underline{}$ $95\% = \underline{}$

B

Write Fractions as Percentages

To write a fraction as a percentage, write an equivalent fraction with 100 as the denominator. Then, write the matching percentage.

Ex. $\dfrac{2}{5}$ of the children in the orchestra play the violin. What percentage of the children play the violin?

$$\dfrac{2}{5} \xrightarrow{\times 20} \dfrac{40}{100} = \mathbf{40\%}$$ (× 20)

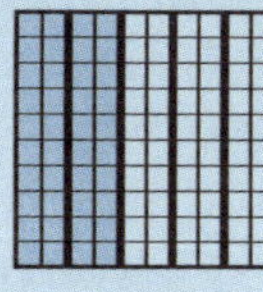

To write a percentage as a fraction, write the percentage as a fraction with 100 as the denominator. Then, simplify the fraction.

Ex. 8% of the children in the orchestra play the string bass. What fraction of the children play the string bass?

$$8\% = \dfrac{8}{100} \xrightarrow{\div 4} \dfrac{2}{25}$$ (÷ 4)

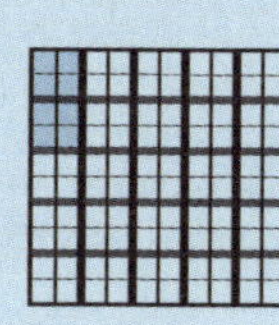

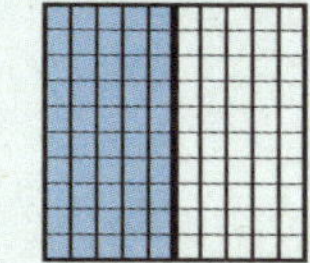 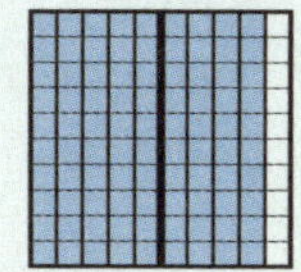 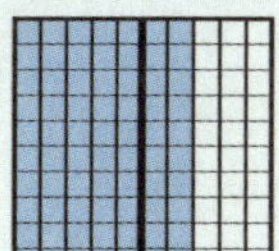 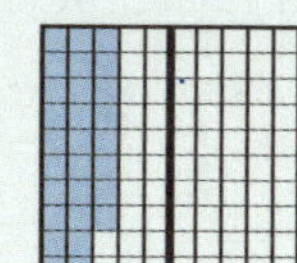

$\dfrac{1}{2} = \dfrac{}{100} = \underline{}\%$ $\dfrac{9}{10} = \dfrac{}{100} = \underline{}\%$ $70\% = \dfrac{}{100} = \dfrac{}{}$ $28\% = \dfrac{}{100} = \dfrac{}{}$

C

✱ ✱ ✱ Park Improvement Survey ✱ ✱ ✱			
What improvement would you most like to see at the park?	**Number of People**	**Fraction**	**Percent**
New swings	4		
Splash pad	9		
Pickleball court	5		
More trees	2		

Practice

**Convert the fractions to percentages.
(Use equivalent fractions as needed.)**

$\frac{1}{4} = \frac{25}{100} = 25\%$

$\frac{3}{10} =$

$\frac{9}{20} =$

$\frac{13}{50} =$

$\frac{3}{4} =$

$\frac{7}{10} =$

$\frac{11}{20} =$

$\frac{37}{50} =$

Convert the percentages to fractions. Write the fractions in simplest form.

$80\% = \frac{80}{100} = \frac{4}{5}$

$95\% =$

$32\% =$

$1\% =$

$20\% =$

$5\% =$

$68\% =$

$99\% =$

Answer the questions. Write fractions in simplest form.

The Penguins hockey team played 25 games this season. They won 18 games and lost the rest.

What fraction of the games did they win?

What fraction of the games did they lose?

What percentage of the games did they win?

What percentage of the games did they lose?

Jiang plays the piano. He has learned how to play 13 of the songs in his practice book. There are a total of 20 songs in the book.

What fraction of the songs does he know how to play?

What fraction of the songs does he have left to learn?

What percentage of the songs does he know how to play?

What percentage of the songs does he have left to learn?

Maddie earns money pet-sitting. She makes the following budget for her earnings.

What fraction of her money does she save?

What fraction of her money does she give to charity?

What fraction of her money does she spend?

Review

Simplify each expression. Then, answer the questions.

$$3y - 2y$$

What is the value of the expression if $y = 8$?

$$a + a + b + b$$

What is the value of the expression if $a = 5$ and $b = 20$?

$$c + 3 + d + c$$

What is the value of the expression if $c = 3$ and $d = 7$?

Compare with <, >, or =.

$-2.78 \bigcirc -3.94$	$5.4 \bigcirc -0.7$	$-1\frac{3}{4} \bigcirc \frac{5}{6}$	$-2\frac{2}{3} \bigcirc -4\frac{1}{5}$
$-\frac{1}{2} \bigcirc 0.65$	$2\frac{1}{4} \bigcirc 2.25$	$3\frac{3}{4} \bigcirc 3.6$	$-7\frac{1}{5} \bigcirc 7.2$

Solve. Write the equations you use.

At the track meet, Ilona threw the shotput 6.45 m. She threw the shotput 2.68 m further than Callie. How far did Callie throw the shotput?

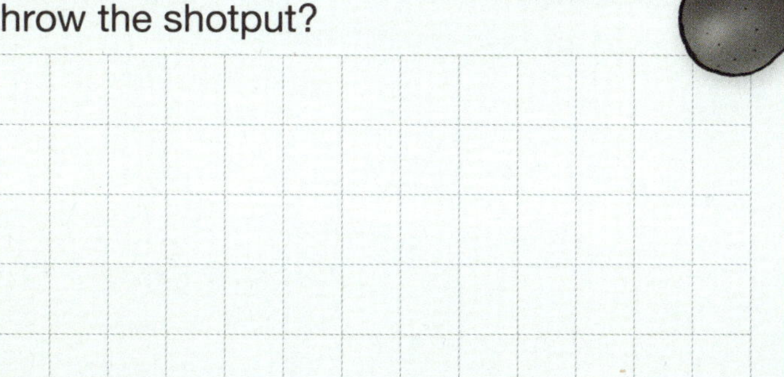

Mira threw the shotput 1.93 m. Grace threw the shotput 3 times as far as Mira did. How far did Grace throw the shotput?

Lesson Activities

A

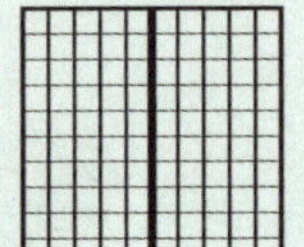 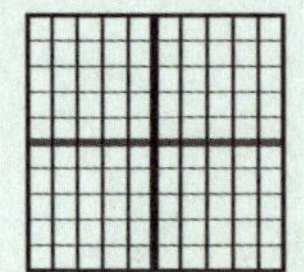 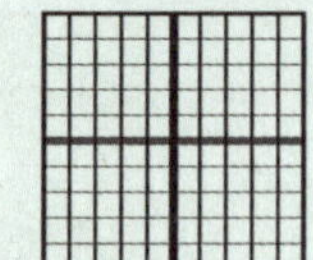 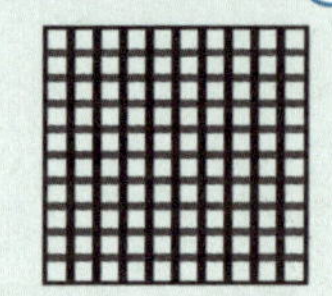

$\frac{1}{2}$ = _____ % $\frac{1}{4}$ = _____ % $\frac{3}{4}$ = _____ % $\frac{1}{100}$ = _____ %

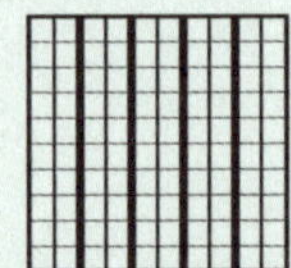

$\frac{1}{5}$ = _____ %

$\frac{2}{5}$ = _____ %

$\frac{3}{5}$ = _____ %

$\frac{4}{5}$ = _____ %

$\frac{5}{5}$ = _____ %

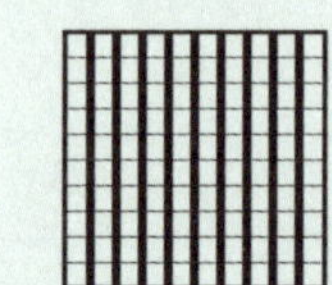

$\frac{1}{10}$ = _____ % $\frac{6}{10}$ = _____ %

$\frac{2}{10}$ = _____ % $\frac{7}{10}$ = _____ %

$\frac{3}{10}$ = _____ % $\frac{8}{10}$ = _____ %

$\frac{4}{10}$ = _____ % $\frac{9}{10}$ = _____ %

$\frac{5}{10}$ = _____ % $\frac{10}{10}$ = _____ %

B

What Percentage Equals $\frac{1}{3}$ or $\frac{2}{3}$?

If we divide a percent square into 3 equal parts, there are $33\frac{1}{3}$ small squares in each part.

$$\frac{1}{3} = 33\frac{1}{3}\%$$

$$\frac{2}{3} = 66\frac{2}{3}\%$$

We often use approximations for these percentages.

$$\frac{1}{3} \approx 33\%$$

$$\frac{2}{3} \approx 67\%$$

Ex.

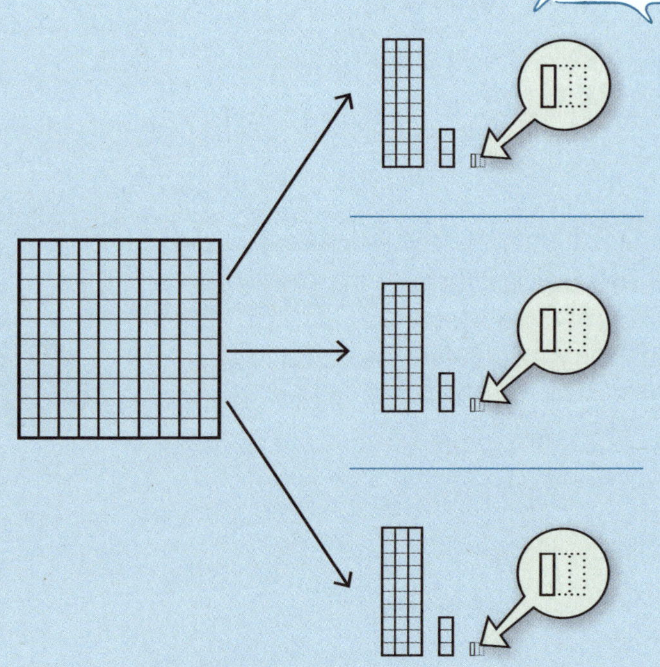

Practice 

Write the fraction that is equivalent to each percentage. You will use each fraction once.

$\frac{4}{5}$ $\frac{3}{10}$ $\frac{1}{10}$ $\frac{9}{10}$ $\frac{2}{5}$ $\frac{1}{5}$ $\frac{1}{3}$ $\frac{1}{4}$ $\frac{1}{2}$ $\frac{3}{4}$ $\frac{2}{3}$ $\frac{7}{10}$

30% =	90% =	50% =	$33\frac{1}{3}$% =
20% =	25% =	40% =	75% =
$66\frac{2}{3}$% =	80% =	10% =	70% =

Circle the percentages that match the description in the star.

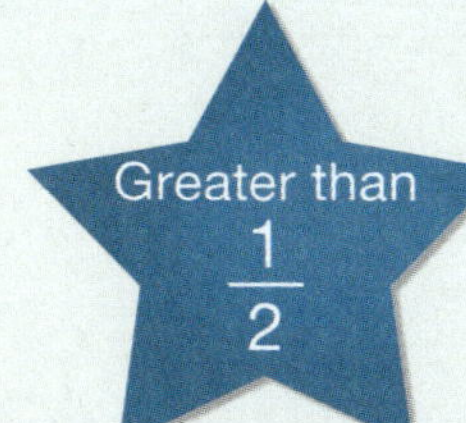

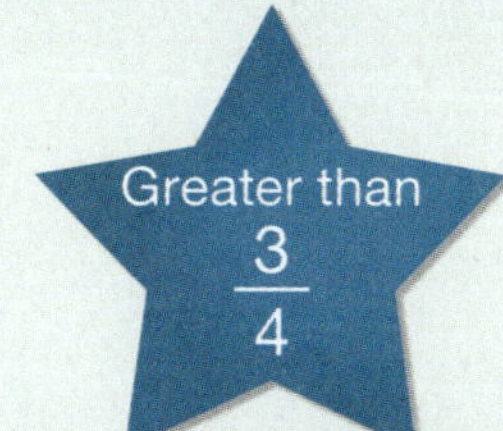

17%	40%	20%	77%
71%	51%	26%	67%
62%	35%	23%	73%
54%	92%	30%	81%
48%	87%	17%	99%

Sadie surveyed her friends about their favorite beach activity. Complete the chart to match the pie graph.

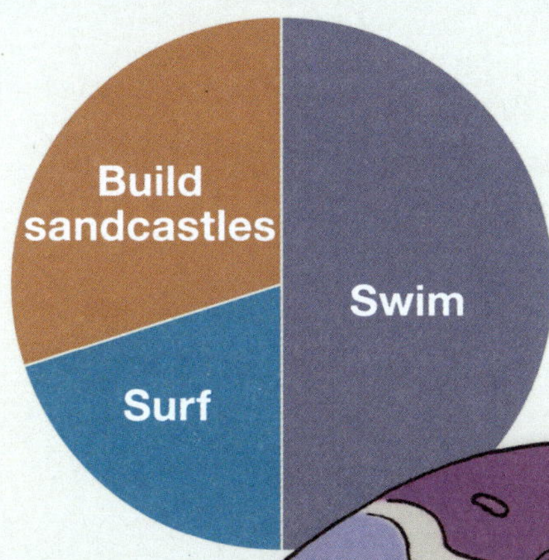

Activity	Fraction	Percent
Swim	$\frac{1}{2}$	
Build sandcastles	$\frac{3}{10}$	
Surf	$\frac{1}{5}$	

Review

Graph the points and connect them to create a quadrilateral. Then, answer the question.

(−1,3) (2,−3) (−2,−3) (−5,3)

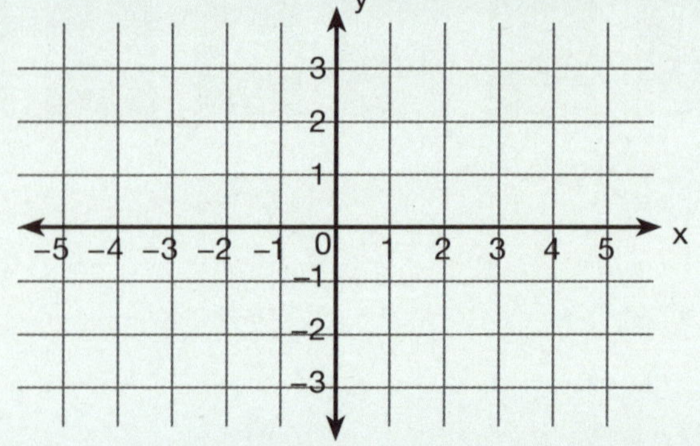

What is the area of the quadrilateral?

Use mental math to complete.

$\frac{1}{3}$ of 210 = _____________

$\frac{1}{4}$ of 800 = _____________

$\frac{1}{5}$ of 350 = _____________

$\frac{2}{3}$ of 210 = _____________

$\frac{3}{4}$ of 800 = _____________

$\frac{4}{5}$ of 350 = _____________

$\frac{1}{10}$ of 80 = _____________

$\frac{1}{10}$ of 90 = _____________

$\frac{1}{10}$ of 200 = _____________

$\frac{3}{10}$ of 80 = _____________

$\frac{7}{10}$ of 90 = _____________

$\frac{9}{10}$ of 200 = _____________

Solve. Write the equations you use. Write your answers in simplest form.

Nova has 6 boards. Each board is $4\frac{2}{3}$ ft. long. What is the total length of the boards?

Maverick makes 3 pizzas for 10 people. If each person eats the same amount of pizza, what fraction of a pizza does each person eat?

Asher makes $5\frac{1}{2}$ L of hot apple cider. He pours $\frac{1}{4}$ L into each mug. How many mugs does he fill?

Mila practices soccer for $1\frac{3}{4}$ hr. each day. How many hours does she practice soccer in 5 days?

Lesson Activities 

Find a Percentage of a Number

In math, "of" often means multiply. We can use fractions to find a percentage of a number.

1. Convert the percentage to a fraction. Use the simplest fraction possible.

2. Multiply the fraction by the number. Or, use mental math to find the fraction of the number.

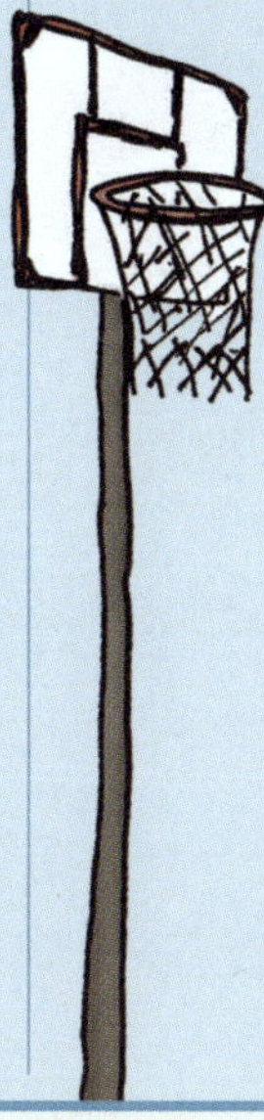

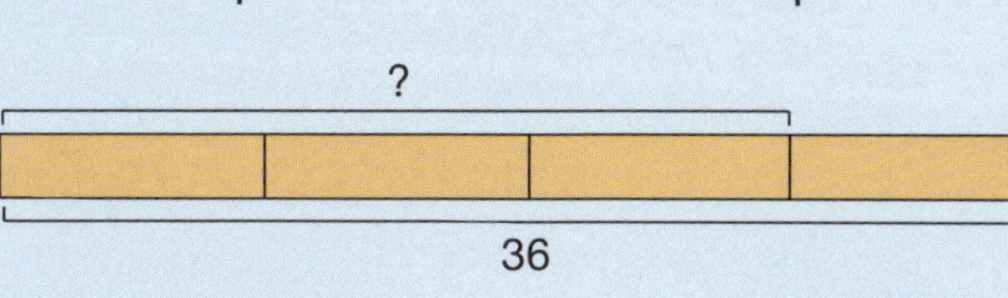

A

Ex. Caitlin tried to make 36 baskets. She made 75% of her baskets. How many baskets did she make?

$75\% = \dfrac{3}{4}$, so we want to find $\dfrac{3}{4}$ of 36.

?

36

Mental Math

$36 \div 4 = 9$

$9 \times 3 = 27$

$\dfrac{3}{4}$ of 36 = **27 baskets**

Fraction Multiplication

$\dfrac{3}{\cancel{4}_1} \times \cancel{36}^{9} = \textbf{27 baskets}$

$33\dfrac{1}{3}\%$ of 60

90% of 30

80% of 400

B

Spin a Percentage (2-Player Game)

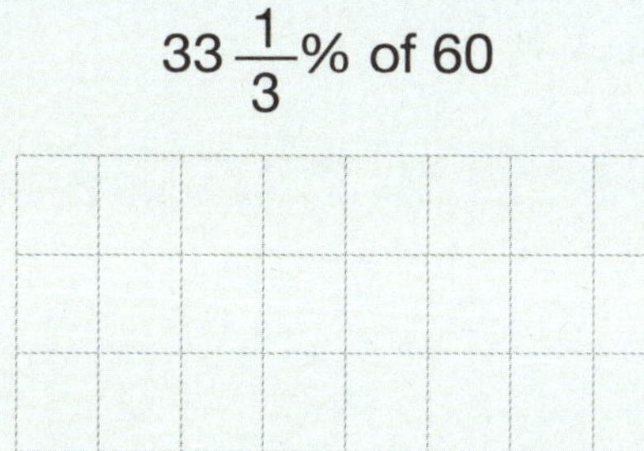

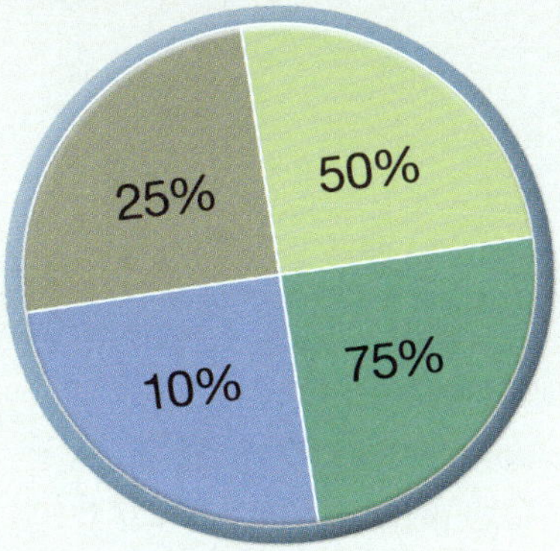

of

80	300	140	20
200	40	180	60
120	400	100	160

							Total
Player 1							
Player 2							

Practice

Write a fraction that is equivalent to each percentage. Use the simplest form possible for the fraction.

25% =	75% =	$33\frac{1}{3}\%$ =	$66\frac{2}{3}\%$ =
10% =	20% =	30% =	40% =
50% =	60% =	70% =	80% =

Use mental math to complete.

50% of 60 = __________	25% of 12 = __________	$33\frac{1}{3}\%$ of 9 = __________
50% of 100 = __________	25% of 80 = __________	$33\frac{1}{3}\%$ of 30 = __________
50% of 400 = __________	25% of 100 = __________	$33\frac{1}{3}\%$ of 45 = __________
50% of 150 = __________	25% of 200 = __________	$33\frac{1}{3}\%$ of 90 = __________

Use mental math or written equations to complete.

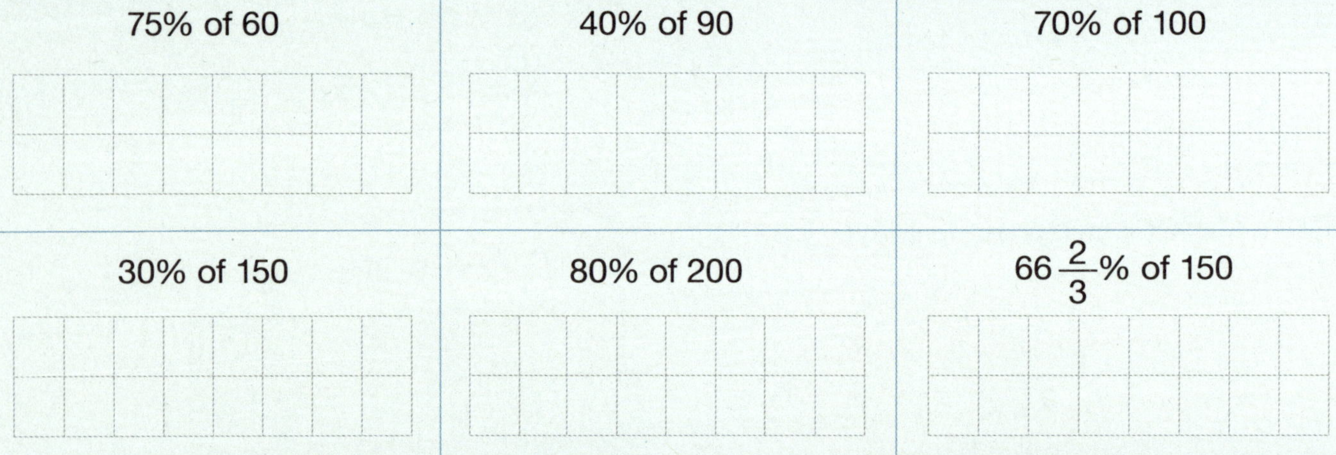

75% of 60	40% of 90	70% of 100

30% of 150	80% of 200	$66\frac{2}{3}\%$ of 150

Solve. Write the equations you use.

At batting practice, the coach pitched 30 balls to Alejandro. Alejandro hit 60% of the balls. How many balls did he hit?

 The coach pitched 24 balls to Will. Will hit the same number of balls as Alejandro. What percentage of the balls did Will hit?

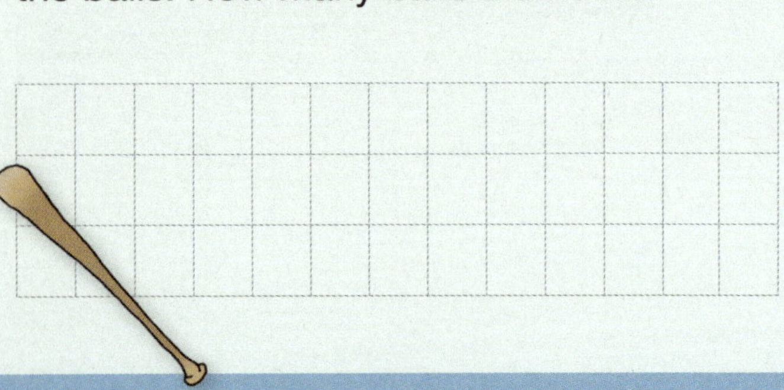

Review  

Complete the charts.

n	$n + 4$
5	
	12
32	
	104

x	$2x$
8	
	12
30	
	40

s	t	$s + t$
8	4	
10	5	
4		20
	1	100

Use the chart to complete the conversions.
(Think carefully about whether to multiply or divide.)

1 cm = 10 mm

1 m = 100 cm

1 km = 1,000 m

74.5 cm = __________ m

3.8 cm = __________ mm

999 m = __________ km

2.5 km = __________ m

Use bar models to answer the questions.

The lacrosse team's ratio of wins to losses is 3 to 2. They have won 4 more games than they have lost.

Wins

Losses

How many games has the team won?

What fraction of the games has the team won?

What fraction of the games has the team lost?

What percentage of the games has the team won?

What percentage of the games has the team lost?

Lesson Activities

A

10% of 50 = _______________   10% of 200 = _______________   10% of 380 = _______________

50 ÷ 10 = ?   200 ÷ 10 = ?   380 ÷ 10 = ?

B

Use 10% to Mentally Find Other Percentages

Ex. Dinner at the restaurant cost \$80. Taylor's mom wants to leave a 20% tip. How much money should she leave as a tip?

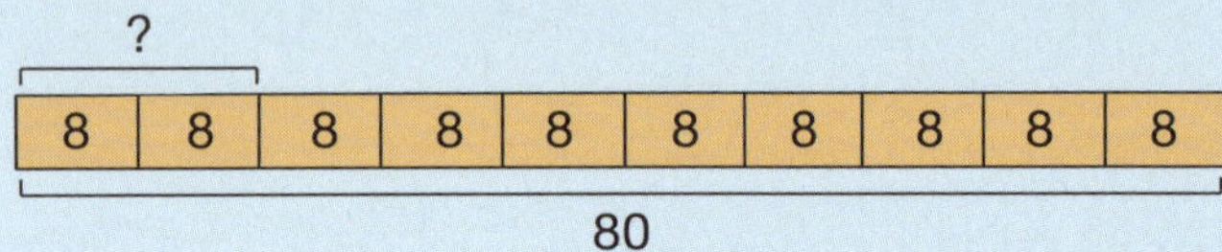

$\frac{1}{10}$ of 80 = 8 → 10% of 80 = 8

2 × 8 = 16 → 20% of 80 = **\$16**

Ex. Lunch at the restaurant cost \$40. Brendan's dad wants to leave a 15% tip. How much money should he leave as a tip?

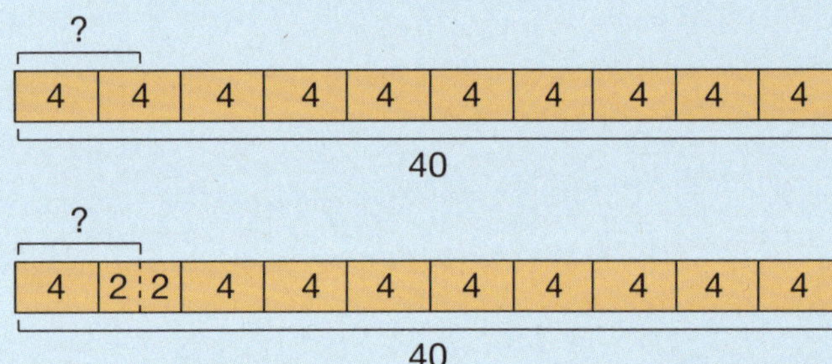

$\frac{1}{10}$ of 40 = 4 → 10% of 40 = 4

$\frac{1}{2}$ of 4 = 2 → 5% of 40 = 2

4 + 2 = 6 → 15% of 40 = **\$6**

C

Climb the Ladder (2-Player Game)

Practice

Complete.

10% of 100 = ____________

40% of 100 = ____________

70% of 100 = ____________

100% of 100 = ____________

10% of 20 = ____________

20% of 20 = ____________

30% of 20 = ____________

40% of 20 = ____________

10% of 50 = ____________

20% of 50 = ____________

50% of 50 = ____________

90% of 50 = ____________

10% of 300 = ____________

20% of 300 = ____________

40% of 300 = ____________

5% of 300 = ____________

10% of 280 = ____________

20% of 280 = ____________

5% of 280 = ____________

15% of 280 = ____________

10% of 1,000 = ____________

5% of 1,000 = ____________

90% of 1,000 = ____________

★ 95% of 1,000 = ______

Solve. Write the equations you use.

Jade's family spends $90 on a meal at a restaurant. Jade's dad wants to leave a 20% tip. How much money should he leave as a tip?

Ezekiel buys an electronics kit that costs $60. The sales tax is 5% of the price. How much is the sales tax for the kit?

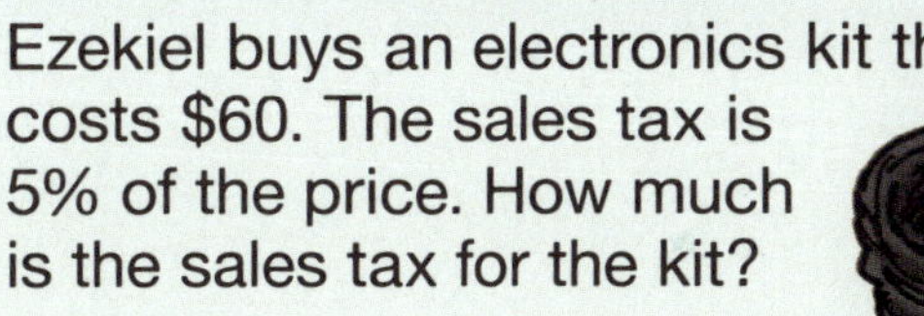

The regular price for a ticket to the amusement park is $80. Michael has a coupon for 10% off the regular price. How many dollars does he save?

The regular price for a ticket to the amusement park is $80. Emilia has a coupon for 30% off the regular price. How many dollars does she save?

What is the final price of his ticket?

What is the final price of her ticket?

Review

Complete.

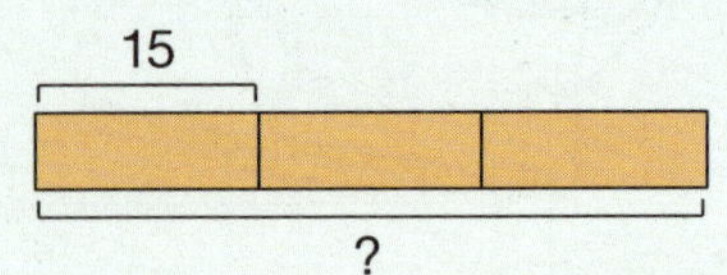

$\dfrac{1}{3}$ of __________ = 15

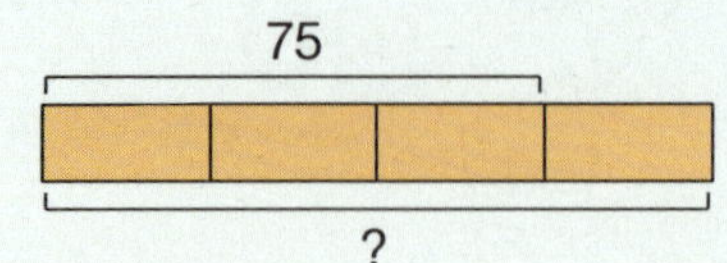

$\dfrac{3}{4}$ of __________ = 75

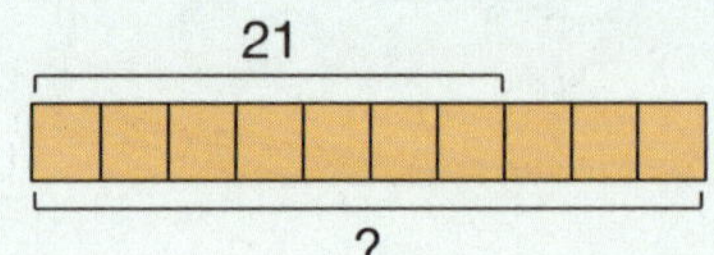

$\dfrac{7}{10}$ of __________ = 21

Find the perimeter and area of each shape. Write the equations you use.

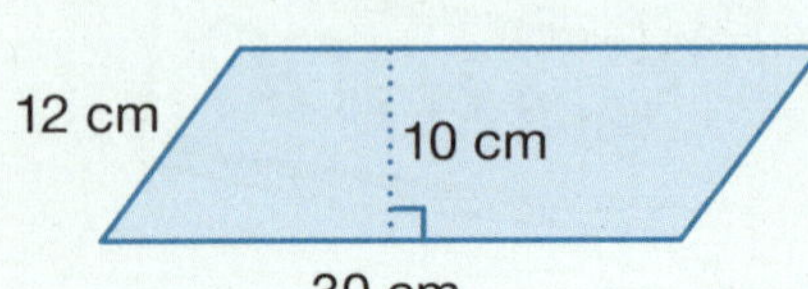

Perimeter: __________

Area: __________

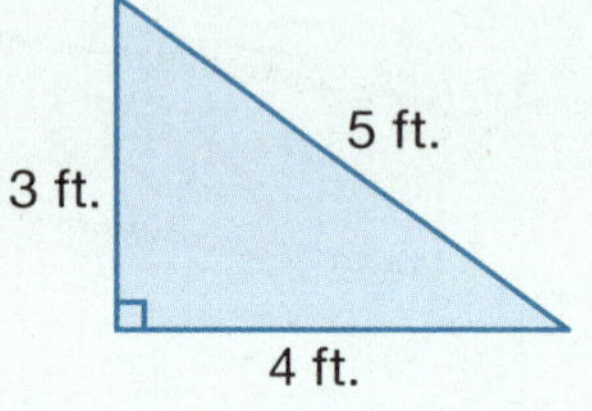

Perimeter: __________

Area: __________

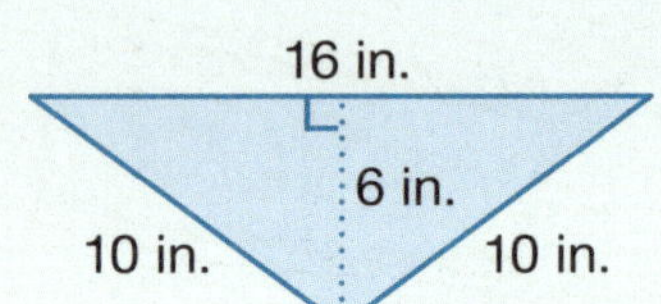

Perimeter: __________

Area: __________

Solve. Write your equations in the work space.

The bakery uses 0.54 kg of flour for each loaf of bread. How much flour do they need to bake 24 loaves of bread?

WORK SPACE

The scientist makes 1.95 L of a chemical solution. She divides it equally into 6 beakers. How much solution is in each beaker? Write your answer with 2 decimal digits.

Lesson Activities 

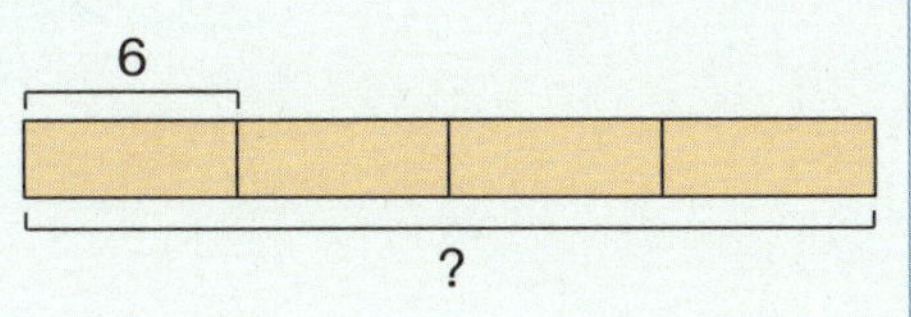
6

?

$\frac{1}{4}$ of __________ = 6

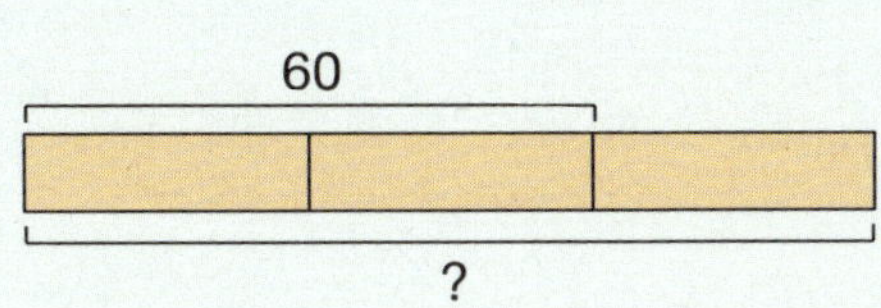
60

?

$\frac{2}{3}$ of __________ = 60

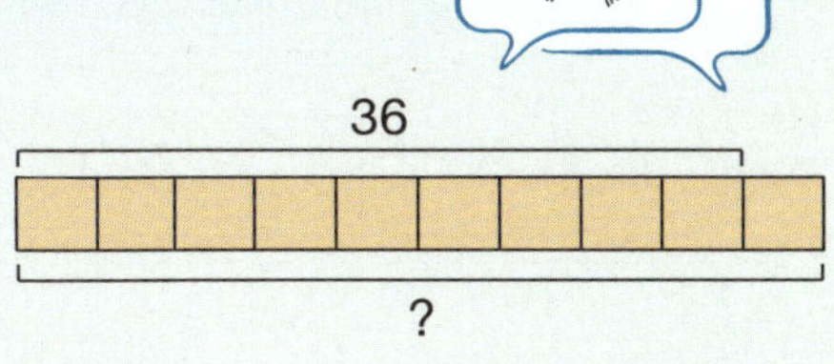
36

?

$\frac{9}{10}$ of __________ = 36

Use a Percentage to Find the Total Amount

Ex. Brynn scored 12 points at the basketball game. She scored 30% of her team's points. How many points did her team score in all?

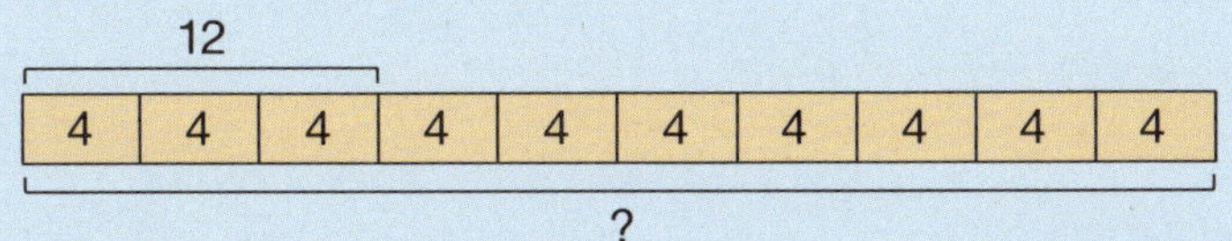
12

| 4 | 4 | 4 | 4 | 4 | 4 | 4 | 4 | 4 | 4 |

?

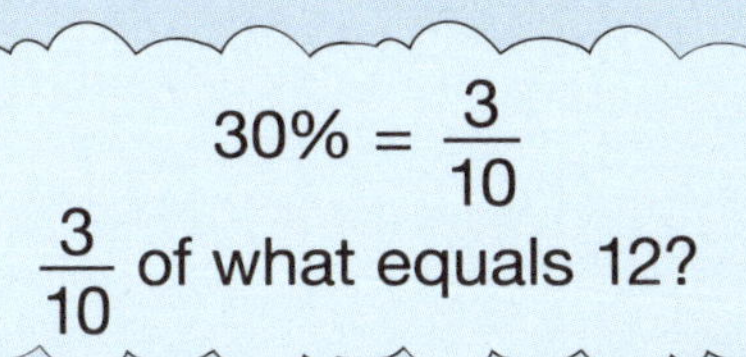

$$30\% = \frac{3}{10}$$

$\frac{3}{10}$ of what equals 12?

$12 \div 3 = 4$

$4 \times 10 = \textbf{40 points}$

In a survey, 8 people said pancakes are their favorite breakfast food. These 8 people were 40% of all the people surveyed. How many people were surveyed?

Brian has read 75% of his library book. He has read 150 pages so far. How many pages long is the book?

How many people did not choose pancakes?

How many pages does he have left to read?

Practice

Use the bar models to complete.

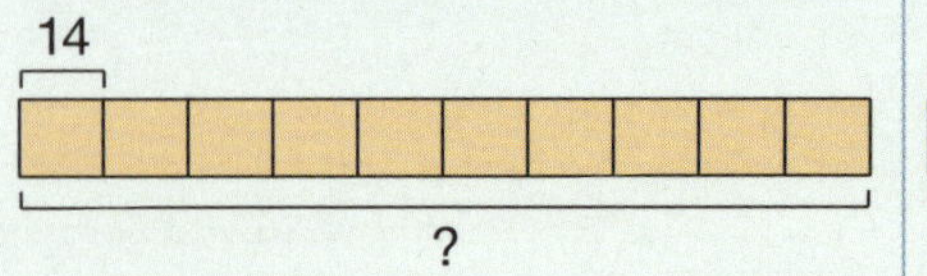

10% of _________ = 14

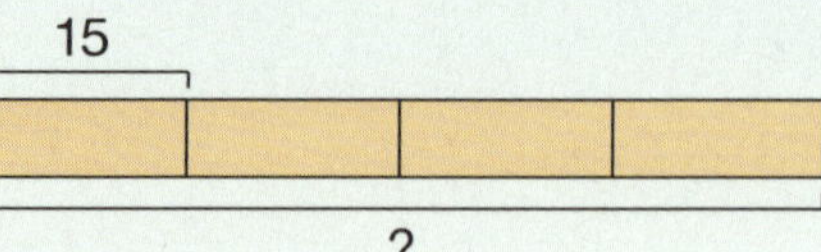

20% of _________ = 11

15

25% of _________ = 15

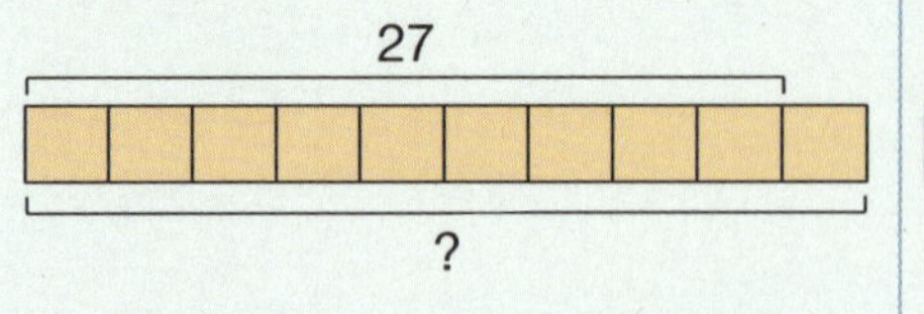

90% of _________ = 27

15

75% of _________ = 15

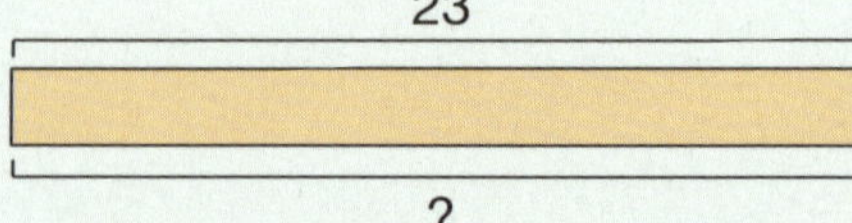

100% of _________ = 23

Use the bar models to complete. Split and label each bar to match the problem.

50% of _________ = 45

$33\frac{1}{3}$% of _________ = 40

10% of _________ = 60

60% of _________ = 90

30% of _________ = 15

$66\frac{2}{3}$% of _________ = 24

Use the bar models to complete. Split and label each bar to match the problem.

Steven helped his parents plant spring flowers. He planted 25% of the flowers, and his parents planted the rest. Steven planted 30 flowers. How many flowers did they plant in all?

Evie spent 60% of her money on a movie ticket and the rest on snacks. The movie ticket cost $9. How much did she spend in all? 

How many flowers did his parents plant?

How much did she spend on snacks?

Review   **Simplify each expression.**

$8(5t)$	$2(h + 1)$	$3(4s + 7)$
$c + 3c + 5c$	$9d - 4d$	$3x + x + y + 2y + 7$

Use the survey results to answer the questions.

What is your favorite sport to watch in the Winter Olympics?

Sport	Number of People
Ice skating	10
Skiing	6
Snowboarding	4
Total	20

What percentage of people chose ice skating?

What percentage of people chose skiing?

What percentage of people chose snowboarding?

Solve. Write the equations you use.

The table runner is $\frac{3}{4}$ ft. wide and 6 ft. long. What is the area of the table runner?

Wendell has $1\frac{1}{4}$ m of wire. He cuts it into pieces that are each $\frac{1}{4}$ m long. How many pieces does he get?

Lesson Activities

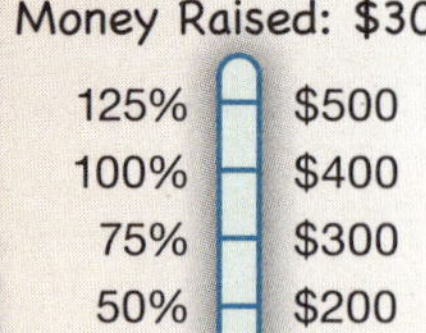

Goal: $400

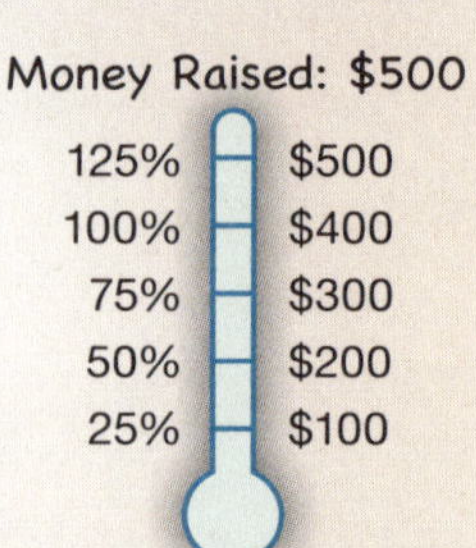

Money Raised: $300

125%	$500
100%	$400
75%	$300
50%	$200
25%	$100

Money Raised: $400

125%	$500
100%	$400
75%	$300
50%	$200
25%	$100

Money Raised: $500

125%	$500
100%	$400
75%	$300
50%	$200
25%	$100

Percentages Greater Than 100%

We use percentages greater than 100% to stand for more than a whole amount.

Ex. Write 150% as a whole number or mixed number.

 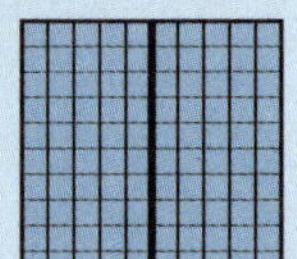

100% = 1 whole $50\% = \frac{1}{2}$

100% + 50% = 150%

$1 + \frac{1}{2} = 1\frac{1}{2}$

Ex. Write 200% as a whole number or mixed number.

 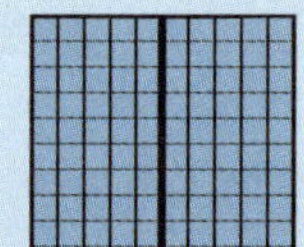

100% = 1 whole   100% = 1 whole

100% + 100% = 200%

$1 + 1 = 2$

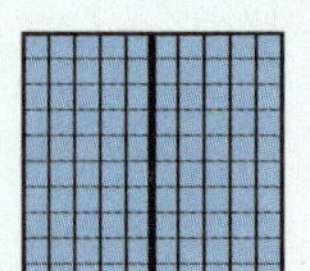 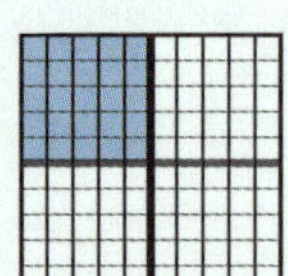

125% =

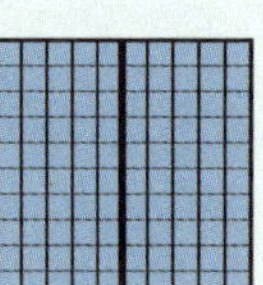 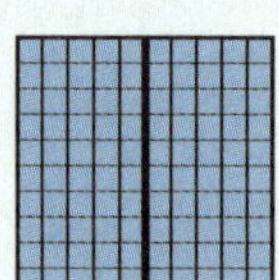 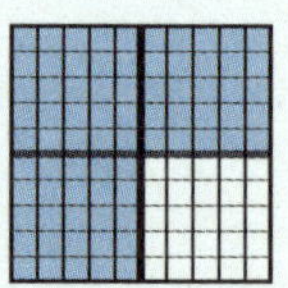

275% =

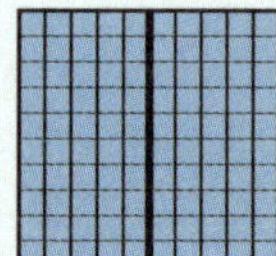 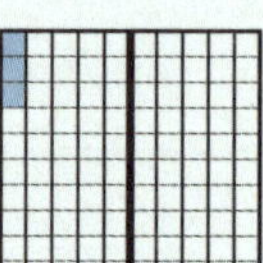

103% =

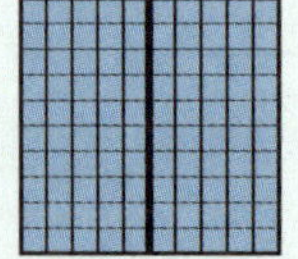 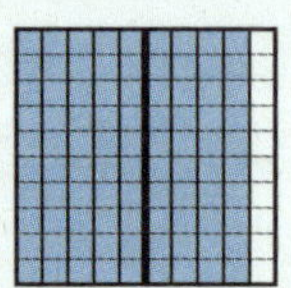

190% =

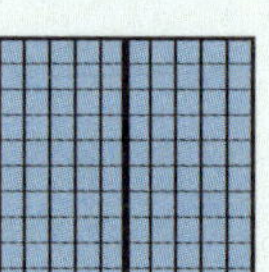 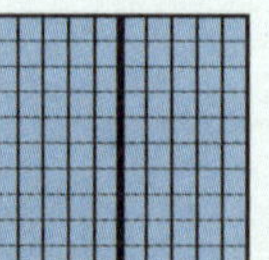 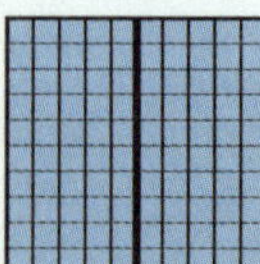

300% =

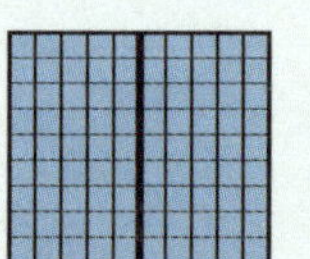 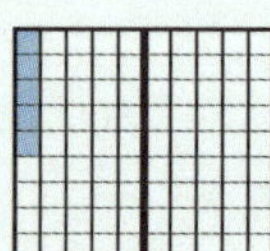

105% =

Practice 

Write each percentage as a mixed number in simplest form.

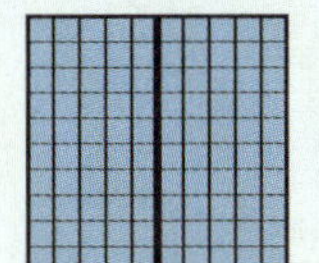 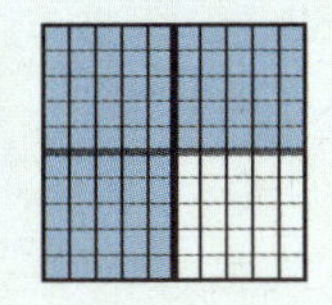

175% = 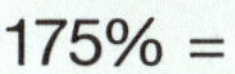

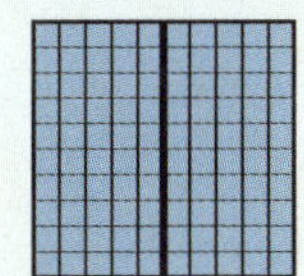 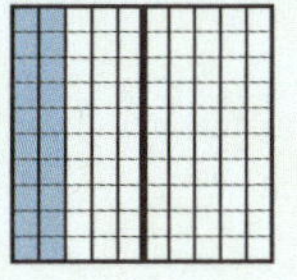

120% =

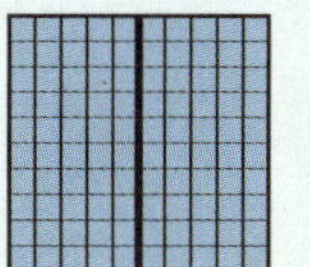 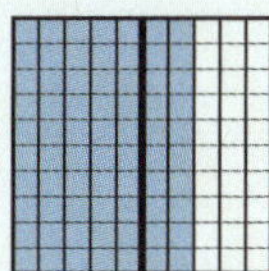

170% =

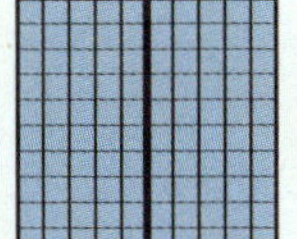 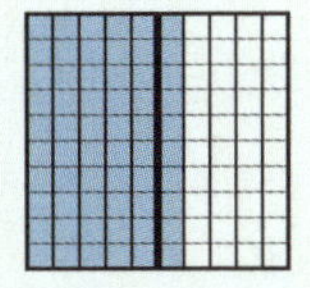

160% =

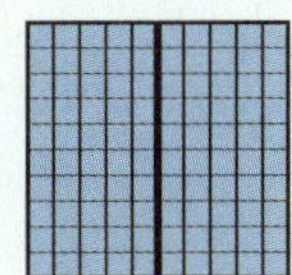

140% = 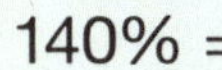

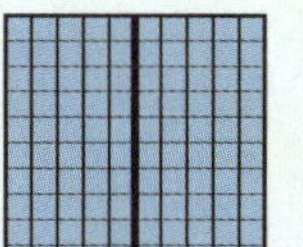

199% =

Match each percentage with the equivalent mixed number.

250%	$166\frac{2}{3}\%$	225%	$133\frac{1}{3}\%$	101%	$333\frac{1}{3}\%$

$2\frac{1}{4}$	$2\frac{1}{2}$	$1\frac{1}{3}$	$1\frac{2}{3}$	$3\frac{1}{3}$	$1\frac{1}{100}$

Complete.

100% of 60 = __________ 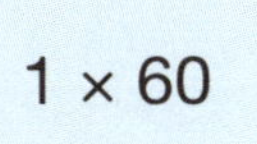

1×60

200% of 60 = __________ 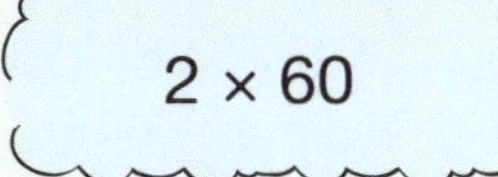

2×60

300% of 60 = __________ 

_____ $\times$ 60

400% of 60 = __________ 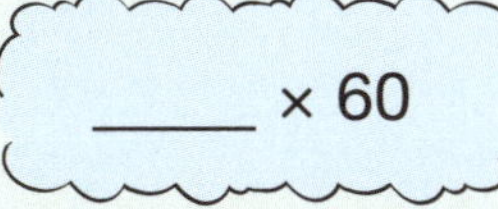

_____ $\times$ 60

100% of 400 = __________ 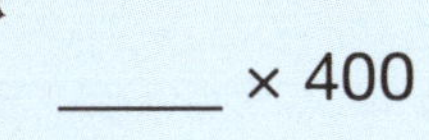

_____ $\times$ 400

200% of 400 = __________ 

_____ $\times$ 400

300% of 400 = __________ 

_____ $\times$ 400

400% of 400 = __________ 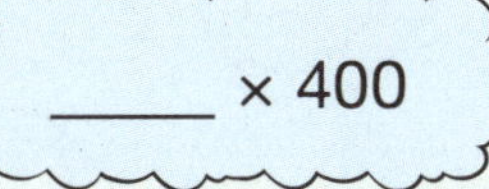

_____ $\times$ 400

100% of 150 = __________ 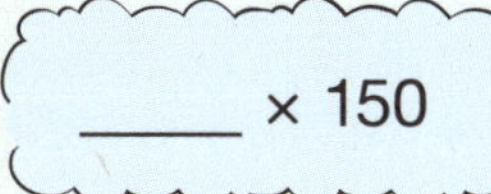

_____ $\times$ 150

200% of 150 = __________ 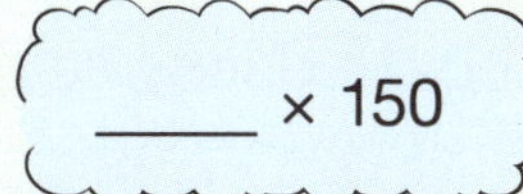

_____ $\times$ 150

300% of 150 = __________ 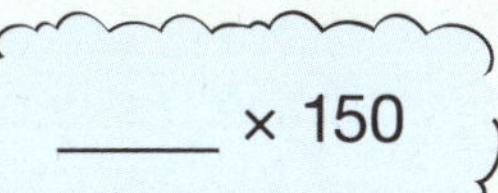

_____ $\times$ 150

400% of 150 = __________

_____ $\times$ 150

10.7

Move the decimal point to find the product or quotient.

3.6 × 1,000 = _______

0.45 × 100 = _______

0.087 × 10 = _______

1.2 × 100 = _______

0.009 × 10 = _______

2.34 × 100 = _______

407 ÷ 100 = _______

1,001 ÷ 1,000 = _______

63.4 ÷ 10 = _______

2.75 ÷ 100 = _______

0.7 ÷ 10 = _______

19 ÷ 10 = _______

Complete.

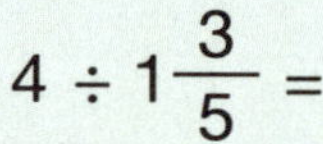

10% of 30 = _______

20% of 30 = _______

30% of 30 = _______

90% of 30 = _______

5% of 30 = _______

Rewrite as a multiplication problem and solve. Write your answers in simplest form. Convert improper fractions to whole numbers or mixed numbers.

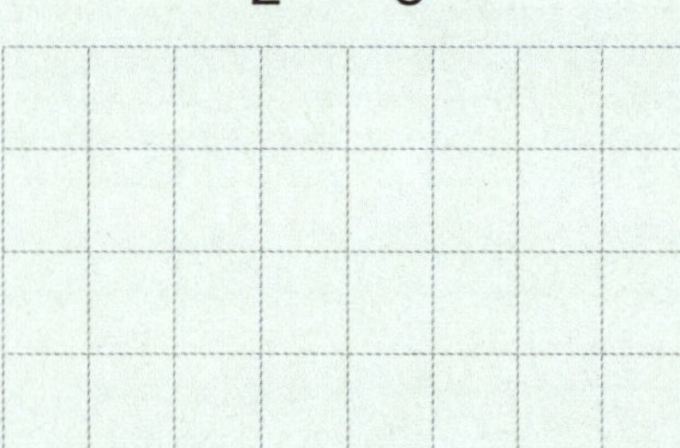

$$3\frac{1}{2} \div \frac{2}{3} =$$

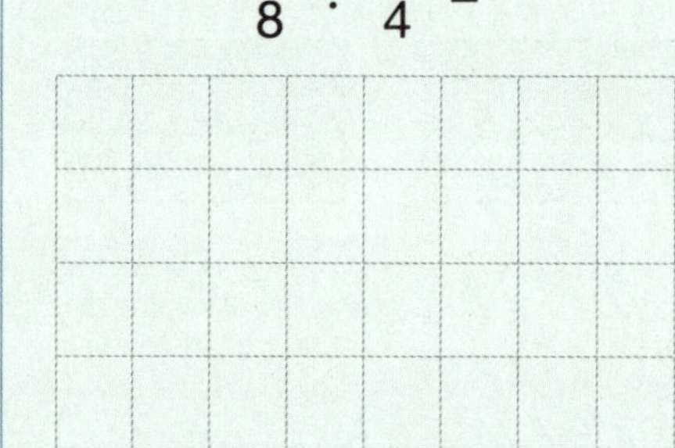

$$\frac{3}{8} \div \frac{3}{4} =$$

$$4 \div 1\frac{3}{5} =$$

Solve. Write the equations you use.

Julie buys 36 boxes of candy hearts. She gives $\frac{2}{3}$ of the boxes to her friends. How many boxes does she have left?

Julie keeps $\frac{1}{4}$ of the remaining boxes for herself and gives the rest to her family. How many boxes does she give to her family?

The ratio of white candy hearts to pink candy hearts in each box is 3:2. If there are 15 white candy hearts in each box, how many pink candy hearts are there? Make a ratio table to find the answer.

Lesson Activities 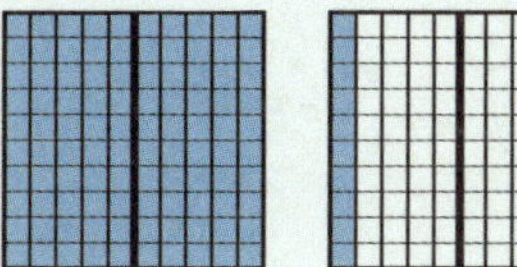

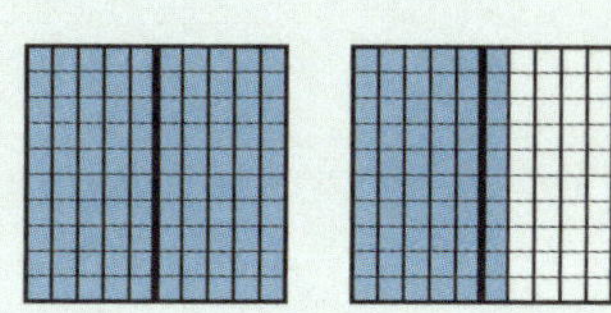

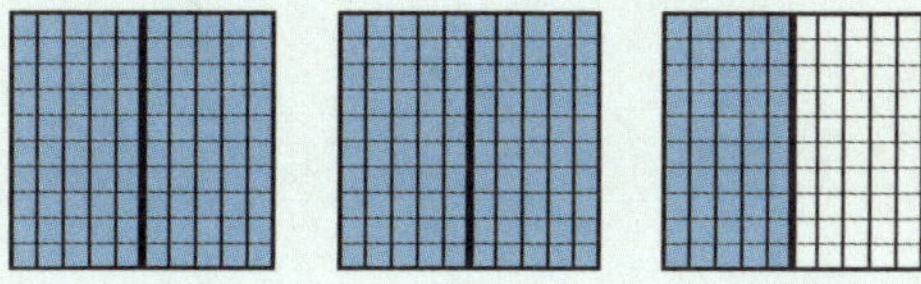

110% =

250% =

160% =

Percentages Greater Than 100%

 **Ex.** Marc set a goal of raising $40 for the charity fundraiser. He ended up raising 150% of his goal. How much money did he raise?

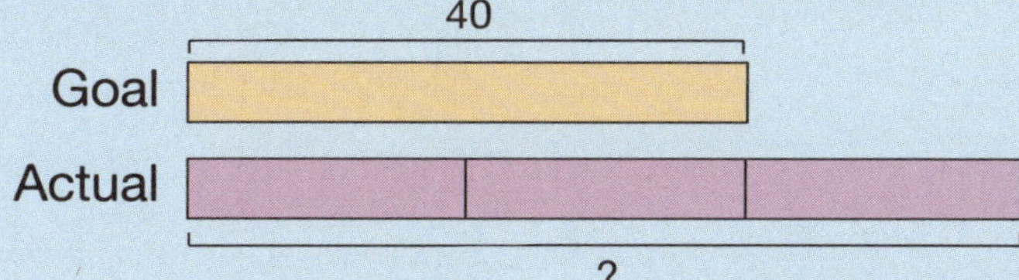

Mental Math

100% of 40 equals 40.

50% of 40 equals 20.

40 + 20 = 60, so Marc raised **$60**.

Fraction Multiplication

150% of 40 $\rightarrow$ $1\frac{1}{2} \times 40$

$$\frac{3}{\cancel{2}_{1}} \times \cancel{40}^{20} = \frac{60}{1} = \textbf{\$60}$$

Climb the Ladder (2-Player Game) 

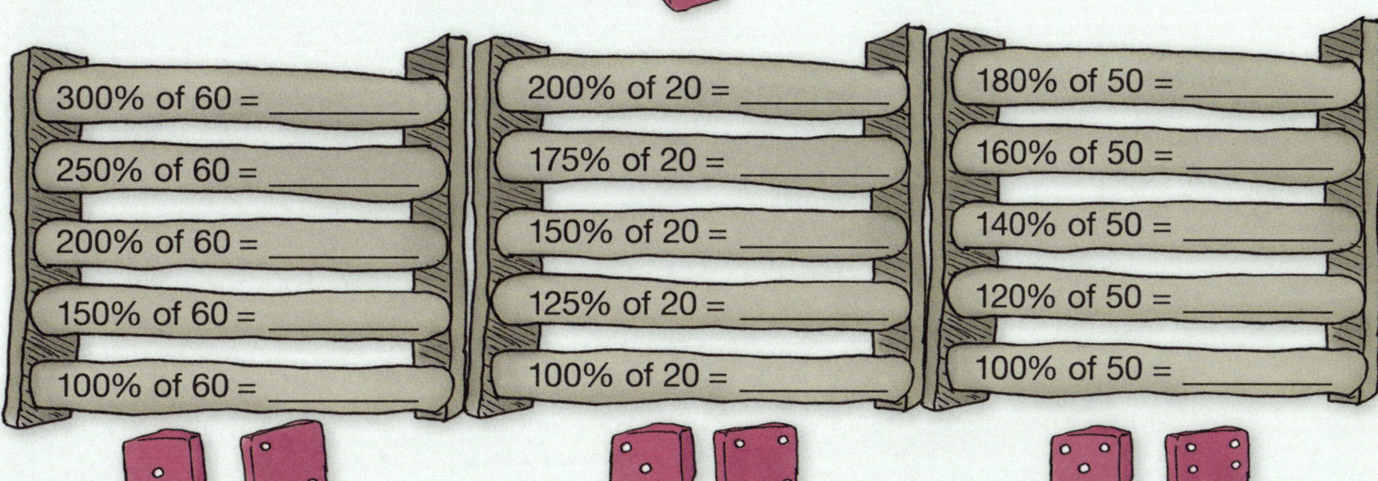

Practice   Complete.

100% of 50 = __________	100% of 80 = __________	100% of 60 = __________
120% of 50 = __________	110% of 80 = __________	150% of 60 = __________
140% of 50 = __________	120% of 80 = __________	200% of 60 = __________
160% of 50 = __________	130% of 80 = __________	250% of 60 = __________
180% of 50 = __________	140% of 80 = __________	300% of 60 = __________
200% of 50 = __________	150% of 80 = __________	350% of 60 = __________

Complete.

125% of 20 = __________   200% of 25 = __________   250% of 20 = __________

175% of 24 = __________   140% of 30 = __________ $166\frac{2}{3}\%$ of 12 = __________

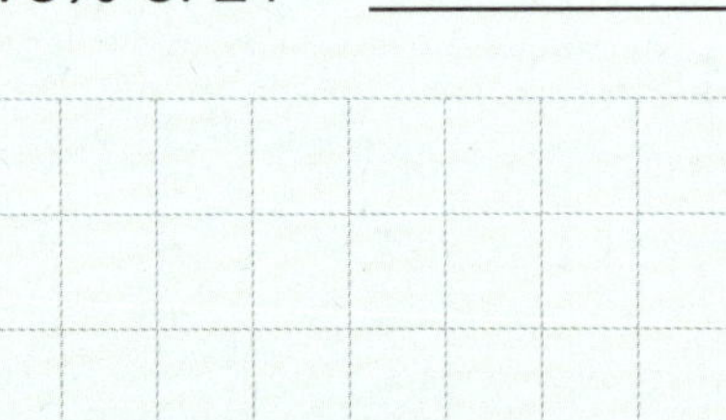
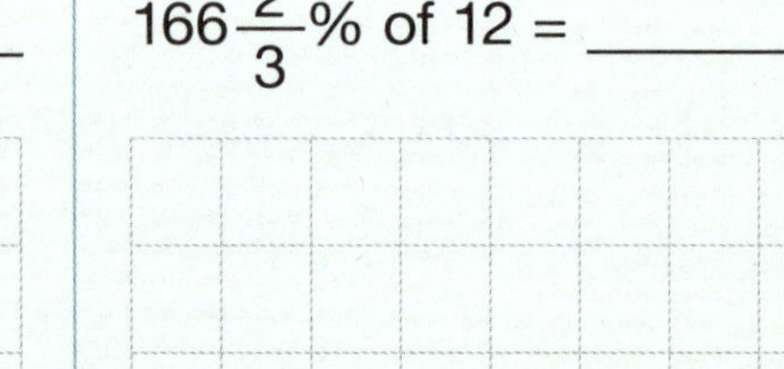

Solve. Write the equations you use.

Seattle's average rainfall is approximately 40 in. per year. In 2021, the rainfall was 110% of the average amount. How many inches of rain fell on Seattle that year?

In 2012, Seattle's rainfall was 80% of the average amount. How many inches of rain fell on Seattle that year?

Review — Match.

| –3 |	–3	–(–3)
| 3 |	3	–(3)
| –5 |	–5	–(–5)
| 5 |	5	–(5)

Evaluate each expression for $n = 7$.

$4n$	$4n + 2$	$6(4n + 2)$

$\dfrac{4n}{2}$	$\dfrac{4n + 2}{2}$	$\dfrac{6(4n + 2)}{2}$

Plot the points. Then, connect the points in order with straight lines to create a shape.

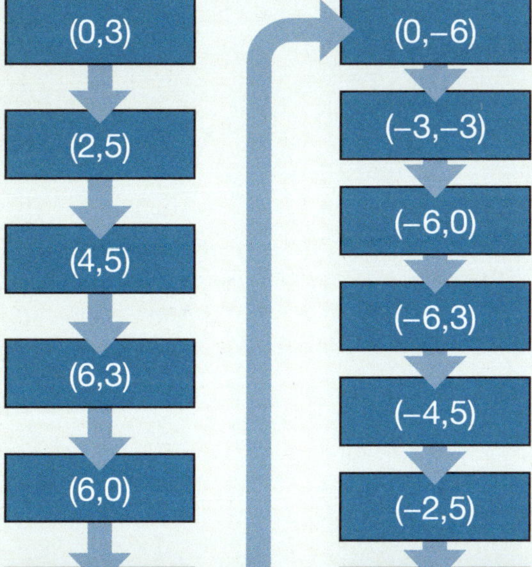

(0,3)
(2,5)
(4,5)
(6,3)
(6,0)
(3,–3)
(0,–6)
(–3,–3)
(–6,0)
(–6,3)
(–4,5)
(–2,5)
(0,3)

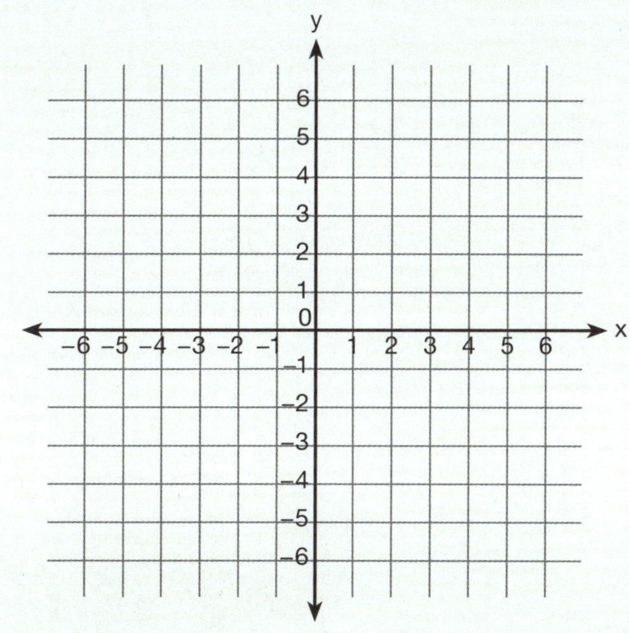

Lesson Activities 

Increase and Decrease Problems

1. Use the percentage to find the amount of the increase or decrease.

2. If the problem involves an increase, add the increase to the original amount.

3. If the problem involves a decrease, subtract the decrease from the original amount.

Ex. The sweater's regular price is $40. Today, the sweater is on sale for 25% off the regular price. How much does it cost?

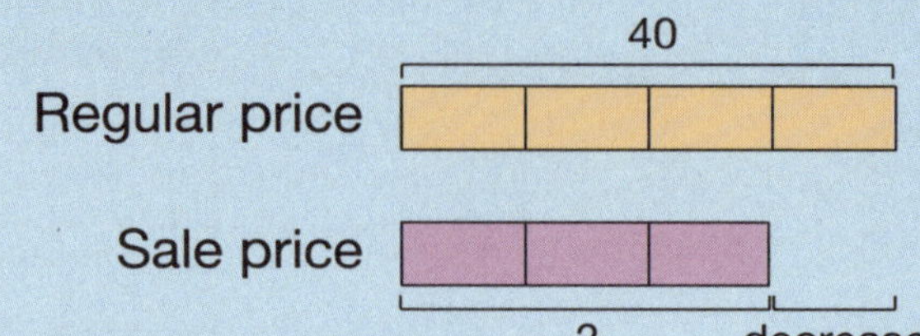

$25\% = \dfrac{1}{4}$

25% of 40 → $\dfrac{1}{4} \times 40 = \$10$

$40 - 10 = \mathbf{\$30}$

Last year, there were 130 children in the soccer league. This year, there are 10% fewer children in the league. How many children are in the league this year?

The baby elephant weighed 210 pounds when it was born. After one month, it weighed 50% more. How much did the elephant weigh after one month?

Birth weight

One-month weight

Practice

Use mental math to complete.

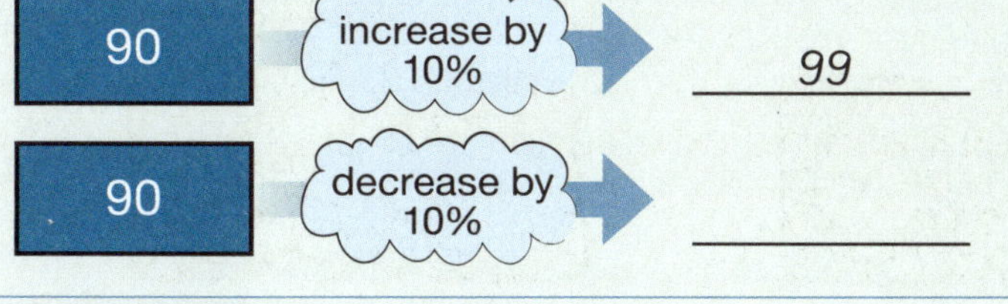

| 90 | increase by 10% → | 99 |
| 90 | decrease by 10% → | ____ |

| 75 | increase by 100% → | ____ |
| 75 | decrease by 100% → | ____ |

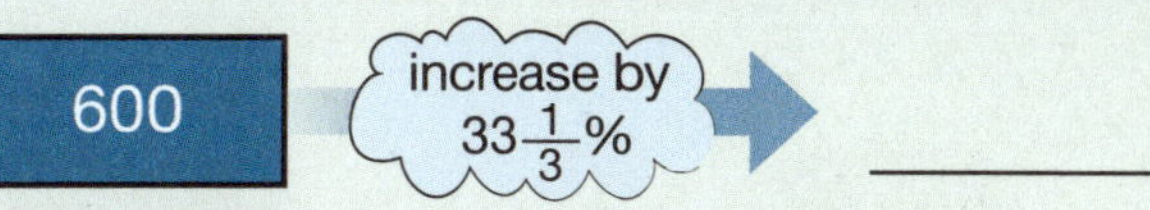
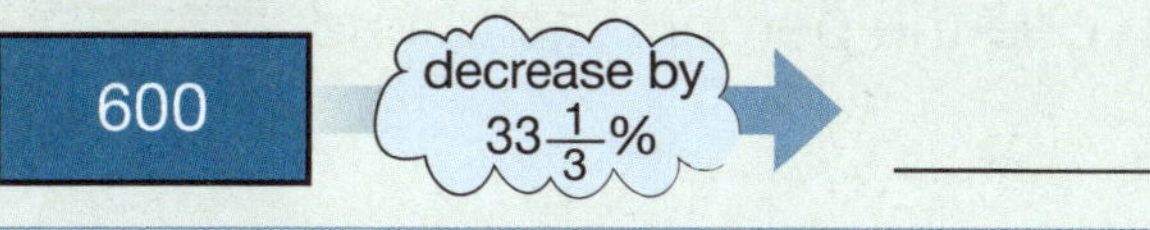
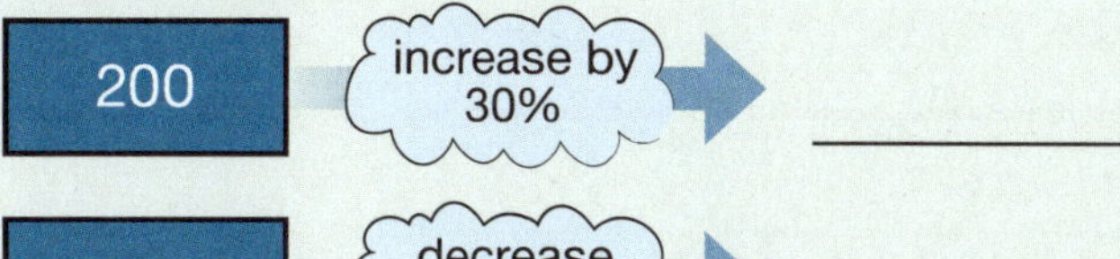

| 600 | increase by $33\frac{1}{3}\%$ → | ____ |
| 600 | decrease by $33\frac{1}{3}\%$ → | ____ |

| 200 | increase by 30% → | ____ |
| 200 | decrease by 30% → | ____ |

Use bar models to solve.

The rug normally costs $800. Today, it is on sale for 30% off the normal price. How much does the rug cost?

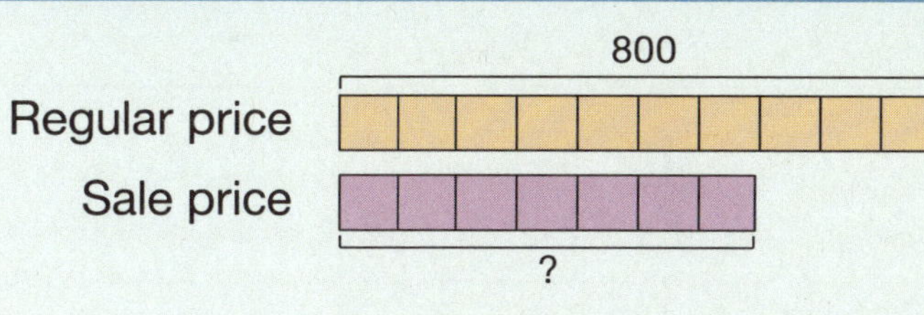

The bill for breakfast was $40. Maya's mom paid the bill and also left a 20% tip. How much did she pay in all?

Original bill

Total amount paid

Last week, Lainey practiced the trumpet for 120 minutes. This week, she'd like to practice 25% more minutes than she practiced last week. How many minutes does she need to practice to meet her goal?

Last week

This week

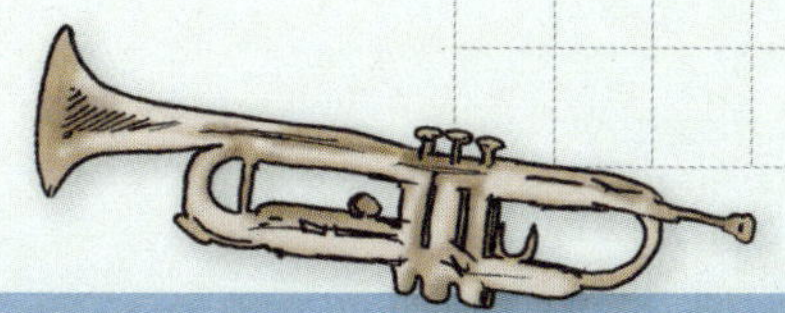

Review

Complete the charts.

v	$v + 5$
1	
	16
30	
	100

w	$3w$
10	
	24
15	
	120

x	y	$x + 2y$
4	10	
10	4	
20		32
	9	58

Find the product. Use cancelling where possible. Write your answers in simplest form. Convert improper fractions to mixed numbers.

$$1\frac{1}{2} \times \frac{3}{4} \times 2$$

$$\frac{3}{\cancel{2}_1} \times \frac{3}{4} \times \frac{\cancel{2}^1}{1} = \frac{9}{4} = 2\frac{1}{4}$$

$$2\frac{1}{2} \times 1 \times \frac{3}{5}$$

$$2 \times 4 \times 1\frac{3}{4}$$

$$3\frac{1}{8} \times \frac{4}{5} \times 2$$

Solve. Write the equations you use.

Stephen received the following scores at the gymnastics competition.

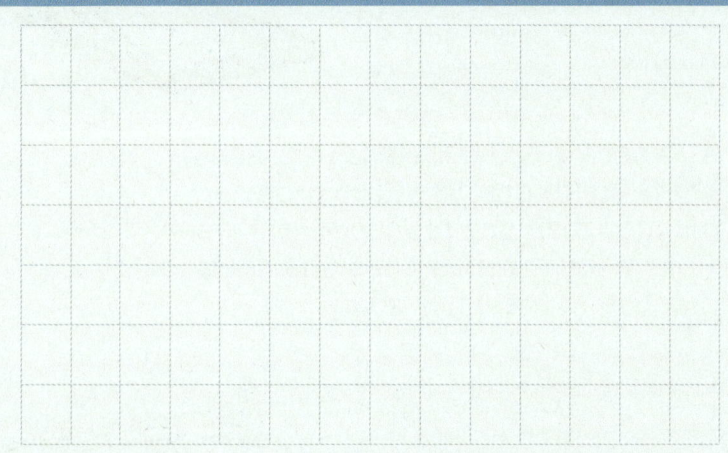

What is his mean (average) score?
Write your answer with 2 decimal digits.

Unit Wrap-Up

Write a fraction that is equivalent to each percentage. Write the fractions in simplest form.

25% =	75% =	$33\frac{1}{3}\%$ =	$66\frac{2}{3}\%$ =
10% =	20% =	30% =	40% =
50% =	60% =	70% =	80% =

Convert the percentages to decimals.

37% = __________   99% = __________

10% = __________   6% = __________

Convert the fractions to percentages.

$\dfrac{49}{100}$ =

$\dfrac{7}{20}$ =

$\dfrac{3}{100}$ =

$\dfrac{8}{25}$ =

Use mental math to complete.

50% of 160 = __________   25% of 200 = __________ $33\frac{1}{3}$ % of 900 = __________

25% of 160 = __________   75% of 200 = __________ $66\frac{2}{3}$ % of 900 = __________

10% of 70 = __________   20% of 25 = __________   10% of 40 = __________

30% of 70 = __________   120% of 25 = __________   5% of 40 = __________

Use mental math or written equations to complete.

75% of 320

80% of 300

150% of 110

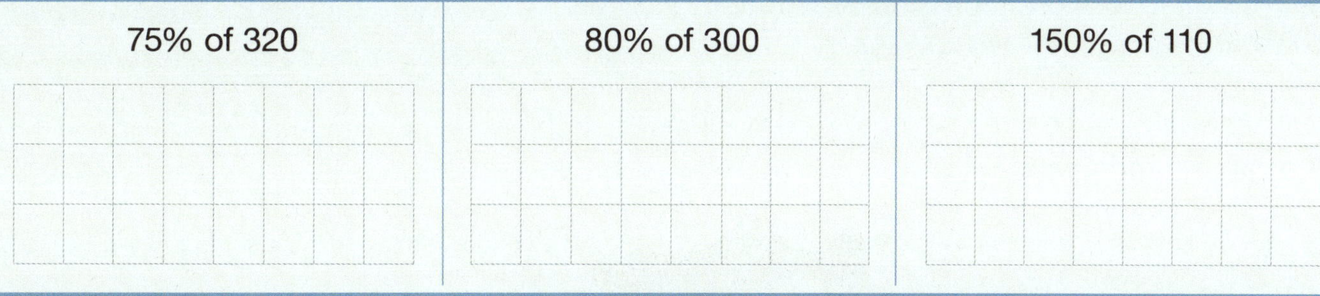

Use the bar models to complete.

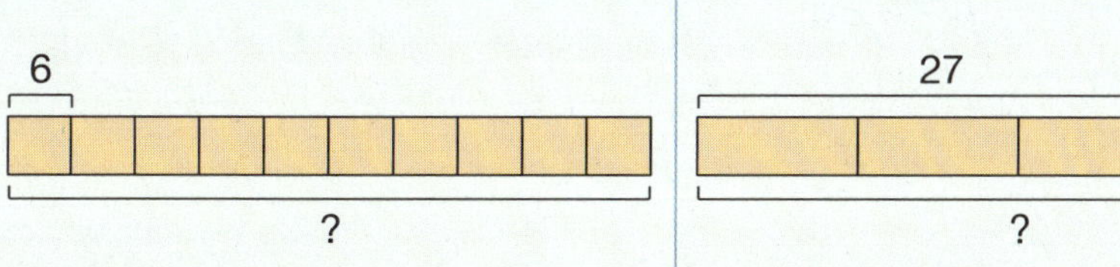
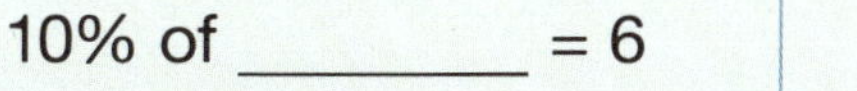

10% of __________ = 6

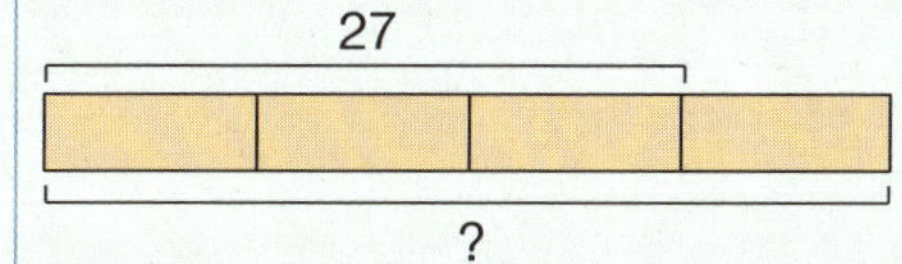

75% of __________ = 27

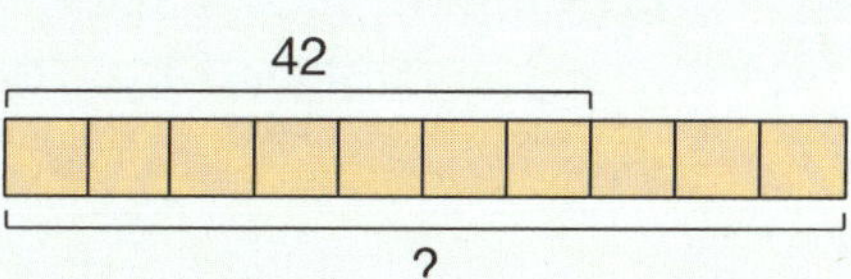

70% of __________ = 42

Unit Wrap-Up

Use bar models to solve.

Annabel and Lydia both collect mugs. Annabel has 15 mugs. Lydia has 20% fewer mugs than Annabel. How many mugs does Lydia have?

How many more mugs does Annabel have than Lydia?

15

Annabel

Lydia

Zach and Tyler are on the swim team. At the last practice, Zach swam 60 laps. He swam 75% as many laps as Tyler. How many laps did Tyler swim?

Zach

Tyler

Stella, Brayden, and Amir are on the track team. Last week, Stella ran 50 laps. Brayden ran 90% as many laps as Stella. How many laps did Brayden run?

Amir ran $33\frac{1}{3}$% more laps than Brayden. How many laps did Amir run?

Who ran the most laps?

Stella

Brayden

Amir

 Last month, Nova spent 60% of her money and saved the rest. She saved $36. How much money did she spend?

Lesson Activities 👥

Equation Expression Inequality	$-2 < 1$	$3 \times 5 - 7$	$11 = 3 + 8$
	__________	__________	__________

Inequalities

Inequalities are mathematical statements that compare unequal quantities. We can use variables in inequalities.

$a < 6$ $b > -2$ $c \geq 1$ $d \leq 0$

a is less than 6.

b is greater than -2.

c is greater than or equal to 1.

d is less than or equal to 0.

Ex. The bag of candy weighs more than 2 lb. (Use w to stand for the weight.)

$$w > 2$$

Any number greater than 2 is a possible value for w.

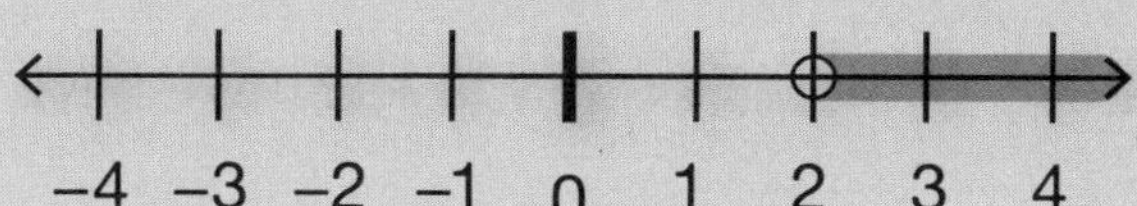

$$-4 \quad -3 \quad -2 \quad -1 \quad 0 \quad 1 \quad 2 \quad 3 \quad 4$$

The open circle means that 2 is not included in the graph.

Ex. The temperature is less than or equal to $-1°$. (Use t to stand for the temperature.)

$$t \leq -1$$

Any number less than -1 is a possible value for t. -1 is also a possible value for t.

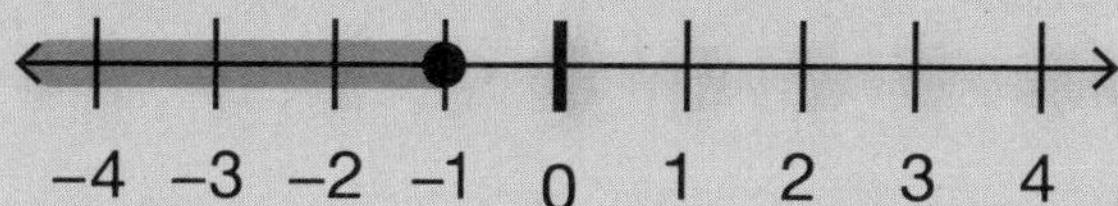

$$-4 \quad -3 \quad -2 \quad -1 \quad 0 \quad 1 \quad 2 \quad 3 \quad 4$$

The closed circle means that -1 is included in the graph.

My secret number is greater than -2. (Use n to stand for the secret number.)

Inequality: _________________________

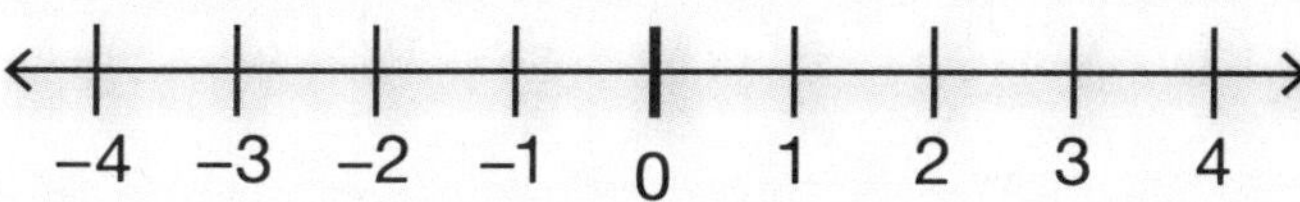

$$-4 \quad -3 \quad -2 \quad -1 \quad 0 \quad 1 \quad 2 \quad 3 \quad 4$$

Which of these could be the secret number?

-1	$1\frac{1}{2}$	-3	0

I have at least \$1 in my bank account. (Use m to stand for the money.)

Inequality: _________________________

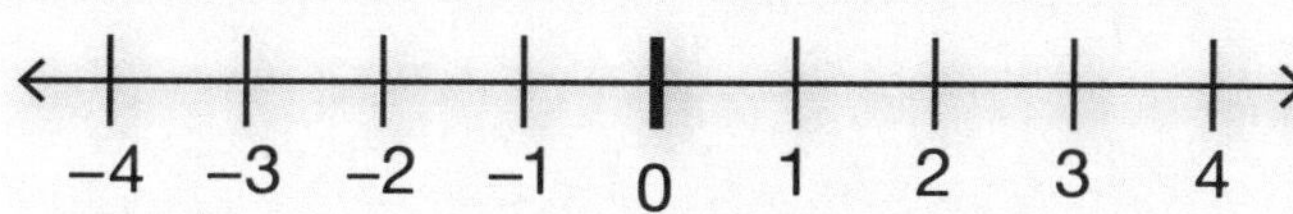

$$-4 \quad -3 \quad -2 \quad -1 \quad 0 \quad 1 \quad 2 \quad 3 \quad 4$$

Which of these could be the bank account balance?

\$0.99	\$1.00	\$1.01	$-\$1.00$

Practice

Match each inequality with its graph on the number line.

$a \leq 0$

$b < 2$

$c > -1$

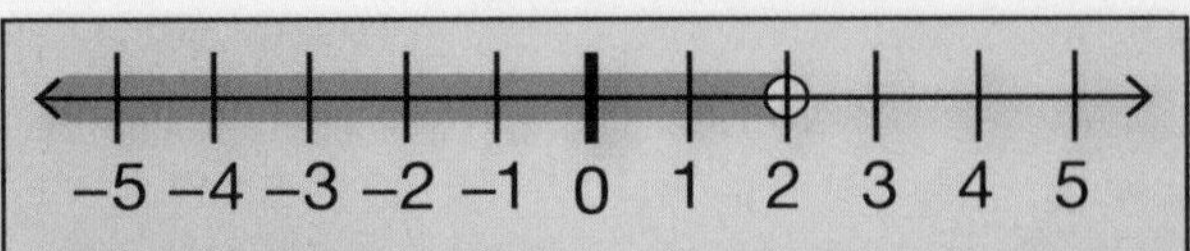

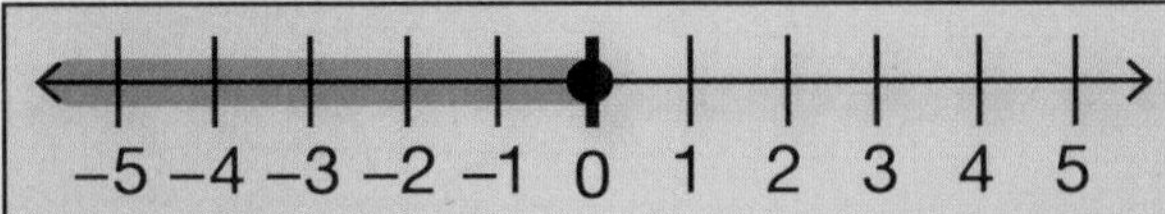

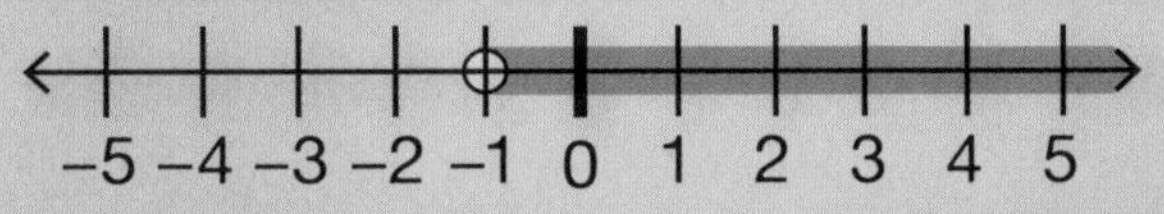

Graph each inequality on the number line. Then, circle the numbers that make the inequality true. X the numbers that do not make the inequality true.

$p \geq -2\frac{1}{2}$

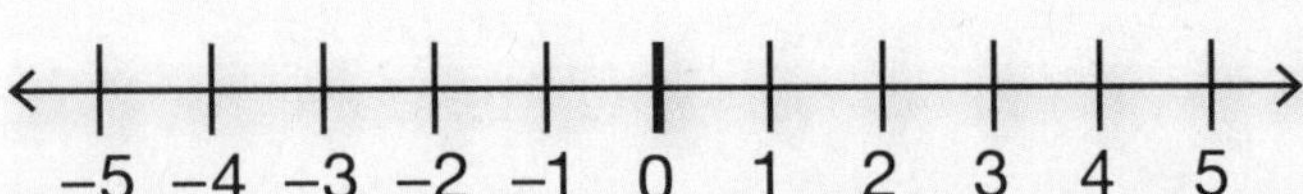

| 0 | −5 | 3 | $-1\frac{1}{4}$ |

$t < 3$

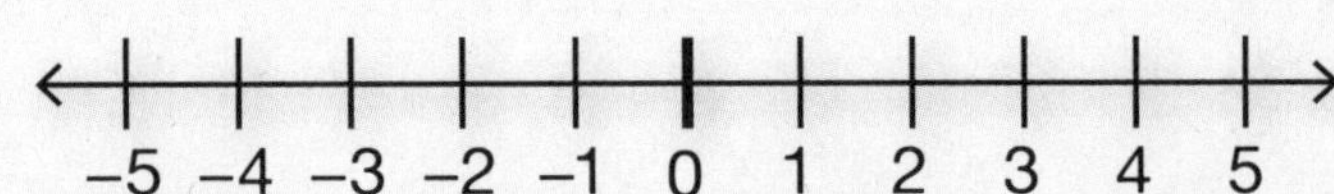

| −3 | 2 | $\frac{1}{2}$ | 0 |

Use the printed variable to write an inequality to match each situation. Graph the inequality on the number line. Then, write three numbers that make the inequality true. (Many answers are possible.)

Inequality: _____ w _____________

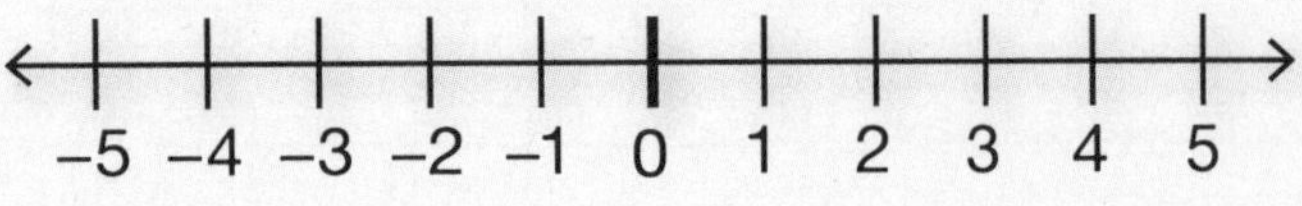

Inequality: _____ t _____________

Review   **Use mental math to complete.**

10% of 20 = _____________

10% of 50 = _____________

10% of 300 = _____________

30% of 20 = _____________

70% of 50 = _____________

90% of 300 = _____________

130% of 20 = _____________

100% of 50 = _____________

190% of 300 = _____________

230% of 20 = _____________

170% of 50 = _____________

300% of 300 = _____________

Circle the most reasonable answer for each product or quotient.

81.5×9

| 7.35 | 73.5 | 733.5 |

0.815×9

| 7.35 | 73.5 | 733.5 |

8.15×9

| 7.35 | 73.5 | 733.5 |

$2.934 \div 3$

| 0.0978 | 0.978 | 9.78 |

$29.34 \div 3$

| 0.0978 | 0.978 | 9.78 |

$0.2934 \div 3$

| 0.0978 | 0.978 | 9.78 |

Use bar models to complete the blanks and answer the questions.

Xander used blue and green beads to make bracelets. The ratio of blue beads to green beads was 2 to 5. He used 150 more green beads than blue beads.

Blue

Green

Number of blue beads: _____________

Number of green beads: _____________

Total number of beads: _____________

Express the number of blue beads as a fraction of the total number of beads.

Express the number of green beads as a fraction of the total number of beads.

Lesson Activities

Equations

An equation is a mathematical statement with an equals sign. The two sides of the equation are like the two sides of a scale. The equals sign tells that the two sides equal each other and are in balance.

A solution to an equation is a value for the variable that makes the equation true. To check whether a number is a solution to an equation, substitute the number into the equation. Evaluate both sides and check whether the two sides are equal.

Ex. Is $a = 4$ a solution to this equation?

$$6 = 2a$$
$$6 \overset{?}{=} 2 \cdot 4$$
$$6 \neq 8 \qquad \textbf{No.}$$

Ex. Is $b = 3$ a solution to this equation?

$$2b + 1 = 7$$
$$2 \cdot 3 + 1 \overset{?}{=} 7$$
$$6 + 1 \overset{?}{=} 7$$
$$7 = 7 \qquad \textbf{Yes.}$$

__________ = __________

Is $c = 7$ a solution to the equation?

__________ = __________

Is $d = 8$ a solution to the equation?

__________ = __________

Is $e = 5$ a solution to the equation?

Write an equation to match the statement. Use n to stand for the secret number.

__________ = __________

Which of these numbers is the secret number?

11	12	13

Practice

Use mental math to check whether each number is a solution to the equation. Circle the numbers that are the solutions to the equation. (Some equations will have more than one solution.)

$4a = 24$			$b = 20 - 18$			$c + 3 = 3 + c$		
4	5	6	1	2	3	8	9	10

$\dfrac{35}{d} = 7$			$e + e + e = 3e$			$2f = f + 7$		
5	6	7	4	5	6	6	7	8

Match.

32 equals the sum of x and 5.	$\dfrac{4x}{5} = 32$
4 times x, plus 5, equals 32.	$4x + 5 = 32$
4 times x, divided by 5, equals 32.	$32 = 4(x + 5)$
32 equals 4 times the quantity x plus 5.	$32 = x + 5$

Substitute the number into the equation to check whether the number is a solution to the equation.

Is $x = 27$ a solution to this equation?

$$32 = x + 5$$

Is $x = 25$ a solution to this equation?

$$\frac{4x}{5} = 32$$

Is $x = 3$ a solution to this equation?

$$32 = 4(x + 5)$$

Is $x = 3$ a solution to this equation?

$$4x + 5 = 32$$

Review

Use mental math to complete.

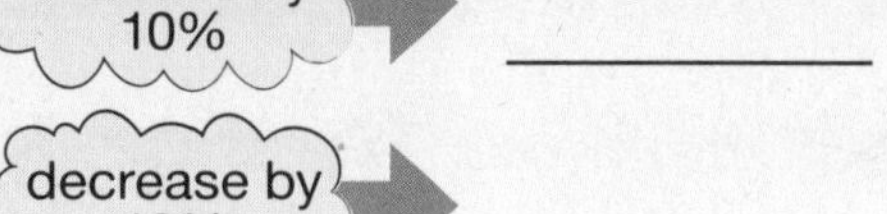
50 — increase by 10% → _______

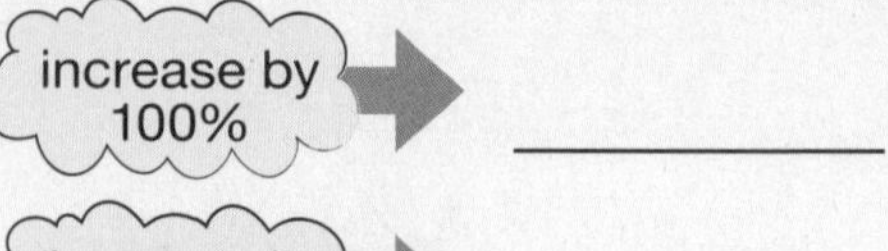
125 — increase by 100% → _______

50 — decrease by 10% → _______

125 — decrease by 100% → _______

80 — increase by 10% → _______

80 — increase by 20% → _______

80 — decrease by 10% → _______

80 — decrease by 20% → _______

Evaluate each expression for $b = 10$.

b^2	$b^2 + 1$	$4(b^2 + 1)$
b^3	$b^3 + 1$	$4(b^3 + 1)$

Use bar models to solve. Write the equations you use.

Dominic has \$75. He uses $\frac{3}{5}$ of his money on new headphones. How much does he spend on the headphones?

Zara spends $\frac{3}{4}$ of the money in her savings account on a new speaker. The speaker costs \$84. How much money did she have in her savings account to start?

Lesson Activities 👥

A

Cross out 3 loose marbles on each side of the scale.

$a =$ _____________

Cross out 1 loose marble on each side of the scale.

$b =$ _____________

Cross out 4 loose marbles on each side of the scale.

$c =$ _____________

B

Solve Equations, Part 1

To solve an equation, we change both sides until we have the variable by itself on one side of the equation.

The two sides of an equation are like the two sides of a scale. If you change one side of the equation, you must change the other side in the same way.

1. Identify what happens to the variable in the equation. Do the opposite operation to both sides of the equation.

2. Simplify both sides.

3. Substitute the solution into the equation to check your answer.

Ex. Solve: $x + 18 = 27$

In this equation, 18 is added to x. So, we subtract 18 from both sides to get x by itself on one side of the equation.

$$x + 18 = 27$$
$$-18 \quad -18$$
$$x = 9$$

Check:
$$9 + 18 \stackrel{?}{=} 27$$
$$27 = 27 ✓$$

$p + 12 = 47$

Check:

$29 = n + 15$

Check:

Practice

Solve each equation. Show all your steps. Then, substitute the solution into the equation to check that it is correct.

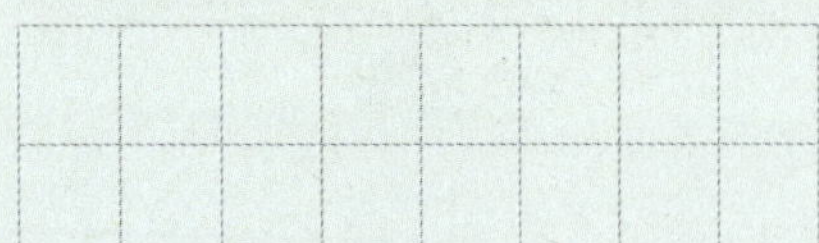

$a + 3 = 15$

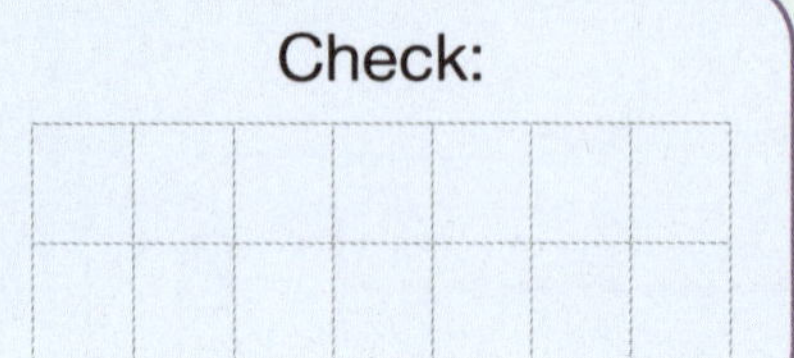

Check:

$30 = b + 1$

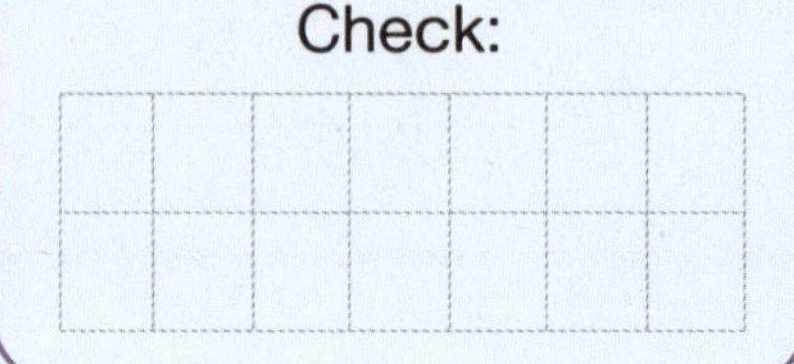

Check:

$c + 4 = 4$

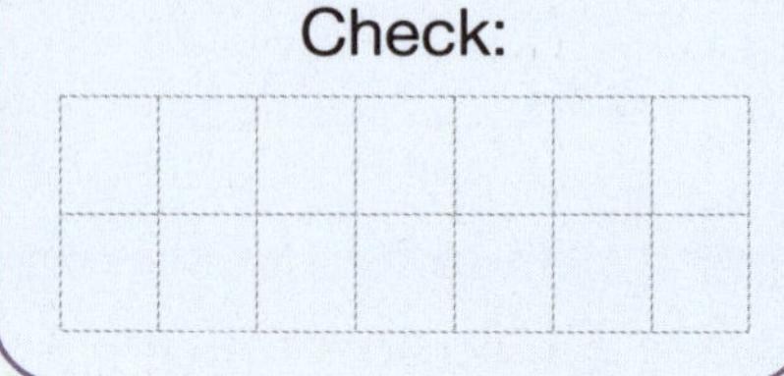

Check:

$8 = d + 2$

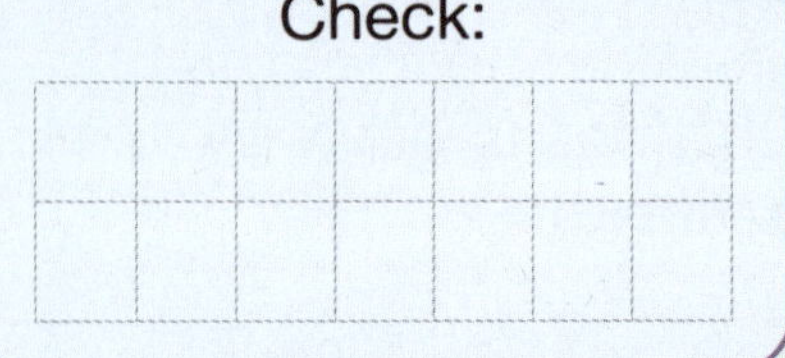

Check:

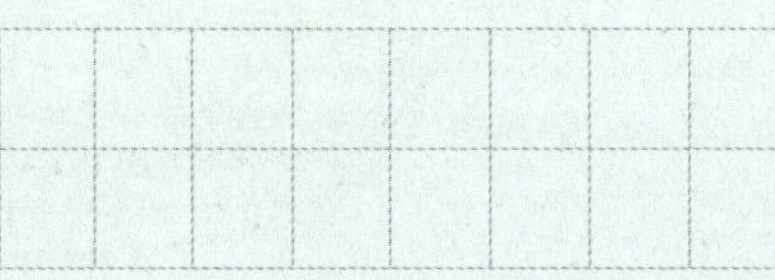

$46 = e + 22$

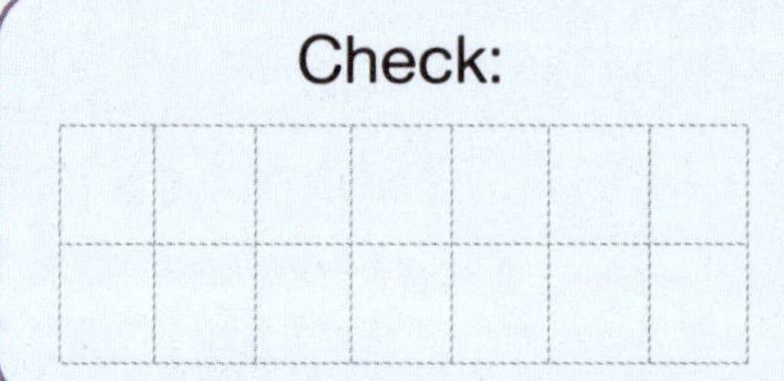

Check:

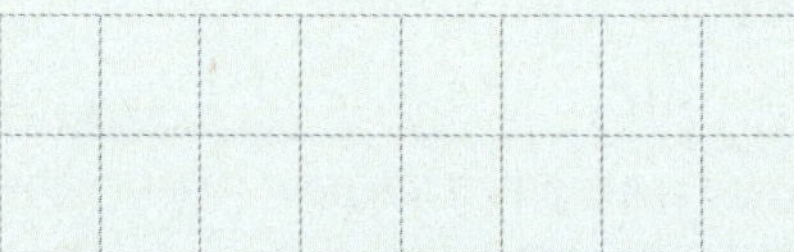

$100 = 85 + f$

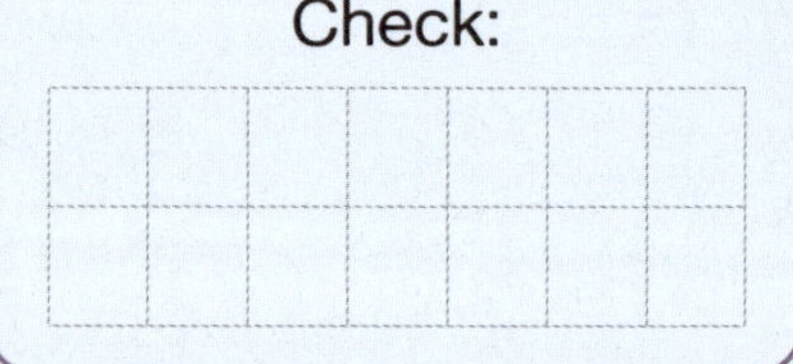

Check:

Follow the directions.

Write an equation to match the clue.
Use m to stand for the secret number.

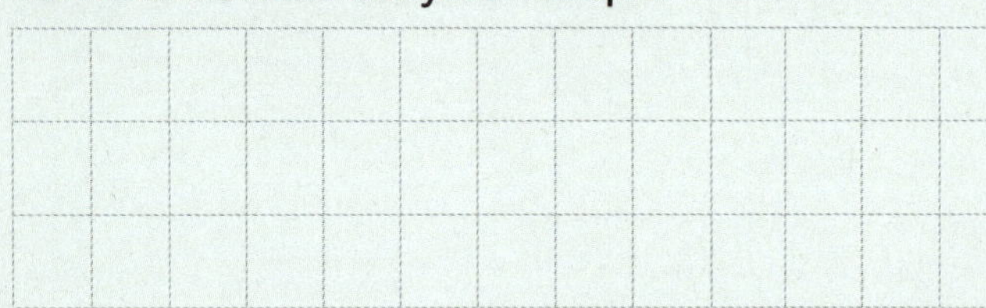

Solve the equation to find the secret number. Show all your steps.

Write an equation to match the clue.
Use n to stand for the secret number.

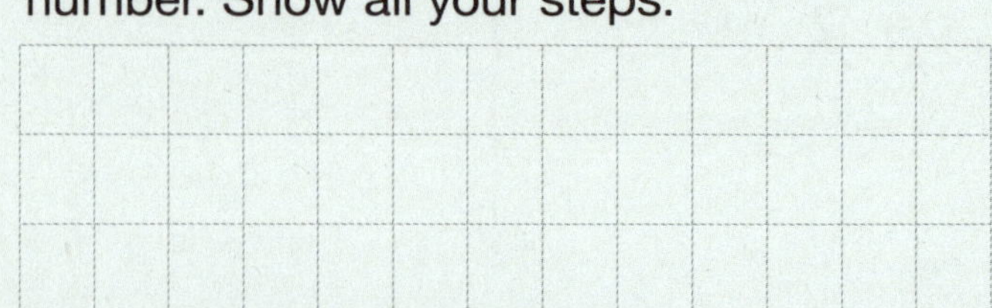

Solve the equation to find the secret number. Show all your steps.

Review   Follow the directions.

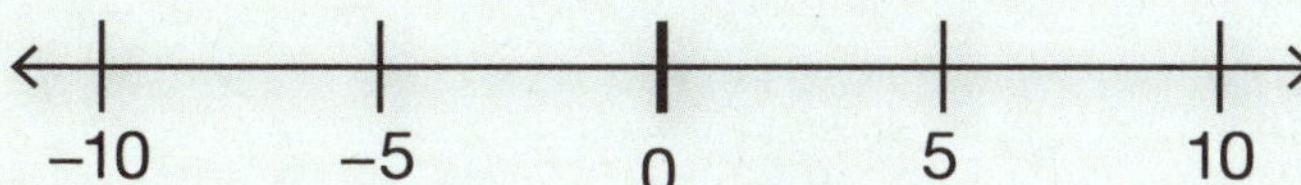

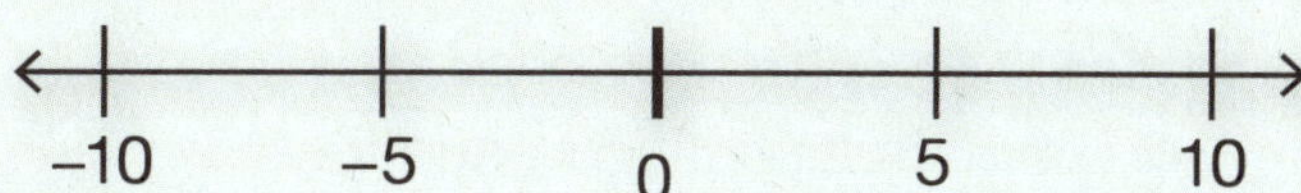

Write an inequality to match the statement. Use *m* to stand for the amount of money.	Write an inequality to match the statement. Use *t* to stand for the temperature.
Graph the inequality on the number line.	Graph the inequality on the number line.

–10   –5   0   5   10   –10   –5   0   5   10

Circle the numbers that make the inequality true. X the numbers that do not make the inequality true.

–5	0	5	10

Circle the numbers that make the inequality true. X the numbers that do not make the inequality true.

–5	0	5	10

Rewrite each division problem as a multiplication problem and solve. Write your answers in simplest form. Convert improper fractions to whole numbers or mixed numbers.

$3 \div \dfrac{1}{4} =$

$3 \div \dfrac{3}{4} =$

$3 \div 1\dfrac{1}{4} =$

Use mental math to complete the chart.

- 16 children play the guitar.
- 25% more children play the piano than play the guitar.
- 50% fewer children play the drums than play the piano.
- 20% fewer children play the clarinet than play the drums.

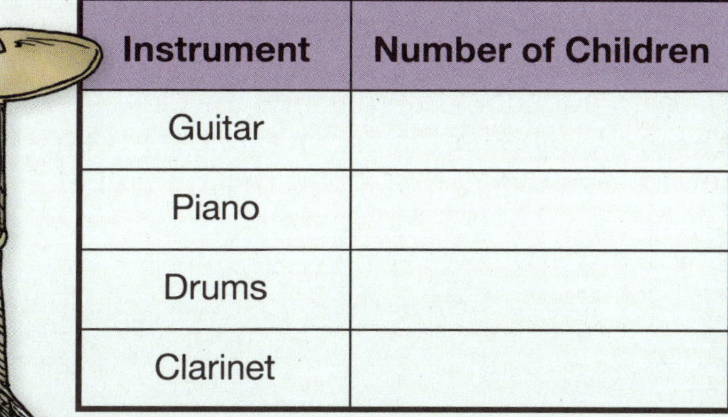

Instrument	Number of Children
Guitar	
Piano	
Drums	
Clarinet	

Lesson Activities

A

$p =$ ___________

$r =$ ___________

B

Solve Equations, Part 2

We solve multiplication equations with the same steps we use to solve addition equations. We change both sides in the same way until we have the variable by itself on one side of the equation.

1. Identify what happens to the variable in the equation. Do the opposite operation to both sides of the equation.

2. Simplify both sides.

3. Substitute the solution into the equation to check your answer.

Ex. Solve: $3z = 21$

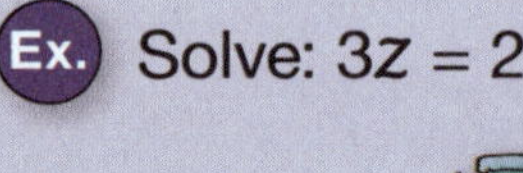

In this equation, z is multiplied by 3. So, we divide both sides by 3 to get z by itself on one side of the equation.

$$3z = 21$$
$$\frac{3z}{3} = \frac{21}{3}$$
$$z = 7$$

Check:
$$3 \cdot 7 \overset{?}{=} 21$$
$$21 = 21 \checkmark$$

$8g = 240$

Check:

$24 = 2h$

Check:

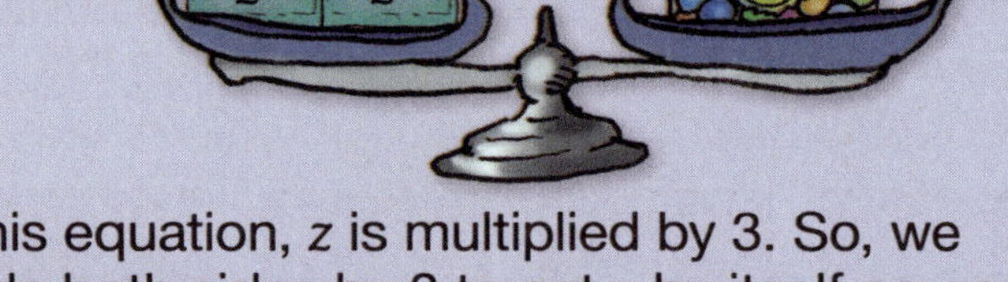

C

Write an equation that matches the clue. (Use n to stand for the secret number.) Then, solve the equation to find the secret number.

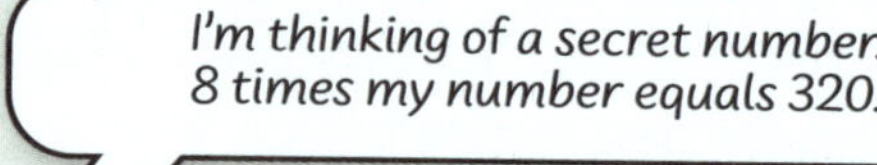

Write an equation that matches the clue. (Use m to stand for the secret number.) Then, solve the equation to find the secret number.

Practice

Solve each equation. Show all your steps. Then, substitute the solution into the equation to check that it is correct.

$2d = 16$

Check:

$28 = 4e$

Check:

$3f = 120$

Check:

$5g = 40$

Check:

$180 = 9h$

Check:

$400 = 8i$

Check:

Follow the directions.

I'm thinking of a secret number. The product of my number and 4 equals 32.

Write an equation to match the clue. Use x to stand for the secret number.

Solve the equation to find the secret number. Show all your steps.

I'm thinking of a secret number. Double my number equals 80.

Write an equation to match the clue. Use y to stand for the secret number.

Solve the equation to find the secret number. Show all your steps.

Review Match.

$\frac{4}{100}$		4%		0.3
$\frac{3}{10}$		5%		0.04
$\frac{2}{5}$		30%		0.4
$\frac{1}{2}$		40%		0.05
$\frac{5}{100}$		50%		0.5

Rewrite as a multiplication problem and solve. Write your answers in simplest form. Convert improper fractions to whole numbers.

$$\frac{9}{10} \div \frac{1}{5} =$$

$$4\frac{1}{6} \div \frac{5}{6} =$$

$$1\frac{5}{9} \div 2 =$$

Complete the ratios and answer the questions. Write your fractions and ratios in simplest form.

Daisy earned $45 in March.
She saved $20 and spent the rest.

Money saved : Total earnings

______ : ______

Money spent : Total earnings

______ : ______

Money saved : Money spent

______ : ______

Money spent : Money saved

______ : ______

What fraction of her earnings did Daisy save?

What fraction of her earnings did Daisy spend?

Lesson Activities

Did you know a cricket's chirps can tell you the temperature? To find the temperature, count the number of times a cricket chirps in 15 seconds. Then, add 40 to your count. The sum is the approximate temperature in Fahrenheit!

A

Number of Chirps	Temperature
10	
20	
30	
40	

B

Equations with Two Variables

Some equations express the relationship between two variables. To write an expression with two variables, describe what you do to one variable to get the other variable. Then, translate the words into mathematical symbols.

Ex. Write an equation that tells the relationship between the number of times a cricket chirps in 15 seconds and the temperature. Use n to stand for the number of chirps and t to stand for the temperature.

The number of chirps plus 40 equals the temperature.

$$n + 40 = t$$

Ex. If the cricket chirps 25 times, what is the temperature?

$$n + 40 = t$$
$$25 + 40 = t$$
$$65 = t$$

The temperature is **65° F**.

Xander starts with \$20. Write an equation that shows the relationship between how many dollars he spends (s) and how many dollars he has remaining (r).

If Xander spends \$18, how much money does he have remaining? Use your equation to find the answer.

Dollars spent (s)	Dollars remaining (r)
1	
2	
3	
4	
5	
6	
7	

Practice

Use the information to complete the charts and answer the questions.

Nina and Peter have the same birthday. Nina is 5 years older than Peter.

Peter's age (p)	1	2	3	4	5	6
Nina's age (n)	6					

Write an equation that shows the relationship between Peter's age (p) and Nina's age (n).

When Peter is 12, how old is Nina? Use your equation to find the answer.

When Nina is 16, how old is Peter?

Ezra has a lawn-mowing business. He earns $20 for each lawn he mows.

Lawns mowed (n)	1	2	3	4	5	6
Dollars earned (d)	20					

Write an equation that shows the relationship between the number of lawns he mows (n) and the number of dollars he earns (d).

Use your equation to predict how much Ezra makes if he mows 12 lawns.

Ezra wants to earn $200 this summer. How many lawns does he need to mow to reach his goal?

Use the equation to complete the chart and answer the questions.

$3x + 1 = y$

x	0	1	2	3	4	5	6	7
y	1	4						

If $x = 20$, what does y equal?

If $x = 100$, what does y equal?

★ If $y = 31$, what does x equal?

Review

Use the bar models to complete. Draw lines to split each bar to match the percentage.

35

?

50% of _________ = 35

75% of _________ = 24

$66\frac{2}{3}$% of _________ = 30

10% of _________ = 7

20% of _________ = 8

30% of _________ = 18

Use mental math to check whether each number is a solution to the equation. Circle the numbers that are the solutions to the equation. (Some equations will have more than one solution.)

$7a = 35$

| 4 | 5 | 6 |

$20 = h + 7$

| 11 | 12 | 13 |

$2i + 5 = 19$

| 7 | 8 | 9 |

$j + 4 = 4 + j$

| 5 | 6 | 7 |

$k - 6 = 8$

| 12 | 13 | 14 |

$2(l + 1) = 2l + 2$

| 3 | 4 | 5 |

Solve. Write the equations you use.

Tom made this shield from cardboard. He wants to cover the front of the shield with aluminum foil. How many square inches of aluminum foil does he need?

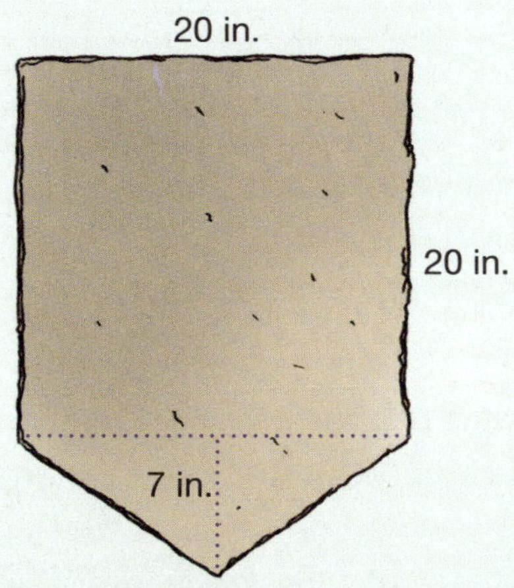

Lesson Activities

A

Isabella's minivan needs 1 gallon of gas to drive 20 miles.

$$20g = m$$

Gallons (g)	0	1	2	3	4	5
Miles (m)						

George's car needs 1 gallon of gas to drive 40 miles.

$$40g = m$$

Gallons (g)	0	1	2	3	4	5
Miles (m)						

B

How to Graph Equations

1. Make a chart that shows a few solutions to the equation.
2. Plot points for the ordered pairs that match the solutions in your chart.
3. Connect the points with a line.

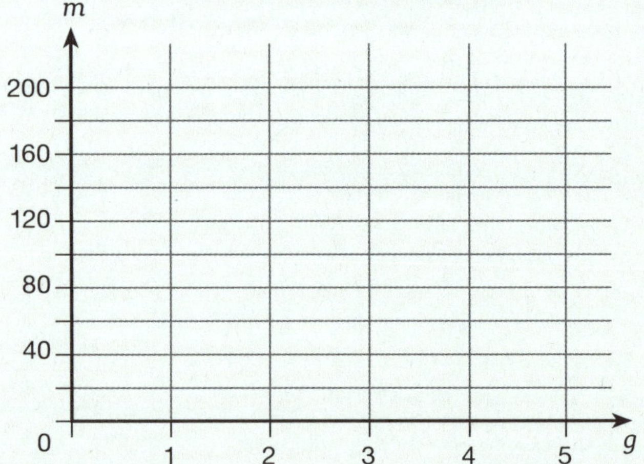

Isabella's Minivan

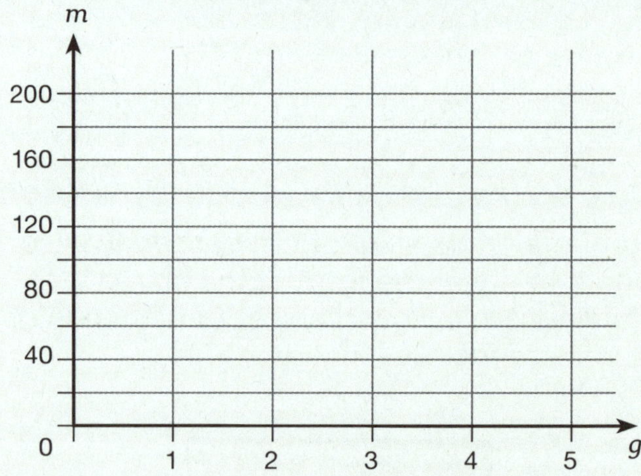

George's Car

Draw a point on each graph where $g = 2\frac{1}{2}$.

If Isabella has $2\frac{1}{2}$ gallons of gas, how far can she drive?

If George has $2\frac{1}{2}$ gallons of gas, how far can he drive?

Draw a point on each graph where $m = 60$.

How much gas does Isabella need to drive 60 miles?

How much gas does George need to drive 60 miles?

Practice

Use the information and equations to complete the charts and create matching graphs. Then, answer the questions.

Eve's Savings Plan

I already have \$10.
I will save \$4 per day.

$$10 + 4d = m$$

Number of days (d)	Money in dollars (m)
0	10
1	14
2	
3	
4	
5	

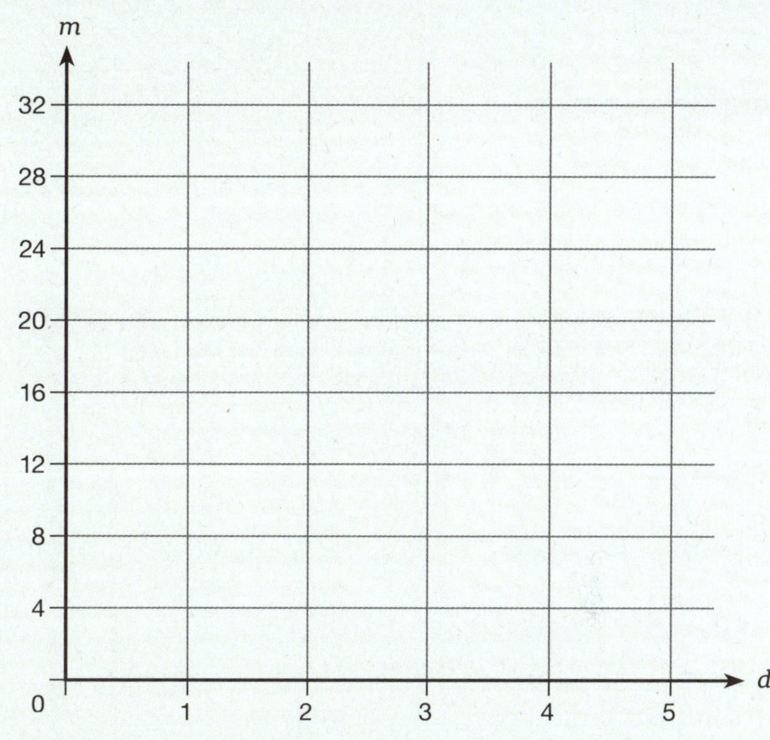

Cameron's Spending Plan

I already have \$30.
I spend \$6 per day.

$$30 - 6d = m$$

Number of days (d)	Money in dollars (m)
0	30
1	24
2	
3	
4	
5	

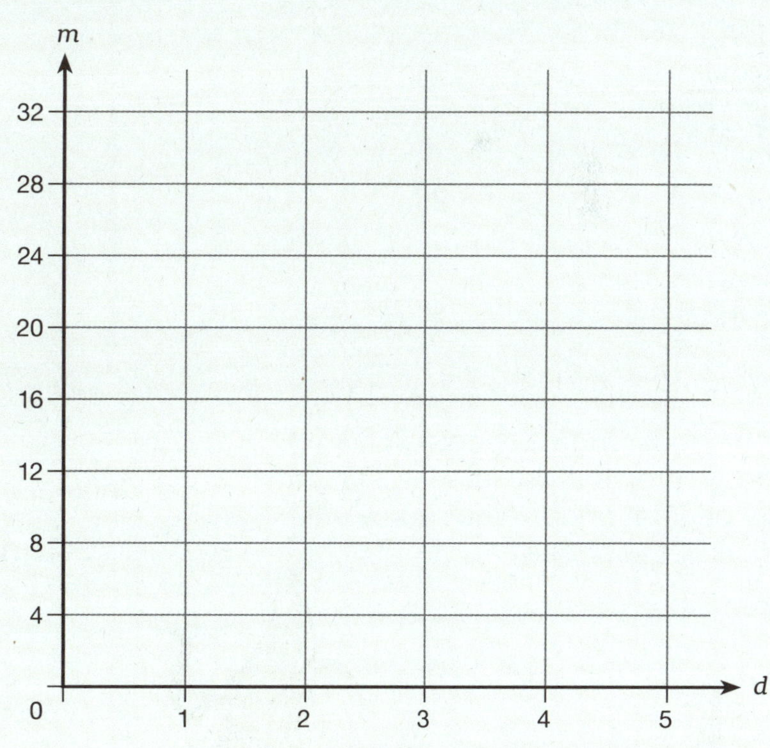

Who has more money to start?

Who has more money on day 5?

Which day do Eve and Cameron have the same amount of money?

Review

Solve each equation. Show all your steps. Then, substitute the solution into the equation to check that it is correct.

$99 = f + 37$

Check:

$10n = 170$

Check:

Convert the percentages to decimals. Convert the fractions to percentages.

59% = __________   8% = __________

30% = __________   11% = __________

130% = __________   111% = __________

$\dfrac{25}{100} =$ $\dfrac{1}{100} =$

$\dfrac{48}{50} =$ $\dfrac{2}{25} =$

$1\dfrac{2}{5} =$ $2\dfrac{1}{2} =$

Find the area. Write the equations you use.

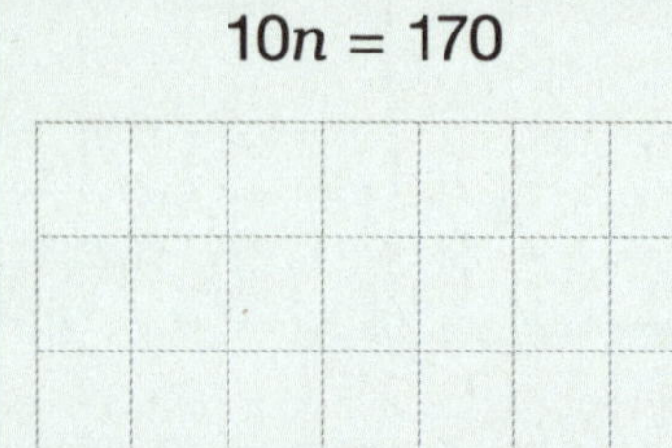

Use bar models to solve.

The shoes originally cost $60. Today, they are on sale for 25% off the original price. What is the sale price of the shoes?

Original price

Sale price

Unit Wrap-Up

Write whether each mathematical statement is an equation, expression, or inequality.

$2(4 + a)$	$b < 8$	$6c = 30$
_____________	_____________	_____________

Graph each inequality on the number line. Then, circle the numbers that make the inequality true. X the numbers that do not make the inequality true.

$e > -3$

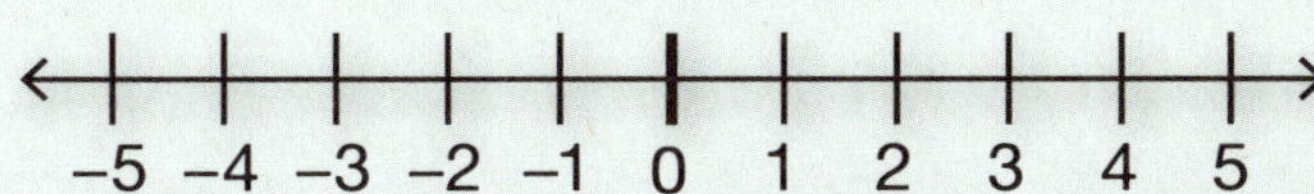

$f \leq 4$

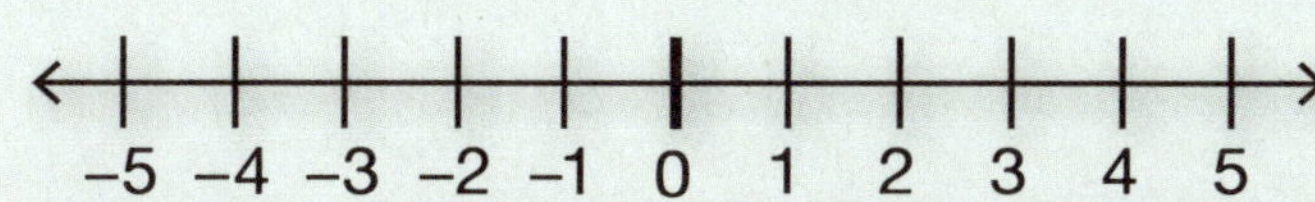

-5	3	-3	$-2\frac{1}{2}$	2	4	0	-5

Use mental math to check whether each number is a solution to the equation. Circle the numbers that are the solutions to the equations. (Some equations will have more than one solution.)

$8 + u = 19$	$16 = 20 - v$	$w \cdot 0 = 0$
11 12 13	2 3 4	7 8 9

$\dfrac{x}{5} = 2$	$y + y = 2y$	$2(z + 4) = 20$
9 10 11	4 5 6	6 7 8

Solve each equation. Show all your steps. Then, substitute the solution into the equation to check that it is correct.

$x + 6 = 25$	$78 = y + 17$	$110 = 99 + z$
	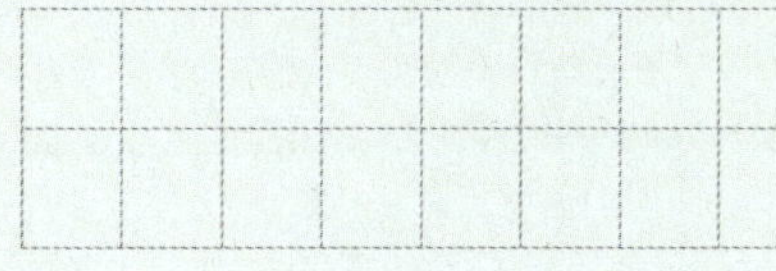	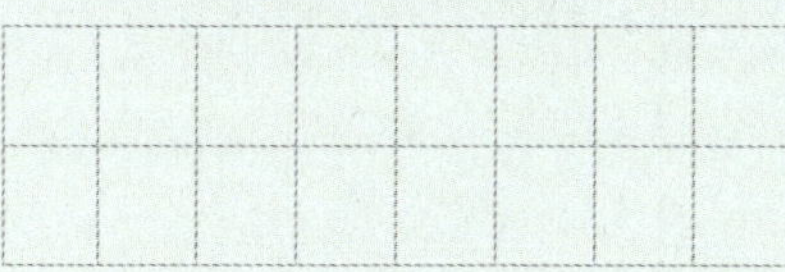
Check: 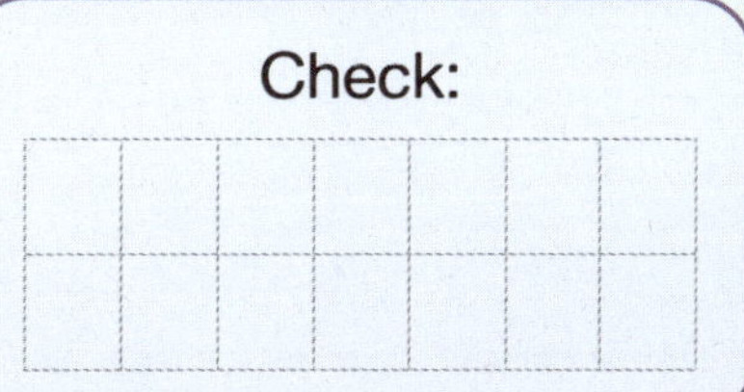	Check:	Check: 

Unit Wrap-Up

Solve each equation. Show all your steps. Then, substitute the solution into the equation to check that it is correct.

$4g = 100$

Check:

$10h = 230$

Check:

$28 = 2x$

Check:

Use the information to complete the chart and create a graph to match. Then, answer the questions.

Pounds of rice (r)	0	1	2	3	4	5
Cost in dollars (c)	0	4				

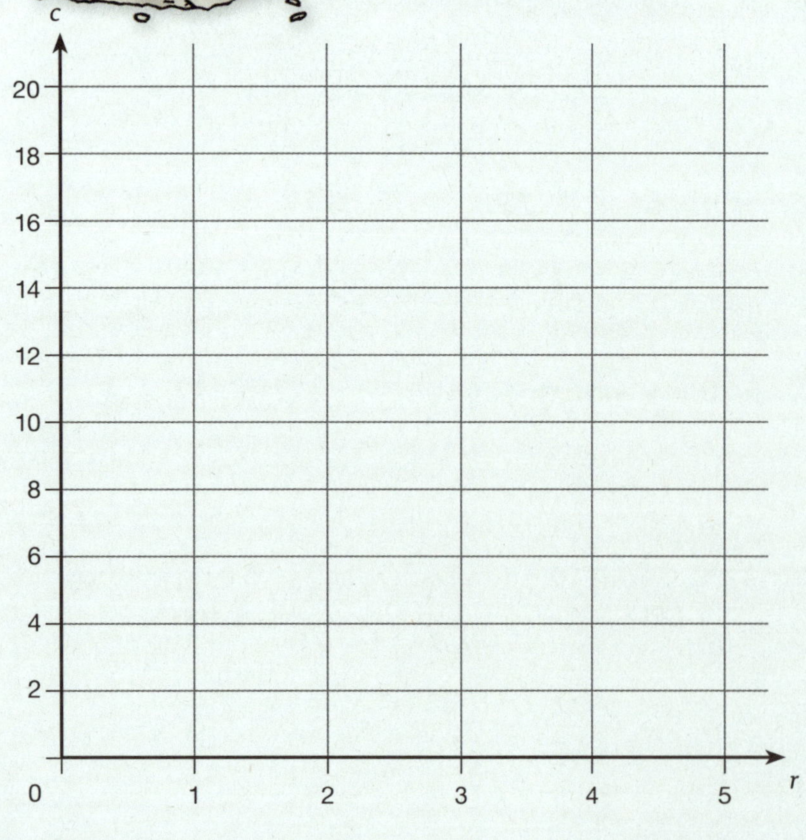

Write an equation that shows the relationship between the number of pounds of rice (r) and the cost (c).

Use your equation to find how much 8 pounds of rice cost.

Draw a point on the graph where $r = 3\frac{1}{2}$. How much do $3\frac{1}{2}$ pounds of rice cost?

Lesson Activities

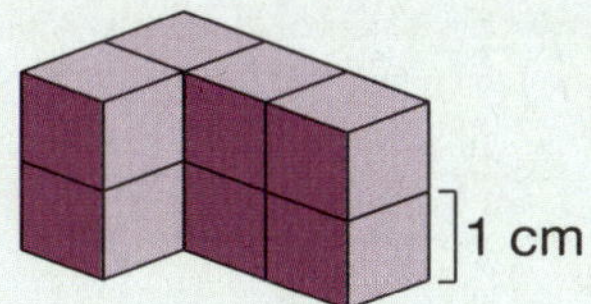

Volume: _________ cubic cm

Volume: _________ cubic cm

Volume: _________ cubic cm

A

B

Review Volume

A rectangular prism is a three-dimensional shape with 6 rectangular faces. We use these formulas to find the volume (V) of a rectangular prism.

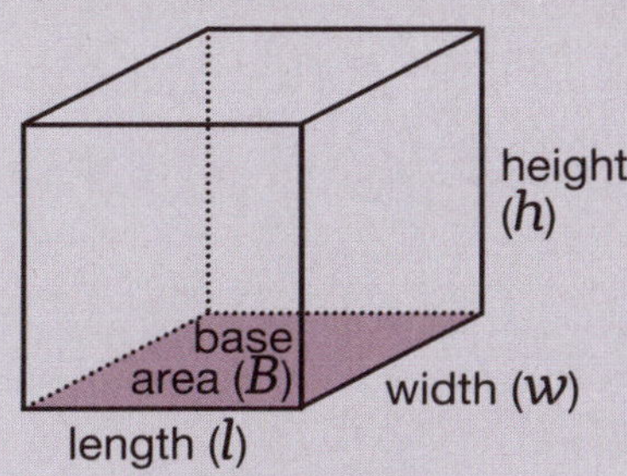

$$l \cdot w \cdot h = V$$

$$\downarrow$$

$$B \cdot h = V$$

We can choose any face to be the base, as long as we measure the height perpendicular to the chosen base.

Ex. The jewelry box is 25 cm long, 10 cm wide, and 10 cm tall. What is its volume?

$$l \cdot w \cdot h = V$$

$$25 \text{ cm} \cdot 10 \text{ cm} \cdot 10 \text{ cm} = \textbf{2,500 cm}^3$$

Ex. The wardrobe sticks out 2 ft. from the wall. The back of the wardrobe covers 60 ft.² of the wall. What is the volume of the wardrobe?

$$B \cdot h = V$$

$$60 \text{ ft.}^2 \cdot 2 \text{ ft.} = \textbf{120 ft.}^3$$

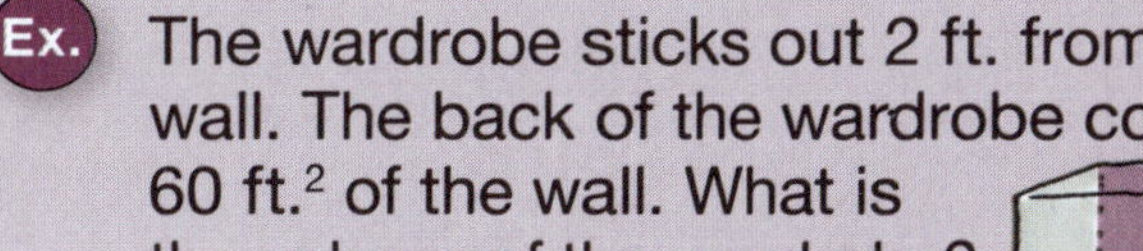

C

Design a Clubhouse!

The area of the floor must be less than 100 ft.².

You may only use straight lines and right angles.

The walls are 6 ft. tall.

Clubhouse Floor Plan

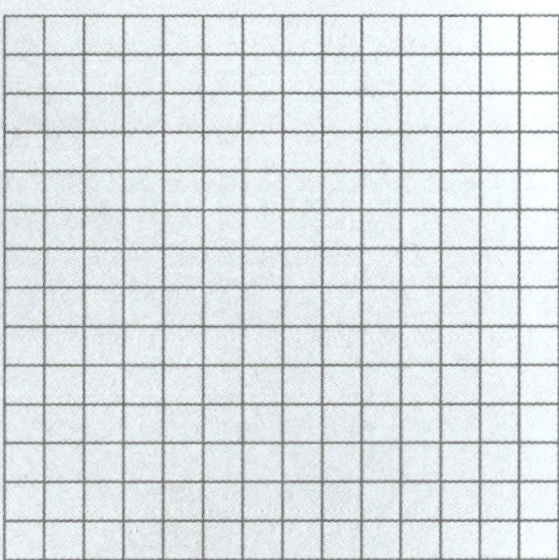

What is the area of the clubhouse floor?

What is the volume of the clubhouse?

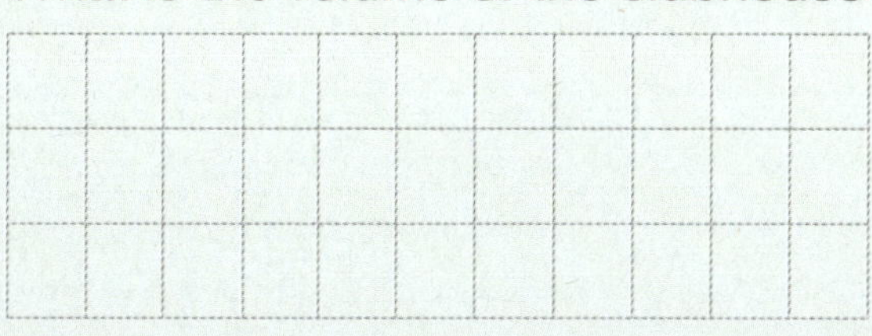

Practice

Find the base area and volume for each solid.
(Use the highlighted side as the base.)
Make sure to include the correct units in your answers.

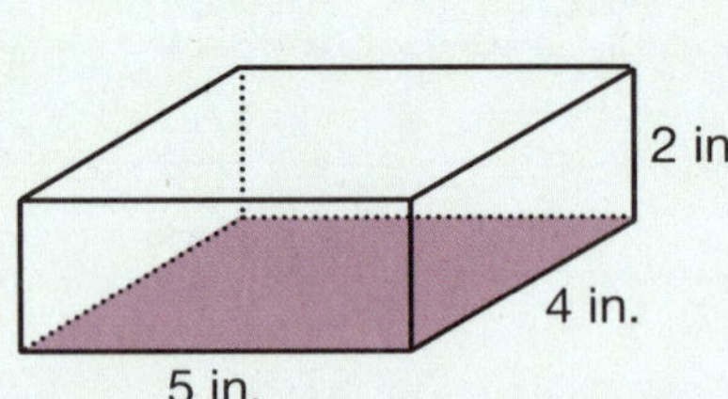

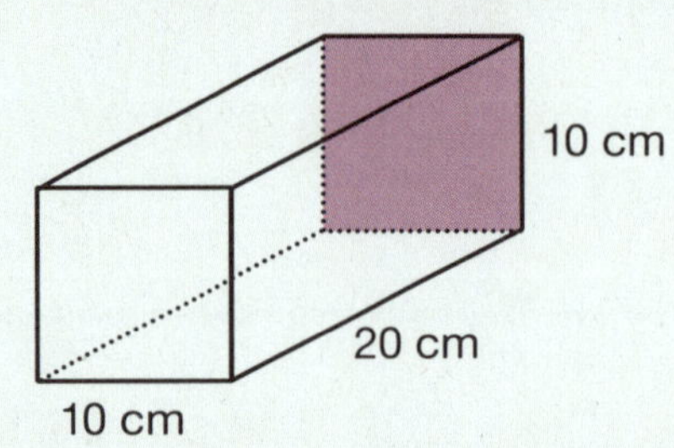

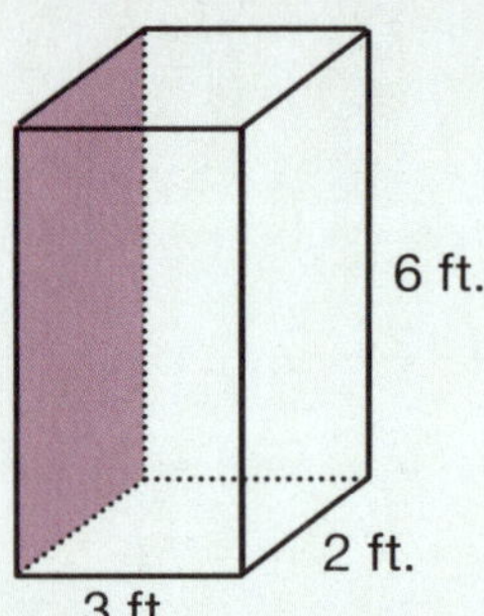

Base area: _______________

Volume: _______________

Base area: _______________

Volume: _______________

Base area: _______________

Volume: _______________

Complete the missing units. Use exponents for square and cubic units.

This box is 8 cm by 2 cm by 5 cm.
What is its volume?

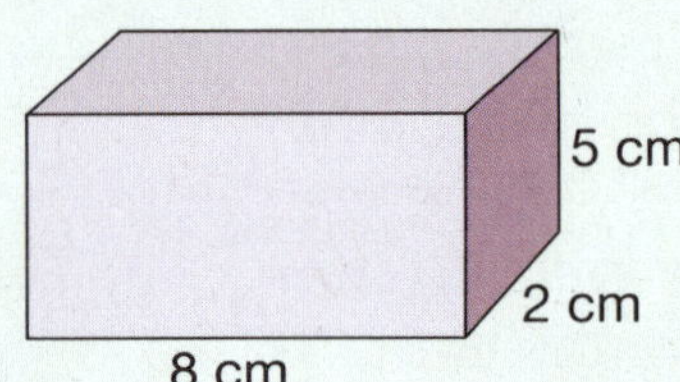

$8\ \boxed{} \cdot 2\ \boxed{} \cdot 5\ \boxed{} = 80\ \boxed{}$

This box is 3 ft. tall. Its bottom covers an area of 5 ft.^{2}. What is its volume?

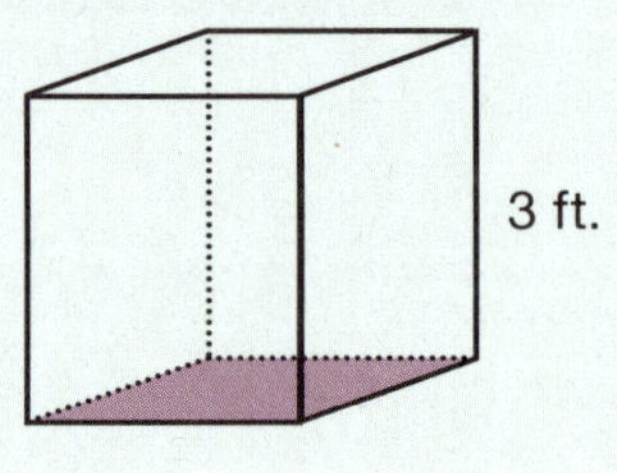

$5\ \boxed{} \cdot 3\ \boxed{} = 15\ \boxed{}$

Solve. Write the equations you use.

The water tank is 30 cm by 25 cm by 40 cm. What is its volume?

1,000 cm^3 equals 1 liter. How many liters of water can the water tank hold?

The kiddie pool's bottom covers an area of 15 ft.^{2}. Rebekah fills the pool 2 ft. deep with water. What is the volume of the water in the pool?

1 cubic foot of water equals approximately 7.5 gallons. How many gallons of water does Rebekah put in the pool?

Review   Find the products.

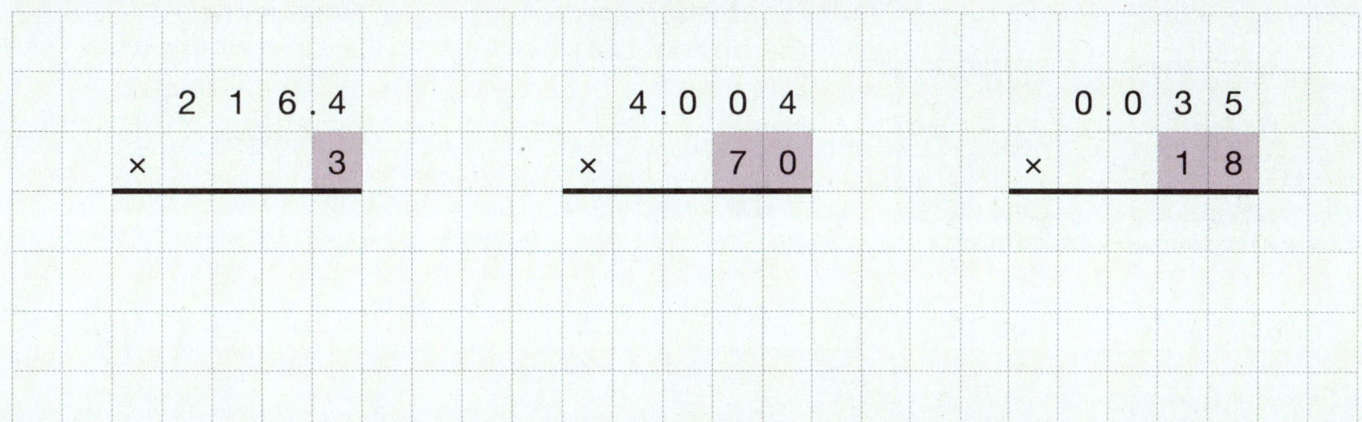

Write the fraction that is equivalent to each decimal. You will use each fraction once.

$$\frac{3}{10} \qquad \frac{4}{5} \qquad \frac{1}{2} \qquad \frac{9}{10} \qquad \frac{2}{5} \qquad \frac{7}{10} \qquad \frac{1}{5} \qquad \frac{3}{5} \qquad \frac{1}{10}$$

0.1 = _____________ 0.2 = _____________ 0.3 = _____________

0.4 = _____________ 0.5 = _____________ 0.6 = _____________

0.7 = _____________ 0.8 = _____________ 0.9 = _____________

Complete the chart.

Expression	Number of Terms	Number of Constants	Simplest Form
$m + m + m + 5 + 1$			
$9b - b + 3$			
$5a + 6 + 1 + 4a + 2$			

Use bar models to complete the ratios and answer the question.

Adam's age is $\frac{4}{5}$ of Morgan's age.

Adam's age : Morgan's age

_______ : _______

Morgan's age : Adam's age

_______ : _______

Adam is 24 years old. How old is Morgan?

Lesson Activities

20 in.   15 in.   10 in.

What is the area of the bottom of the aquarium?

What is the volume of the water in the aquarium?

Divide to Find Base Area or Height

If you know the volume of a rectangular prism and its height, you can divide the volume by the height to find the area of the base.

$$V = B \cdot h \quad \rightarrow \quad \frac{V}{h} = B$$

If you know the volume of a rectangular prism and the area of its base, you can divide the volume by the area of the base to find the height.

$$V = B \cdot h \quad \rightarrow \quad \frac{V}{B} = h$$

Ex. At the aquarium, the jellyfish tank is 4 ft. tall. It has a volume of 48 ft.^{3}. What is the area of the bottom of the jellyfish tank?

$$\frac{48 \text{ ft.}^3}{4 \text{ ft.}} = \frac{48 \text{ ft.} \cdot \text{ft.} \cdot \text{ft.}}{4 \text{ ft.}} = \textbf{12 ft.}^2$$

4 ft.

Ex. The tropical fish tank covers an area of 3 m^2. It has a volume of 3 m^3. What is its height?

$$\frac{3 \text{ m}^3}{3 \text{ m}^2} = \frac{3 \text{ m} \cdot \text{m} \cdot \text{m}}{3 \text{ m} \cdot \text{m}} = \textbf{1 m}$$

The stingray tank's bottom has an area of 300 ft.^{2}. The tank holds 1,500 ft.^{3} of water. How tall is the tank?

The largest tank at the aquarium is 7 m tall. It holds 686 m^3 of water. What is the area of the bottom of the tank?

Practice

All of these rectangular prisms have a volume of 60 cm³.
Find the base area or height. Make sure to use the correct units.
Use mental math or write equations in the work space.

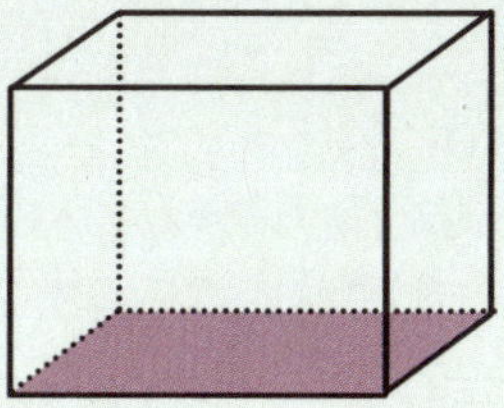

5 cm

Base area: _______________

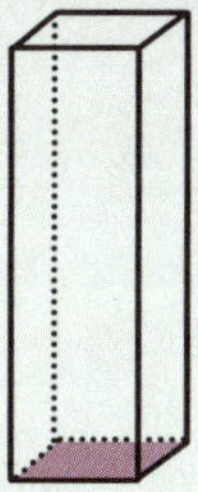

10 cm

Base area: _______________

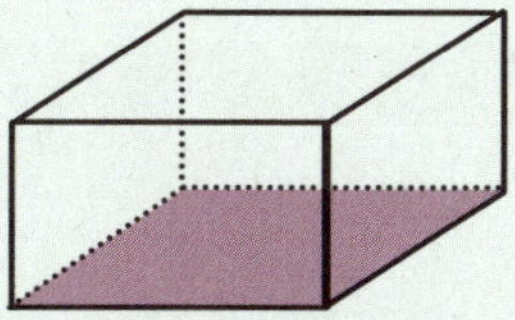

WORK SPACE

Base area: 20 cm²

Height: _______________

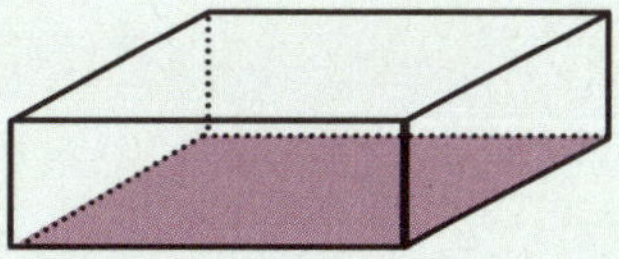

Base area: 30 cm²

Height: _______________

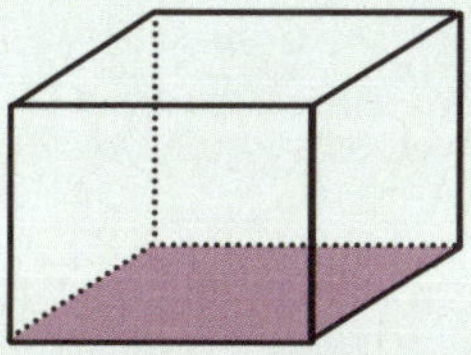

Base area: 15 cm²

Height: _______________

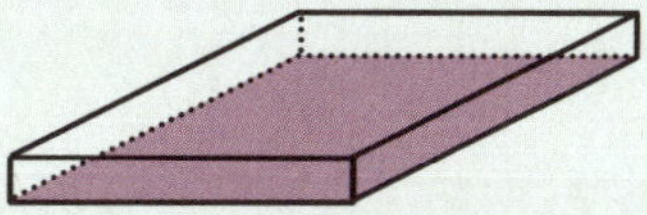

Base area: 60 cm²

Height: _______________

Solve. Write the equations you use.

Zeke rents a storage unit. The unit is 10 ft. long by 10 ft. wide. What is the area of the storage unit's floor?

The flyer for the storage unit says that it holds 800 ft.³ of household items. What is the height of the storage unit?

The mason pours 180 in.³ of cement into a mold. The cement fills the mold to a depth of 3 in. What is the base area of the mold?

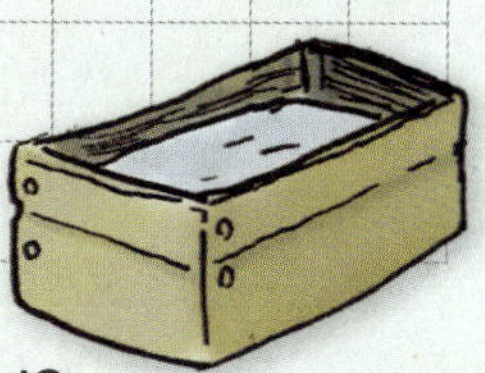

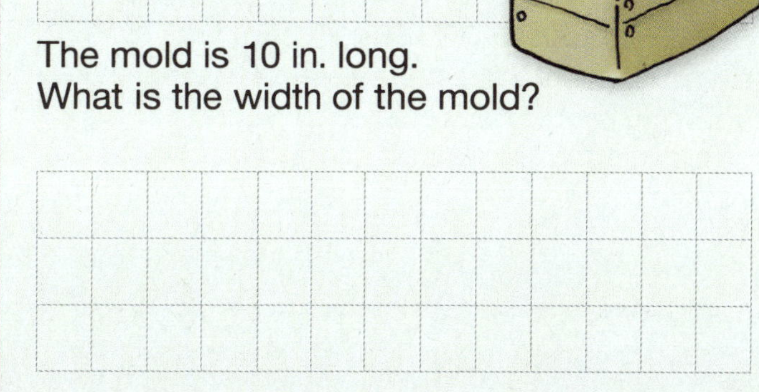

The mold is 10 in. long.
What is the width of the mold?

Review   Use mental math to complete.

50% of 80 = _______	25% of 32 = _______	$33\frac{1}{3}$% of 240 = _______
25% of 80 = _______	75% of 32 = _______	$66\frac{2}{3}$% of 240 = _______
10% of 90 = _______	20% of 35 = _______	10% of 160 = _______
40% of 90 = _______	80% of 35 = _______	5% of 160 = _______

**Solve each equation. Show all your steps.
Then, substitute the solution into the equation to check that it is correct.**

$25 = m + 6$

Check:

$140 = 7n$

Check:

Solve. Write the equations you use in the work space.

At the grocery store, a 5-pound bag of rice costs $3.79. What is the unit cost of 1 pound of rice? Write your answer with 2 decimal digits.

At the wholesale club, a 25-pound bag of rice costs $17.88. The restaurant owner buys 4 bags. How much does she pay?

Lesson Activities

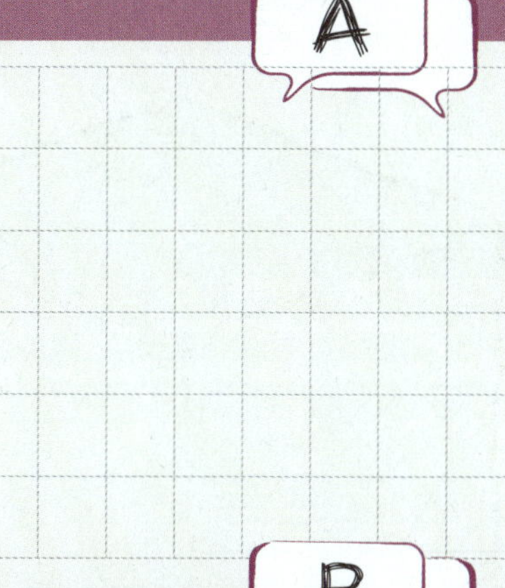

A

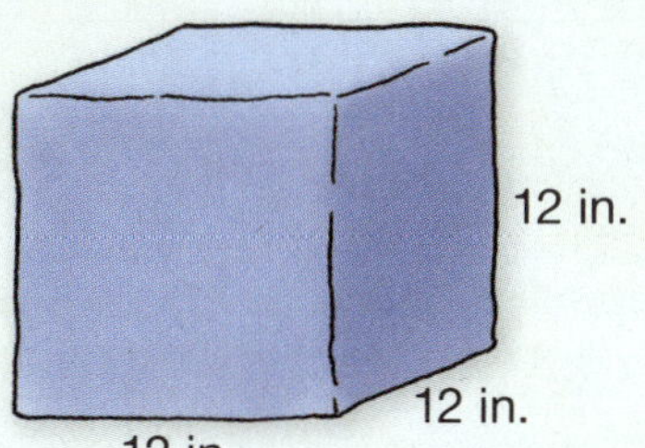

How many cubic inches are in 1 cubic foot?

1 cubic inch equals what fraction of a cubic foot?

12 in.

12 in.

12 in.

Use Fractions to Find Volume

B

Ex. The foam dice company cuts foam into cubes to make foam dice. What is the volume of a foam die that is $\frac{1}{2}$ ft. long on each side?

$\frac{1}{2}$ ft.

$$\frac{1}{2} \text{ ft.} \times \frac{1}{2} \text{ ft.} \times \frac{1}{2} \text{ ft.} = \frac{1}{8} \textbf{ ft.}^3$$

Ex. How many $\frac{1}{2}$-foot dice can the company cut from a foam cube that is 1 ft. long on each side?

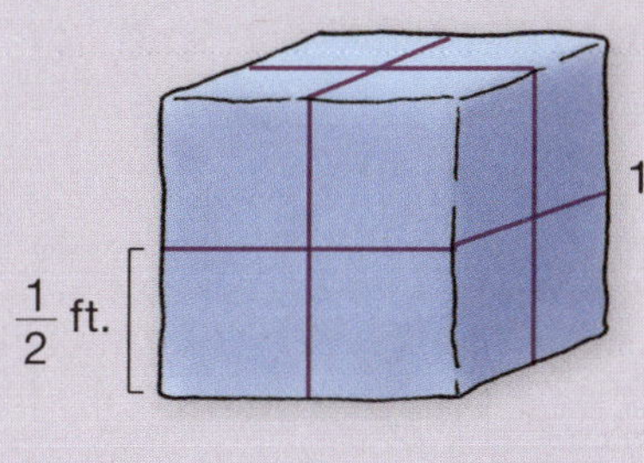

1 ft.

$\frac{1}{2}$ ft.

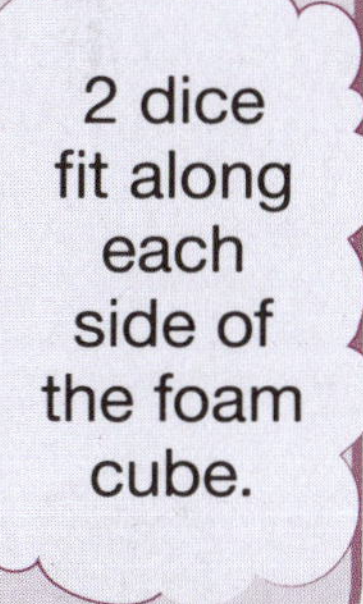

$$2 \times 2 \times 2 = \textbf{8 dice}$$

What is the volume of a die that is $\frac{1}{3}$ ft. long on each side?

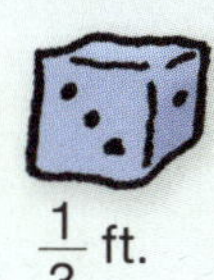

$\frac{1}{3}$ ft.

How many $\frac{1}{3}$-foot dice can the company cut from a foam cube that is 1 ft. long on each side?

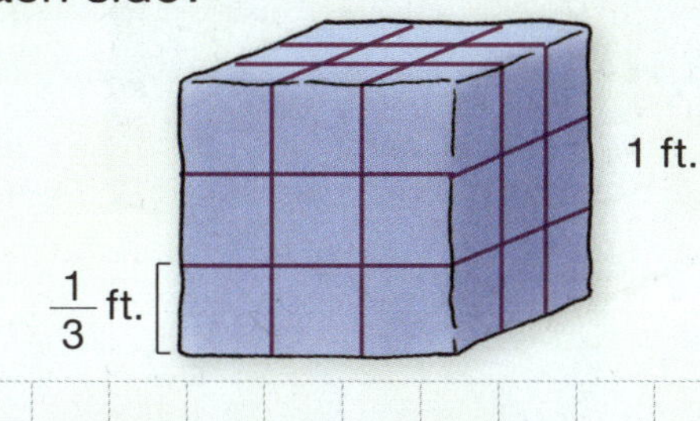

1 ft.

$\frac{1}{3}$ ft.

What is the volume of a die that is $\frac{1}{4}$ ft. long on each side?

$\frac{1}{4}$ ft.

How many $\frac{1}{4}$-foot dice can the company cut from a foam cube that is 1 ft. long on each side?

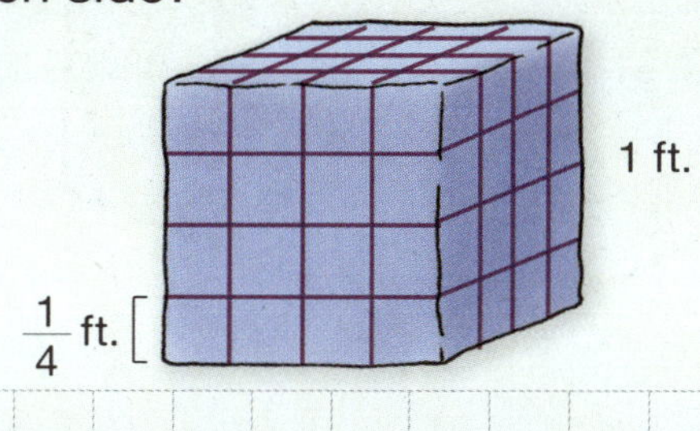

1 ft.

$\frac{1}{4}$ ft.

Practice

Answer the questions. Write the equations you use.

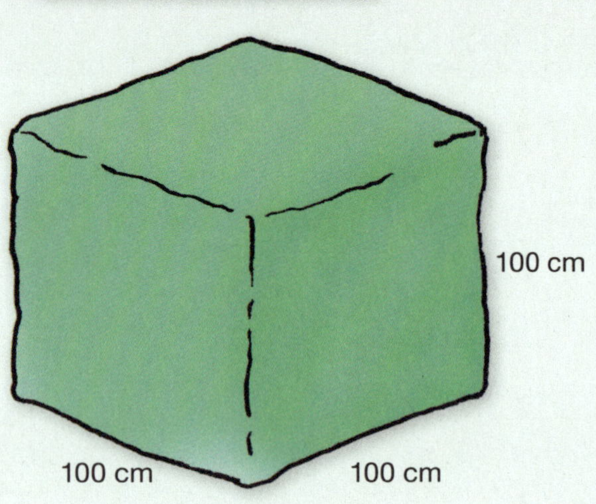

How many cubic centimeters are in 1 cubic meter?

1 cubic centimeter equals what fraction of a cubic meter?

Solve. Write the equations you use.

What is the volume of a foam die that is $\frac{1}{5}$ m long on each side?

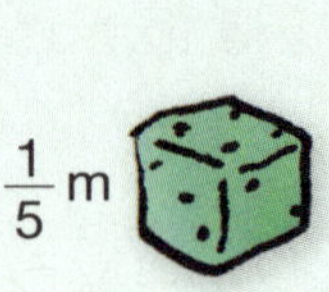

How many $\frac{1}{5}$-meter dice can the company cut from a foam cube that is 1 m long on each side?

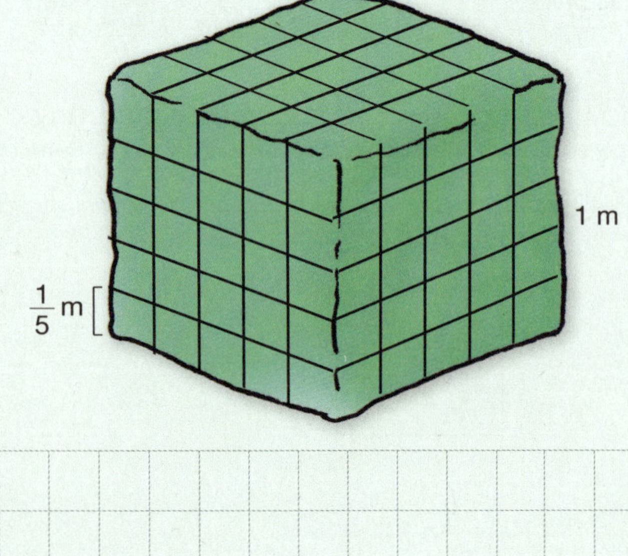

What is the volume of a foam die that is $\frac{1}{10}$ m long on each side?

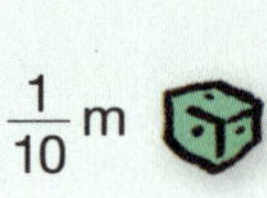

How many $\frac{1}{10}$-meter dice can the company cut from a foam cube that is 1 m long on each side?

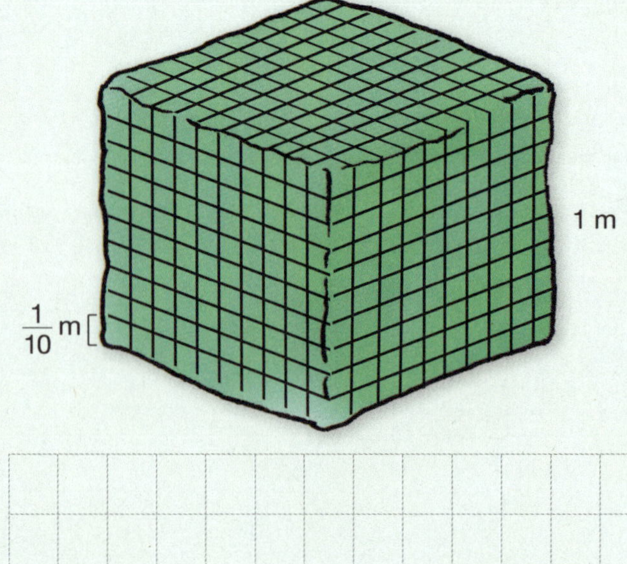

Review   Complete the chart.

c	1	2	3	4	5	6	7	8	9	10
c^2	1	4								
$c^2 + 1$	2	5								
$2 \cdot c^2$	2	8								

Use the decimal squares to complete the blanks.

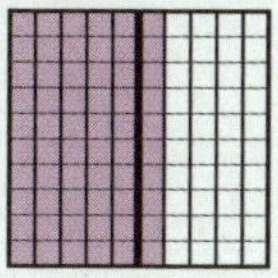

Half of 0.6: ___0.3___

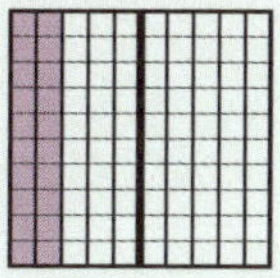

Half of 0.2: _________

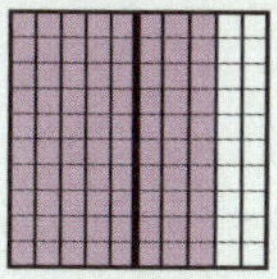

Half of 0.8: _________

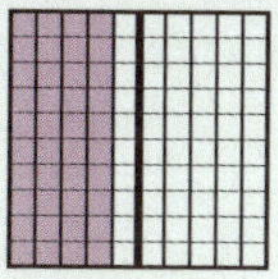

Half of 0.4: _________

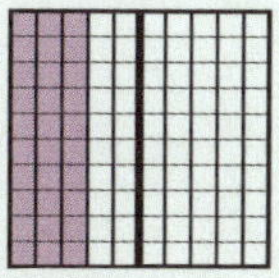

Half of 0.3: _________

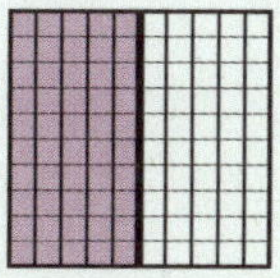

Half of 0.5: _________

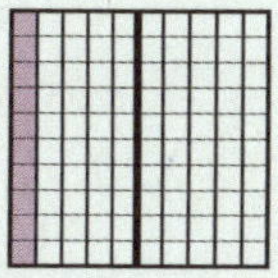

Half of 0.1: _________

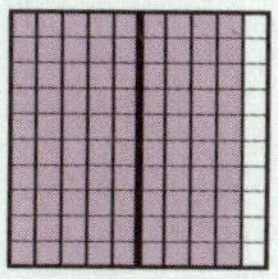

Half of 0.9: _________

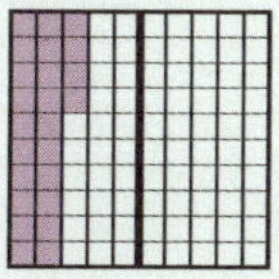

Half of 0.24: _________

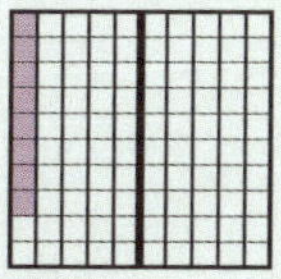

Half of 0.08: _________

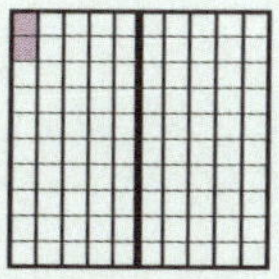

Half of 0.02: _________

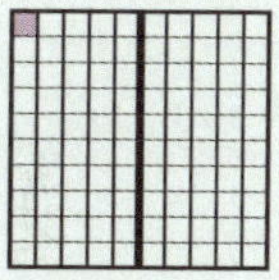

★ Half of 0.01: _________

Answer the questions.

The rectangle's length is 2 times its width. Write an expression (in simplest form) for the perimeter of the rectangle. Use w to stand for the rectangle's width.

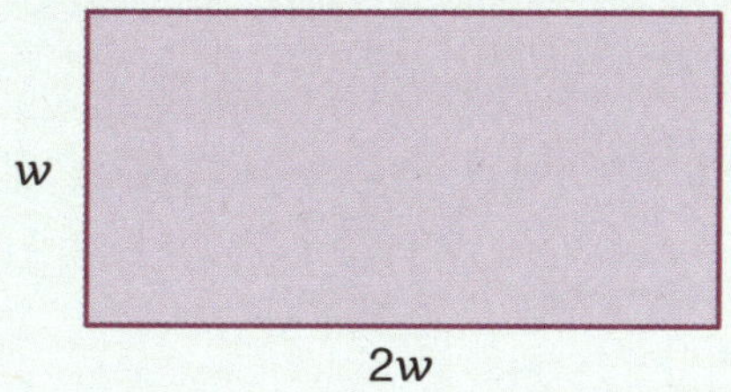

w

$2w$

The perimeter of the rectangle is 60 cm. What are its length and width?

What is the area of the rectangle?

Lesson Activities

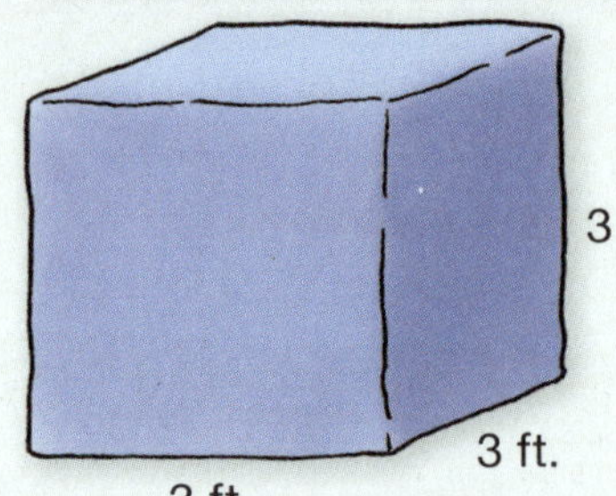

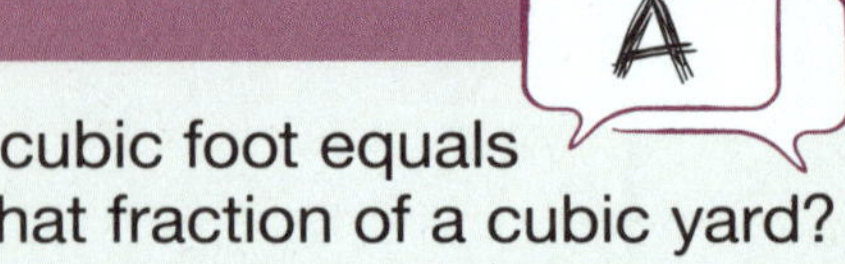

How many cubic feet are in 1 cubic yard?

1 cubic foot equals what fraction of a cubic yard?

Use Fractions and Mixed Numbers to Find Volume

 **Ex.** What is the volume of this box?

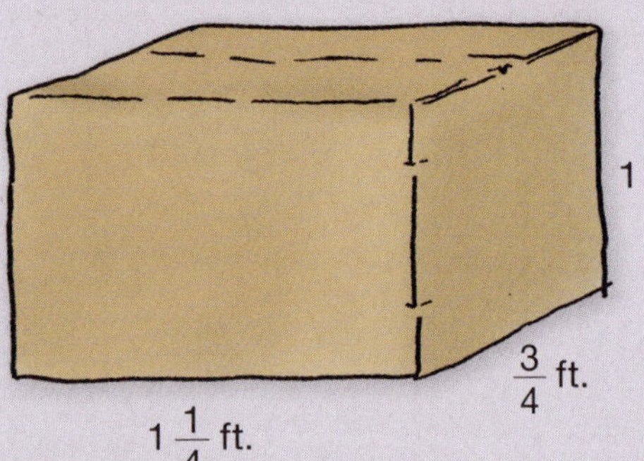

$$l \cdot w \cdot h = V$$

$$1\frac{1}{4} \text{ ft.} \times \frac{3}{4} \text{ ft.} \times 1 \text{ ft.}$$

$$\frac{5}{4} \text{ ft.} \times \frac{3}{4} \text{ ft.} \times \frac{1}{1} \text{ ft.} = \frac{15}{16} \text{ ft.}^3$$

Alana's family packs their Christmas ornaments in this storage box. What is the volume of the box?

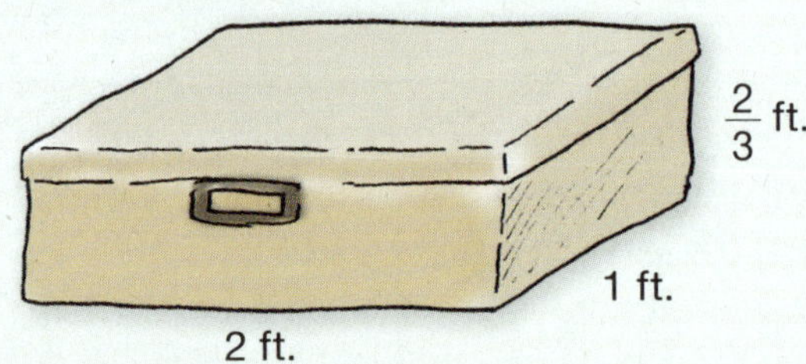

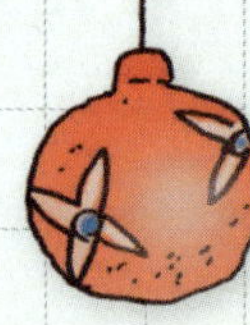

 They pack each ornament in a small box that is $\frac{1}{3}$ ft. long on each side. How many ornaments can they pack in the storage box? (Think about how many ornaments fit along each side of the storage box.)

Practice

Find the volume of each box. Write your equations in the work space. Then, answer the questions.

Small Box

Volume: _______________

Medium Box

Volume: _______________

Large Box

Volume: _______________

Extra-Large Box

Volume: _______________

Lamp Box

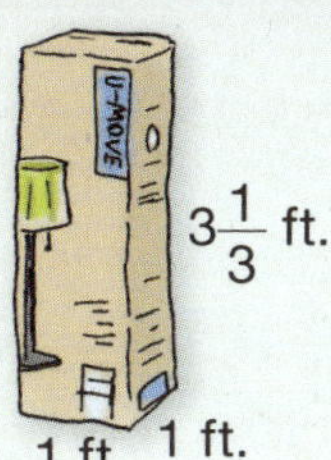

Volume: _______________

Wardrobe Box

Volume: _______________

Orion's older sister is packing to go to college. She uses 4 small boxes, 3 medium boxes, and 1 wardrobe box. What is the total volume of all her boxes?

★ How many small boxes does it take to hold the same volume of items as the extra-large box?

Review

Convert the measurements.
Write your answers as fractions in simplest form.

1 in. = $\frac{1}{12}$ ft.

$$\frac{1}{12}$$

2 in. = __________ ft.

$$\frac{2}{12} = \frac{1}{6}$$

3 in. = __________ ft.

4 in. = __________ ft.

5 in. = __________ ft.

6 in. = __________ ft.

7 in. = __________ ft.

8 in. = __________ ft.

9 in. = __________ ft.

10 in. = __________ ft.

11 in. = __________ ft.

12 in. = 1 ft.

Move the decimal point to find the product or quotient.

$0.623 \times 100 =$ __________

$0.081 \times 10 =$ __________

$0.041 \times 1{,}000 =$ __________

$0.09 \div 10 =$ __________

$0.84 \div 100 =$ __________

$0.5 \div 1{,}000 =$ __________

Solve. Write the equations you use.

Ava uses $\frac{2}{3}$ c. yogurt to make a smoothie each morning. How much yogurt does she use in one week?

Ava also uses $\frac{3}{4}$ c. blueberries in each smoothie. There are $3\frac{3}{4}$ c. frozen blueberries in the bag. How many days does it take her to eat the whole bag of blueberries?

Lesson Activities 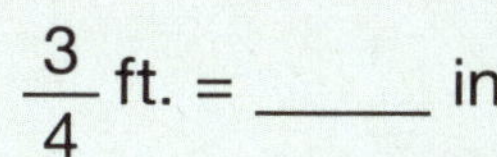

$\dfrac{3}{4}$ ft. = _____ in.

$\dfrac{1}{2}$ ft. = _____ in.

4 in. = _____ ft.

10 in. = _____ ft.

A

B

Convert Measurement Units to Find Volume

When we multiply measurements to find volume, the measurements must have the same unit.

If the measurements have different units, first convert them all to the same unit. Then, solve like usual.

Ex. What is the volume of this gift box?

$1\dfrac{1}{2}$ ft. × 1 ft. × 3 in.

3 in. = $\dfrac{1}{4}$ ft.

$\dfrac{3}{2}$ ft. × $\dfrac{1}{1}$ ft. × $\dfrac{1}{4}$ ft. = $\dfrac{3}{8}$ **ft.³**

C

Length (ft.)	Width (ft.)	Height (ft.)	Volume (ft.³)

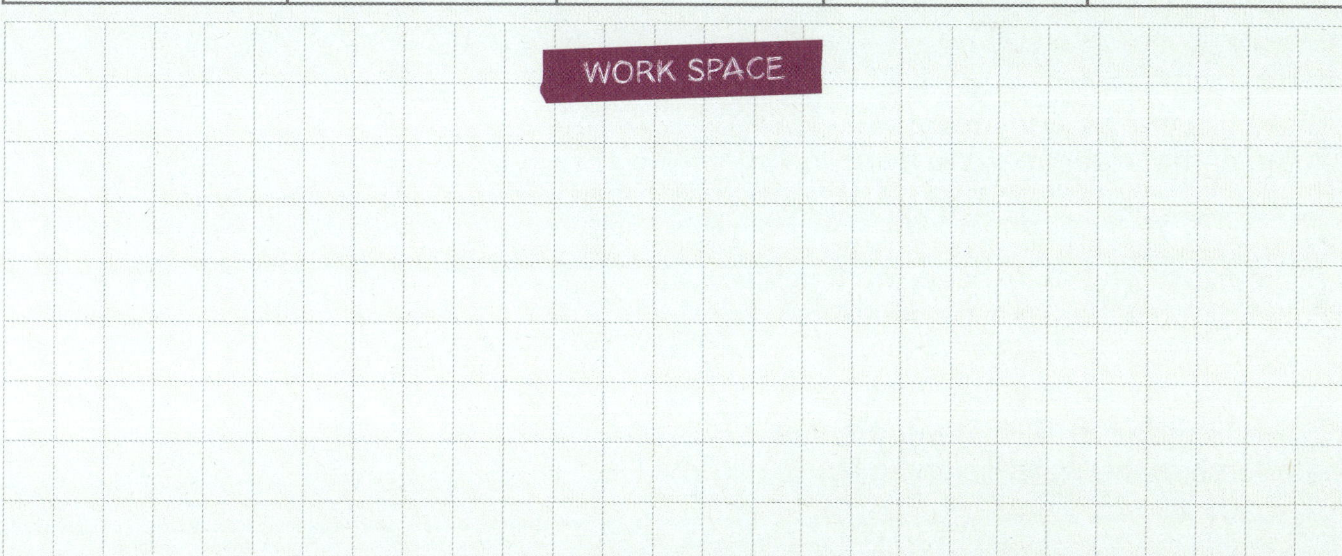

WORK SPACE

Practice

Solve. Write the equations you use in the work space.

What is the volume of this wrapping paper box?

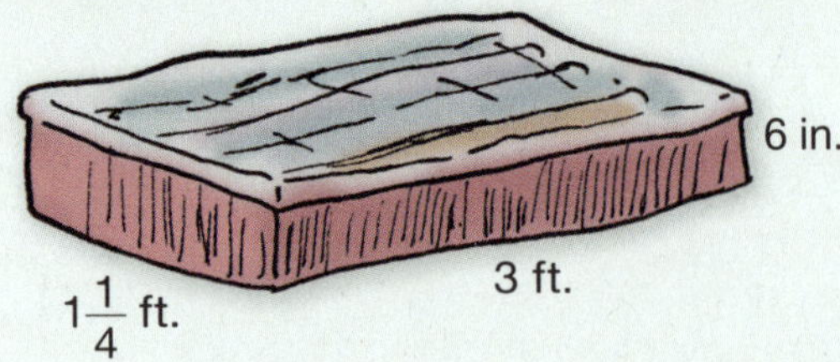

Tiana wants to fill this garden bed with dirt. How many cubic feet of dirt does she need?

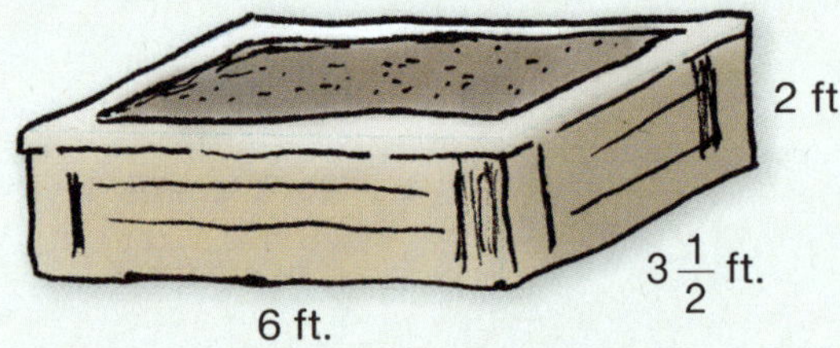

Blake has a rectangular bathtub. The inside of the tub is 5 ft. long and $2\frac{1}{2}$ ft. wide. What is the area of the bottom of the tub?

If Blake fills the tub 3 in. deep, what is the volume of the water (in cubic feet)?

If Blake fills the tub 6 in. deep, what is the volume of the water (in cubic feet)?

If Blake fills the tub 12 in. deep, what is the volume of the water (in cubic feet)?

WORK SPACE

Review 👤 Use mental math to complete.

100% of 20 = _____________   100% of 15 = _____________   100% of 35 = _____________

125% of 20 = _____________ $133\frac{1}{3}$% of 15 = _____________   200% of 35 = _____________

150% of 20 = _____________ $166\frac{2}{3}$% of 15 = _____________   300% of 35 = _____________

175% of 20 = _____________   200% of 15 = _____________   400% of 35 = _____________

Use the distributive property to complete the blanks. You do not need to evaluate.

$80 \cdot (30 + 7) =$ ________ $\cdot\, 30 +$ ________ $\cdot\, 7$ $35 \cdot 46 + 35 \cdot 4 = 35 \cdot (46 +$ ________ $)$

$200 \cdot (60 + 4) = 200 \cdot 60 + 200 \cdot$ ________ $77 \cdot 1 + 77 \cdot 39 = 77 \cdot ($ ________ $+ 39)$

Use the information to complete the chart, draw a graph, and answer the questions.

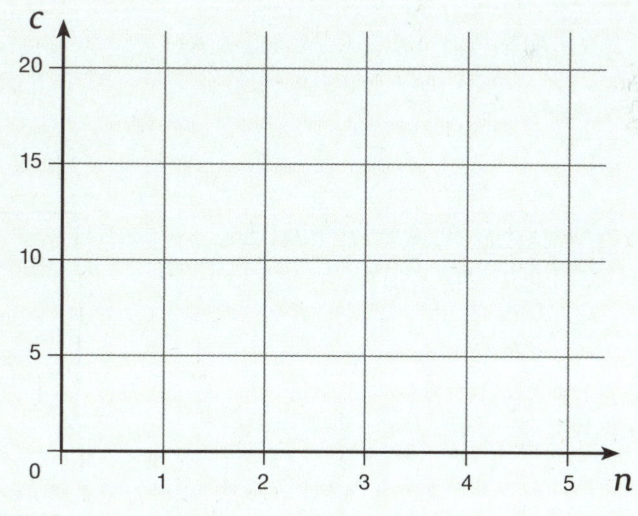

Pounds	Cost ($)
0	0
1	4
2	
3	
4	
5	

Write an equation that shows the relationship between the number of pounds of strawberries (n) and their total cost (c).

How much do 15 pounds of strawberries cost? Use your equation to find the answer.

 How many pounds of strawberries can you buy for $80? Use your equation to find the answer.

Lesson Activities 👥

A

What is the volume of the planter (in cubic feet)?

B

How many cubic feet of water fit inside the pond if you fill it to the top?

1 cubic foot equals approximately 7.5 gallons. How many gallons of water does it take to fill the pond?

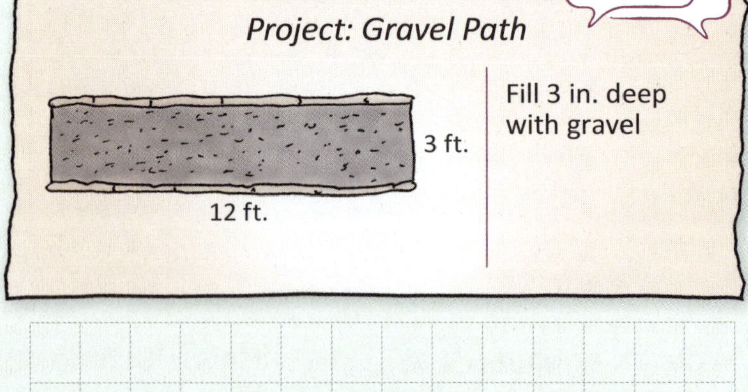

C

How many cubic feet of gravel are needed to fill in the path?

Gravel comes in bags that each hold $\frac{1}{2}$ ft.³. How many bags are needed to fill in the path?

Practice

Use the diagrams to answer the questions. Write the equations you use.

Sadie is helping her dad build a sandbox.

What is the volume of the sandbox?

Each bag of sand holds $\frac{3}{4}$ ft.^{3} of sand. How many bags do they need to fill the sandbox?

Noah buys this block of foam for a craft project.

What is the volume of the foam block in cubic inches?

Noah cuts the block into 6 equal pieces. What is the volume of each piece in cubic inches?

Hope is making a snow fort. She uses this mold to make blocks of snow.

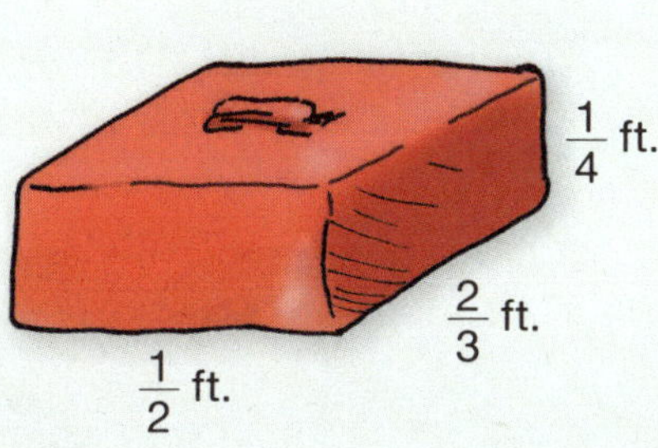

What is the volume of each block of snow in cubic feet?

Hope uses 30 blocks to make her snow fort. What is the total volume of the snow she uses to build the fort?

Review · Simplify each expression.

$a + 4 + 2a + 6$

$3f - 2f + f$

$z + z + z + z$

$6(3x + 4)$

$8(7r)$

$m + n + 3n + m + m$

Graph each inequality on the number line. Then, circle the numbers that make the inequality true. X the numbers that do not make the inequality true.

$a \geq 0$

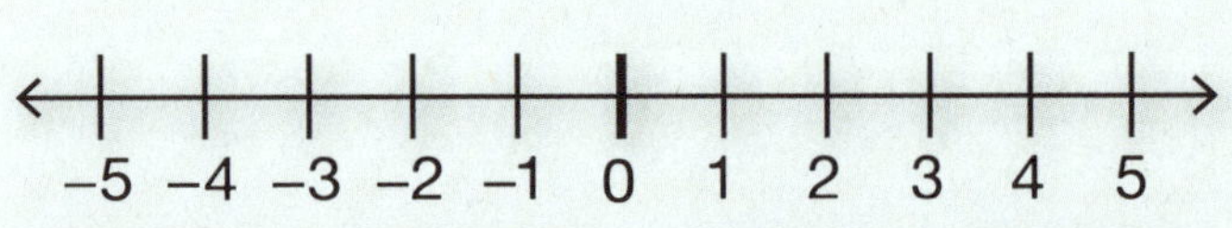

| 0 | −5 | 3 | 1.75 |

$b < -3$

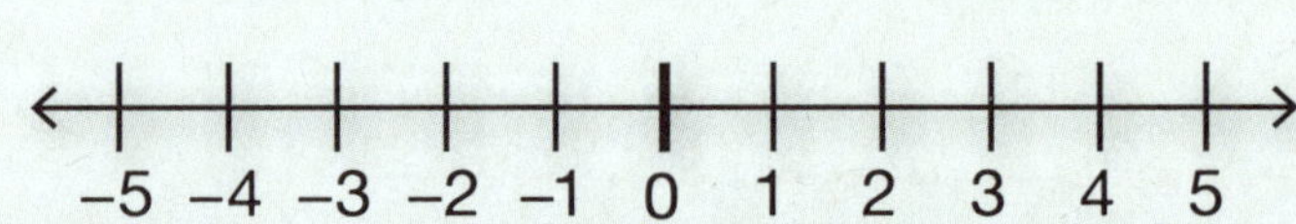

| −2 | 1 | −4.3 | 0 |

Use bar models to solve.

The bakery baked 75% as many sugar cookies as chocolate chip cookies. They baked 240 sugar cookies. How many chocolate chip cookies did they bake?

Sugar

Chocolate chip

How many more chocolate chip cookies than sugar cookies did they bake?

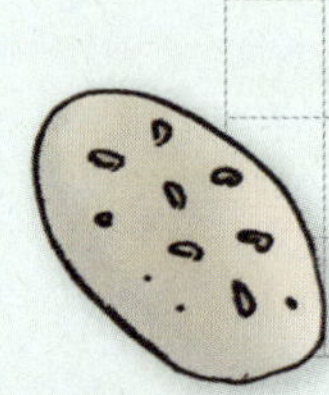

Unit Wrap-Up

Complete the blanks for each solid. Make sure to include the correct units in your answers.

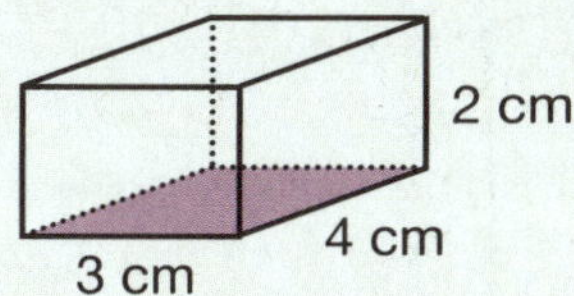

Base area: _______________

Height: _______________

Volume: _______________

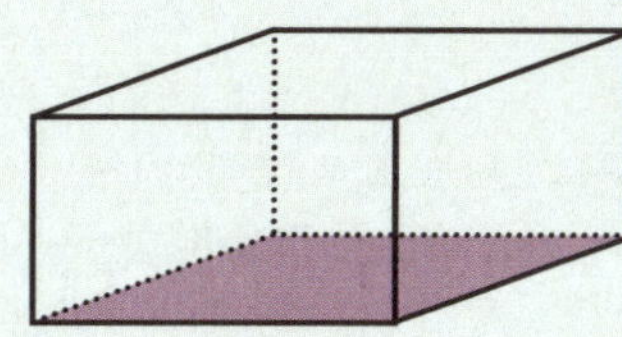

Base area: 25 cm^2

Height: _______________

Volume: 75 cm^3

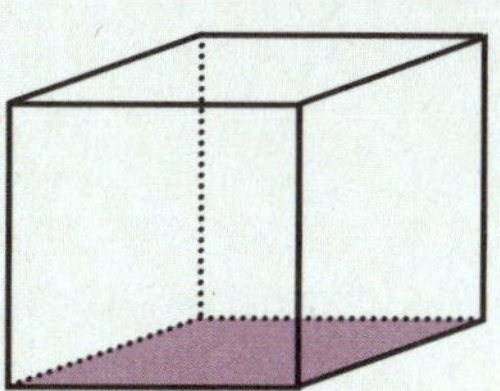

Base area: _______________

Height: 4 cm

Volume: 64 cm^3

Find the volume of each cube. Then, answer the question.

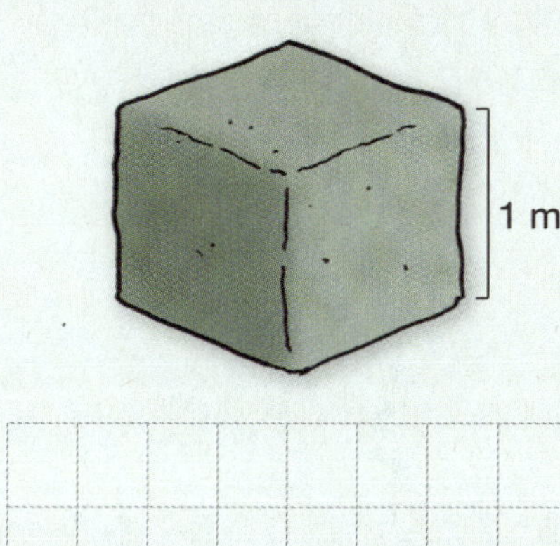

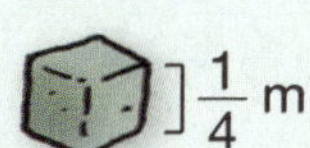

How many small cubes fit inside the large cube?

Find the volume of each box.

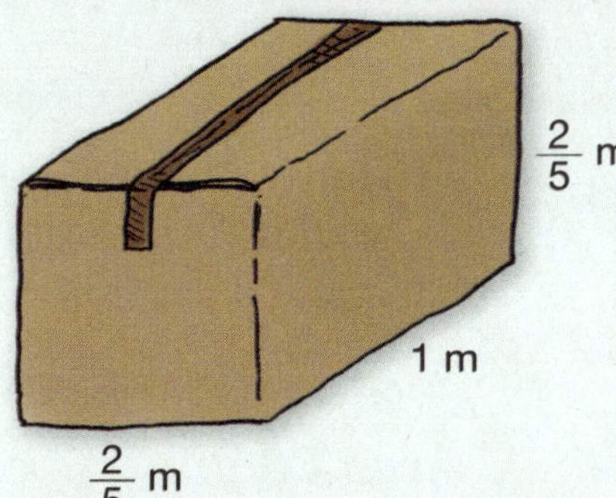

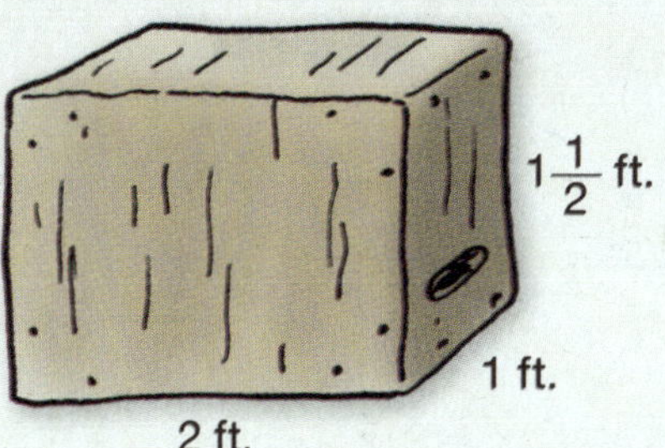

Unit Wrap-Up

Jonathan and his dad built this storage bench for their back hall. Use the diagram to answer the questions.

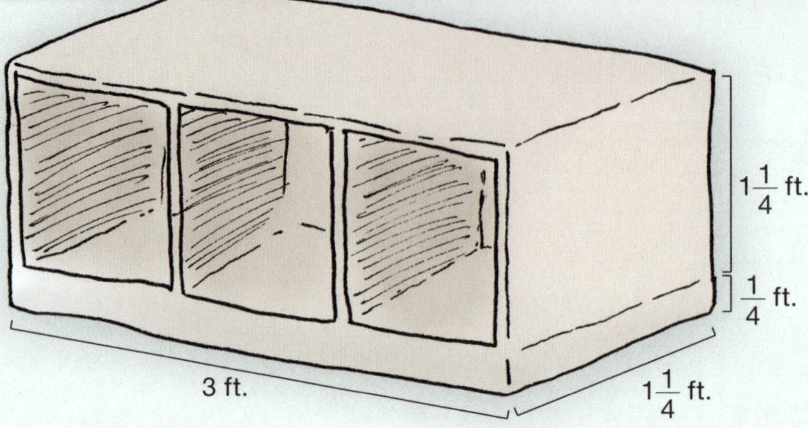

What is the total volume of the bench?

The space under the storage area is called "dead space," because it can't be used for anything. What is the volume of the dead space at the bottom of the bench?

Norah's family is shopping for a new medicine cabinet. Find the volume of each medicine cabinet in cubic feet. Then, answer the question.

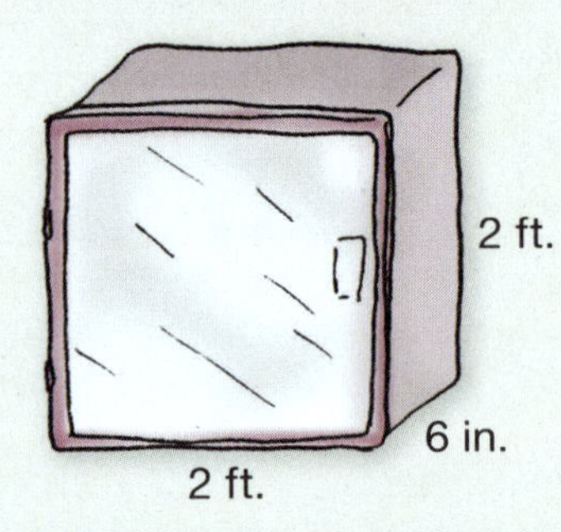

Norah's family wants to buy the medicine cabinet with the greater volume. Which cabinet should they buy?

Lesson Activities 👥

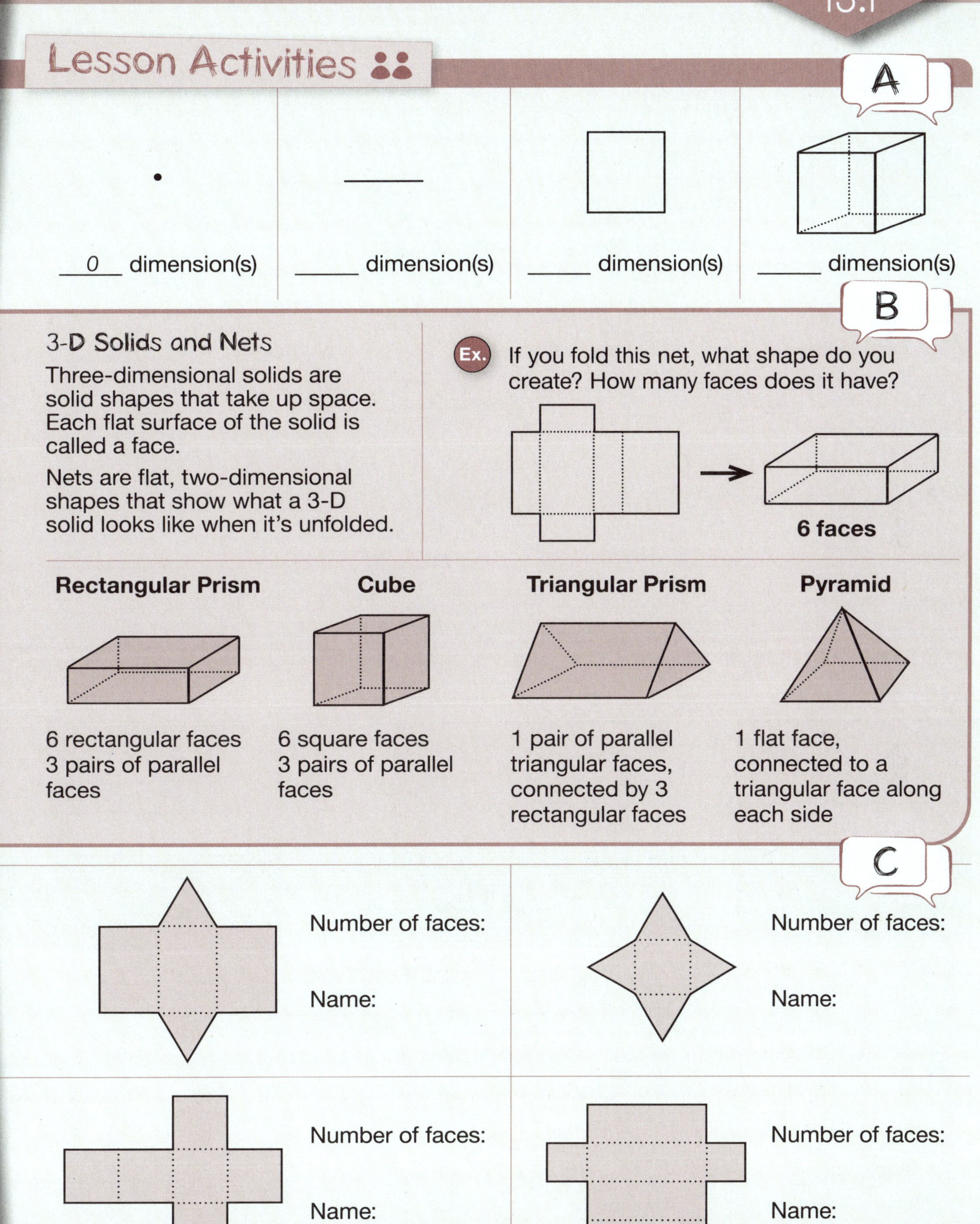

A

___0___ dimension(s)   ______ dimension(s)   ______ dimension(s)   ______ dimension(s)

B

3-D Solids and Nets

Three-dimensional solids are solid shapes that take up space. Each flat surface of the solid is called a face.

Nets are flat, two-dimensional shapes that show what a 3-D solid looks like when it's unfolded.

Ex. If you fold this net, what shape do you create? How many faces does it have?

6 faces

Rectangular Prism	**Cube**	**Triangular Prism**	**Pyramid**
6 rectangular faces 3 pairs of parallel faces	6 square faces 3 pairs of parallel faces	1 pair of parallel triangular faces, connected by 3 rectangular faces	1 flat face, connected to a triangular face along each side

C

Number of faces:

Name:

Number of faces:

Name:

Number of faces:

Name:

Number of faces:

Name:

Practice

Write the name of each 3-D solid and tell how many faces it has.

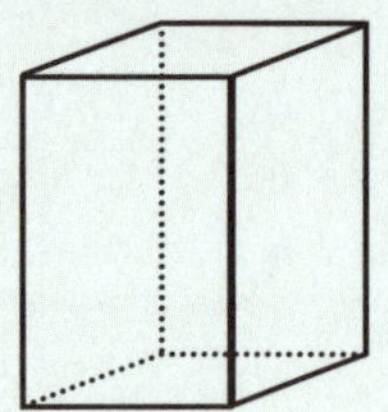

Name: _________________

Number of faces: _________

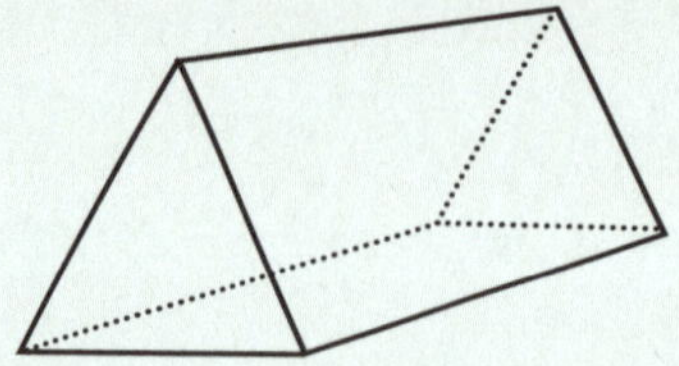

Name: _________________

Number of faces: _________

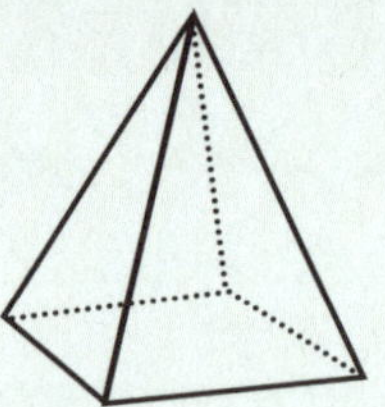

Name: _________________

Number of faces: _________

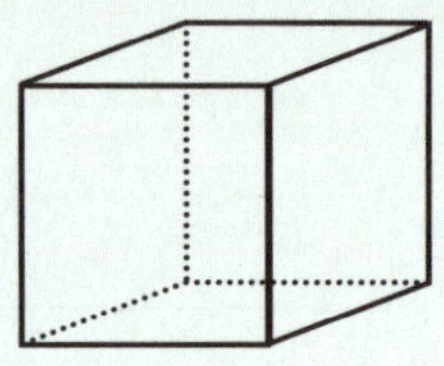

Name: _________________

Number of faces: _________

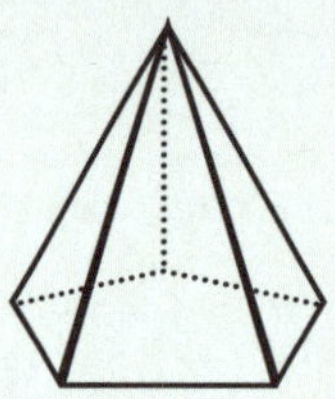

Name: _________________

Number of faces: _________

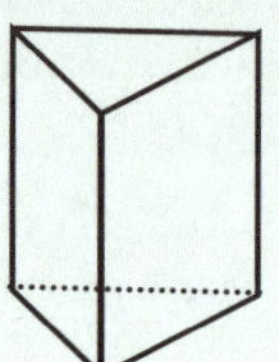

Name: _________________

Number of faces: _________

Match each net with its solid. Then, find the volume of the solid. Each small square is 1 cm by 1 cm.

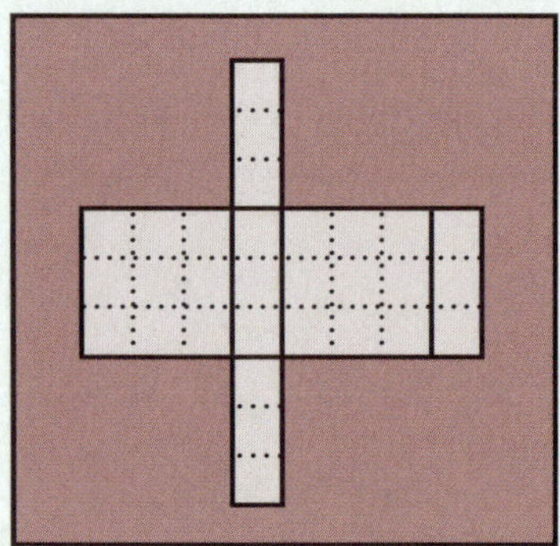

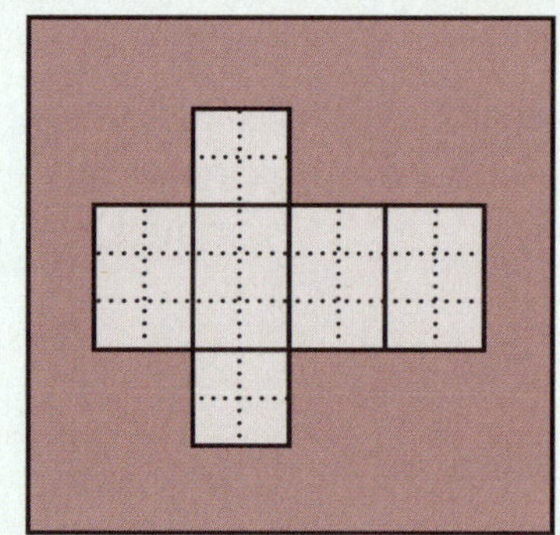

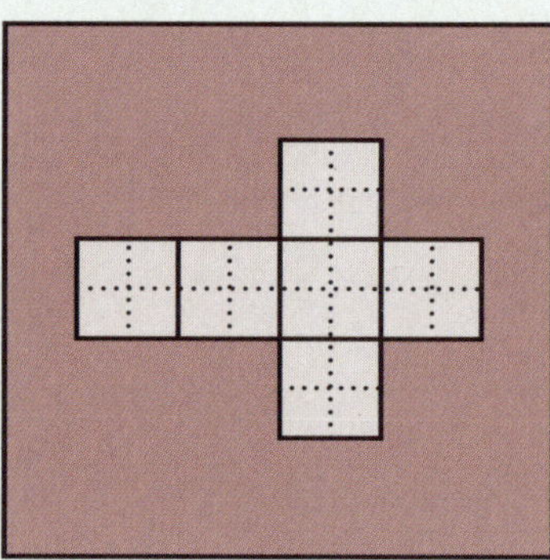

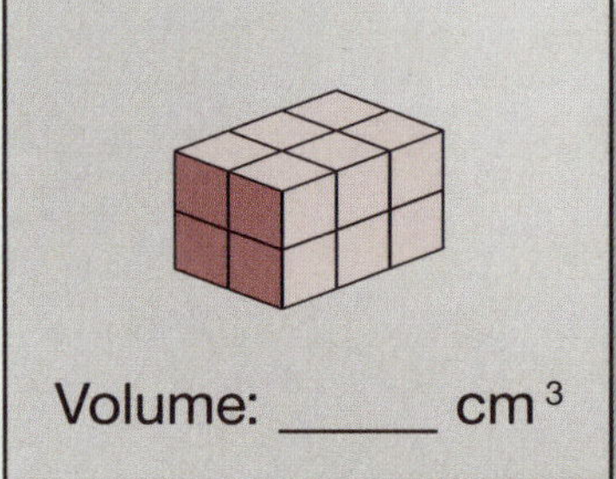

Volume: _______ cm^3

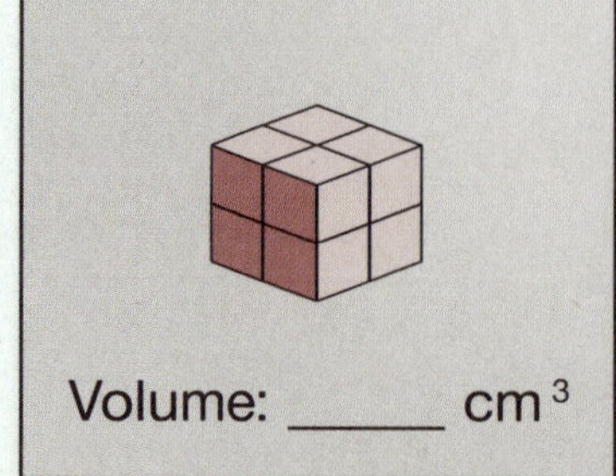

Volume: _______ cm^3

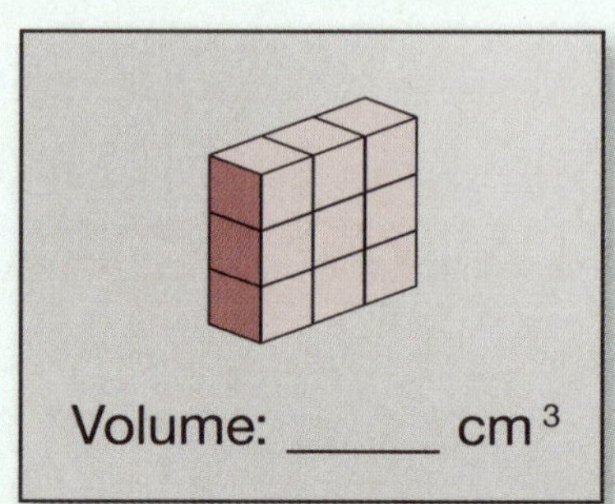

Volume: _______ cm^3

Review

Use long division to find the unit price of each item. Round your answer to the hundredths-place.

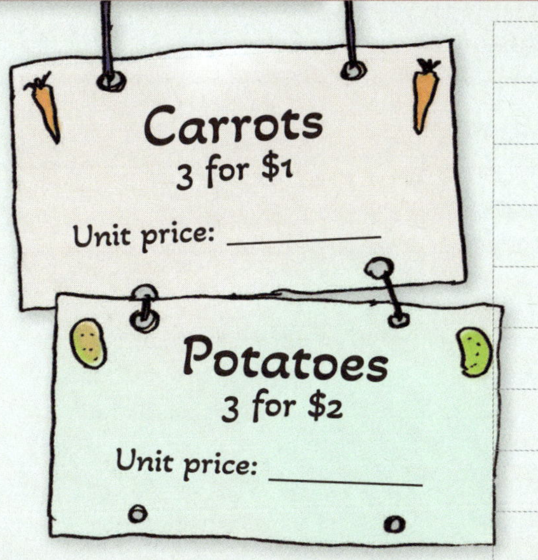

Use mental math to check whether each number is a solution to the equation. Circle the numbers that are solutions to the equation. (Some equations will have more than one solution.)

$8 + m = 40$			$30 = 6n$			$3p = p + 2p$		
30	31	32	4	5	6	10	20	30

$q + 0 = q$			$1 \cdot r = r$			$s + s = s$		
5	6	7	22	23	24	0	1	2

Use bar models to solve.

The bike normally costs $280. Today, it is on sale for 25% off the regular price. What is the sale price of the bike?

Regular price

Sale price

Lesson Activities

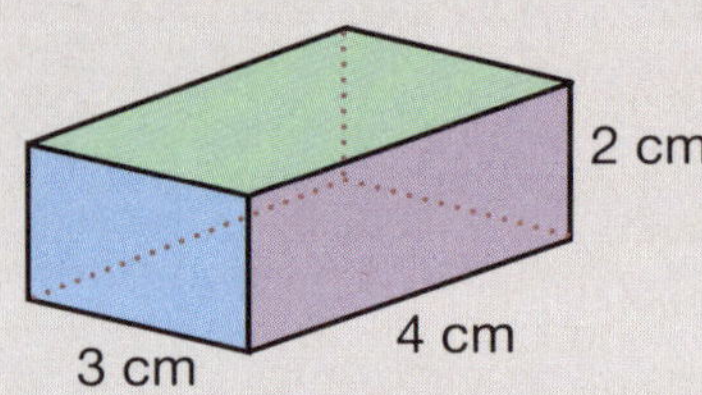

A

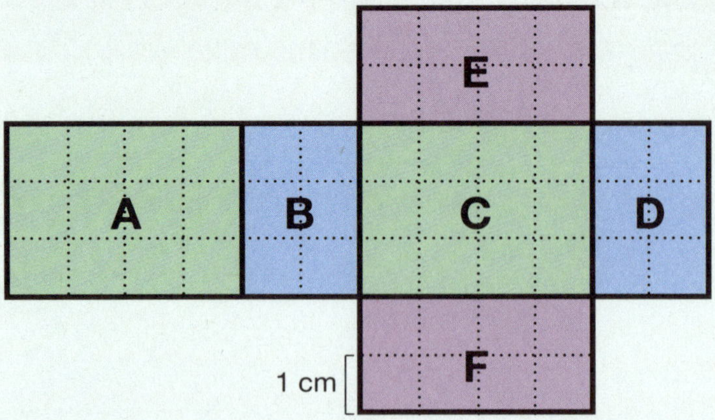

	Area (cm²)			Area (cm²)
A			D	
B			E	
C			F	

Total area: _______________________

B

Surface Area of Rectangular Prisms and Cubes

The surface area of a 3-D solid is the total area of all its faces. To find surface area, we find the area of each face and then add the areas.

Ex. What is the surface area of the box?

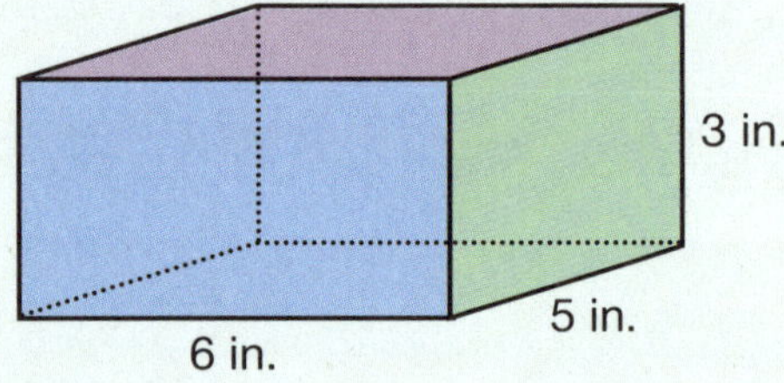

Area of each green face: 4 cm × 3 cm = 12 cm²

Area of each blue face: 2 cm × 3 cm = 6 cm²

Area of each purple face: 4 cm × 2 cm = 8 cm²

12 cm² + 12 cm² + 6 cm² + 6 cm² + 8 cm² + 8 cm² = **52 cm²**

Surface area: _______________________

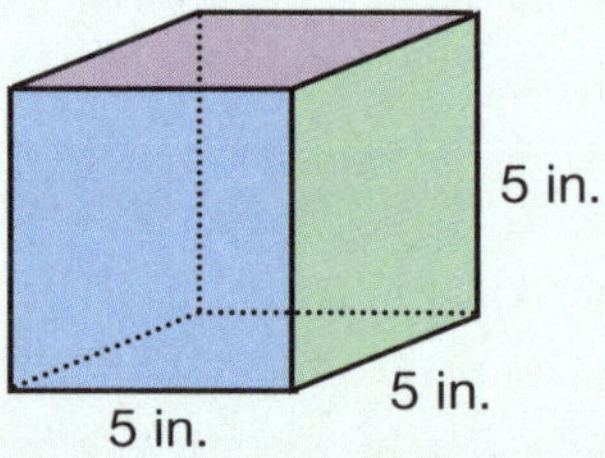

Surface area: _______________________

Practice

Use the net to find the surface area of the matching 3-D solid. Each small square represents 1 cm.²

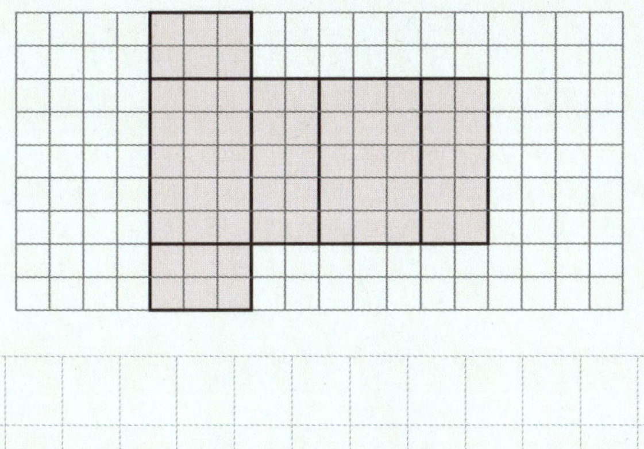

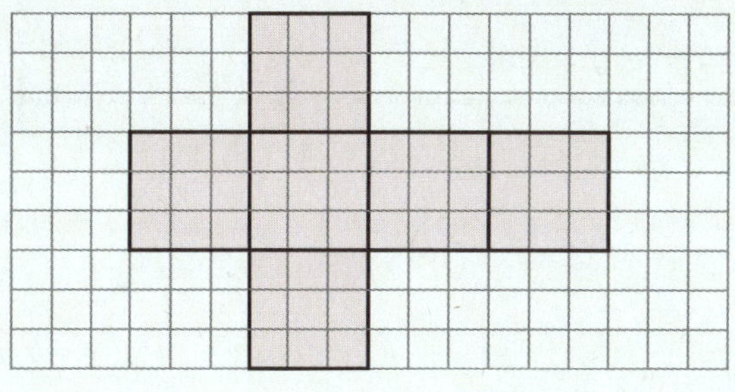

Find the surface area of each solid.

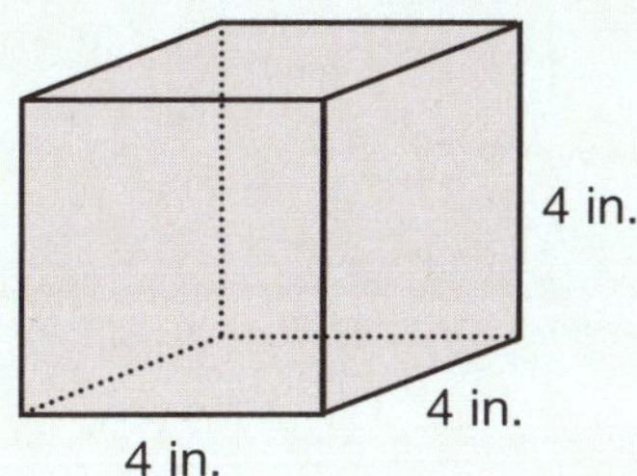

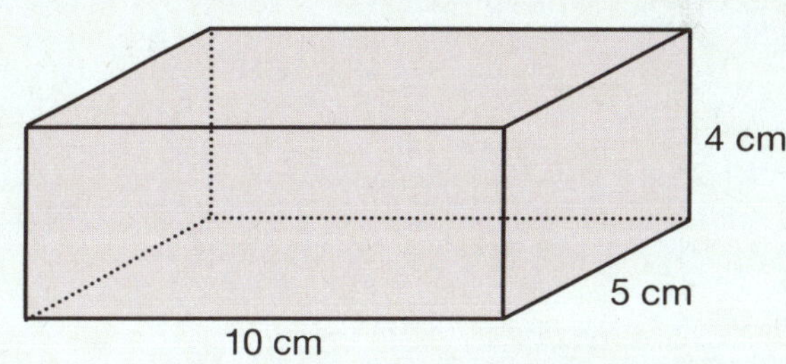

Solve. Write the equations you use.

What is the surface area of the cardboard box?

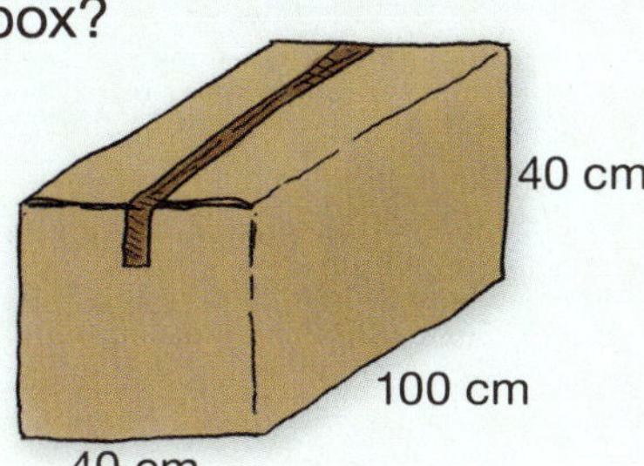

Willow builds this closed box out of wood. What is the surface area of the box?

Review

Solve each equation. Show all your steps. Then, substitute the solution into the equation to check that it is correct.

$125 = s + 46$

Check:

$8t = 72$

Check:

Find the area. Write the equations you use.

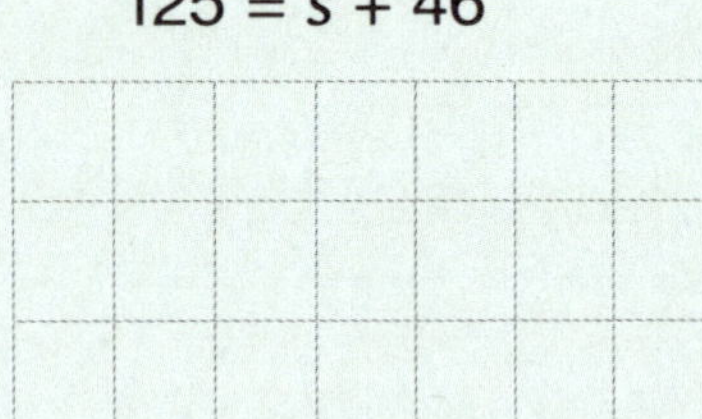

Area: __________ sq. cm

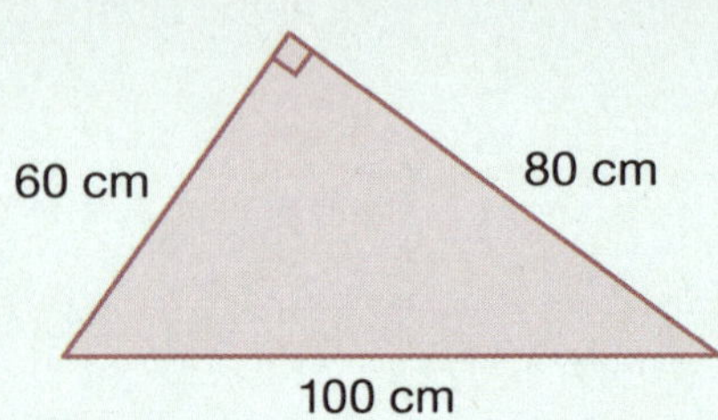

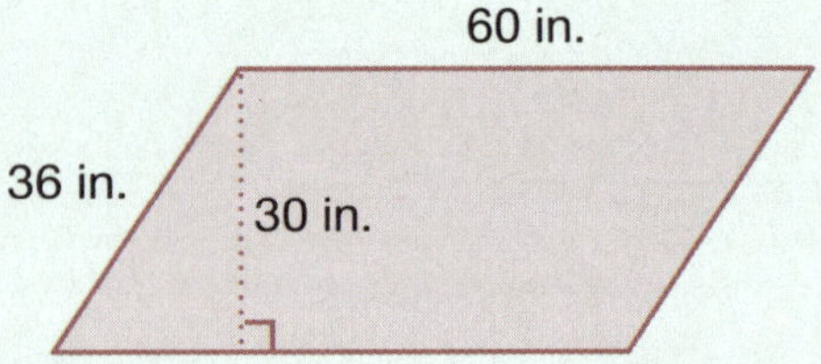

Area: __________ sq. in.

Evaluate.

$2^4 =$ __________

$7^2 =$ __________

$4^3 =$ __________

$1^9 =$ __________

$34^1 =$ __________

$10^4 =$ __________

$7 \times 10^3 =$ __________

$2^3 \times 10^2 =$ __________

$5^2 \times 10^6 =$ __________

Solve. Write the equations you use.

What is the volume of the aquarium in cubic feet?

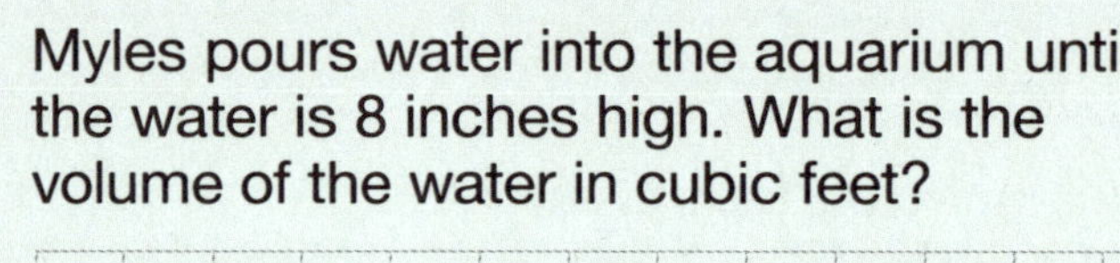

Myles pours water into the aquarium until the water is 8 inches high. What is the volume of the water in cubic feet?

Lesson Activities

Surface area: _______________________________

Volume: _______________________________

A

B

Pasta Perfecto Meeting Agenda

1 pound of penne pasta has a volume of 60 in.^{3}
Which box holds 1 pound of penne and uses the least amount of cardboard?

BOX A
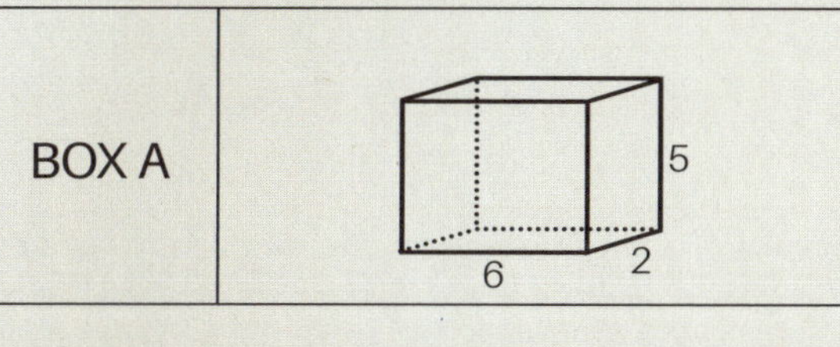

BOX B
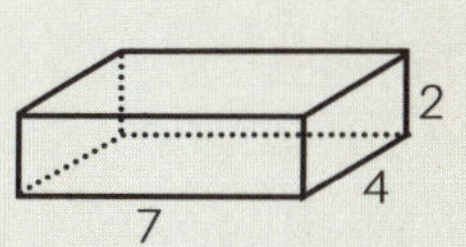

BOX C
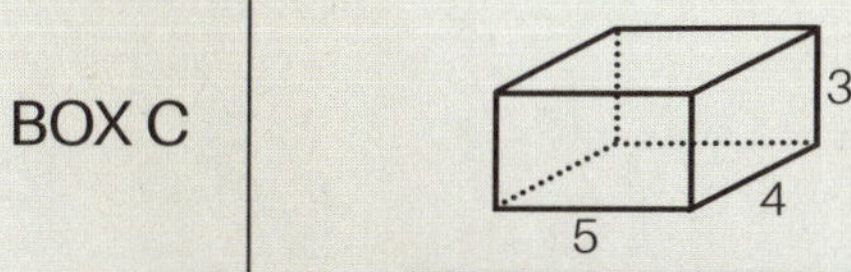

BOX D
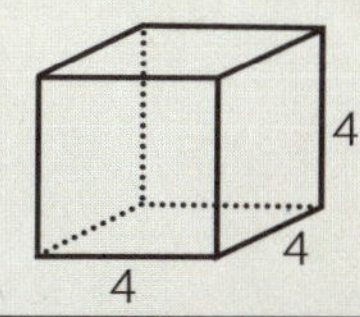

	Box A	Box B	Box C	Box D
Volume (in.^{3})				
Surface area (in.^{2})				

Practice

Complete the chart. Write your equations in the work space. All measurements are in centimeters.

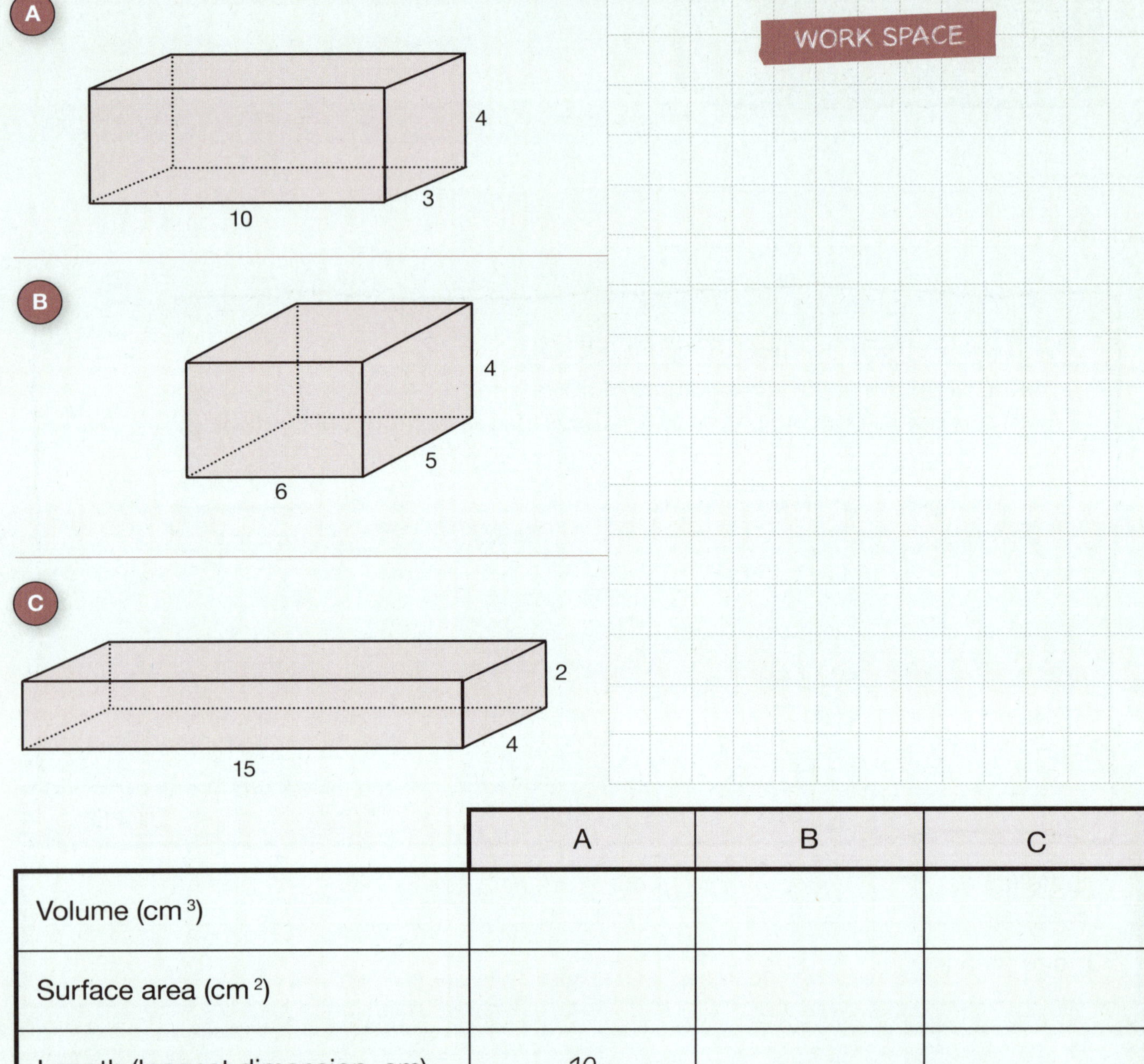

	A	B	C
Volume (cm^3)			
Surface area (cm^2)			
Length (longest dimension, cm)	10		

What do the solids' volumes have in common?

Which solid has the highest surface area?

Which solid has the lowest surface area?

Which solid has the longest length?

Which solid has the shortest length?

Review   Match.

n > –2

n ≤ –2

n < –2

n ≥ –2

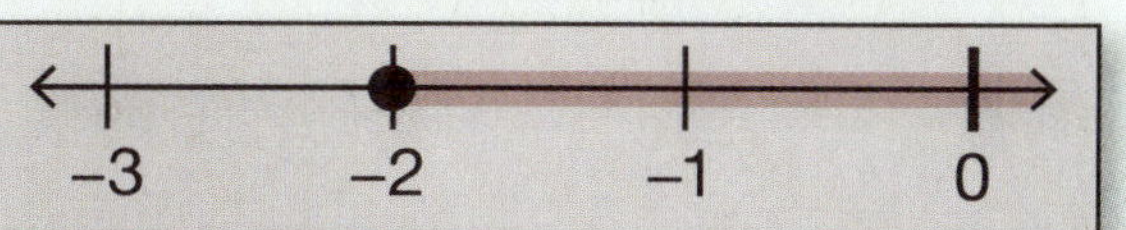

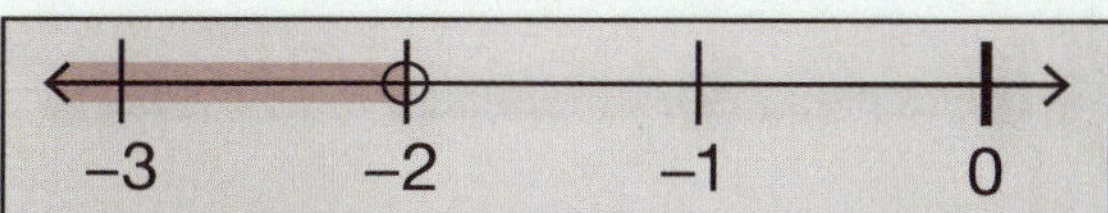
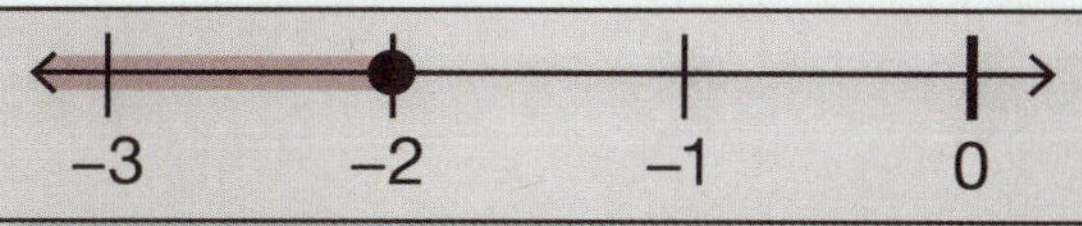

Use a factor tree to find the prime factorization for each number. (Write the prime factors in order from least to greatest.) Then, find the GCF.

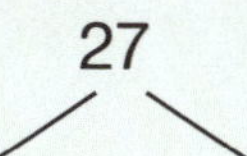

27

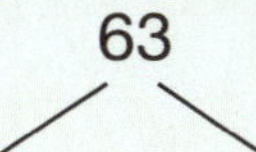

63

Prime Factorizations

27 = _______________________

63 = _______________________

What is the GCF of 27 and 63?

Solve. Write the equations you use.

Anja cuts this foam block into 9 equal pieces. What is the volume of each piece in cubic inches?

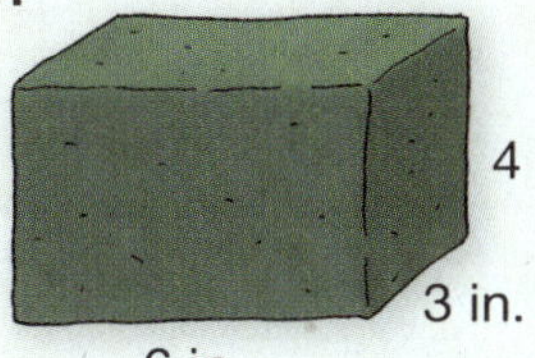

4 in.

3 in.

6 in.

What is the area of the flag?

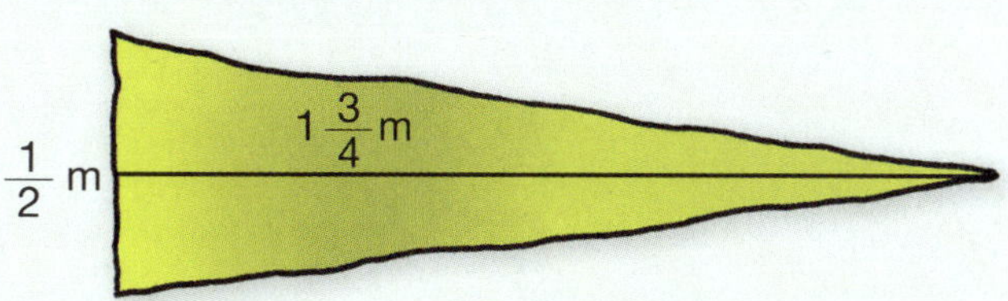

Lesson Activities

Backyard Family Pool

Length: 20 ft. • Width: 10 ft.

Depths available: 4 ft., 6 ft., 8 ft., or 10 ft.

Tile for the bottom and sides of the pool costs $10 per square foot.

Depth	Volume (ft.³)	Area of the Bottom (ft.²)	Area of the Sides (ft.²)	Total Area of the Bottom and Sides (ft.²)	Tile Cost
4 ft.					
6 ft.					
8 ft.					
10 ft.					

When the depth increases by 2 ft., the volume increases by ___________ ft.³

When the depth increases by 2 ft., the area of the bottom increases by ___________ ft.²

When the depth increases by 2 ft., the area of the sides increases by ___________ ft.²

Luka's family is building a pool. They have a budget of $7,000 for the tile, and they want the pool to be as deep as possible. What depth should they choose?

Practice

Leah and her parents want to build a chicken run for their chickens. They plan to build the frame from wood and then cover the frame with wire mesh. The chicken run will be open on the bottom. Answer the questions to help them decide which design to use.

How many square feet of wire mesh do they need to cover the top and sides of this chicken run?

Wire mesh costs $0.30 per square foot. How much will it cost to cover this chicken run with wire mesh?

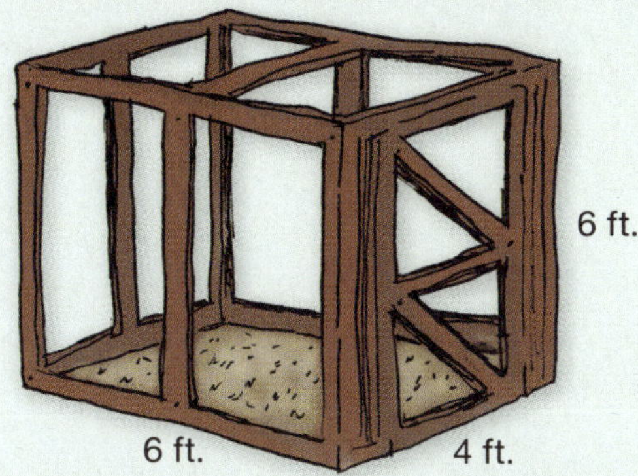

How many square feet of wire mesh do they need to cover the top and sides of this chicken run?

Wire mesh costs $0.30 per square foot. How much will it cost to cover this chicken run with wire mesh?

Review

Find the products.

	0 . 2 5			0 . 7 5
×	1 6		×	4 0

Circle the prime numbers. X the composite numbers.

1	2	3	4	5	6
7	8	9	10	11	12
13	14	15	16	17	18
19	20	21	22	23	24

Circle the words that best describe each decimal.

0.472

about $\frac{1}{4}$ about $\frac{1}{2}$

0.739

about $\frac{3}{5}$ about $\frac{3}{4}$

0.9104

about $\frac{3}{4}$ about $\frac{9}{10}$

0.023

about 0   about $\frac{1}{4}$

0.996

about $\frac{1}{10}$ about 1

0.0996

about $\frac{1}{10}$ about 1

Use bar models to solve.

In February, Jasper's family's electricity bill was $150. Their March bill was $\frac{4}{5}$ as much as their February bill. How much did they pay for electricity in all in February and March?

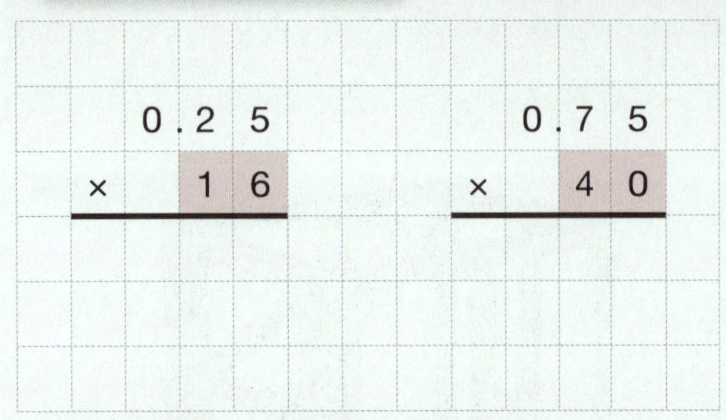

February

March

The ratio of girls to boys in the play is 3:2. There are 27 girls. How many boys are there?

Lesson Activities 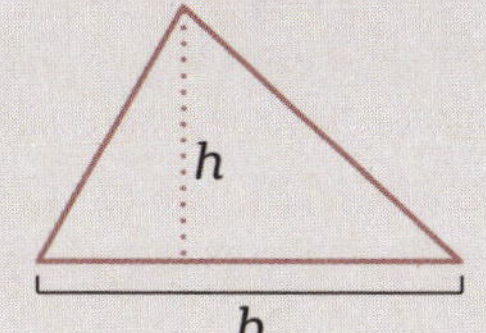

A

Formula for the Area of a Triangle

$$\frac{b \cdot h}{2}$$

$$\frac{1}{2} \cdot b \cdot h$$

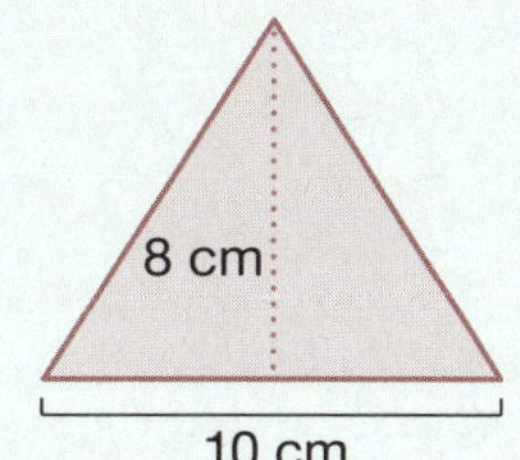

Area: _______________

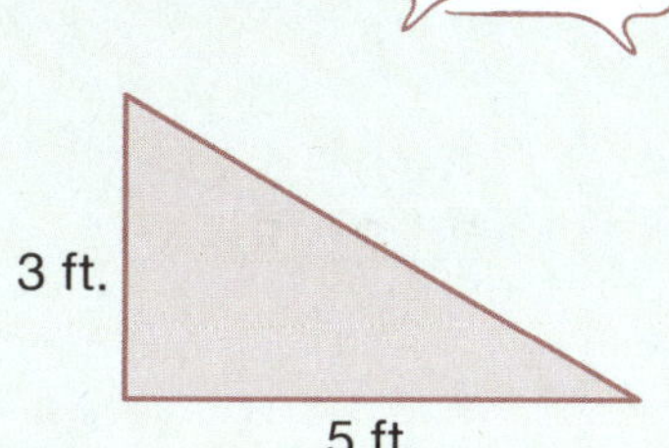

Area: _______________

B

Surface Area of Triangular Prisms and Pyramids

Ex. What is the surface area of the chocolate bar's box? (All measurements are in centimeters.)

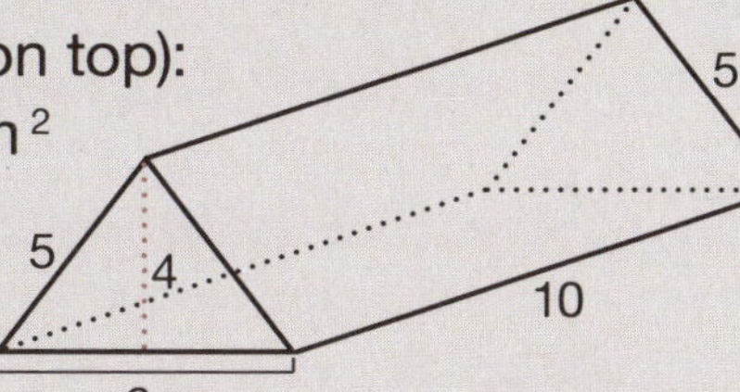

2 rectangular faces (on top):
5 cm · 10 cm = 50 cm^2

Rectangular face (on bottom):
6 cm · 10 cm = 60 cm^2

2 triangular faces:
$$\frac{1}{2} \cdot 6 \text{ cm} \cdot 4 \text{ cm} = 12 \text{ cm}^2$$

2 · 50 cm^2 + 2 · 12 cm^2 + 60 cm^2
100 cm^2 + 24 cm^2 + 60 cm^2
184 cm^2

C

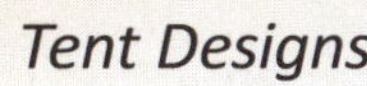

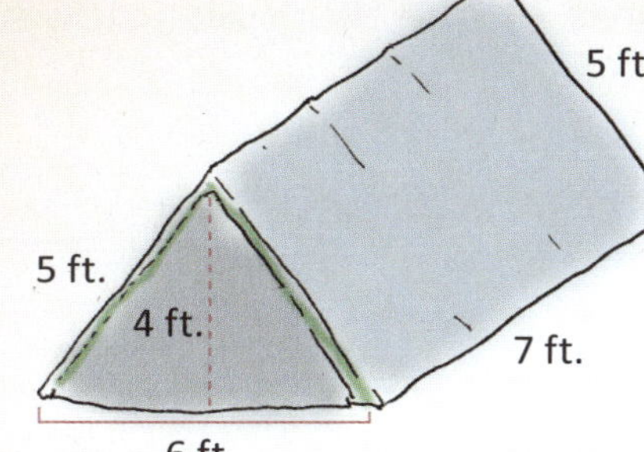

Surface area: _______________

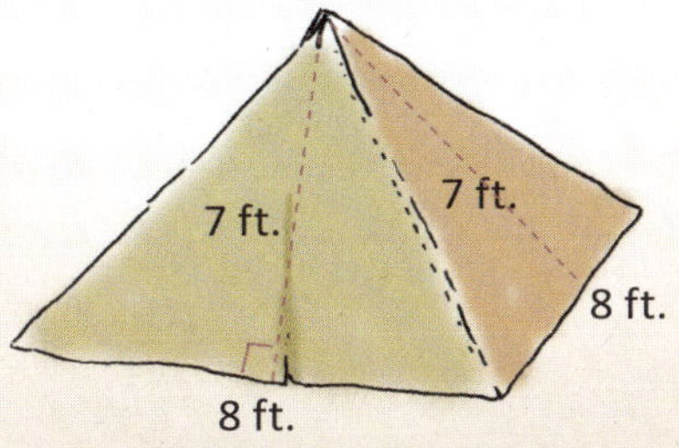

Surface area: _______________

Practice

Find the surface area of the triangular prism. Write the equations you use.

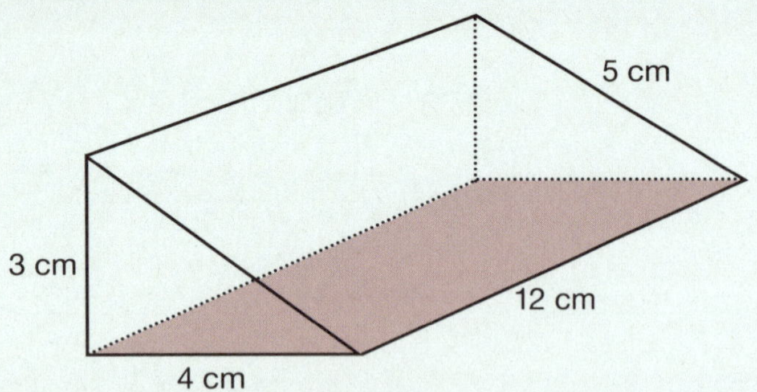

Each side of this pyramid is an identical equilateral triangle. Use its net to find the surface area of the pyramid. Express your answer with 1 decimal digit.

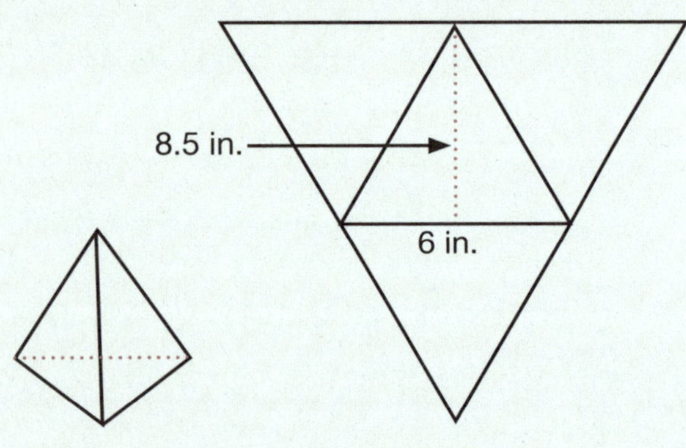

Solve. Write the equations you use.

The Great Pyramid of Giza has 4 triangular sides. Each face has a height of approximately 150 m. The base of each face is approximately 230 m long.

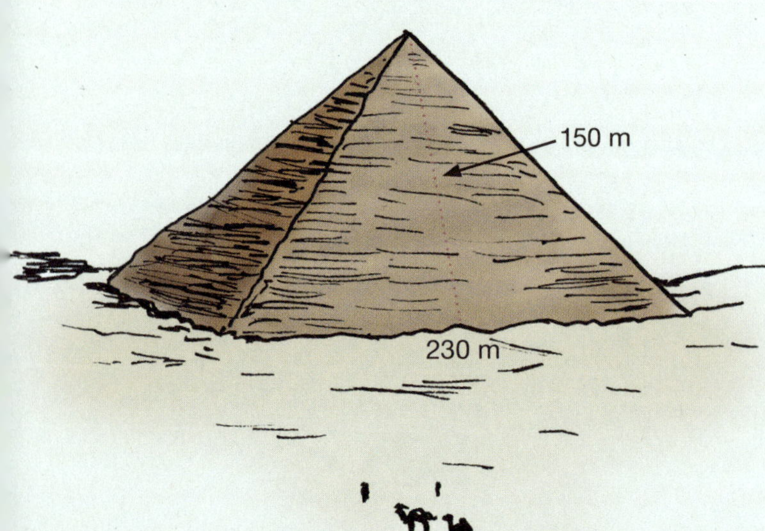

What is the area of one triangular side of the pyramid?

What is the total area of all 4 triangular sides of the pyramid?

Review

Use mental math to find the quotient.

900 ÷ 10 = _____________ | 380 ÷ 10 = _____________ | 8,237 ÷ 10 = _____________

900 ÷ 100 = _____________ | 380 ÷ 100 = _____________ | 8,237 ÷ 100 = _____________

900 ÷ 1,000 = _____________ | 380 ÷ 1,000 = _____________ | 8,237 ÷ 1,000 = _____________

Find the distance between each pair of numbers.

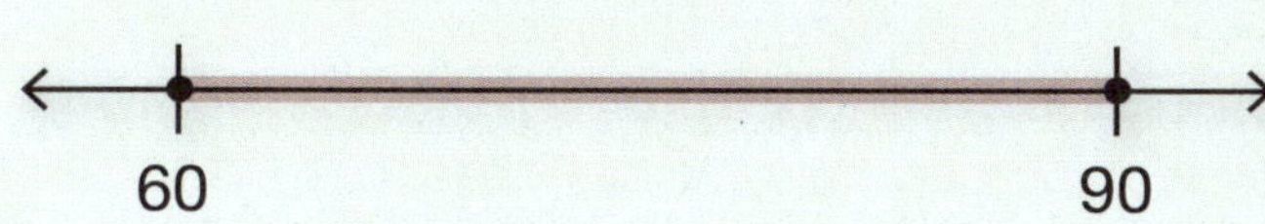

60   90

Distance: _____________ units

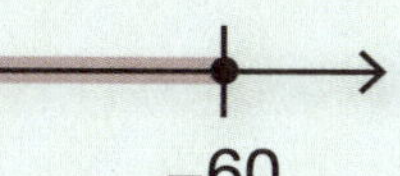

−90   −60

Distance: _____________ units

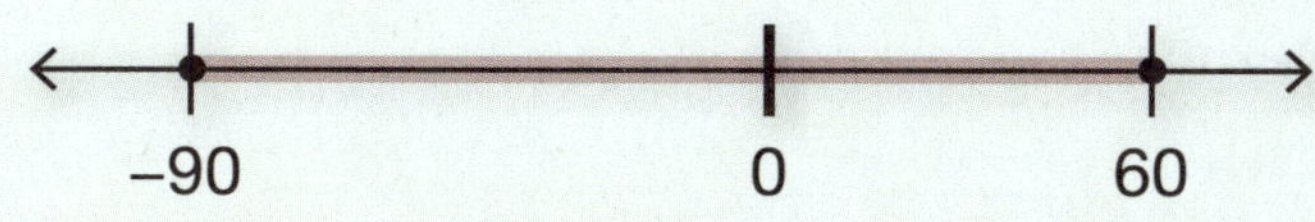

−90   0   60

Distance: _____________ units

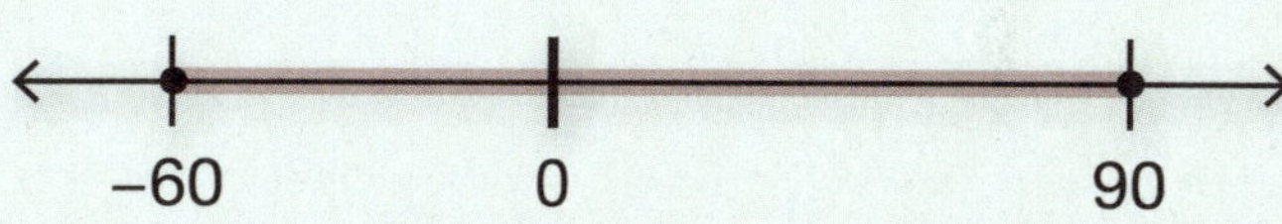

−60   0   90

Distance: _____________ units

Answer the questions.

Write an expression (in simplest form) for the volume of the rectangular prism. Use h to stand for its height.

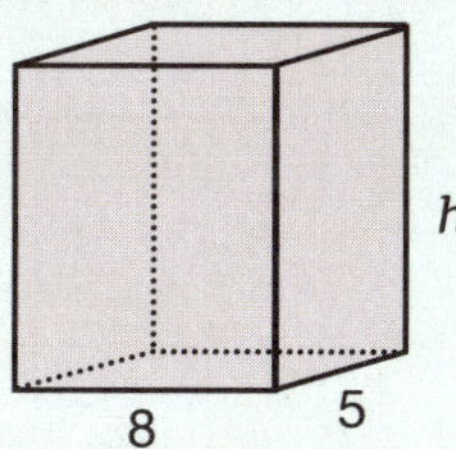

The volume of the rectangular prism is 400 cm.³ What is its height?

What is the volume of the box (in cubic ft.)?

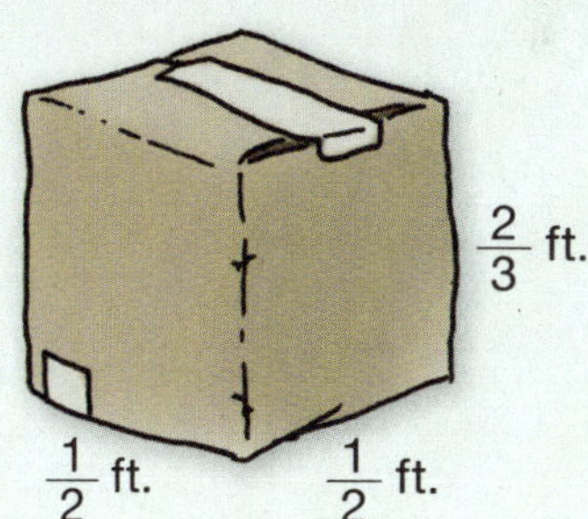

Unit Wrap-Up

Use the net to find the surface area of the matching 3-D solid. (Each small square represents 1 cm.²) Then, use the word bank to write the name of the matching 3-D solid.

rectangular prism ∘ cube ∘ triangular prism ∘ pyramid

Surface area: ______________________

Name: ______________________

Surface area: ______________________

Name: ______________________

Surface area: ______________________

Name: ______________________

Surface area: ______________________

Name: ______________________

Unit Wrap-Up

Solve. Write the equations you use.

The roof and sides of this shipping container are made from steel. The floor is made from plywood. What is the area of the shipping container's roof and sides?

What is the area of the shipping container's floor?

What is the volume of the shipping container?

This small satellite is shaped like a cube. It has a surface area of 600 cm.^{2}

 What is the area of each face?

 What is the length of each face?

 What is the volume of the satellite?

Lesson Activities

How many times does your heart beat in 15 seconds?

_________ times

A

Beats								
Seconds	15	30	45	60	75	90	105	120

B

Rate

A rate is a special type of ratio that compares two quantities with different units. We write rates with the word "per," a fraction bar, or a slash. Per means "for each."

Ex. The cow's heart beats 50 times in 1 minute.

50 beats per min.

50 beats/min.

$$50 \frac{\textbf{beats}}{\textbf{min.}}$$

Unit Rate

A unit rate compares a certain number of units of one quantity to one unit of the other quantity.

To find a unit rate, use a fraction bar to divide one quantity by the other. Use the quantities' units to decide which quantity to write above the fraction bar and which quantity to write below the fraction bar.

Ex. The whale's heart beats 35 times in 5 minutes. What is its heart rate in beats per minute?

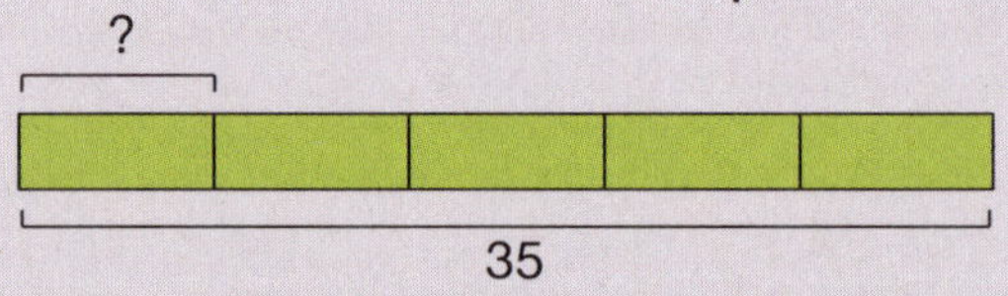

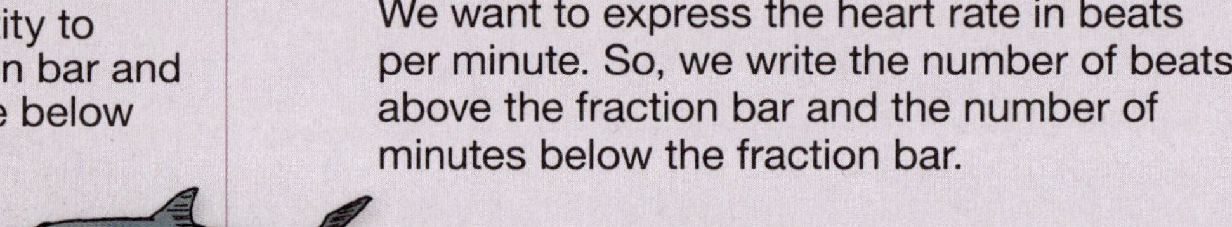

We want to express the heart rate in beats per minute. So, we write the number of beats above the fraction bar and the number of minutes below the fraction bar.

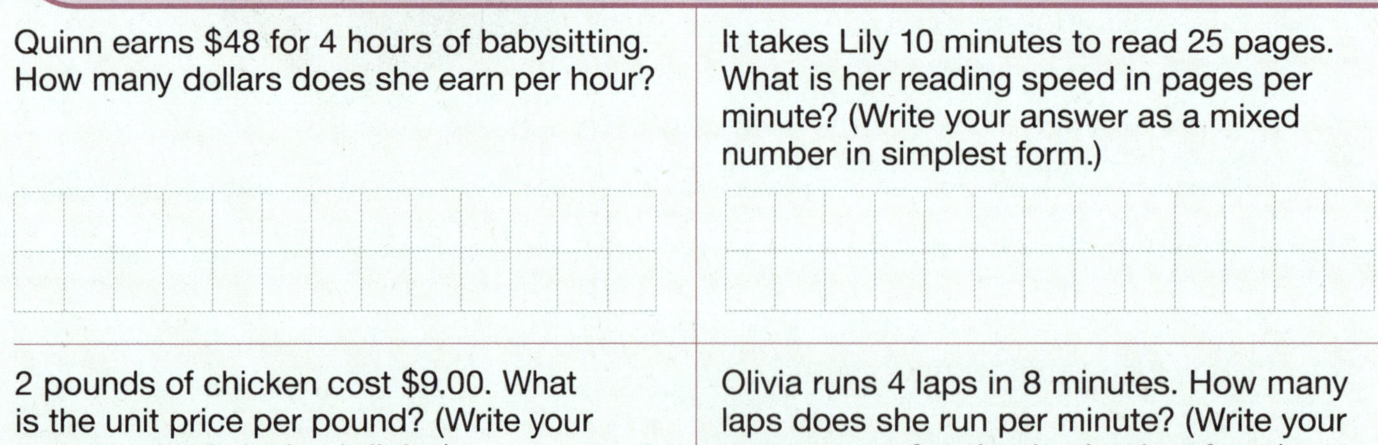

$$\frac{35 \textbf{ beats}}{5 \textbf{ min.}} = 7 \frac{\textbf{beats}}{\textbf{min.}} \qquad \text{7 beats per min.}$$

Quinn earns \$48 for 4 hours of babysitting. How many dollars does she earn per hour?

It takes Lily 10 minutes to read 25 pages. What is her reading speed in pages per minute? (Write your answer as a mixed number in simplest form.)

2 pounds of chicken cost \$9.00. What is the unit price per pound? (Write your answer with 2 decimal digits.)

Olivia runs 4 laps in 8 minutes. How many laps does she run per minute? (Write your answer as a fraction in simplest form.)

Practice 

Circle the rates that are equivalent to the unit rate in the box.

100 beats per min.	300 beats per 3 min.	500 beats per 4 min.	600 beats per 6 min.	200 beats per 1 min.	200 beats per 2 min.
 $5/hr.	$\dfrac{\$20}{6\ \text{hr.}}$	$\dfrac{\$15}{3\ \text{hr.}}$	$\dfrac{\$10}{2\ \text{hr.}}$	$\dfrac{\$100}{20\ \text{hr.}}$	$\dfrac{\$150}{15\ \text{hr.}}$
 20 miles per gallon	$\dfrac{30\ \text{mi.}}{2\ \text{gal.}}$	$\dfrac{60\ \text{mi.}}{4\ \text{gal.}}$	$\dfrac{40\ \text{mi.}}{2\ \text{gal.}}$	$\dfrac{100\ \text{mi.}}{5\ \text{gal.}}$	$\dfrac{180\ \text{mi.}}{9\ \text{gal.}}$

Answer the questions. Make sure to include the correct units in your answers.

The carousel makes 24 rotations in 4 minutes. How many rotations does it make per minute?

10 ounces of potato chips cost $3.70. What is the unit price per ounce?

Joseph mows 8 lawns in 2 hours. How many lawns does he mow per hour?

Maura blows up 7 balloons in 6 minutes. How many balloons does she blow up per minute? (Write your answer as a fraction or mixed number in simplest form.)

Liam mows 9 lawns in 3 hours. How many lawns does he mow per hour?

Winnie blows up 8 balloons in 10 minutes. How many balloons does she blow up per minute? (Write your answer as a fraction or mixed number in simplest form.)

Who is faster at mowing lawns, Joseph or Liam?

Who is faster at blowing up balloons, Maura or Winnie?

Review 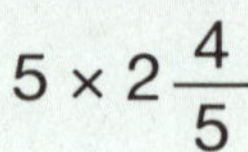

Find the product or quotient.

$1\frac{3}{4} \times \frac{3}{4}$	$5 \times 2\frac{4}{5}$	$1\frac{2}{3} \times 30$

$2\frac{1}{2} \div 1\frac{1}{8}$	$3\frac{1}{3} \div \frac{5}{6}$	$6\frac{2}{5} \div 2$

Complete the charts.

n	$n + 3$
10	
56	
	43
	25

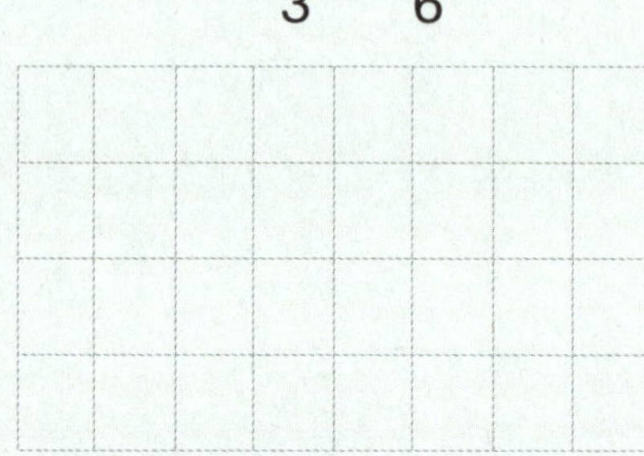

x	$2x$
5	
15	
	40
	100

c	d	$c - d$
8	4	
10	5	
20		19
	10	25

Use ratio tables to solve.

The chef mixes 3 parts olive oil with 1 part vinegar to make salad dressing. If he uses 450 mL of olive oil, how much vinegar should he use?

The photo has a length of 8 in. and a width of 6 in. Tiana enlarges the photo without changing the ratio of the length to the width. If the large photo has a length of 24 in., what is its width?

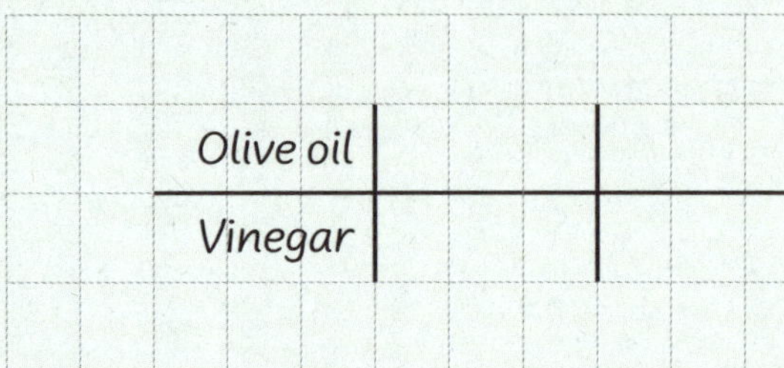

Olive oil		
Vinegar		

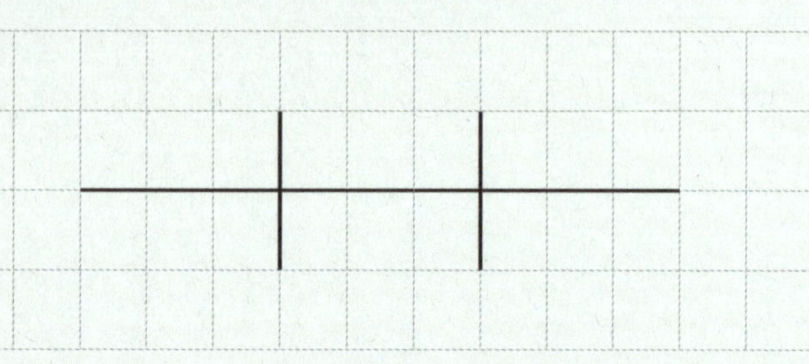

Lesson Activities 👥

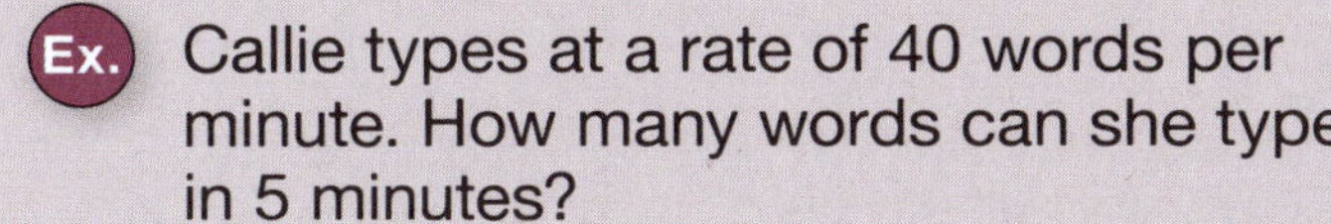

How many jumping jacks can you do in 10 seconds? _____ jumping jacks	Jumping jacks						
	Seconds	10	20	30	40	50	60

A

B

Solve Rate Problems

Ex. Callie types at a rate of 40 words per minute. How many words can she type in 5 minutes?

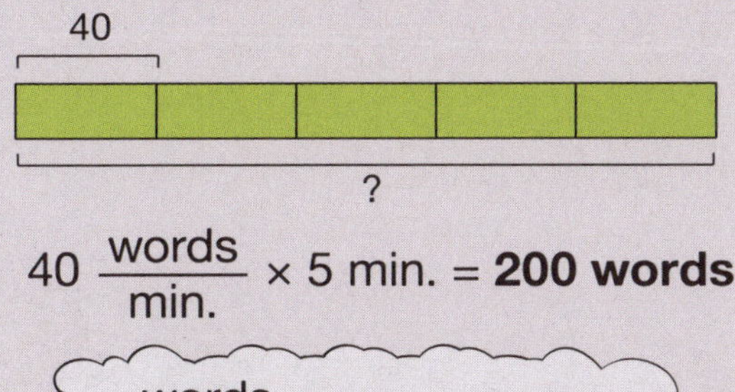

$$40 \ \frac{\text{words}}{\text{min.}} \times 5 \text{ min.} = \textbf{200 words}$$

$$\frac{\text{words}}{\text{min.}} \times \cancel{\text{min.}} = \text{words}$$

Ex. Callie types at a rate of 40 words per minute. How long does it take her to type 320 words?

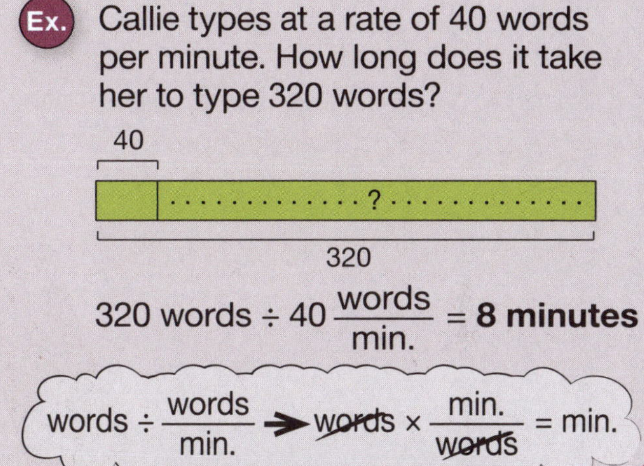

$$320 \text{ words} \div 40 \ \frac{\text{words}}{\text{min.}} = \textbf{8 minutes}$$

$$\text{words} \div \frac{\text{words}}{\text{min.}} \rightarrow \cancel{\text{words}} \times \frac{\text{min.}}{\cancel{\text{words}}} = \text{min.}$$

HOSE FLOW RATE
50 liters per minute

If you leave the hose on for 10 minutes, how many liters of water do you use?

How many minutes does it take to fill a 200-liter water barrel?

How many minutes does it take to fill a 310-liter water barrel? Write your answer as a mixed number in simplest form.

Car Gas Mileage
30 miles per gallon

How many gallons of gas do you need to drive 240 miles?

If you have 5 gallons of gas in your tank, how many miles can you drive?

If you have 7.6 gallons of gas in your tank, how many miles can you drive? Write your answer as a decimal.

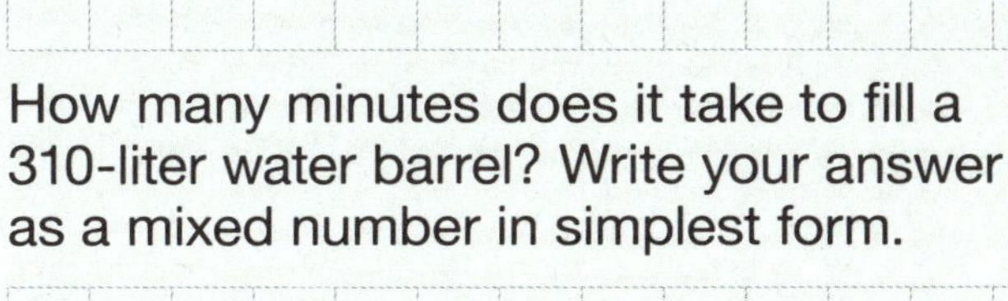

Practice

Solve. Write the equations you use.

A mouse's heart beats 500 times per minute. How many times does its heart beat in 5 minutes?

Polly is knitting a scarf with 180 rows. It takes her 1 hour to knit 9 rows. How long will it take her to complete the scarf?

The factory produces 300 chocolate bars per hour. How long does it take the factory to produce 2,400 chocolate bars?

The leaky faucet wastes $2\frac{1}{2}$ gallons of water per day. How many gallons of water does the leaky faucet waste in 1 week? Write your answer as a mixed number in simplest form.

Solve. Write the equations you use.

The crayon factory produces 100 crayons in 5 minutes. How many crayons does it produce per minute?

Aaron earns $150 for 5 hours of work. How many dollars per hour does he earn?

How many crayons does the factory produce in 1 hour? (60 minutes equal 1 hour.)

How much money does Aaron earn for 18 hours of work?

How many minutes does it take the factory to produce 4,000 crayons?

How many hours does it take Aaron to earn $900?

Review — Find the product or quotient.

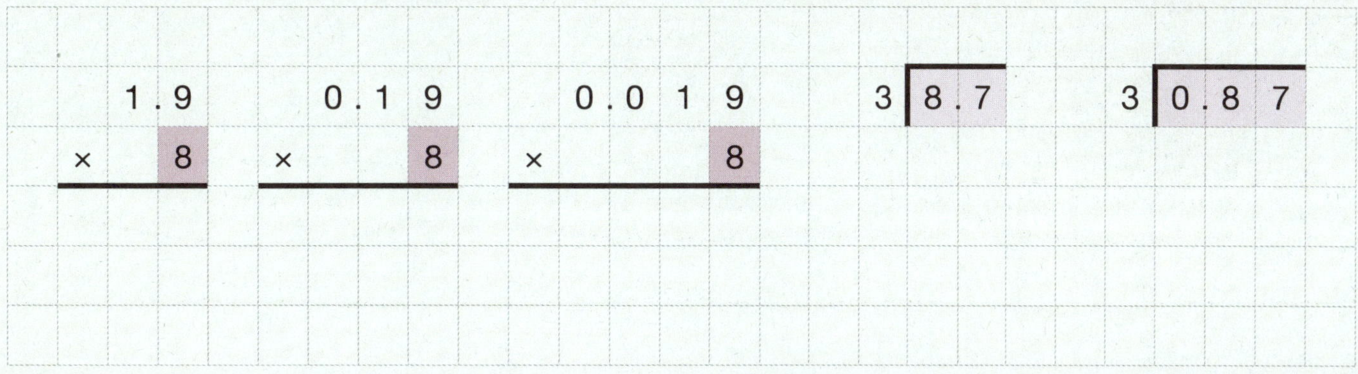

1.9 × 8	0.19 × 8	0.019 × 8	3) 8.7	3) 0.87

Label the numbers on the number line.

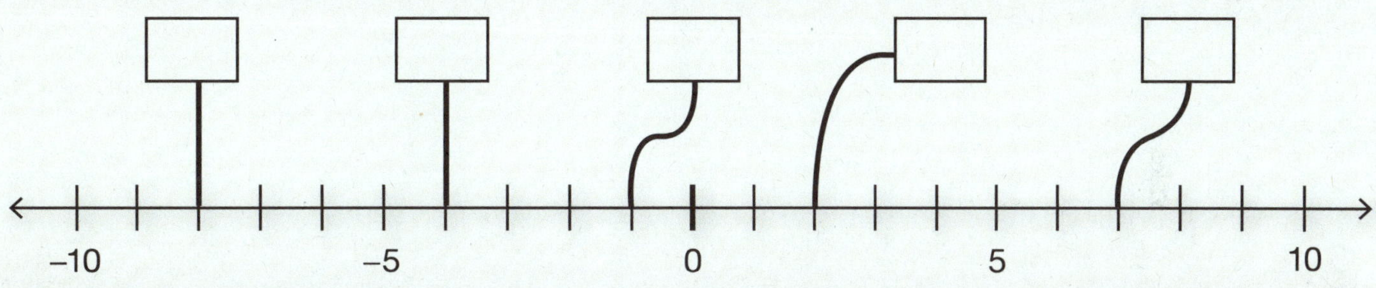

Rani wants to make a play tent for her little sister. Use the directions to answer the questions. Write the equations you use.

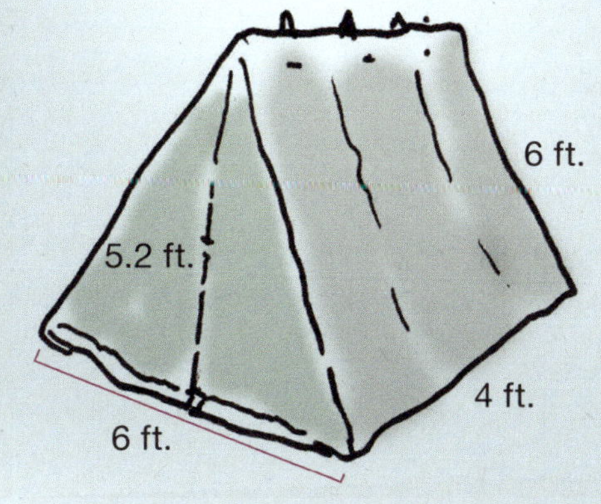

What is the total area of the front, back, and sides of the tent?

Fabric costs $6 per square foot. How much does it cost to buy enough fabric for the front, back, and sides of the tent?

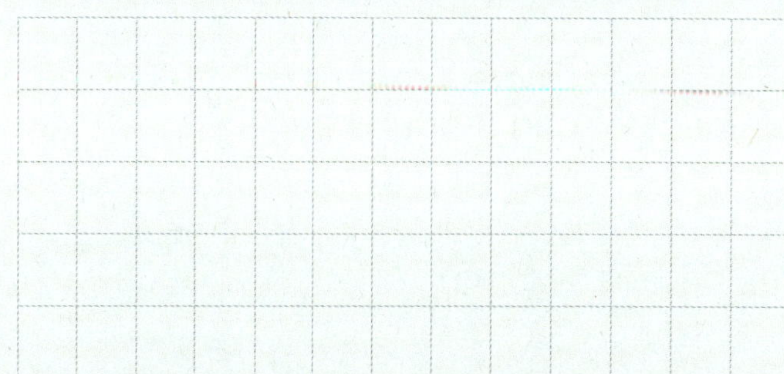

Lesson Activities

A

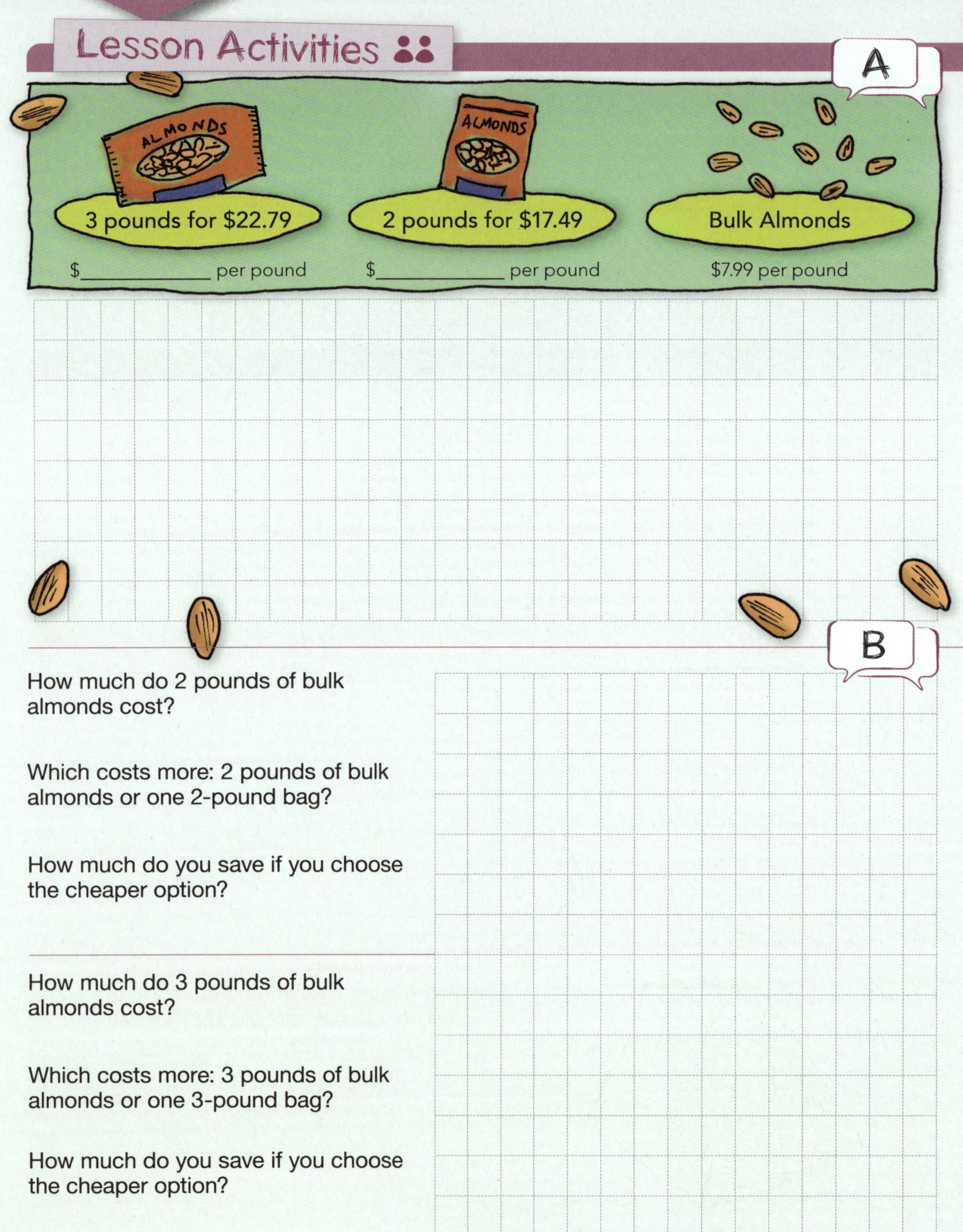

B

How much do 2 pounds of bulk almonds cost?

Which costs more: 2 pounds of bulk almonds or one 2-pound bag?

How much do you save if you choose the cheaper option?

How much do 3 pounds of bulk almonds cost?

Which costs more: 3 pounds of bulk almonds or one 3-pound bag?

How much do you save if you choose the cheaper option?

Practice

Use estimation to circle the words that best describe each unit price. You do not need to find the exact unit prices.

10 granola bars for $4.79

more than $0.50 per granola bar	less than $0.50 per granola bar

6 bottles for $7.19

more than $1 per bottle	less than $1 per bottle

8 oranges for $6.49

more than $1 per orange	less than $1 per orange

Solve. Write the equations you use.

10 oz. of Krunchies potato chips cost $4.70. What is the unit price per ounce?

WORK SPACE

8 oz. of Snacktastic potato chips cost $3.96. What is the unit price per ounce?

Which brand of potato chips has a lower unit price per ounce?

A 5-pound bag of flour costs $5.80. What is the unit price per pound?

Bulk flour costs $0.99 per pound. How much do 5 pounds cost?

How much do you save if you buy 5 pounds of bulk flour instead of buying a 5-pound bag?

Review

Use estimation to circle the words that best describe each quotient. You do not need to find the exact quotient.

$357.8 \div 2$	$72.98 \div 7$	$17.003 \div 3$
less than 100 / greater than 100	less than 10 / greater than 10	less than 5 / greater than 5

$1.98 \div 4$	$6.325 \div 3$	$0.891 \div 6$
less than 1 / greater than 1	less than 1 / greater than 1	less than 1 / greater than 1

Evaluate. Write your answers in simplest form. Convert improper fractions to mixed numbers.

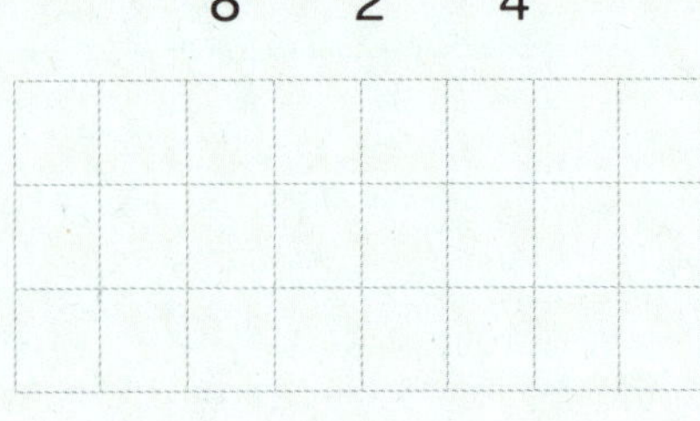

$$\frac{5}{8} + \frac{5}{2} - \frac{3}{4}$$

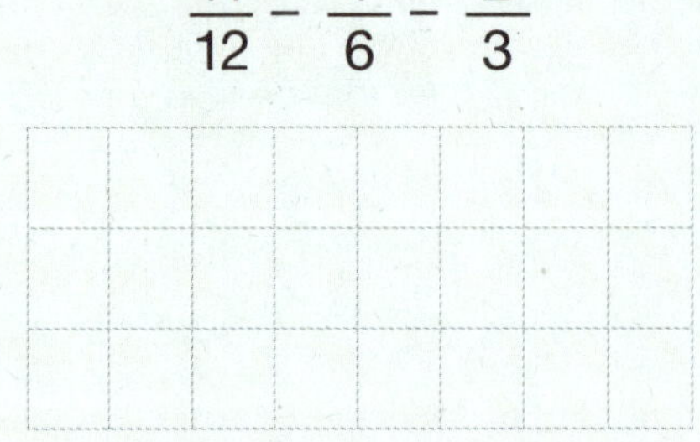

$$\frac{11}{12} - \frac{1}{6} - \frac{2}{3}$$

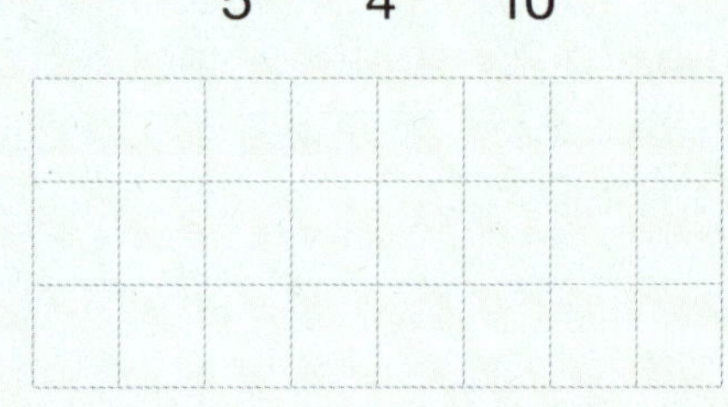

$$\frac{4}{5} + \frac{3}{4} + \frac{7}{10}$$

Complete the circles with <, >, or =.

$9 \bigcirc 5$

$9 \bigcirc -5$

$-9 \bigcirc -5$

$3 \bigcirc -4$

$-3 \bigcirc -4$

$-3 \bigcirc 4$

$0 \bigcirc 2$

$0 \bigcirc -2$

$2 \bigcirc -2$

Find the volume and surface area of the box. Write the equations you use in the work space.

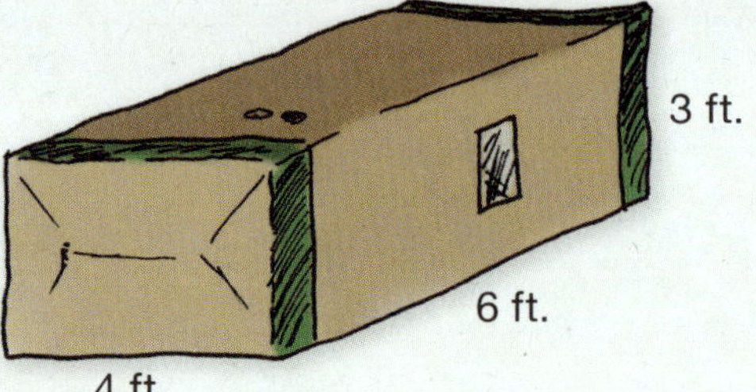

Volume: ______________________

Surface Area: ______________________

Lesson Activities

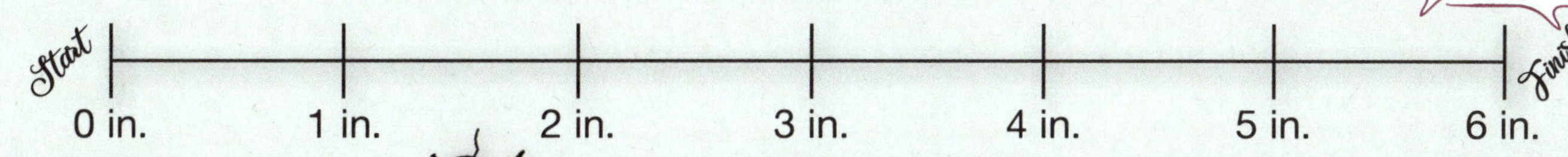

A

The ladybug travels 6 inches in 6 seconds.

The snail travels 6 inches in 12 seconds.

The ant travels 6 inches in 3 seconds.

__________ inches per second

__________ inches per second

__________ inches per second

B

Speed

Speed is a special type of unit rate that compares distance to one unit of time.

$$\frac{\text{distance}}{\text{time}} = \text{speed}$$

Measurement units for speed always include both a distance unit and a time unit. We sometimes use p to stand for "per" in measurement units for speed.

miles per hour

miles/hour

mph

Ex. James is training for a marathon. On Sunday, he ran 12 miles. It took him 2 hours. What was his speed (in miles per hour)?

$$\frac{12 \text{ miles}}{2 \text{ hours}} = \textbf{6 miles per hour}$$

Ex. On Monday, James ran 10 miles. It took him $1\frac{1}{2}$ hours. What was his speed (in miles per hour)?

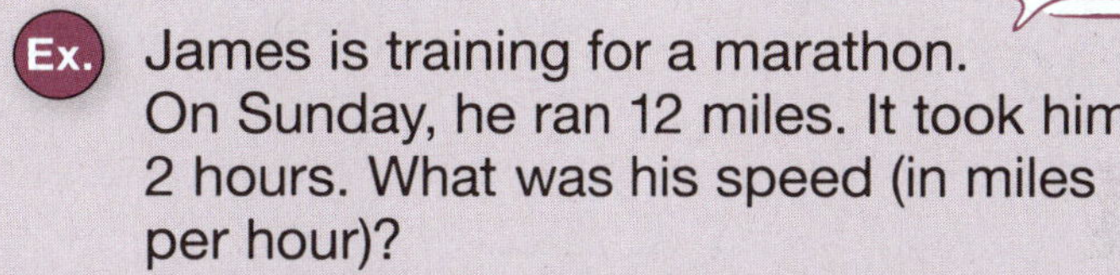

$$\frac{10 \text{ miles}}{1\frac{1}{2} \text{ hours}} \longrightarrow 10 \div 1\frac{1}{2}$$

$$\frac{10}{1} \div \frac{3}{2} \longrightarrow \frac{10}{1} \times \frac{2}{3} = \frac{20}{3} = 6\frac{2}{3} \text{ mph}$$

Running Log	Distance (mi.)	Time (hr.)	Speed (mph)
Tuesday	18	3	
Wednesday	19	3	
Thursday	21	$4\frac{2}{3}$	
Saturday	10	$1\frac{1}{4}$	

Practice

Circle the speeds that are equivalent to the speed in the box.

40 miles per hour	$\frac{80 \text{ mi.}}{2 \text{ hr.}}$	$\frac{60 \text{ mi.}}{3 \text{ hr.}}$	$\frac{120 \text{ mi.}}{3 \text{ hr.}}$	$\frac{40 \text{ mi.}}{1 \text{ hr.}}$	$\frac{40 \text{ km}}{1 \text{ hr.}}$
30 kilometers per hour	$\frac{10 \text{ km}}{2 \text{ hr.}}$	$\frac{90 \text{ km}}{3 \text{ hr.}}$	$\frac{300 \text{ km}}{10 \text{ hr.}}$	$\frac{60 \text{ km}}{2 \text{ hr.}}$	$\frac{60 \text{ km}}{2 \text{ min.}}$
10 feet per second	$\frac{50 \text{ ft.}}{5 \text{ sec.}}$	$\frac{80 \text{ ft.}}{10 \text{ sec.}}$	$\frac{20 \text{ mi.}}{2 \text{ hr.}}$	$\frac{40 \text{ ft.}}{4 \text{ sec.}}$	$\frac{100 \text{ ft.}}{10 \text{ sec.}}$

Jennie made a chart of her bike rides. Use the chart to find her speed for each ride. Write your answers as whole numbers or mixed numbers in simplest form.

Day	Distance (km)	Time (hr.)	Speed (km/hr.)
Saturday	48	3	
Monday	35	$2\frac{1}{2}$	
Wednesday	27	2	
Friday	60	5	

Solve. Write the equations you use.

The Olympic sprinter runs 100 meters in 10 seconds. What is the sprinter's speed in meters per second?

The cheetah runs 24 meters in 2 seconds. What is its speed in meters per second?

Which is faster, the cheetah or the sprinter?

Review

Use long division to solve. Use the multiplication table to help.

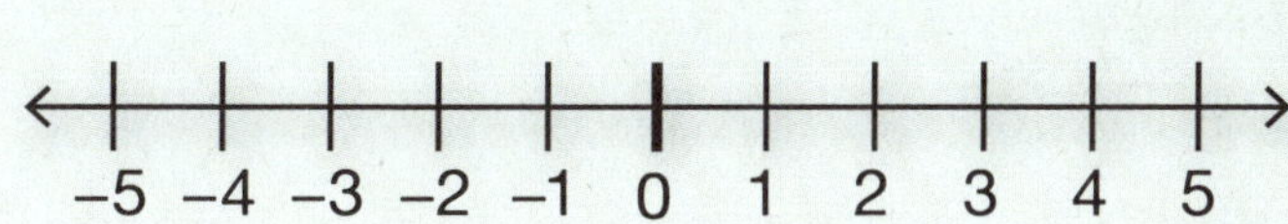

$3\ 5\ \overline{)2\ 8\ 7}$

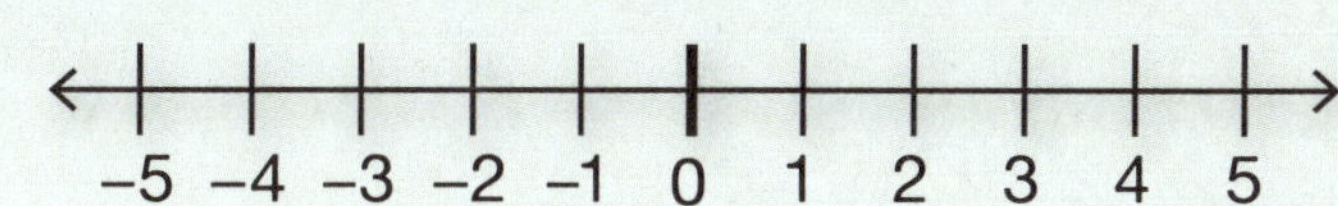

$3\ 5\ \overline{)2,8\ 7\ 6}$

$3\ 5\ \overline{)8\ 2\,.\,9\ 5}$

× 35	
1	35
2	70
3	105
4	140
5	175
6	210
7	245
8	280
9	315

Graph each inequality on the number line. Then, circle the numbers that make the inequality true. X the numbers that do not make the inequality true.

$t > -4$

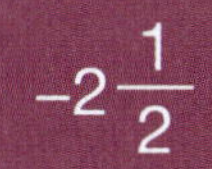

$-5\ -4\ -3\ -2\ -1\ \ 0\ \ 1\ \ 2\ \ 3\ \ 4\ \ 5$

3.6	$-2\frac{1}{2}$	-4	-5

$m \leq -1$

$-5\ -4\ -3\ -2\ -1\ \ 0\ \ 1\ \ 2\ \ 3\ \ 4\ \ 5$

$-3\frac{3}{4}$	-1	1	0

Find the surface area.

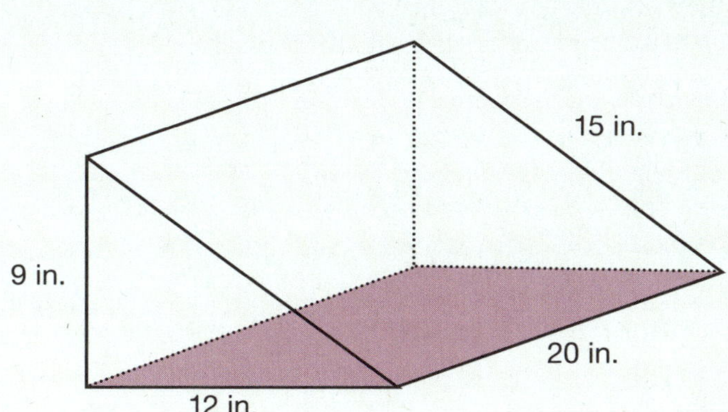

Surface area: ___________________________

Lesson Activities 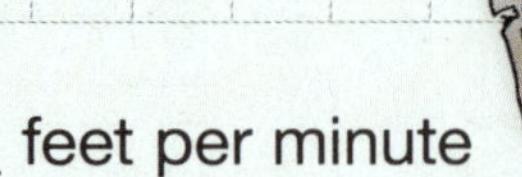

The turtle crawls 15 feet in 3 minutes.

_______ feet per minute

The space station travels 20 miles in 4 seconds.

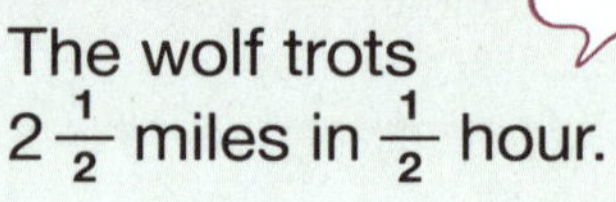

_______ miles per second

The wolf trots $2\frac{1}{2}$ miles in $\frac{1}{2}$ hour.

_______ miles per hour

Ex. The airplane travels at a speed of 600 miles per hour. If the plane flies for $1\frac{1}{2}$ hours, how many miles does the plane travel?

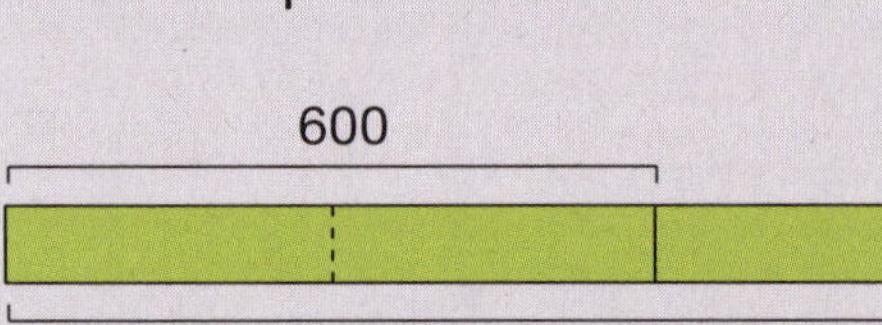

$$600\,\frac{\text{miles}}{\text{hour}} \times 1\frac{1}{2}\text{ hours}$$

$$\overset{300}{\cancel{600}}\,\frac{\text{miles}}{\text{hour}} \times \frac{3}{\cancel{2}}\text{ hours} = \textbf{900 miles}$$

speed × time = distance

Ex. The airplane travels at a speed of 600 miles per hour. How long does it take the plane to travel 2,400 miles?

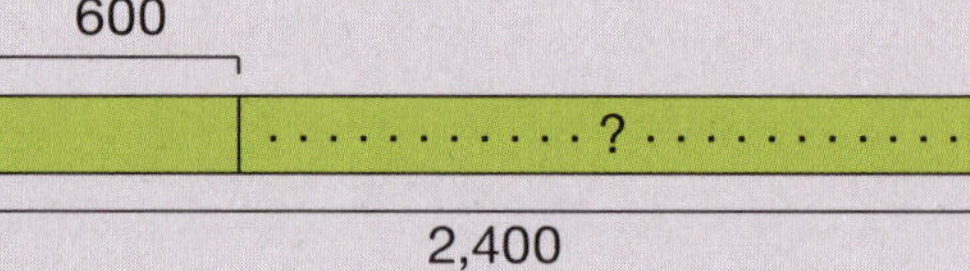

$$2{,}400\text{ miles} \div 600\,\frac{\text{miles}}{\text{hour}} = \textbf{4 hours}$$

distance ÷ speed = time

Hannah rides her bike at a speed of 9 miles per hour. How far does she bike in $2\frac{1}{2}$ hours?

Aaron swims 50 yards per minute. How many minutes does it take him to swim 400 yards?

Lee paddles his canoe at a speed of 6 kilometers per hour. How long does it take him to travel 10 kilometers?

Imani rows at a speed of 250 meters per minute. How far does she row in 20 minutes?

Practice

Complete the chart. Write your equations in the work space. Write your answers as whole numbers or mixed numbers in simplest form.

Type of Transportation	Speed (mph)	Time (hr.)	Distance (mi.)
Airplane	550	2	
Car	40	$1\frac{3}{4}$	
Train	50		300
Bike	12		30
Skateboard	8	$\frac{1}{2}$	
Walking	$3\frac{1}{2}$	$2\frac{1}{4}$	

Solve. Write the equations you use.

The sloth travels 12 meters in 3 minutes. What is its speed in meters per minute?

How far does the sloth travel in 8 minutes?

How many minutes does it take the sloth to travel 100 meters?

The banana slug moves 6 inches in 2 hours. What is the banana slug's speed in inches per hour?

How far does the banana slug travel in 5 hours?

How many hours does it take the banana slug to travel 30 inches?

Review   Complete the chart.

Words	Symbols	Value
absolute value of −5	|−5|	
absolute value of 3.7		
opposite of 6	−(6)	
opposite of −2.5		

Find the surface area of the solid.

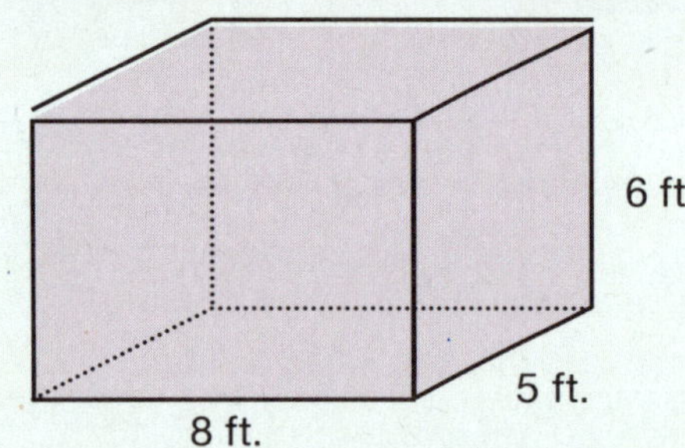

Surface Area: _______________________________________

Find the product.

$$\frac{1}{10} \times \frac{7}{10} =$$

$$\frac{3}{10} \times \frac{7}{10} =$$

$$\frac{1}{100} \times \frac{7}{10} =$$

$$\frac{9}{100} \times \frac{7}{100} =$$

Find the mean and the median of the children's heights. Write your equations in the work space. Express your answers with 2 decimal digits.

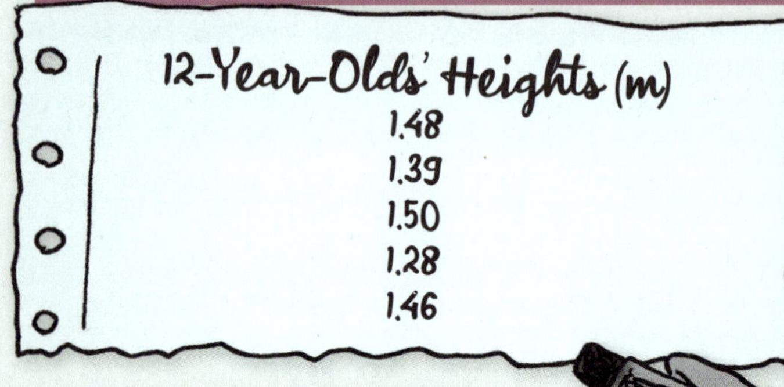

Mean: _____________ Median: _____________

Lesson Activities

speed × time = distance

distance ÷ time = __________

distance ÷ speed = __________

Solve Speed Word Problems

Ex. Thomas runs for $\frac{1}{2}$ hour at a speed of 6 miles per hour. Then, he walks the same distance home at a speed of 3 miles per hour. How long does it take him to walk home?

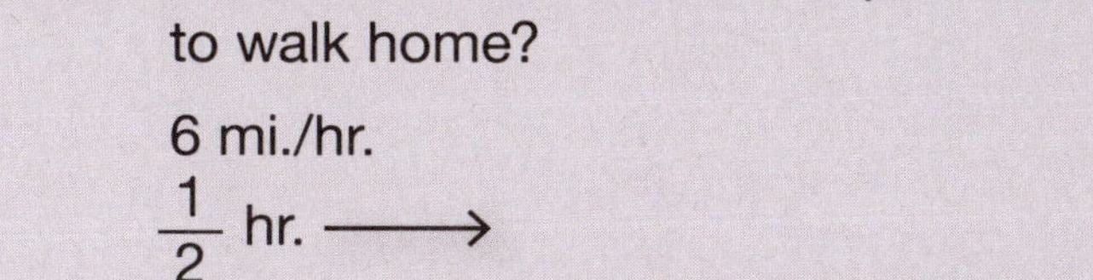

6 mi./hr.

$\frac{1}{2}$ hr. ⟶

?

3 mi./hr.

⟵ ? hr.

3 mi.

First, find the one-way distance Thomas runs.

$$6\,\frac{\text{miles}}{\text{hour}} \times \frac{1}{2}\,\text{hour} = 3\,\text{miles}$$

Then, use the one-way distance to find how long it takes him to walk home.

$$3\,\text{miles} \div 3\,\frac{\text{miles}}{\text{hour}} = \textbf{1 hour}$$

Marianne rode her bike at a speed of 24 kilometers per hour for $1\frac{1}{4}$ hours. Then, she biked the same distance home. It took her 2 hours to bike home. What was Marianne's speed for the return trip?

Marcus runs at a speed of 8 miles per hour for $\frac{1}{2}$ hour. Then, he slows down and jogs at a speed of 6 miles per hour for $\frac{3}{4}$ hour. How far does he run in all?

Practice

Solve. Write the equations you use.

Lauren and her family hike 9 miles from the top of the Grand Canyon to the bottom of the canyon. It takes them 6 hours. What is their speed?

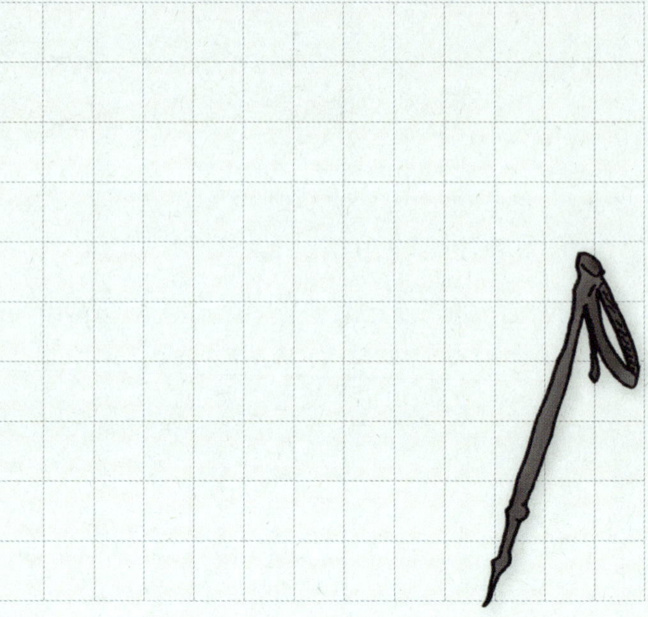

The next day, Lauren and her family hike from the bottom of the canyon back to the top. It takes them 9 hours. What is their speed this day?

Jacob bikes for $\frac{3}{4}$ hour at a speed of 20 miles per hour. Then, he slows down to a speed of 16 miles per hour and bikes for $\frac{1}{2}$ hour longer. How far does he bike in all?

Hailey's family and Amber's family both drive 100 miles to the soccer tournament. Hailey's family drives at a speed of 60 miles per hour. How many hours does it take Hailey's family to get to the soccer tournament?

Amber's family drives at a speed of 50 miles per hour. How many hours does it take Amber's family to get to the soccer tournament?

Which family gets to the tournament more quickly? How much earlier do they arrive?

Review   Write 10, 100, or 1,000 to complete the blanks.

357 ÷ _________ = 3.57	32.6 ÷ _________ = 3.26	6 ÷ _________ = 0.06
604 ÷ _________ = 60.4	19.07 ÷ _________ = 0.1907	4 ÷ _________ = 0.004
195 ÷ _________ = 0.195	80.5 ÷ _________ = 0.0805	8 ÷ _________ = 0.8

Write the name of each 3-D solid and tell how many faces it has.

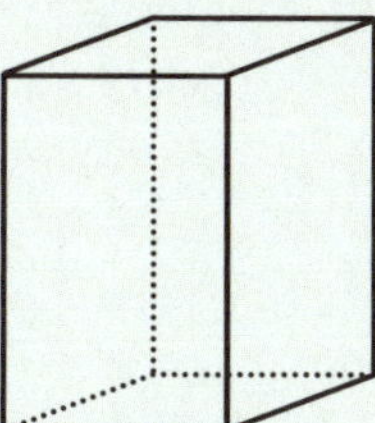

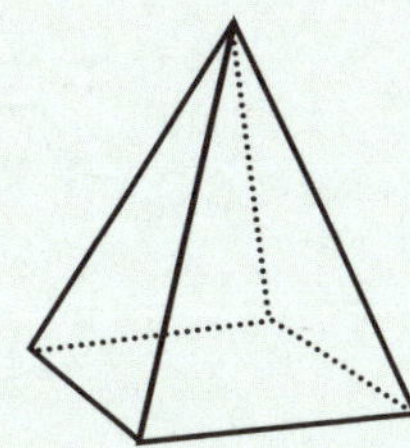

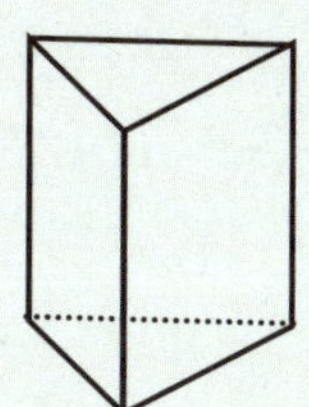

Name: _________________

Number of faces: _________

Name: _________________

Number of faces: _________

Name: _________________

Number of faces: _________

Evaluate each expression for $n = 4$.

$(n - 2)^2$

$(n - 3)^2$

$(n - 4)^2$

$\dfrac{n + 2}{4}$

$\dfrac{n + 3}{4}$

$\dfrac{n + 4}{4}$

Use the net to find the surface area.

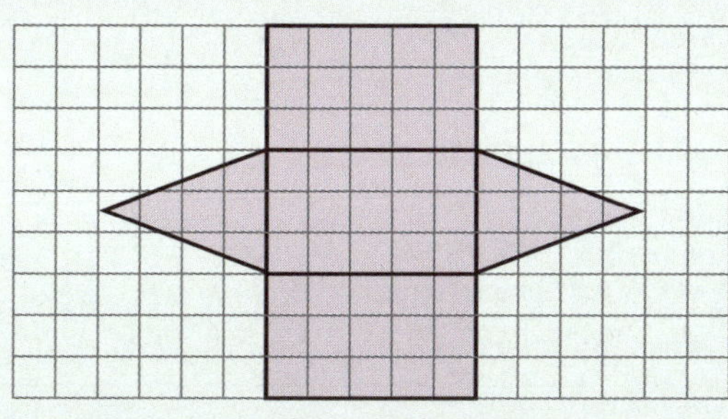

Unit Wrap-Up

Find the unit rate. Then, use the unit rate to answer the other questions.

The factory produces 80 yo-yos in 10 minutes. How many yo-yos does it produce per minute?

Violet uses a hose to fill a 5-gallon bucket. It takes her $\frac{1}{2}$ minute to completely fill the bucket. At what rate does the water flow out of the hose (in gallons per minute)?

How many yo-yos does the factory produce in 60 minutes?

How long does it take the hose to fill a 120-gallon kiddie pool?

How many minutes does it take the factory to produce 1,600 yo-yos?

Violet's little brother accidentally leaves the hose running for 4 minutes. How many gallons of water does he waste?

Solve. Write the equations you use. Use the multiplication table to help with the long division.

A box of 6 granola bars costs $3.72. What is the unit price of each granola bar?

A box of 12 granola bars costs $5.64. What is the unit price of each granola bar?

Andrew wants to buy 24 granola bars to bring to baseball practice. What is the cheapest way to buy 24 granola bars? How much does it cost?

	1	2	3	4	5	6	7	8	9
× 12	12	24	36	48	60	72	84	96	108

Unit Wrap-Up

Jonas is a professional bicyclist. Some days he sprints short distances. Other days, he bikes longer distances at slower speeds. Use mental math or written equations to complete his workout log.

	Speed (mph)	Time (hr.)	Distance (mi.)
Monday	23	3	
Wednesday	28	$2\frac{1}{4}$	
Friday		5	100
Saturday	30		20
Sunday		$\frac{1}{5}$	7

Solve. Write the equations you use.

Simon's family drives 150 miles to an amusement park. The trip takes them 3 hours. What is their speed?

On the way home, they drive at a speed of 60 miles per hour. How long does the trip home take them?

Cora runs at a speed of 10 miles per hour for $\frac{1}{2}$ hour. Then, she slows down and jogs at a speed of 6 miles per hour for $1\frac{1}{2}$ hours. What distance does she travel in all?

Lesson Activities 

10% of $28.00 = __________

28 ÷ 10 = ?

10% of $319.50 = __________

319.5 ÷ 10 = ?

10% of $0.70 = __________

0.70 ÷ 10 = ?

Use 10% to Find Percentages of Decimals

Ex. The cowboy hat originally cost $95.00. Today, it's on sale for 20% off. What is the sale price?

10% of $95.00 = $9.50

$9.50 × 2 = $19.00 ➔ 20% of $95.00 = $19.00

$95.00 − $19.00 = **$76.00**

10% of $72.00 = __________

20% of $72.00 = __________

Sale price: __________

10% of $8.50 = __________

30% of $8.50 = __________

Sale price: __________

10% of $239.90 = __________

40% of $239.90 = __________

Sale price: __________

Practice

Use mental math to complete.

10% of $5.00 = __________	10% of $2.50 = __________	10% of $11.00 =__________
20% of $5.00 = __________	20% of $2.50 = __________	50% of $11.00 =__________
40% of $5.00 = __________	30% of $2.50 = __________	60% of $11.00 =__________
50% of $5.00 = __________	60% of $2.50 = __________	90% of $11.00 =__________

Solve. Write the equations you use.

Sabrina's family spends $98.40 on a meal at a restaurant. Her mom wants to leave a 20% tip. How much money should she leave as a tip? 

What is the total cost of the meal including the tip?

Carlos buys a skateboard that originally cost $127.80. The skateboard is on sale for 30% off. How much does he save if he buys the skateboard on sale?

What is the sale price of the skateboard?

Use bar models to solve.

Last week, Mark earned $28.70. This week, he earned 10% more than last week. How much more did he earn this week than last week?

How much did he earn this week?

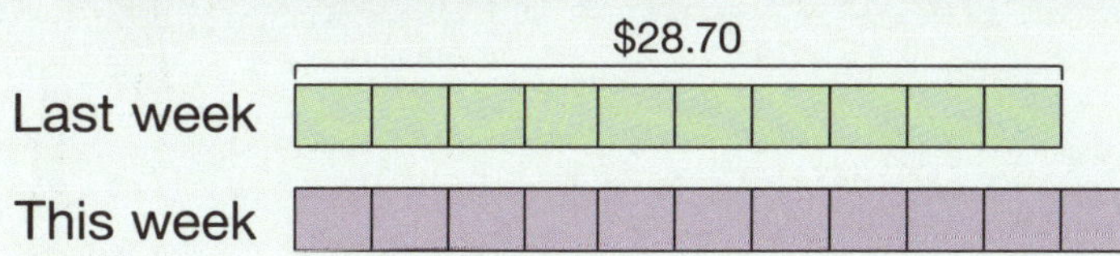

Review   Find the value of each variable. Write the equations you use.

$x + 2 = 20$

$13 = y + 1$

$z + 4 = 31$

Find the distance between each pair of numbers.

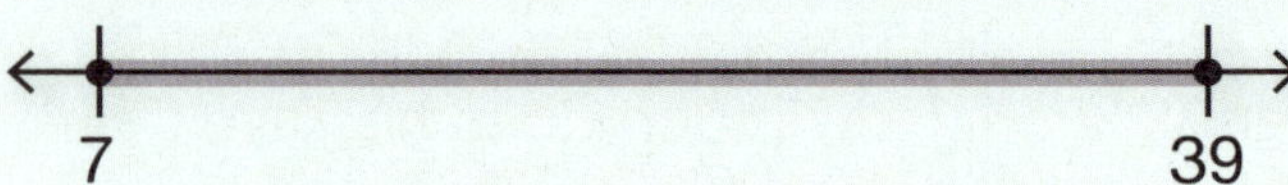

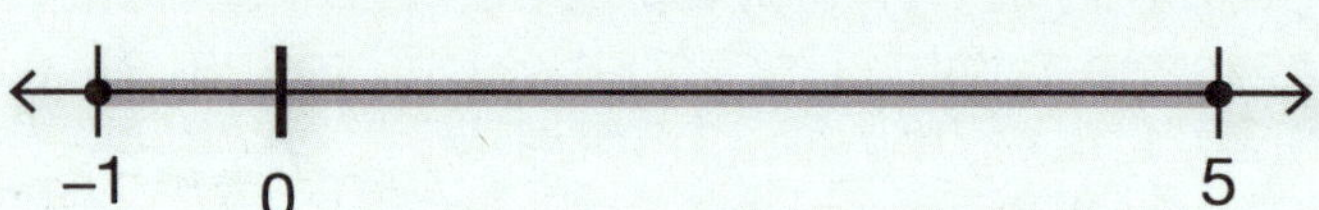

Distance: __________ units

Distance: __________ units

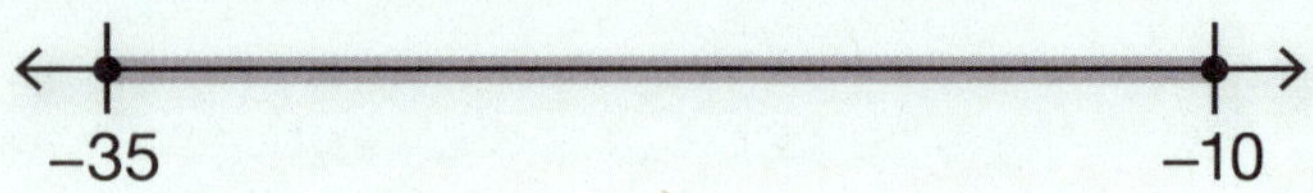

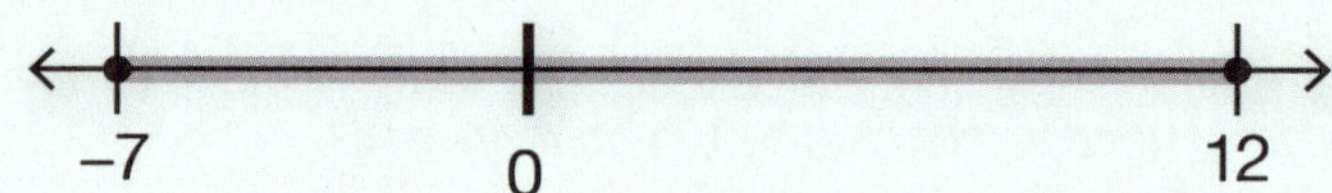

Distance: __________ units

Distance: __________ units

Solve. Write the equations you use.

The factory produces 300 pencils in $\frac{1}{2}$ hour. At what rate does the factory produce pencils (in pencils per hour)?

★ At what rate does the factory produce pencils (in pencils per minute)?

How long does it take the factory to produce 6,000 pencils?

★ How many pencils does the factory produce in 7 minutes?

Lesson Activities

$$53\% = \frac{53}{100} = \underline{0.53}$$

$$9\% = \frac{}{100} = \underline{}$$

$$176\% = \frac{}{100} = \underline{}$$

$$70\% = \frac{}{100} = \underline{}$$

$$41\% = \frac{}{100} = \underline{}$$

$$208\% = \frac{}{100} = \underline{}$$

Use Decimal Multiplication to Find Percentages

In math, "of" often means multiply. We can use decimals to find a percentage of a number.

1. Convert the percentage to a decimal.
2. Multiply the decimal by the number.

Ex. Faith buys a board game for $38. She lives in a state that charges 6% sales tax. How much is the sales tax on the board game?

What is 6% of 38?

$6\% = 0.06$

$$\begin{array}{r} 4 \\ 38 \\ \times\, 0.06 \\ \hline \$2.28 \end{array}$$

Decimal digits

$$\begin{array}{r} 0 \\ +\,2 \\ \hline 2 \end{array}$$

Ex. What is the total cost of the game?

$38.00 + \$2.28 = \mathbf{\$40.28}$

Pop the Percentage (1-Player Game)

53% of $60	6% of $80	176% of $20

Practice

Matthew lives in a state that charges 6% sales tax on all purchases. Find how much sales tax he would need to pay on these items. Write your answers with 2 decimal digits.

$2

Sales tax: _______________

$11

Sales tax: _______________

$70

Sales tax: _______________

$320

Sales tax: _______________

$1,084

Sales tax: _______________

$72,900

Sales tax: _______________

Solve. Write your equations in the work space. Write your answers with 2 decimal digits.

The couch's regular price is $1,799. Today, it is on sale for 45% off. How much do you save if you buy the couch on sale?

What is the sale price of the couch?

Review

Plot the points. Then, connect the points in order with straight lines to create a shape.

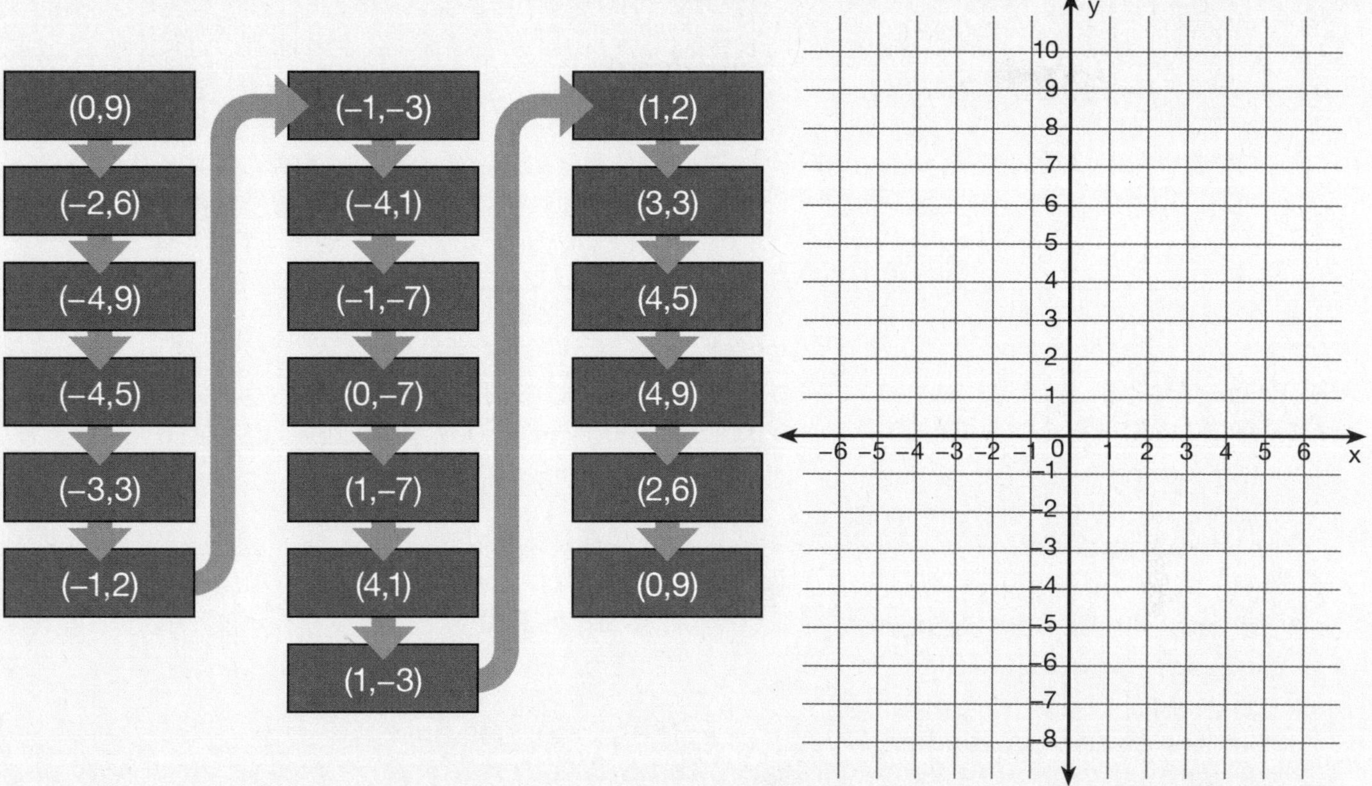

Use mental math to solve.

0.7 + _____________ = 1   1.6 + _____________ = 2   6.5 + _____________ = 10

0.28 + _____________ = 1   1.49 + _____________ = 2   4.25 + _____________ = 10

0.997 + _____________ = 1   1.005 + _____________ = 2   9.875 + _____________ = 10

Complete the chart. Use mental math or write your equations in the work space.

Speed (miles per hour)	Time (hours)	Distance (miles)
60	3	
40	2	
	5	100
	6	60
50		200
40		200

Lesson Activities

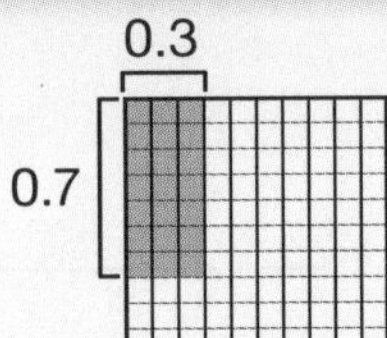

$$\frac{7}{10} \times \frac{3}{10} =$$

0.7 × 0.3 = _______________

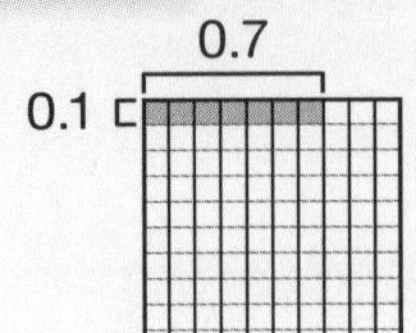

$$\frac{1}{10} \times \frac{7}{10} =$$

0.1 × 0.7 = _______________

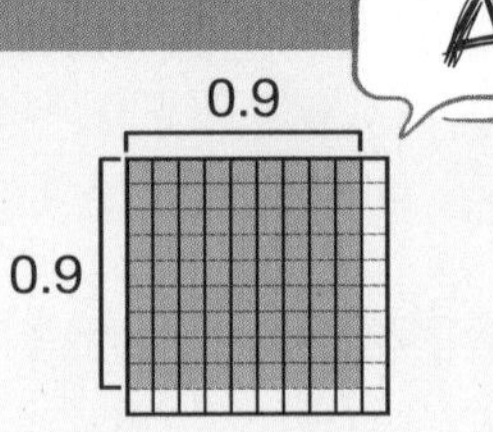

$$\frac{9}{10} \times \frac{9}{10} =$$

0.9 × 0.9 = _______________

Multiply Decimals by Decimals with Mental Math

1. Multiply the non-zero digits. Ignore the decimal point and any leading zeros.
2. Find the total number of decimal digits in the factors.
3. Write a decimal point so the product has the same number of decimal digits as the factors.

Ex. The poster is 0.3 meters wide and 0.5 meters long. What is its area?

0.3 × 0.5 = **0.15**

Decimal digits
1 + 1 = 2

The poster has an area of 0.15 m².

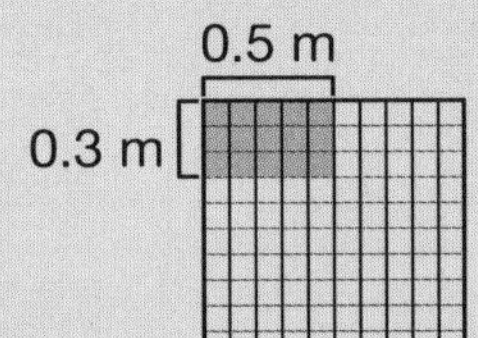

$$\frac{3}{10} \times \frac{5}{10} = \frac{15}{100}$$

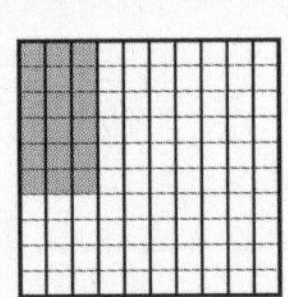

0.6 × 0.3 = _______________

$$\frac{6}{10} \times \frac{3}{10} =$$

0.06 × 0.3 = _______________

$$\frac{6}{100} \times \frac{3}{10} =$$

0.06 × 3 = _______________

$$\frac{6}{100} \times 3 =$$

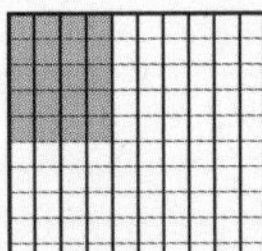

0.5 × 0.4 = _______________

$$\frac{5}{10} \times \frac{4}{10} =$$

0.5 × 0.04 = _______________

$$\frac{5}{10} \times \frac{4}{100} =$$

0.5 × 0.004 = _______________

$$\frac{5}{10} \times \frac{4}{1,000} =$$

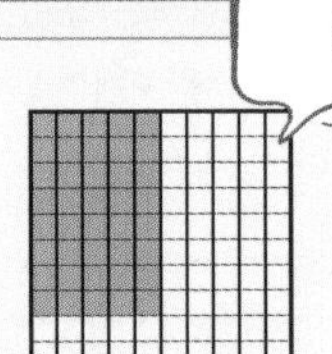

0.8 × 0.5 = _______________

$$\frac{8}{10} \times \frac{5}{10} =$$

0.08 × 0.05 = _______________

$$\frac{8}{100} \times \frac{5}{100} =$$

0.08 × 0.5 = _______________

$$\frac{8}{100} \times \frac{5}{10} =$$

Practice

Find the product.

0.9 × 0.5 = __________	6 × 0.07 = __________	0.08 × 0.09 = __________
0.9 × 0.05 = __________	0.6 × 0.07 = __________	0.8 × 0.09 = __________
0.9 × 0.005 = __________	0.06 × 0.07 = __________	0.8 × 0.9 = __________
0.1 × 0.5 = __________	0.01 × 4 = __________	0.5 × 0.6 = __________
0.1 × 0.05 = __________	0.01 × 0.4 = __________	0.5 × 0.06 = __________
0.1 × 0.005 = __________	0.01 × 0.04 = __________	0.5 × 0.006 = __________

Circle the problems that equal the number in the star.

0.24	0.018	0.10	1.5
0.8 × 0.3	0.6 × 0.03	0.2 × 0.5	3 × 0.05
0.08 × 0.3	0.06 × 3	0.02 × 0.5	3 × 0.5
0.08 × 0.03	0.06 × 0.3	0.02 × 0.05	0.3 × 5
0.08 × 3	0.06 × 0.03	0.02 × 5	0.3 × 0.5

Find the perimeter and area. Write your equations in the work space.

0.08 m

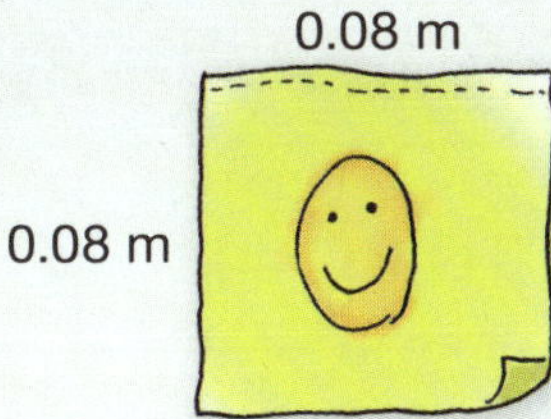

0.08 m

Perimeter: __________   Area: __________

0.8 m

0.4 m

Perimeter: __________   Area: __________

Review   Complete.

$2^2 =$ _______________ $4^2 =$ _______________ $7^2 =$ _______________

$5^2 =$ _______________ $9^2 =$ _______________ $8^2 =$ _______________

$3^2 =$ _______________ $1^2 =$ _______________ $6^2 =$ _______________

Label the coordinates. Then, complete the blanks. Use mental math or write equations in the work space.

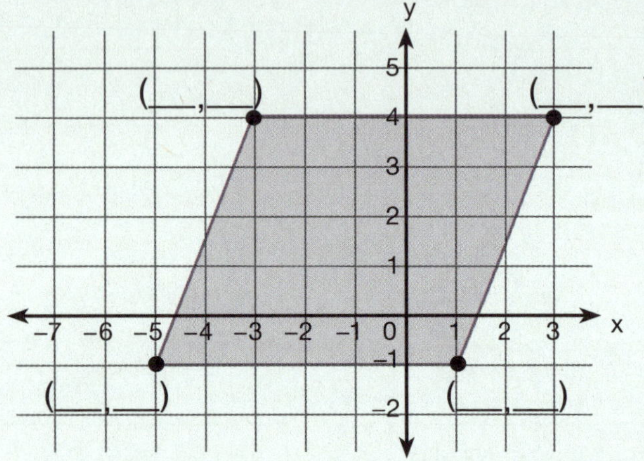

Area: _______________ sq. units

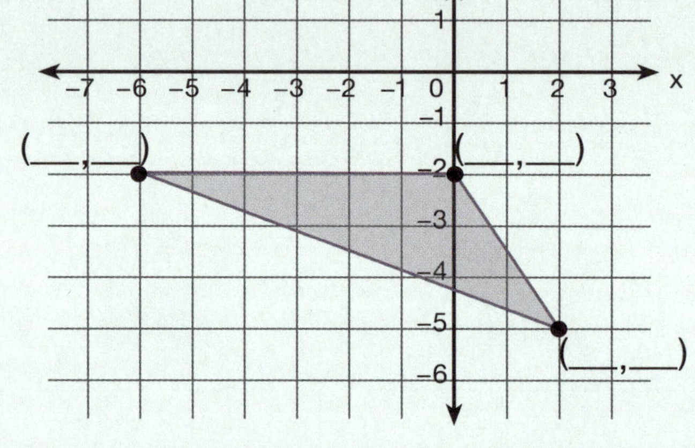

Area: _______________ sq. units

Complete the chart and answer the questions.

12 gallons of water flow out of the hose in 1 minute.

Minutes (t)	1	2	3	4	5	6
Gallons (g)	12					

Write an equation that shows the relationship between the time in minutes (t) and the amount of water in gallons (g).

Use your equation to predict how much water flows out of the hose in 20 minutes.

The kiddie pool has a capacity of 120 gallons. How many minutes will it take to fill the pool?

Lesson Activities

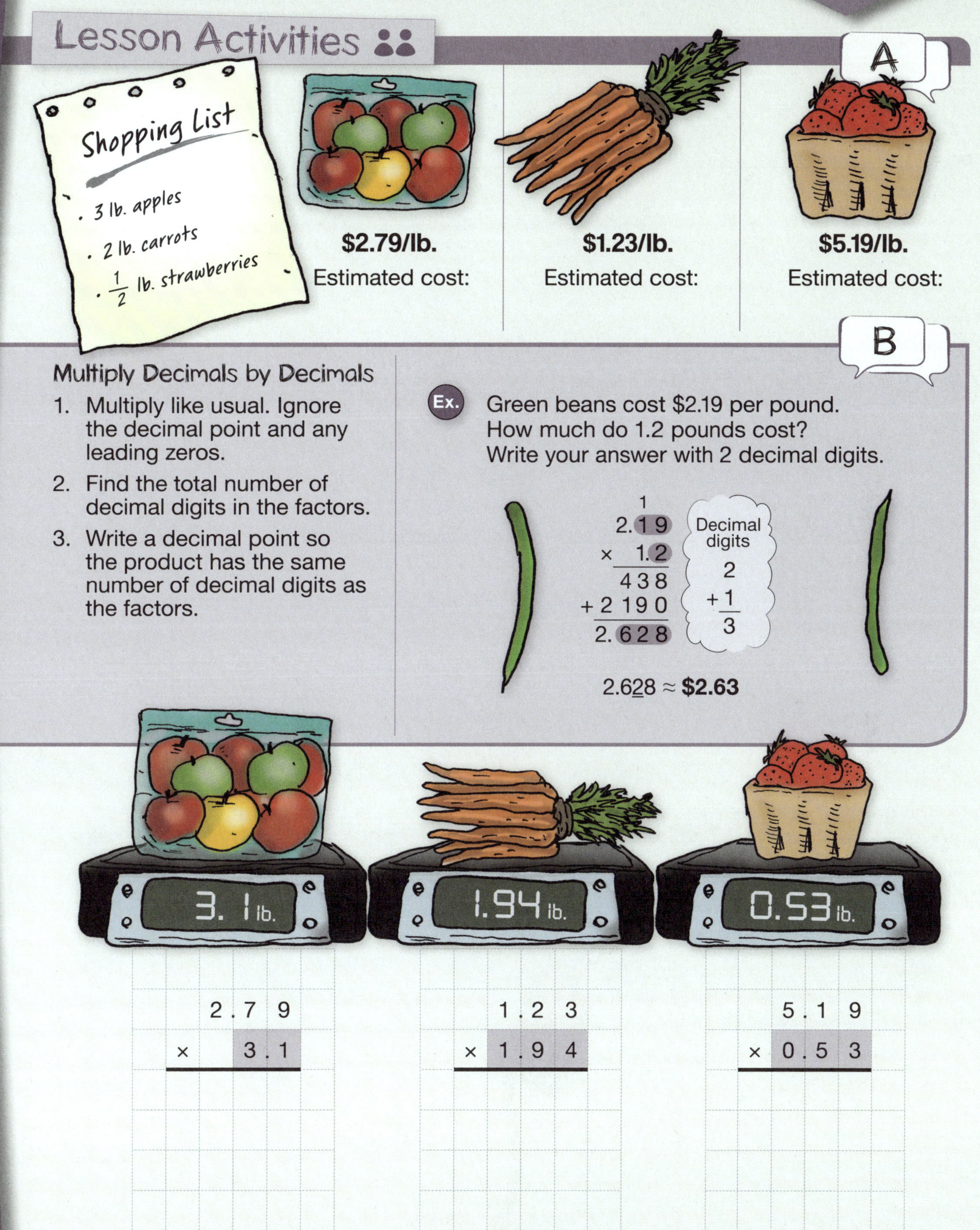

Multiply Decimals by Decimals

1. Multiply like usual. Ignore the decimal point and any leading zeros.

2. Find the total number of decimal digits in the factors.

3. Write a decimal point so the product has the same number of decimal digits as the factors.

Ex. Green beans cost $2.19 per pound. How much do 1.2 pounds cost? Write your answer with 2 decimal digits.

Practice

Circle the most reasonable estimate for each product.

3.9 × 1.15	6.2 × 2.2	4.7 × 3.99
0.4 4 40	0.12 1.2 12	2 20 200

1.3 × 1.04	1.8 × 0.49	0.95 × 5.3
0.01 0.1 1	0.09 0.9 9	0.05 0.5 5

Write the decimal point in the correct place in these products.

```
    2.5 6 4            1.3 9              3 8.7              1.0 4
  ×   0.8          ×     7.3          ×     4.9          ×  2.3 5
  2 0 5 1 2              4 1 7          3 4 8 3                5 2 0
                   + 9 7 3 0        + 1 5 4 8 0              3 1 2 0
                     1 0 1 4 7        1 8 9 6 3        + 2 0 8 0 0
                                                        2 4 4 4 0
```

Solve. Write the equations you use.

At the gas station, gasoline costs $3.29 per gallon. Erica buys 7.2 gallons. How much does she pay? Write your answer with 2 decimal digits.

The fun run is 8.5 kilometers long. Each kilometer equals approximately 0.62 miles. How many miles long is the fun run? Write your answer with 2 decimal digits.

Review

Complete the chart to show 3 ways to write each division problem. (You do not have to find the quotient.)

Division bracket	4 ⟌ 8			9 ⟌ 7
Division symbol	8 ÷ 4	9 ÷ 7		
Fraction bar	$\frac{8}{4}$		$\frac{4}{8}$	

Complete.

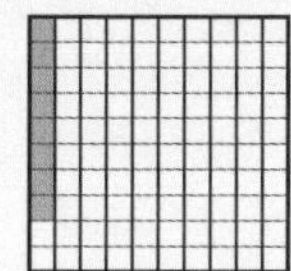

0.08 = _________ hundredths

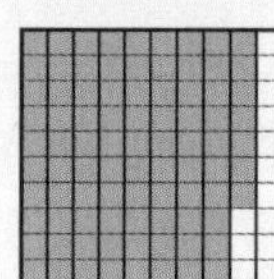

0.87 = _________ hundredths

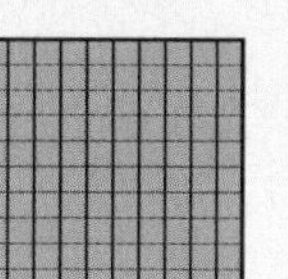

1.29 = _________ hundredths

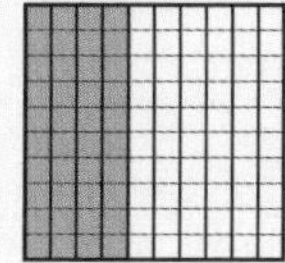

0.4 = _________ hundredths

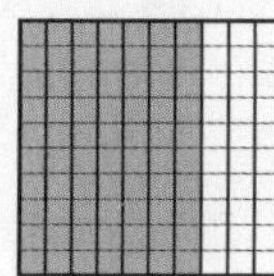

0.7 = _________ hundredths

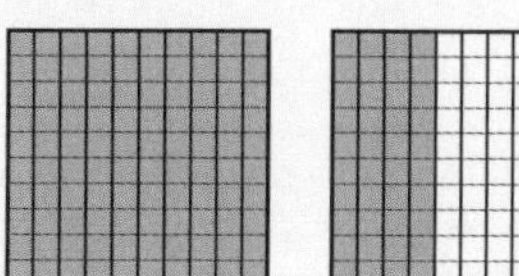

1.4 = _________ tenths

Use mental math to complete.

10% of $4.00 = _________
20% of $4.00 = _________
40% of $4.00 = _________
140% of $4.00 = _________

10% of $3.50 = _________
30% of $3.50 = _________
40% of $3.50 = _________
110% of $3.50 = _________

10% of $13.00 = _________
50% of $13.00 = _________
60% of $13.00 = _________
90% of $13.00 = _________

Use the net to find the surface area of the pyramid.

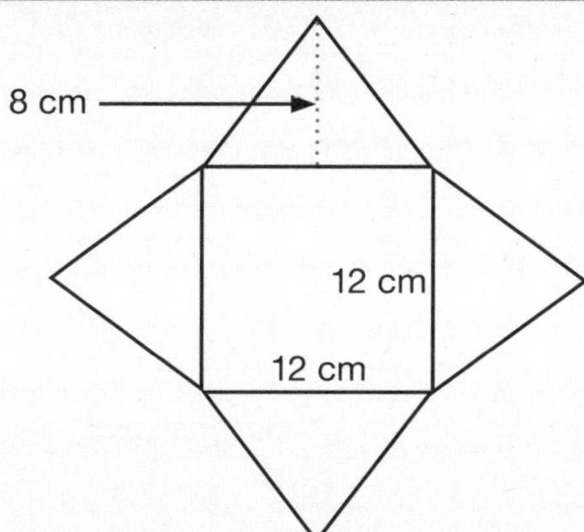

Surface area: _________________________

15.5

A

99% = ___0.99___   1% = __________   38% = __________   90% = __________

75% = __________   20% = __________   15% = __________   7% = __________

B

Use Decimal Multiplication to Find Percentages

Ex. Luis wants to buy a ukulele that costs \$68.50. He lives in a state that charges 5% sales tax. How much is the sales tax on the ukulele? Write your answer with 2 decimal digits.

What is 5% of \$68.50?

5% = 0.05

```
    4 2
  6 8.5
×   0.0 5
  3.4 2 5
```

Decimal digits

1
+2
___
3

3.42̲5 ≈ **\$3.43**

Ex. A guitar costs 40% more than the ukulele. How much does the guitar cost?

What is 140% of \$68.50?

140% = 1.4

```
    6 8.5
×     1.4
  2 7 4 0
+ 6 8 5 0
  9 5.9 0
```

Decimal digits

1
+1
___
2

\$95.90

C

Flip a Percentage (2-Player Game)

Player 1	Player 2
☐☐ % of 3.2 = __________	☐☐ % of 3.2 = __________
☐☐ % of 0.8 = __________	☐☐ % of 0.8 = __________
☐☐ % of 6.54 = __________	☐☐ % of 6.54 = __________
Total: __________	Total: __________

Practice

The sporting goods store is having a sale. Use the regular prices and sale percentages to answer the questions. Write your answers with 2 decimal digits.

How much do you save if you buy the roller skates during the sale?

What is the sale price of the roller skates?

How much do you save if you buy the dumbbells during the sale?

What is the sale price of the dumbbells?

How much do you save if you buy the tennis racket during the sale?

What is the sale price of the tennis racket?

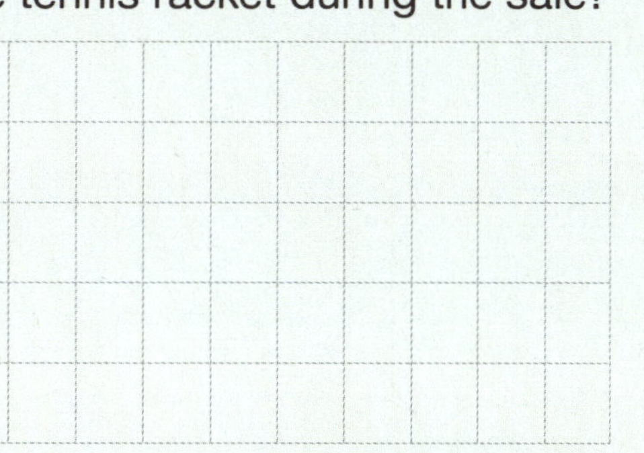

How much do you save if you buy the golf clubs during the sale?

What is the sale price of the golf clubs?

Review

Complete the chart. Write fractions and mixed numbers in simplest form.

Fraction or Mixed Number	Percentage	Decimal
$\frac{7}{100}$		
$1\frac{1}{2}$		
	25%	
	99%	
		0.63
		1.8

Compare with <, >, or =.

$\frac{1}{2}$ ◯ 0.53

$\frac{1}{4}$ ◯ 0.2107

$\frac{1}{10}$ ◯ 0.2

$\frac{3}{4}$ ◯ 0.75

$1\frac{1}{2}$ ◯ 1.3

$2\frac{1}{4}$ ◯ 2.375

$3\frac{4}{5}$ ◯ 3.78

Use the information to complete the chart, draw a graph, and answer the questions.

Gabby runs 1 km in 5 minutes.

Time (minutes)	Distance (km)
0	0
5	1
10	
15	
20	

How far can Gabby run in 9 minutes? Use the graph to approximate the answer. Write the answer as a decimal.

How long does it take Gabby to run 3.1 km? Use the graph to approximate the answer. Write the answer as a decimal.

What is Gabby's speed in kilometers per minute?

Lesson Activities 

Tips for Using a Calculator

1. Type the digits from left to right, in the same order that you would write them.
2. Use estimation to check that the calculator's answer is reasonable.
3. Press the AC button between calculations to clear the calculator's memory. (AC stands for "all clear.")

3.49 + 0.106 = _______________

15.67 − 1.9275 = _______________

4.3 × 1.07 = _______________

0.452 ÷ 4 = _______________

Candy Shopping Spree Order Form

	Unit price per pound	Pounds of candy	Cost (rounded to the hundredths-place)
Jelly beans	$6.79		
Gummy bears	$8.05		
Taffy	$5.49		
Fudge	$17.99		
Red licorice	$3.76		
Malted milk balls	$15.75		
Chocolate-covered pretzels	$10.55		
		Total cost:	

Terms and conditions: You must buy at least $45 and not more than $50 worth of candy. You must buy at least 3 different types of candy.

Practice 

Use a calculator to check whether these answers are correct.

4.08 + 0.685 = _____ 4.765 _____

○ Correct   ○ Incorrect

9.2 – 3.75 = _____ 6.45 _____

○ Correct   ○ Incorrect

0.897 – 0.041 = _____ 0.487 _____

○ Correct   ○ Incorrect

3.6 × 0.25 = _____ 0.975 _____

○ Correct   ○ Incorrect

0.8 × 1.1 = _____ 8.8 _____

○ Correct   ○ Incorrect

10.59 ÷ 3 = _____ 3.53 _____

○ Correct   ○ Incorrect

Meg works as a lifeguard. She makes a chart to record how much money she earns. Use a calculator to complete the chart and answer the questions. Write all money amounts with 2 decimal digits. 

	Hourly wage (dollars per hour)	Number of hours worked	Total pay
Week 1	$15.75	27	
Week 2	$15.75	18.5	
Week 3	$15.75	24.25	

How much more did Meg earn during Week 1 than during Week 2?

How much did Meg earn in all?

On average, how much did Meg earn each week?

 Meg saves 15% of the money she earns. How much money did she save during these 3 weeks?

Review   Complete.

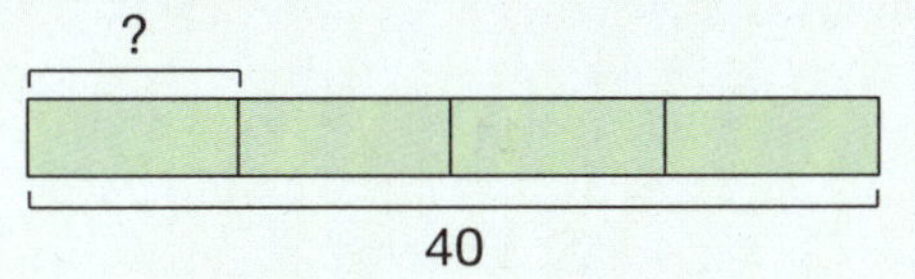

25% of 40 = __________

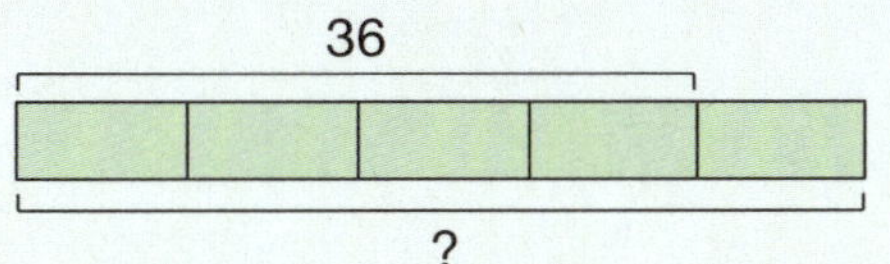

80% of __________ = 36

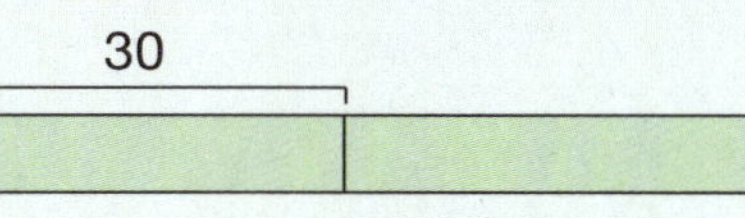

__________ of 60 = 30

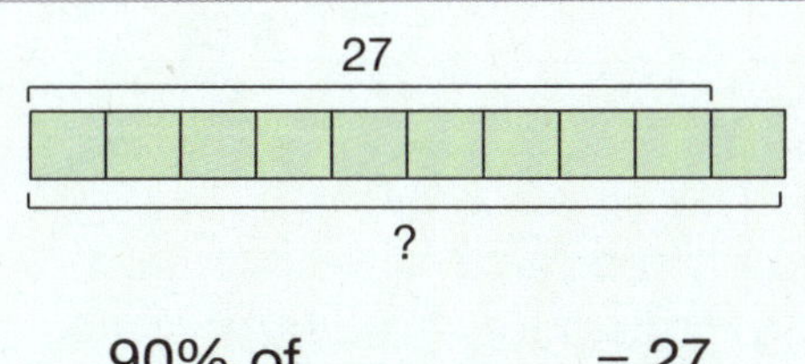

90% of __________ = 27

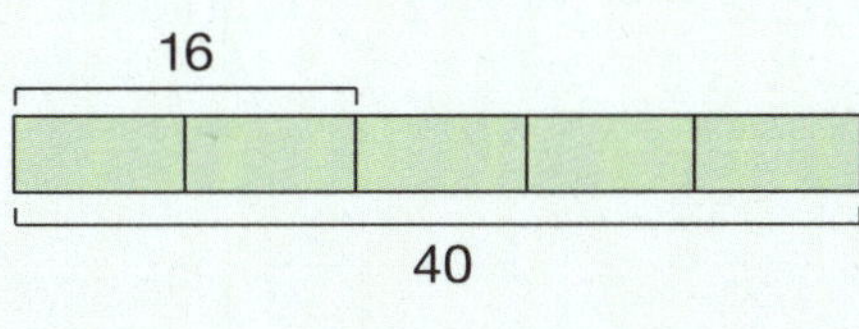

__________ of 40 = 16

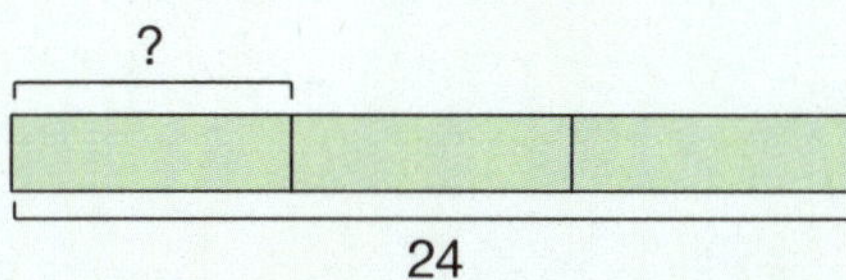

$33\frac{1}{3}$% of 24 = __________

Use mental math to check whether each number is a solution to the equation. Circle the numbers that are solutions to the equation. (Some equations will have more than one solution.)

$2a = 2a$

| 4 | 5 | 6 |

$b = 8 + 7$

| 15 | 16 | 17 |

$16 = 2d + 4$

| 5 | 6 | 7 |

$e + 9 = 9$

| 0 | 1 | 2 |

$9f = 9$

| 0 | 1 | 2 |

$5(g - 1) = 15$

| 3 | 4 | 5 |

Solve. Write the equations you use.

When the puppy was younger, it weighed 3.5 kilograms. Now, it weighs 30% more. How much does it weigh?

A bag of dog food holds 6 pounds. The puppy eats $1\frac{1}{4}$ lb. of dog food each week. How many weeks will it take for the puppy to eat all the food in the bag?

Lesson Activities

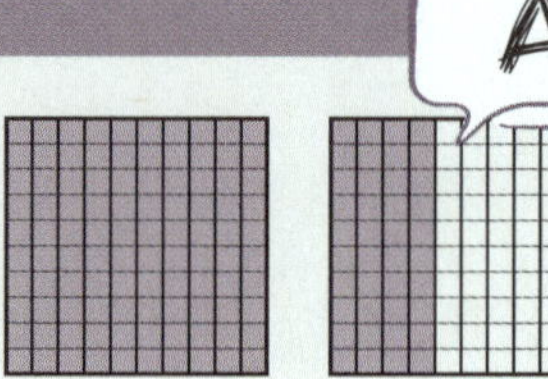

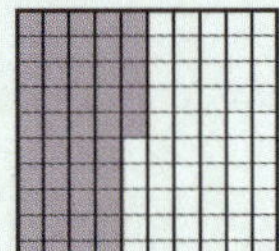

0.45 = _________ hundredths

0.7 = _________ hundredths

1.4 = _________ tenths

Use Place-Value Thinking to Divide Decimals by Decimals

Ex. Chris has a board that is 0.6 m long. He cuts the board into pieces that are each 0.2 m long. How many pieces does he make?

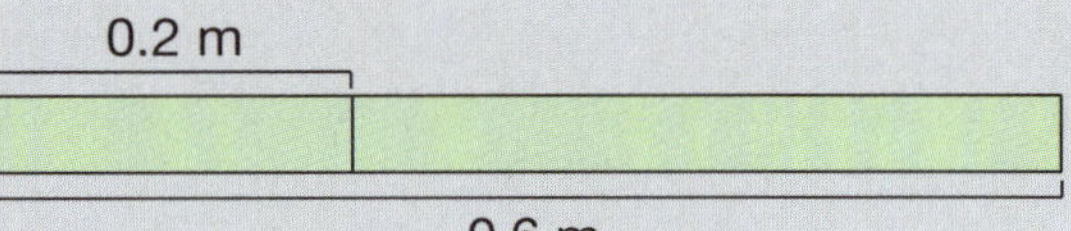

6 tenths ÷ 2 tenths = 3

0.6 ÷ 0.2 = **3**

Ex. Sienna has a piece of wire that is 0.3 m long. She cuts the wire into pieces that are each 0.05 m long. How many pieces does she make?

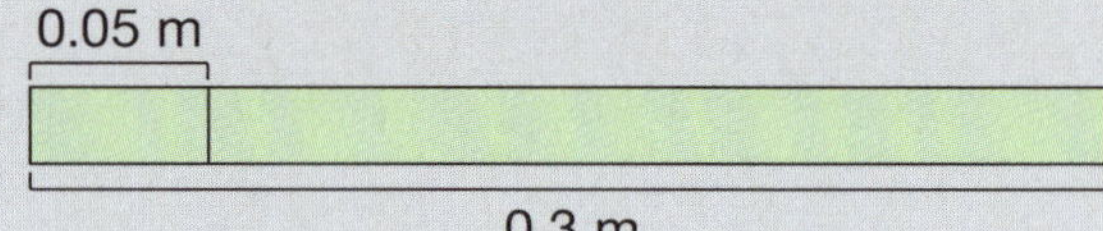

30 hundredths ÷ 5 hundredths = 6

0.3 ÷ 0.05 = **6**

Sam has 0.8 kg of clay. He splits the clay into balls that each weigh 0.2 kg. How many balls of clay does he make?

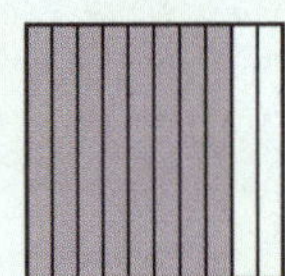

_____ tenths ÷ _____ tenths = _____

0.8 ÷ 0.2 = _________

Eliza has 2 L of grape juice. She pours 0.4 L into each glass. How many glasses does she pour?

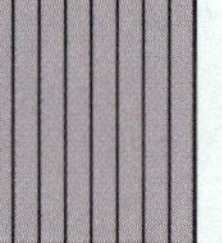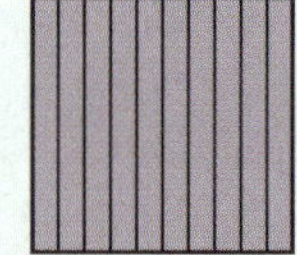

_____ tenths ÷ _____ tenths = _____

2 ÷ 0.4 = _________

Each piece of candy costs $0.05. How many pieces of candy can you buy for $0.35?

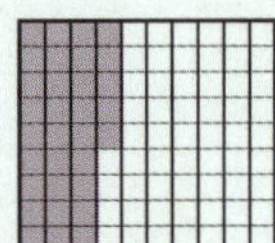

_____ hundredths ÷ _____ hundredths = _____

0.35 ÷ 0.05 = _________

Cassie has 0.4 m of yarn. She splits the yarn into pieces that are each 0.08 m long. How many pieces does she make?

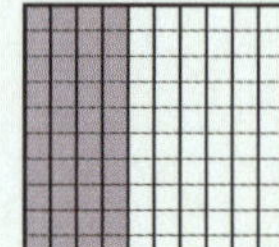

_____ hundredths ÷ _____ hundredths = _____

0.4 ÷ 0.08 = _________

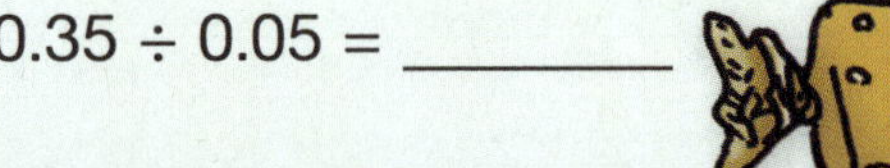

Practice

Find the quotient.

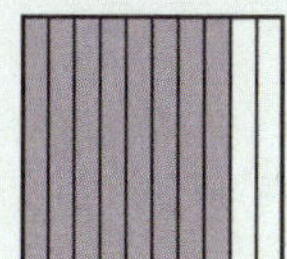

0.8 ÷ 0.4 = _____________

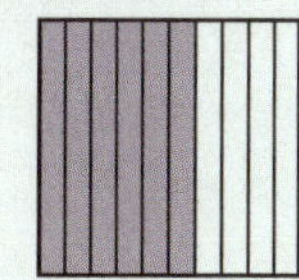

0.6 ÷ 0.1 = _____________

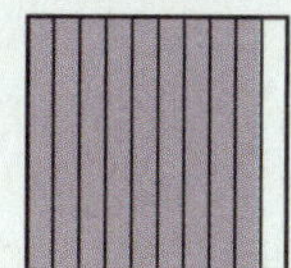

0.9 ÷ 0.3 = _____________

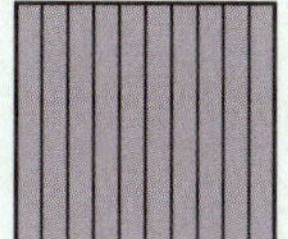 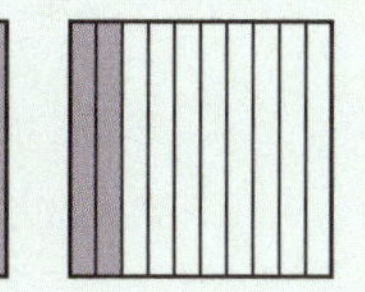

1.2 ÷ 0.3 = _____________

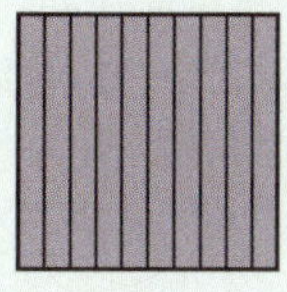

1.8 ÷ 0.2 = _____________

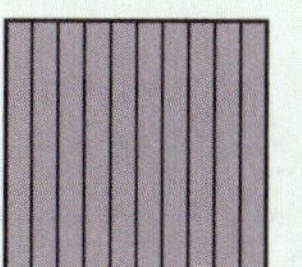

1.5 ÷ 0.5 = _____________

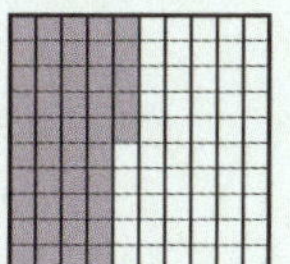

0.45 ÷ 0.09 = _____________

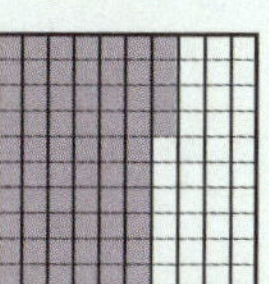

0.64 ÷ 0.08 = _____________

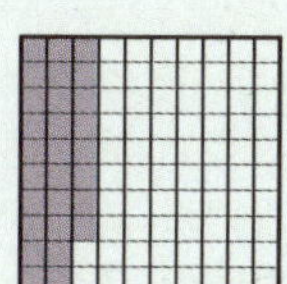

0.28 ÷ 0.04 = _____________

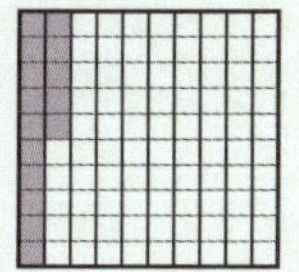

0.15 ÷ 0.01 = _____________

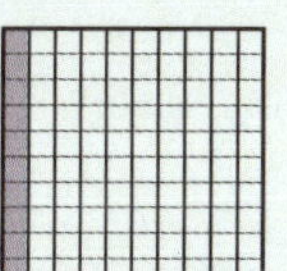

0.1 ÷ 0.05 = _____________

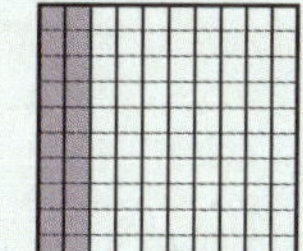

0.2 ÷ 0.05 = _____________

Find the quotient.

0.7 ÷ 0.7 = _____________

0.12 ÷ 0.06 = _____________

1 ÷ 0.5 = _____________

1.4 ÷ 0.7 = _____________

0.18 ÷ 0.06 = _____________

2 ÷ 0.5 = _____________

2.1 ÷ 0.7 = _____________

0.24 ÷ 0.06 = _____________

3 ÷ 0.5 = _____________

Solve. Write the equations you use.

Rachel makes 3.2 lb. of pizza dough. She divides the dough into balls that each weigh 0.8 lb. How many balls of dough does she make?

The restaurant has 4.8 L of iced tea. The waiter pours 0.6 L into each customer's glass. How many glasses can he fill?

Review

Write a number that matches each description. (Many answers are possible.)

Has 3 decimal digits and 2 leading zeros.	Has 4 decimal digits and 1 trailing zero.	Has 2 leading zeros and 1 trailing zero.

Use long division to find the unit price of each item. Write your answers with 2 decimal digits.

Solve. Write the equations you use. Write your answers with 2 decimal digits.

Lucinda earns $135 in April. She saves 40% of the money she earns. How much money does she save?

Lucinda gives away 15% of the money she earns. How much money does she give away?

Lucinda spends the rest of her money. How much does she spend?

Lesson Activities

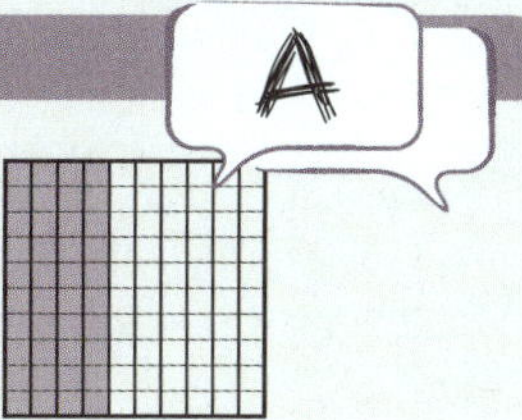

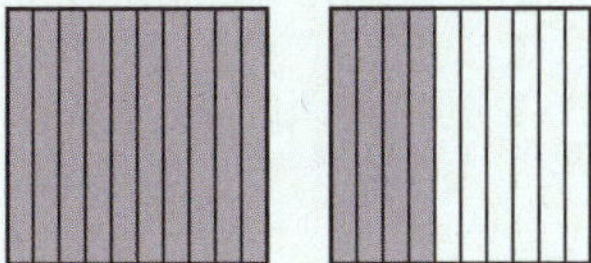

1.4 ÷ 0.7 = __________

0.36 ÷ 0.06 = __________

0.4 ÷ 0.04 = __________

Divide Decimals by Decimals with Long Division

1. Move the divisor's decimal point to the right. Move the decimal point as many places as you need to make the divisor a whole number. Mark the new position with a caret (^).

2. Move the dividend's decimal point the same number of places to the right. Mark the new position with a caret (^).

3. Divide like usual. Ignore any leading zeros.

4. Place the decimal point in the quotient directly above its new place in the dividend.

Ex. Alexandra has 4.2 cubic feet of potting soil. Each flower pot holds 0.3 cubic feet of soil. How many flower pots can she fill?

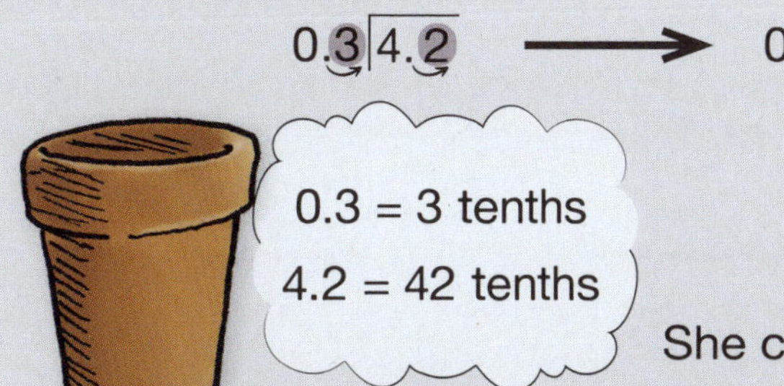

0.3 = 3 tenths

4.2 = 42 tenths

She can fill **14 pots.**

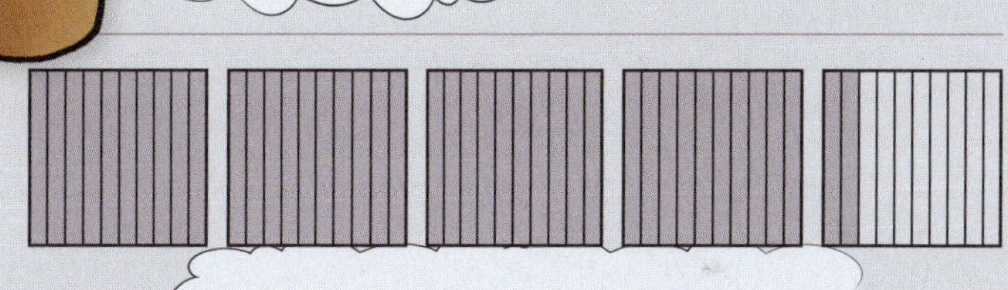

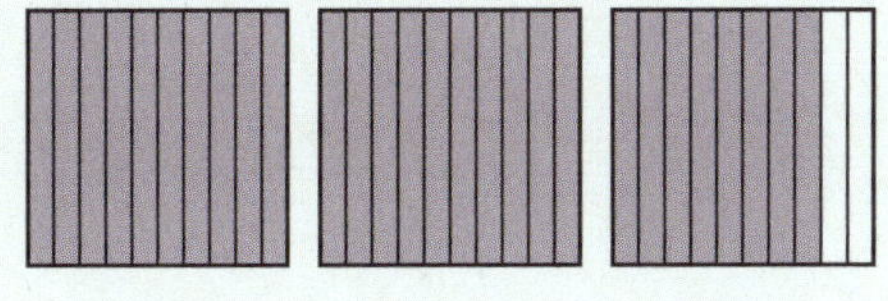

0.2)2.8

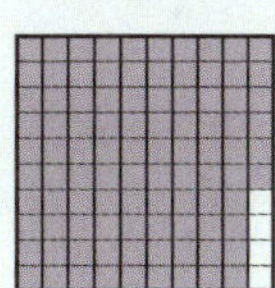

0.0 6)0.9 6

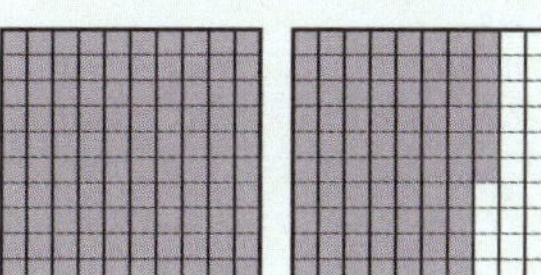

0.0 8)1.7 6

Practice

Use long division to solve.

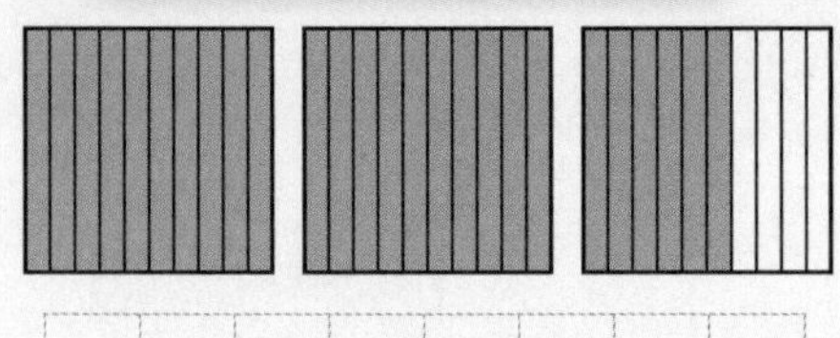

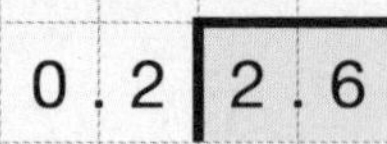

$$0.2\,\overline{)2.6}$$

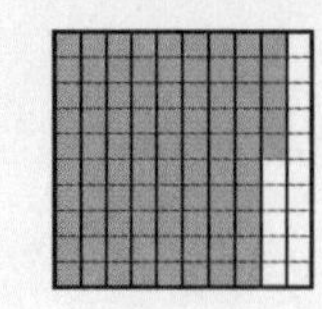

$$0.0\,5\,\overline{)0.8\,5}$$

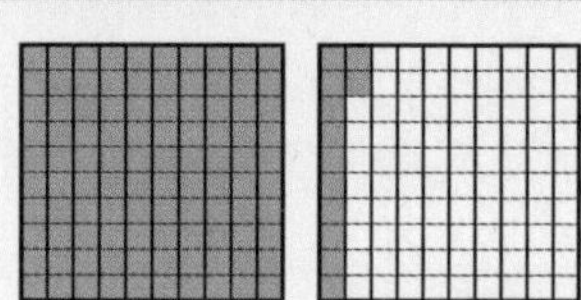

$$0.0\,7\,\overline{)1.1\,2}$$

Use long division to solve. Use the multiplication table to help.

$$0.2\,5\,\overline{)3.7\,5} \qquad 0.2\,5\,\overline{)8.0\,0} \qquad 0.2\,5\,\overline{)9.2\,5}$$

	× 25
1	25
2	50
3	75
4	100
5	125
6	150
7	175
8	200
9	225

Solve. Use the completed problems above to find the answers.

The scientist makes 0.85 L of a chemical solution. He pours 0.05 L into each test tube. How many test tubes does he fill?

1 quarter is worth $0.25. How many quarters are in $9.25?

Each lap around the track is 0.25 miles long. How many laps do you have to run to run a total of 3.75 miles?

Tim buys 2.6 pounds of coffee beans. He uses 0.2 pounds per day. How many days will the coffee beans last?

Review

Match.

| 1 |	–1	–(1)
| –1 |	1	–(–1)
| 14 |	–14	–(14)
| –14 |	14	–(–14)

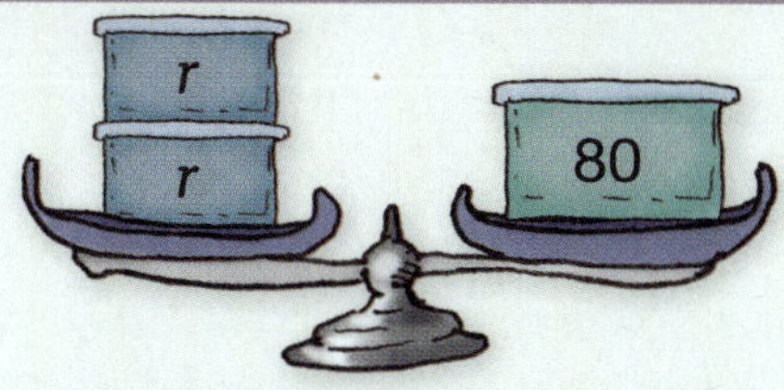

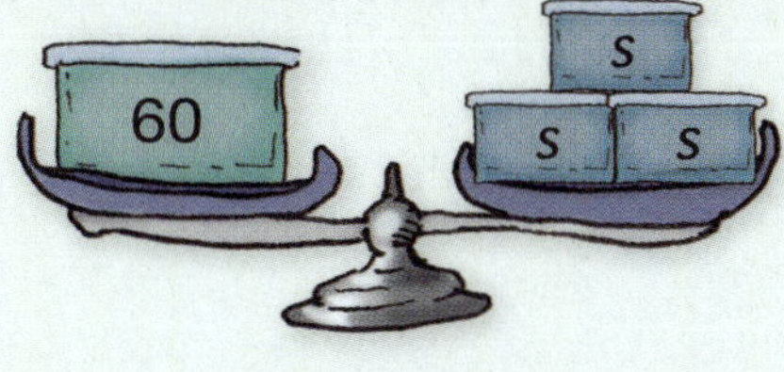

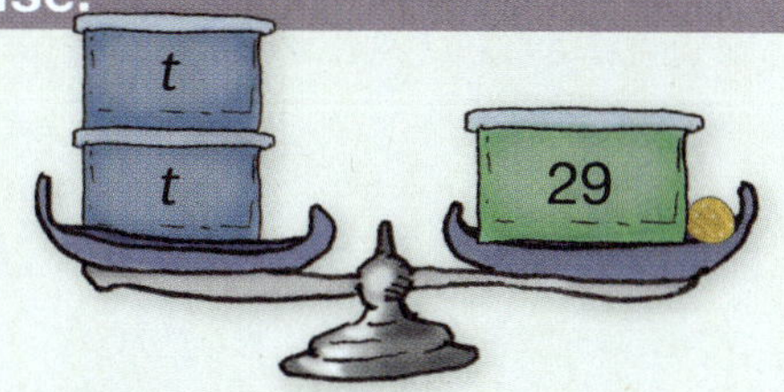

Find the value of each variable. Write the equations you use.

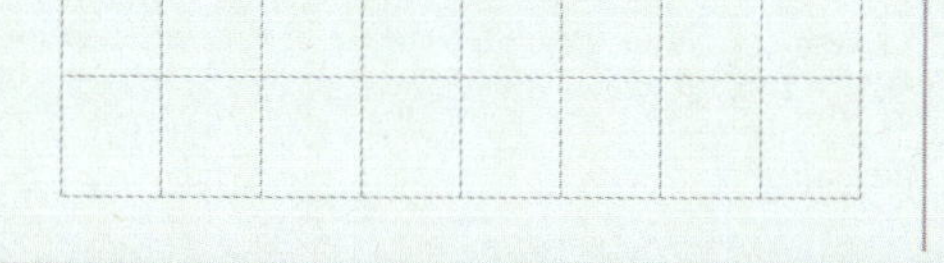

$2r = 80$

$60 = 3s$

★ $2t = 29 + 1$

Find the surface area. Write the equations you use.

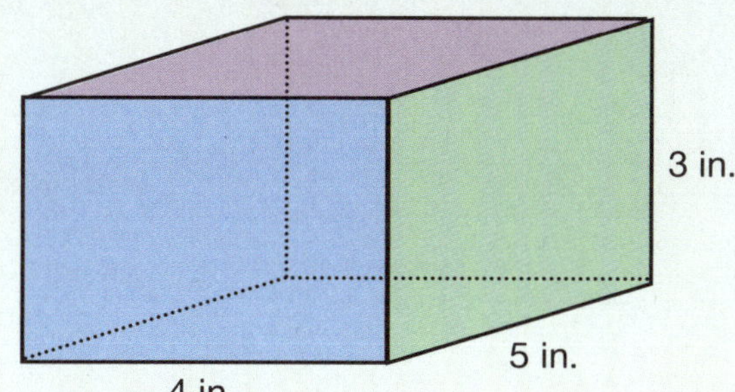

Surface area: ______________________________

Use mental math to complete.

100% of 90 = ____________

$133\frac{1}{3}$% of 90 = ____________

$166\frac{2}{3}$% of 90 = ____________

200% of 90 = ____________

100% of 25 = ____________

200% of 25 = ____________

300% of 25 = ____________

400% of 25 = ____________

Lesson Activities

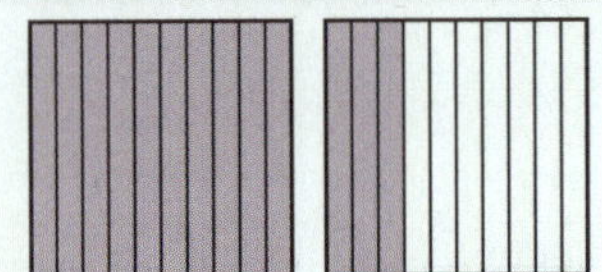

1.3 ÷ 0.5

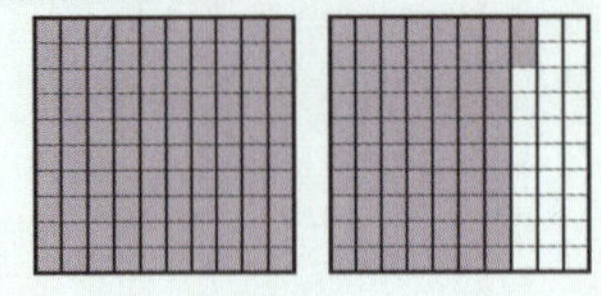

1.72 ÷ 0.8

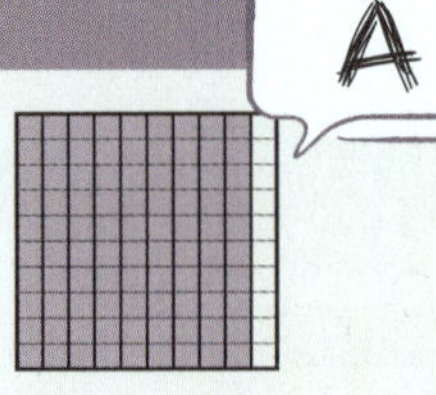

0.9 ÷ 0.12

A

| 1 | 3 | 5 | 1 | 2 | 3 | 4 | 6 | 8 |

B

Tack on Zeros to Divide Decimals

Sometimes, you need to fill in zeros as you move the decimal point.
After you move the decimal point, tack on trailing zeros in the dividend to match the number of decimal digits you want in the answer.

Ex. Prue has 1.1 kg of sugar. She needs 0.25 kg for each batch of brownies. How many batches of brownies can she make? Write your answer with 1 decimal digit.

4.4 batches

$$0.25\overline{)1.10} \rightarrow 0.25\overline{)1.1000}$$
$$-100$$
$$\overline{100}$$
$$-100$$
$$\overline{0}$$

Ex. Paul has 1.74 kg of flour. He needs 0.4 kg for each batch of cookies. How many batches of cookies can he make? Write your answer with 2 decimal digits.

4.35 batches

$$0.4\overline{)1.74} \rightarrow 0.4\overline{)1.740}$$
$$-16$$
$$\overline{14}$$
$$-12$$
$$\overline{20}$$
$$-20$$
$$\overline{0}$$

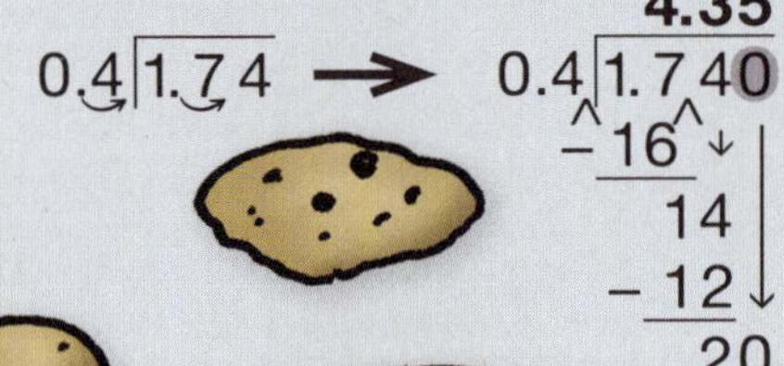

1 decimal digit	2 decimal digits	1 decimal digit	

$$0.5\overline{)1.3}$$

$$0.8\overline{)1.72}$$

$$0.12\overline{)0.9}$$

× 12	
1	12
2	24
3	36
4	48
5	60
6	72
7	84
8	96
9	108

Practice

Circle the best estimate for each division problem.

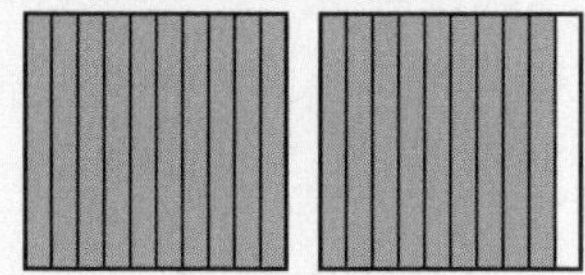

1.9 ÷ 0.5

4	6	8

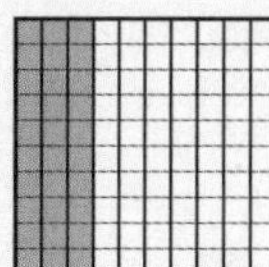

0.3 ÷ 0.04

4	7	10

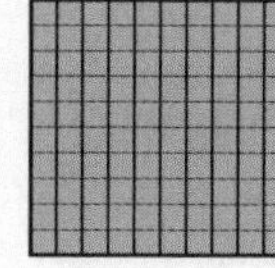

1.49 ÷ 0.3

5	6	7

Write the decimal point in the correct place in these quotients.

```
          7 5                        8 7 5                        3 2
0 . 6 | 4 . 5  0          0 . 0 8 | 0 . 7  0  0  0      0 . 4 5 | 1 . 4  4  0
      - 4 2 ↓                      - 6 4 ↓                      - 1 3 5 ↓
          3 0                            6 0                          9 0
        - 3 0                          - 5 6 ↓                      - 9 0
          ___                            ___                          ___
            0                            4 0                            0
                                       - 4 0
                                         ___
                                           0
```

Use long division to solve. Write your answers with the number of decimal digits listed. Use the multiplication table to help with the final problem.

1 decimal digit	1 decimal digit	2 decimal digits
0 . 5	1 . 7	0 . 6	3 . 3	0 . 3 2	1 . 6 8

× 32	
1	32
2	64
3	96
4	128
5	160
6	192
7	224
8	256
9	288

Review — Use mental math to complete.

| $2.50 | increase by 10% | _____ |
| $2.50 | decrease by 10% | _____ |

| $2.50 | increase by 100% | _____ |
| $2.50 | decrease by 100% | _____ |

| 45 | increase by 10% | _____ |
| 45 | decrease by 10% | _____ |

| 45 | increase by 20% | _____ |
| 45 | decrease by 20% | _____ |

Write each group of numbers in order from least to greatest.

| 1 | −3 | −6 | 2 |

_____ _____ _____ _____
least   greatest

| 0.236 | 0.2365 | 0.237 | 0.2307 |

_____ _____ _____ _____
least   greatest

| 0.45 | $\frac{1}{2}$ | 0.501 | $\frac{2}{5}$ |

_____ _____ _____ _____
least   greatest

| 0.84 | $\frac{3}{4}$ | 0.79 | $\frac{4}{5}$ |

_____ _____ _____ _____
least   greatest

Solve. Write the equations you use.

Kylie runs on the treadmill at a speed of 6.7 miles per hour for 0.5 hours. How far does she run? Write your answer with 2 decimal digits.

The box is $2\frac{1}{2}$ ft. long, $\frac{1}{2}$ ft. wide, and $\frac{1}{3}$ ft. high. What is the volume of the box in cubic feet?

Lesson Activities

1.3<u>8</u>5 ≈ _______________   0.<u>7</u>63 ≈ _______________   16.<u>4</u>99 ≈ _______________

Round Quotients to a Given Number of Decimal Digits

Ex. The bag of chips weighs 6.3 ounces. Each serving is 0.8 ounces. How many servings are in the bag? Write your answer with 1 decimal digit.

1. Set up the problem and move the decimal point. Tack on trailing zeros to match the number of decimal digits you want in the answer.

2. Follow the long division steps.

3. If there is a remainder, tack on 1 more zero and follow the long division steps again. Round your answer to the correct number of decimal digits.

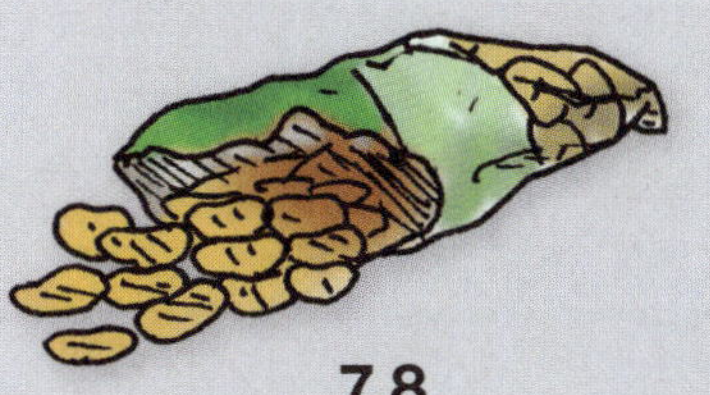

$$0.8\overline{)6.30}$$

$\longrightarrow$

$$\begin{array}{r} 7.8 \\ 0.8\overline{)6.30} \\ -5\,6 \\ \hline 70 \\ -64 \\ \hline 6 \end{array}$$

$\longrightarrow$

$$\begin{array}{r} 7.87 \\ 0.8\overline{)6.300} \\ -5\,6 \\ \hline 70 \\ -64 \\ \hline 60 \end{array}$$

7.87 ≈ **7.9 servings**

The ice cream container weighs 0.84 kg. Each serving of ice cream weighs 0.09 kg. How many servings are in the container? Write your answer with 1 decimal digit.

One bottle of soda holds 2 L. Each serving is 0.22 L. How many servings are in the bottle? Write your answer with 1 decimal digit.

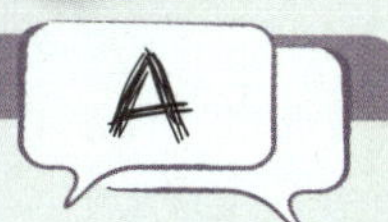

	× 22
1	22
2	44
3	66
4	88
5	110
6	132
7	154
8	176
9	198

Practice

Use long division to find the quotients. Write your answers with the given number of decimal digits. Use the multiplication table at the bottom of the page to help with the last problem.

1.4 ÷ 0.3 = ____________

1 decimal digit

5.1 ÷ 0.28 = ____________

1 decimal digit

Use the recipe to answer the questions. Write your answers with 1 decimal digit. Use the multiplication tables to help.

Play Dough Recipe

- 0.24 kg flour
- 0.28 kg salt
- 0.25 L water

Combine the salt and flour. Gradually stir in the water. Knead for 9 minutes or until the dough is smooth and firm.

The bag of flour weighs 2.3 kg. How many batches of play dough can you make with one bag of flour?

The box of salt weighs 0.74 kg. How many batches of play dough can you make with one box of salt?

	1	2	3	4	5	6	7	8	9
× 24	24	48	72	96	120	144	168	192	216

	1	2	3	4	5	6	7	8	9
× 28	28	56	84	112	140	168	196	224	252

Review

Find the unit rates. Make sure to include the correct units in your answer.

Jude can mow 3 lawns in 2 hours. How many lawns does he mow per hour? Write your answer as a mixed number.

Mimi makes 8 paper airplanes in 4 minutes. How many paper airplanes does she make per minute?

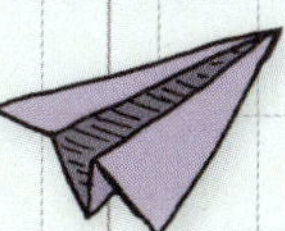

Ollie runs 5 laps in 9 minutes. How many laps does he run per minute? Write your answer as a fraction.

10 ounces of pretzels cost \$2.63. What is the unit price per ounce? Write your answer with 2 decimal digits.

Find the product. Use cancelling where possible. Write your answers in simplest form. Convert improper fractions to mixed numbers.

$$\frac{9}{8} \times \frac{5}{3} \times \frac{4}{5} =$$

$$\frac{2}{7} \times \frac{14}{5} \times \frac{10}{1} =$$

$$\frac{3}{4} \times \frac{4}{3} \times \frac{7}{8} =$$

Use mental math to solve.

3.458 + 1 = _______________

2.793 − 0.1 = _______________

4 − 0.1 = _______________

3.458 + 0.1 = _______________

2.793 − 0.01 = _______________

4 − 0.01 = _______________

3.458 + 0.01 = _______________

2.793 − 0.001 = _______________

4 − 0.001 = _______________

Find the mean and median of the tomato plants' heights. Write your equations in the work space.

Mean: _______________   Median: _______________

Lesson Activities 

A

 1.74 ÷ 0.31 = __________   2.5 ÷ 1.08 = __________   0.84 ÷ 0.029 = __________

| 1 decimal digit | 2 decimal digits | 3 decimal digits |

B

Use a Calculator to Solve Unit Price Problems

Ex. Chicken costs $7.99 per pound. How much do 1.34 pounds of chicken cost? Write your answer with 2 decimal digits.

$7.99/lb. × 1.34 lb. ⟶ `10.7066`

10.7066 ≈ **$10.71**

Ex. Miriam pays $12.85 for a package of chicken. How many pounds of chicken does she buy? Write your answer with 2 decimal digits.

$12.85 ÷ $7.99/lb. ⟶ `1.6082...`

1.6082... ≈ **1.61 lb.**

How much does it cost to buy 14.735 gallons of regular gas? Write your answer with 2 decimal digits.

8.736 gallons of mid-grade gas cost $30.92. What is the price per gallon? Write your answer with 3 decimal digits.

A customer spends $28.92 on premium gas. How many gallons of gas does the customer buy? Write your answer with 3 decimal digits.

How much more does it cost to buy 13.5 gallons of premium gas than to buy 13.5 gallons of regular gas? Write your answer with 2 decimal digits.

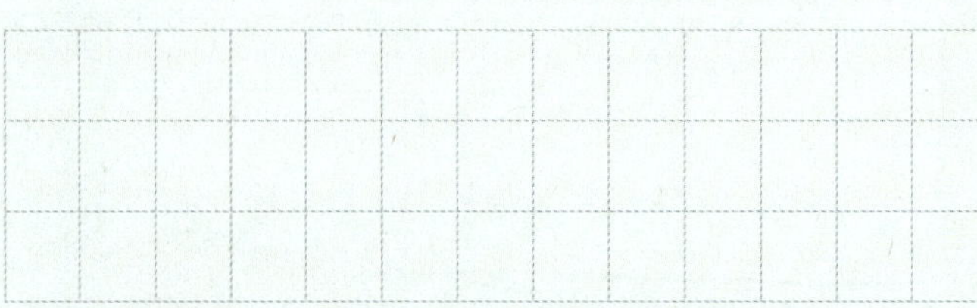

Practice

Use a calculator to find the quotient. Write your answers with the given number of decimal digits.

$6.43 \div 1.98 =$ _____________

2 decimal digits

$0.867 \div 0.041 =$ _____________

3 decimal digits

$1.65 \div 1.45 =$ _____________

2 decimal digits

Find the price per ounce for each bag of pretzels. Use a calculator and write the equations you use. Round your answers to the hundredths-place. Then, answer the question.

13.4 ounces for $5.89

$ _____________ per ounce

7.8 ounces for $3.79

$ _____________ per ounce

Which bag has the lower price per ounce?

Use a calculator and the deli price list to answer the questions. Write the equations you use. Write your answers with 2 decimal digits.

How much does it cost to buy 1.48 pounds of sliced turkey?

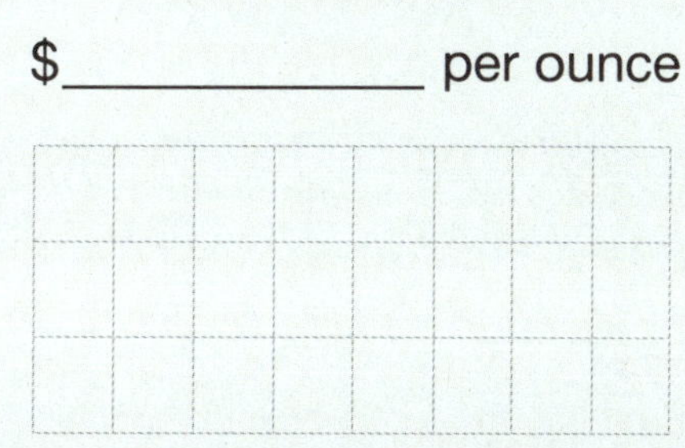

Item	Price per pound
Sliced ham	$9.79
Sliced turkey	$8.49
Sliced cheddar	$6.99

A customer pays $7.35 for a package of sliced cheddar. How many pounds of sliced cheddar are in the package?

How much does it cost to buy 1.25 pounds of sliced turkey and 0.8 pounds of sliced cheddar?

Review
Simplify each expression. Then, answer the questions.

$5a - 2a$

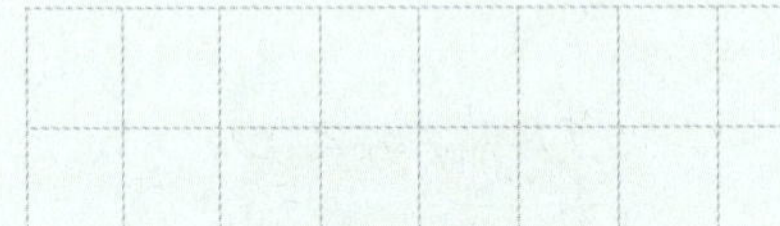

$b + 4 + b + 4$

$c + 2 + d + 1 + c$

What is the value of the expression if $a = 20$?

What is the value of the expression if $b = 7$?

What is the value of the expression if $c = 15$ and $d = 9$?

Rewrite each division problem as a multiplication problem and solve. Write your answers in simplest form and convert improper fractions to mixed numbers.

$4 \div \dfrac{5}{8} =$

$\dfrac{7}{6} \div \dfrac{5}{6} =$

$\dfrac{2}{3} \div \dfrac{1}{4} =$

Use the clues to complete the chart about the survey results.

- 40 people chose red.
- 25% more people chose blue than red.
- 50% fewer people chose green than blue.
- 20% fewer people chose "other" than red.

Favorite Color	Number of People
Blue	
Red	
Green	
Other	

Unit Wrap-Up

Find the product or quotient.

0.3 × 0.4 = _______	0.5 × 0.9 = _______	7 × 0.6 = _______
0.02 × 0.4 = _______	0.07 × 0.03 = _______	9 × 0.04 = _______
0.6 ÷ 0.3 = _______	0.35 ÷ 0.07 = _______	1.00 ÷ 0.25 = _______
1.4 ÷ 0.2 = _______	2.0 ÷ 0.5 = _______	0.4 ÷ 0.05 = _______

Find the product.

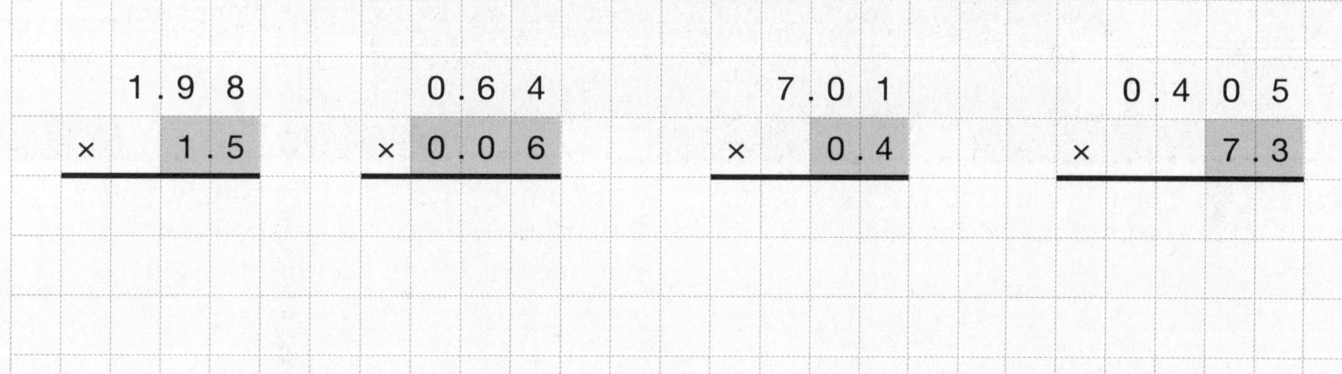

$$\begin{array}{r} 1.98 \\ \times\ 1.5 \\ \hline \end{array} \qquad \begin{array}{r} 0.64 \\ \times\ 0.06 \\ \hline \end{array} \qquad \begin{array}{r} 7.01 \\ \times\ 0.4 \\ \hline \end{array} \qquad \begin{array}{r} 0.405 \\ \times\ 7.3 \\ \hline \end{array}$$

Use long division to find the quotient. Write your answers with the given number of decimal digits. Use the multiplication table to help.

3.7 ÷ 0.6 = _______

2 decimal digits

$$0.6\,\overline{)\,3.7} \qquad\qquad 0.47\,\overline{)\,5.7}$$

5.7 ÷ 0.47 = _______

1 decimal digit

× 47	1	2	3	4	5	6	7	8	9
	47	94	141	188	235	282	329	376	423

Unit Wrap-Up

Use the deli menu and a calculator to answer the questions. Write the equations you use. Write all money amounts with 2 decimal digits.

Item	Price per pound
Tuna salad	$11.98
Chicken salad	$12.39
Potato salad	$6.23
Coleslaw	$5.69
Fruit salad	$8.17

A customer buys 1.74 pounds of tuna salad and 0.83 pounds of chicken salad. How much does he pay?

A customer pays $7.94 for potato salad. How many pounds does she buy? Round your answer to the hundredths-place.

One serving of coleslaw weighs 0.48 pounds. How many servings are in 2.81 pounds of coleslaw? Write your answer with 1 decimal digit.

A package of lobster salad that weighs 0.42 pounds costs $18.46. What is the price per pound?

If you buy 1.07 pounds of fruit salad at the regular price, how much do you pay?

Fruit salad is on sale today. If you buy 1.07 pounds at the sale price, how much do you pay?

Lesson Activities

A

Lee's Results

4, 3, 4, 1, 6, 6, 1, 5,
1, 2, 4, 1, 3, 2, 5, 6

My Results

__, __, __, __, __, __, __, __,
__, __, __, __, __, __, __, __

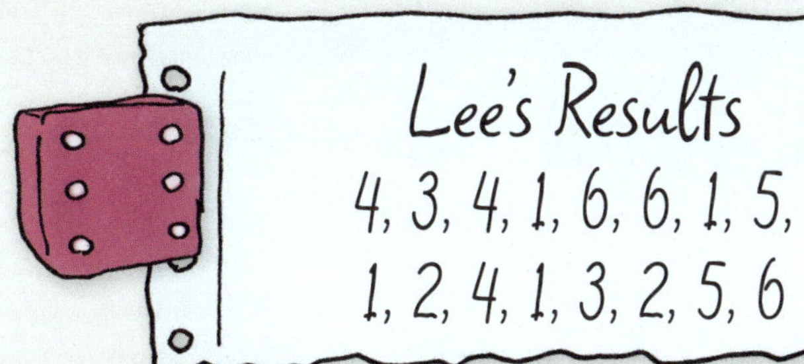

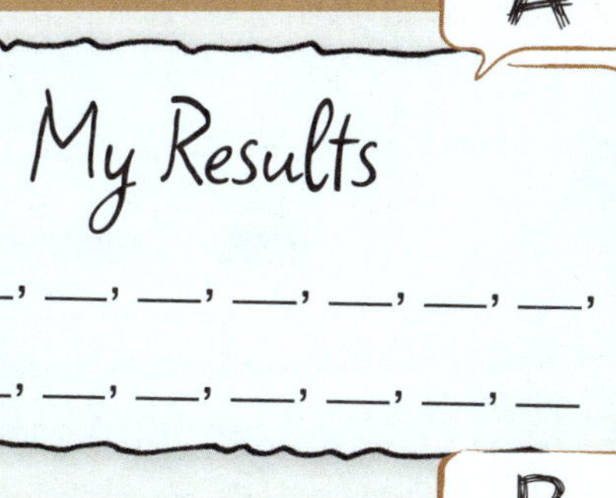

B

Dot Plots

A dot plot is a graph made from dots and part of the number line. The number of dots above each number tells how many times that number occurred in the data set.

Ex. Lee rolled a die 16 times. Make a dot plot to show his results.

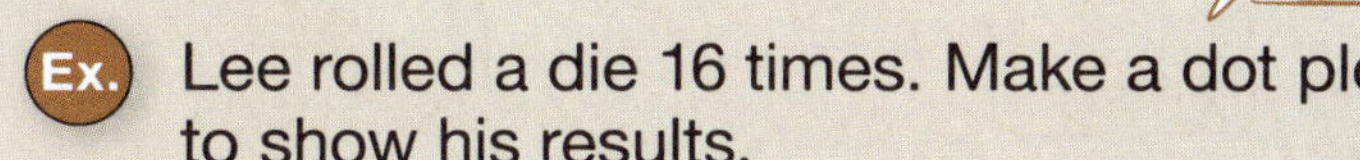

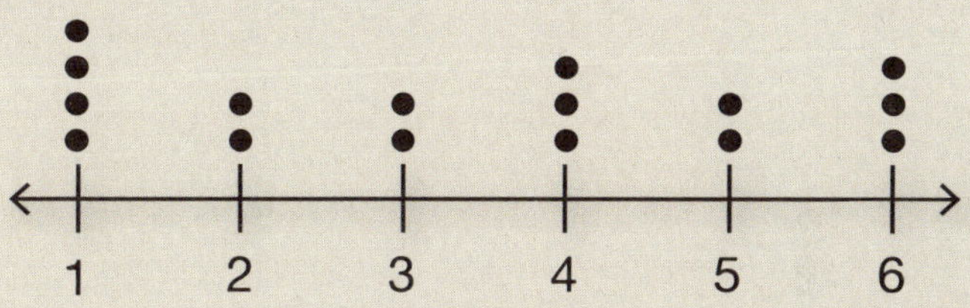

Mean, Median, and Mode

Mean, median, and mode are three different ways to describe the center of a data set:

- The mean is the sum of the values divided by the number of values.
- The median is the value in the middle when you put the values in order.
- The mode is the value that occurs the most frequently.

Ex. Find the mean, median, and mode of Lee's results.

Mean: The sum of Lee's results is 54.
54 ÷ 16 = **3.375**

Median: 1, 1, 1, 1, 2, 2, 3, 3, 4, 4, 4, 5, 5, 6, 6, 6

The two numbers in the middle are 3 and 4. The mean of 3 and 4 is 3.5, so the median is **3.5**.

Mode: The number that occurs the most often is **1**.

Make a dot plot of your results.
Then, find the mean, median, and mode.

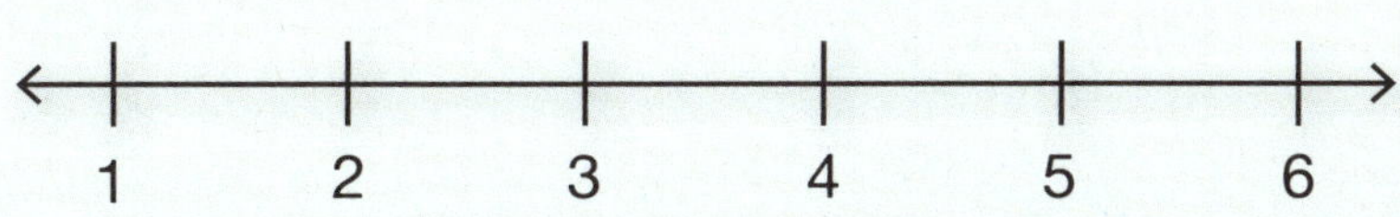

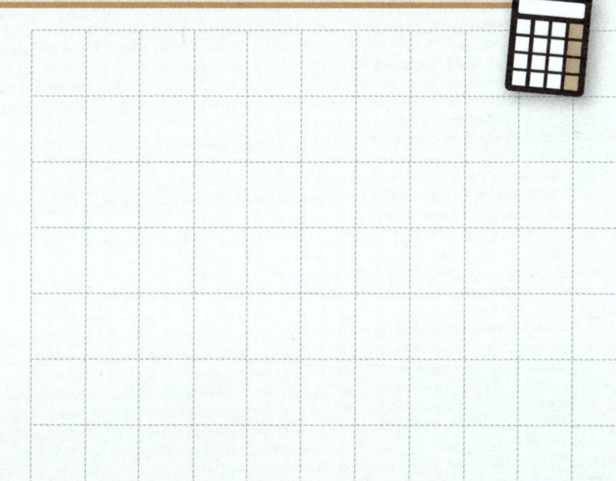

Mean: _______ Median: _______ Mode: _______

Practice

Junie kept track of how many books she checked out from the library each week. Find the mean, median, and mode.

Number of Library Books

4, 2, 6, 3, 3, 9, 3, 5, 8, 6, 4, 7

Mean: _______ Median: _______ Mode: _______

The students in a driver's training class took a 10-question test at the beginning of the class. Then, they took the same test at the end of the class. Find the mean, median, and mode for each dot plot. (Write the mean with 1 decimal digit.) Then, answer the questions.

Number of Questions Correct at the Beginning of the Class

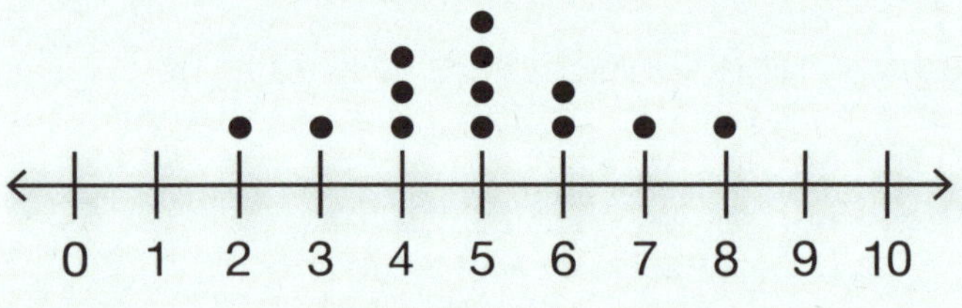

Mean: _____ Median: _____ Mode: _____

Number of Questions Correct at the End of the Class

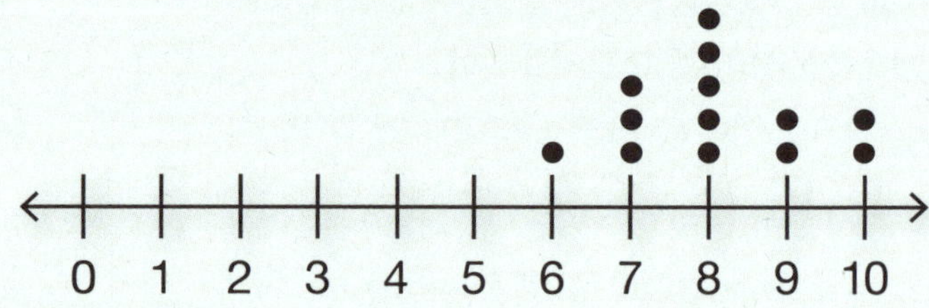

Mean: _____ Median: _____ Mode: _____

At the end of the class, the students had to get 7 or more questions correct to pass. How many students passed?

Based on how the test scores changed, do you think the instructor did a good job? Why or why not?

Review

Complete with <, >, or =.

10^5 ◯ 10^3	$\lvert -4 \rvert$ ◯ -4	$-(8)$ ◯ -8
$3 \cdot 10^4$ ◯ $3{,}000$	$\lvert -4 \rvert$ ◯ 4	$-(8)$ ◯ 8

Convert the fractions to percentages. (Use equivalent fractions as needed.)

$\dfrac{1}{5} = \dfrac{20}{100} = 20\%$	$\dfrac{17}{20} =$	$\dfrac{9}{10} =$	$\dfrac{16}{50} =$
$\dfrac{3}{25} =$	$\dfrac{49}{50} =$	$\dfrac{1}{20} =$	$\dfrac{8}{25} =$

Find how far each number is from 4. Use the number line to help.

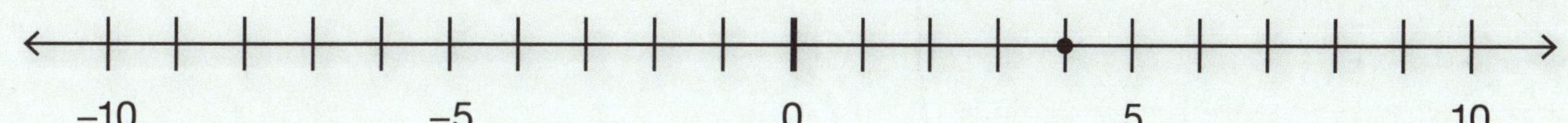

Number	1	−1	8	−8	5	−5	10	−10	2	−2	0
Distance from 4	3	5									

Find the perimeter and area of the backyard. Write your answers with 2 decimal digits.

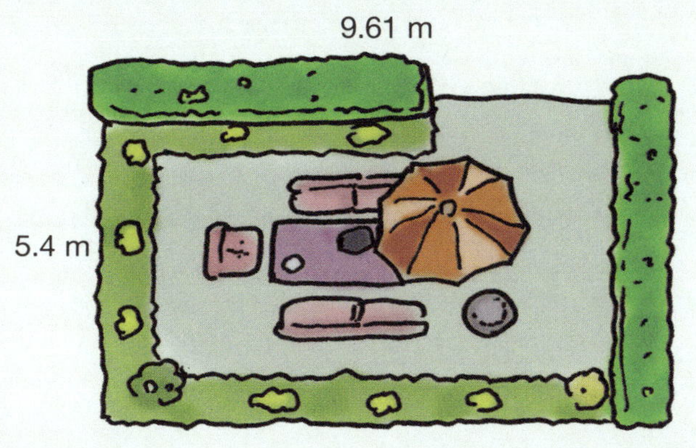

Perimeter: __________   Area: __________

Lesson Activities

A

Ways to Describe the Shape of a Distribution

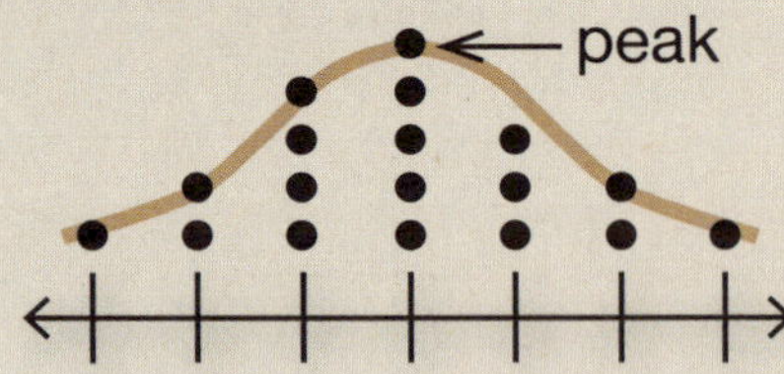

A **symmetric distribution** has two sides that roughly mirror each other.

peak

A **peak** is a value that occurs more frequently than the values around it.

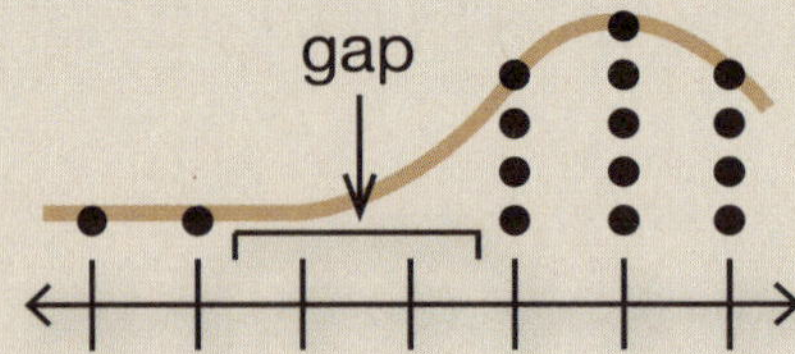

A **left-skewed distribution** has a tail on its left side.

gap

A **gap** is an interval where there are no values.

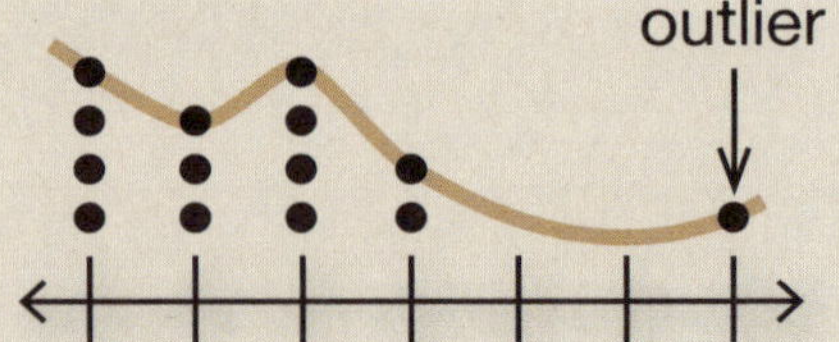

A **right-skewed distribution** has a tail on its right side.

outlier

An **outlier** is a value that is very different from the other values in the data set.

B

Number of Pets

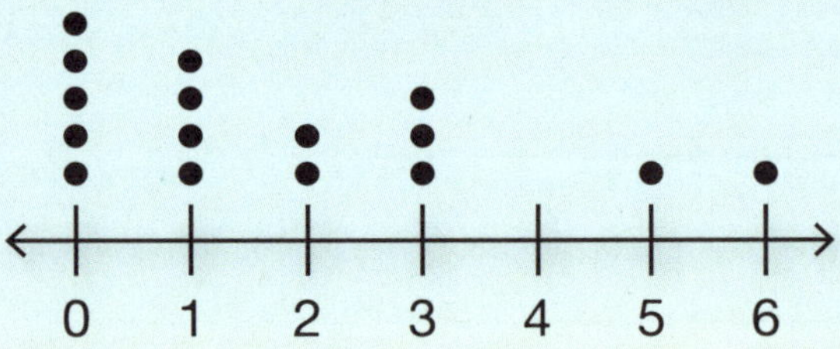
0
1
2
3
4
5
6

Mean: _______ Median: _______ Mode: _______

Questions Correct on Trivia Quiz

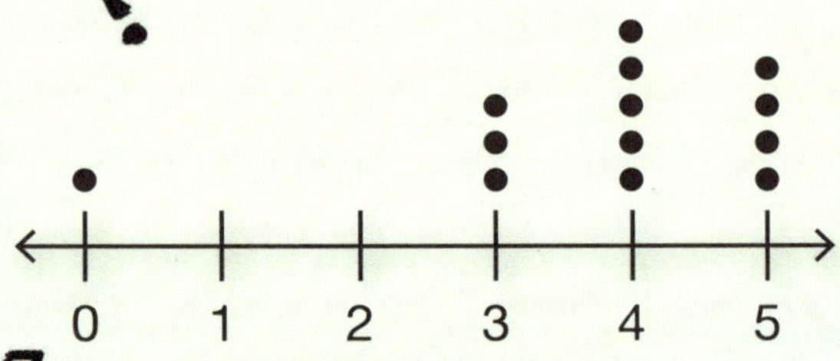
0
1
2
3
4
5

Mean: _______ Median: _______ Mode: _______

Heights of 12-Year-Olds (in.)

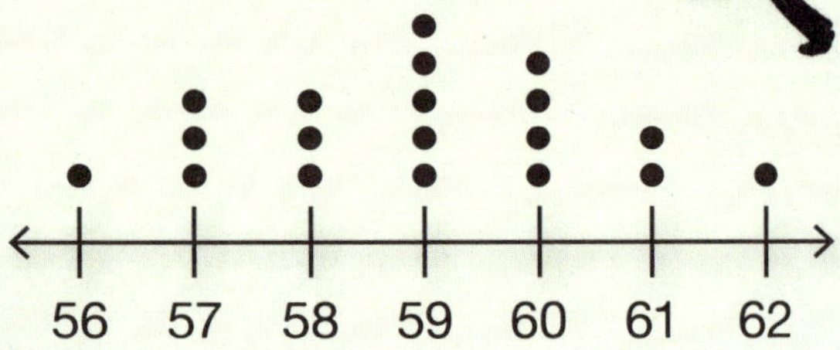
56
57
58
59
60
61
62

Mean: _______ Median: _______ Mode: _______

Practice

Use the dot plots to answer the questions.

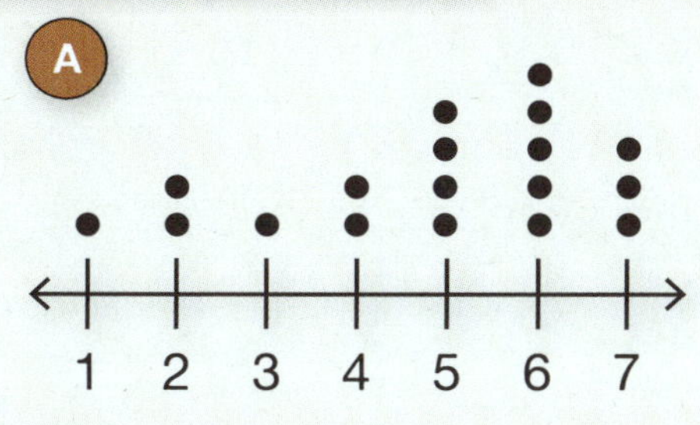

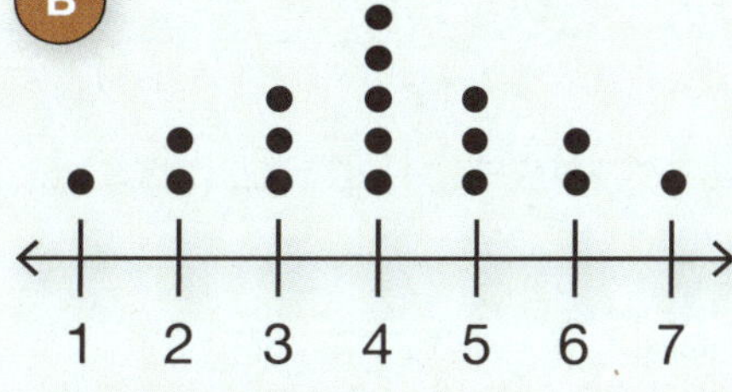

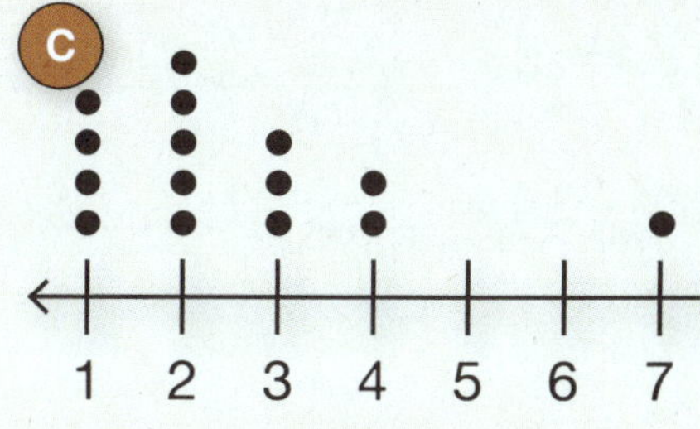

Which distribution is right-skewed?	Which distribution is left-skewed?	Which distribution is symmetric?
Which distribution has a peak at 6?	Which distribution has a peak at 4?	Which distribution has a gap between 4 and 7?

Draw a dot plot to match each description. Include 15-20 dots in each distribution.

Right-skewed, with an outlier of 9

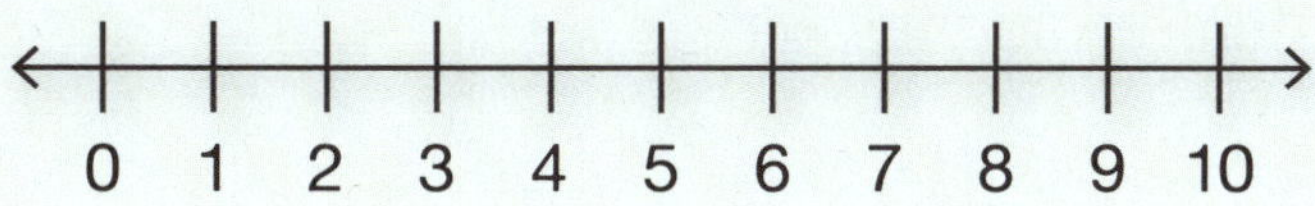

Left-skewed, with a gap from 4 to 7

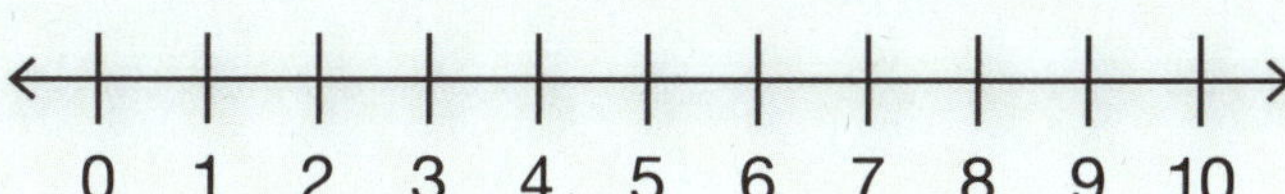

Symmetric, with a mode of 4

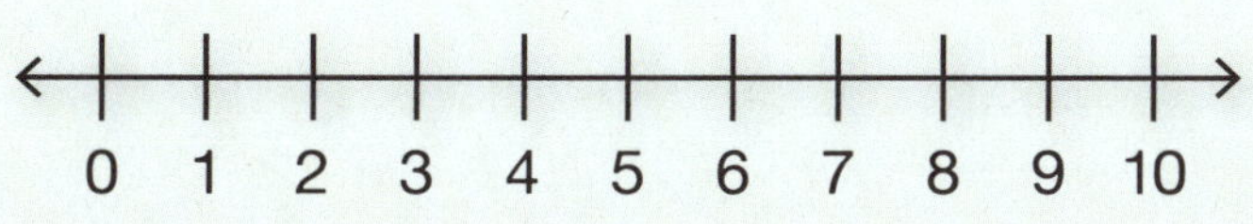

 Symmetric, with a median of 6

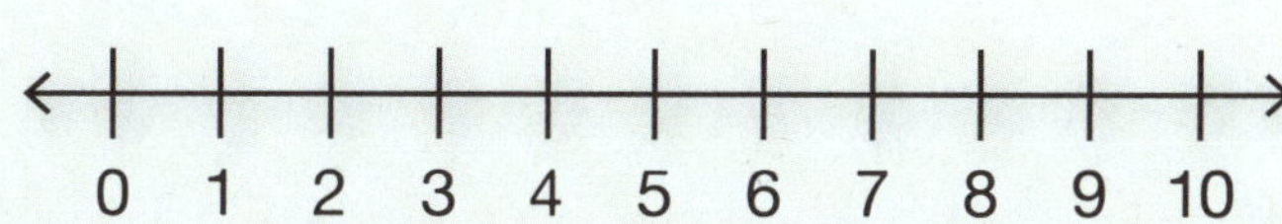

Review

Use mental math to complete.

3.1 + 0.6 = ___________   2.5 − 2.2 = ___________   5.5 − 3 = ___________

4.9 + 0.4 = ___________   3.8 − 3.7 = ___________   6.8 − 2 = ___________

8.7 + 0.3 = ___________   9.0 − 8.5 = ___________   4.3 − 4 = ___________

Use long division to find the quotients. Write your answers with the given number of decimal digits. Use the multiplication table to help with the second problem.

4.1 ÷ 0.3 = ___________

1 decimal digit

2.8 ÷ 0.45 = ___________

1 decimal digit

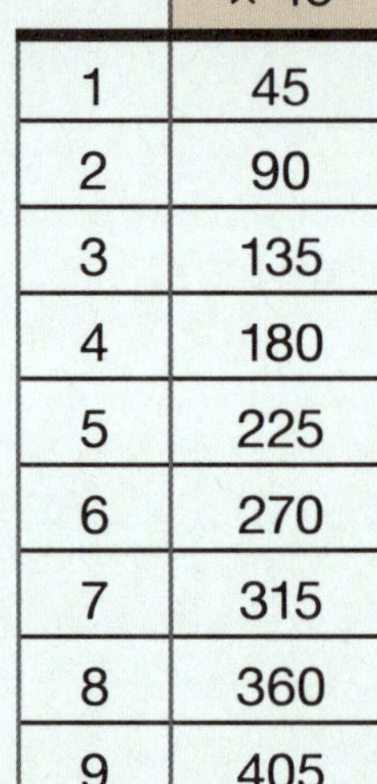

	× 45
1	45
2	90
3	135
4	180
5	225
6	270
7	315
8	360
9	405

Solve. Write all fractions in simplest form.

Savannah played soccer on 12 days in April. What fraction of the days did she play soccer? (April has 30 days.)

What percentage of the days did she play soccer?

What percentage of the days did she not play soccer?

Savannah's soccer team won 70% of their games in April and lost the rest. They played 20 games. What fraction of their games did they win?

How many games did they win?

What fraction of their games did they lose?

Lesson Activities

How many minutes did you spend reading yesterday?

5, 10, 16, 19, 25, 28, 30, 32, 33, 35, 40, 42, 45, 50, 53, 56, 58, 62, 65, 70

Minimum: __________ (lowest value)

Maximum: __________ (highest value)

Range: __________ (maximum − minimum)

Mean: __________

Median: __________

Mode: __________

Histograms and Range

A histogram is like a bar graph that groups data into intervals on the number line. (The intervals must have the same length, and the bars must touch each other.) The height of each bar shows how many values are in the interval.

The range of a data set is the difference between the highest value and the lowest value.

Ex.

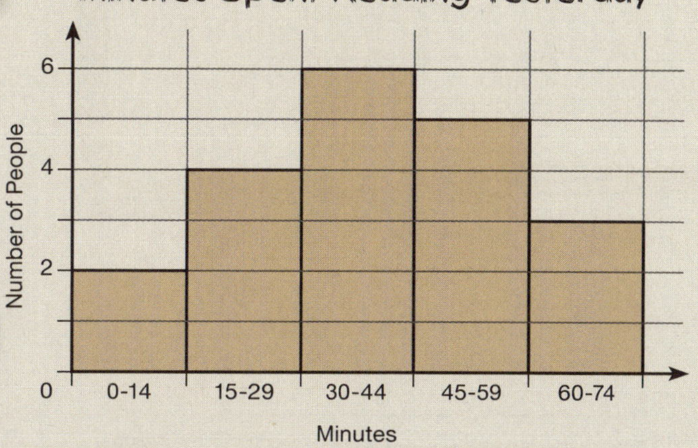

Minutes Spent Reading Yesterday

How many minutes did you spend outside yesterday?

0, 10, 14, 20, 23, 45, 50, 55, 60, 62, 65, 72, 75, 77, 85, 90, 92, 100, 110, 115

Minimum: __________ (lowest value)

Maximum: __________ (highest value)

Range: __________ (maximum − minimum)

Mean: __________

Median: __________

Mode: __________

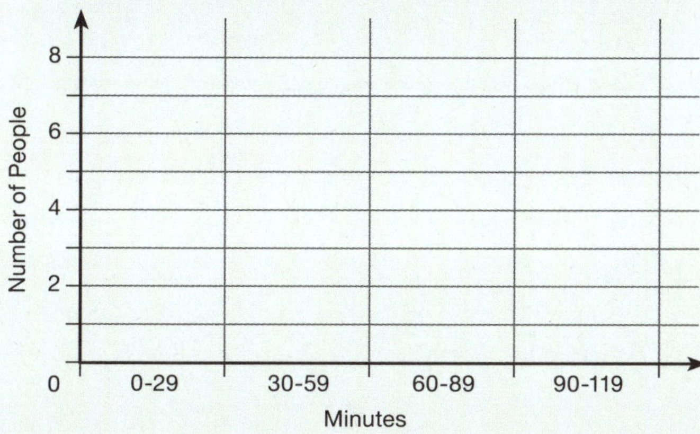

Minutes Spent Outside Yesterday

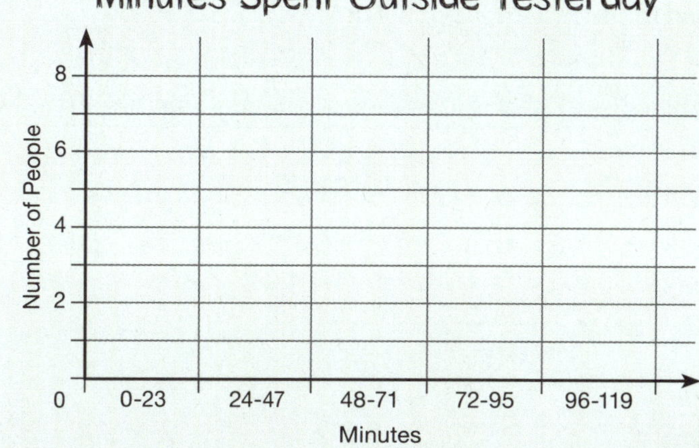

Minutes Spent Outside Yesterday

Practice

The wildlife biologist is studying the weights of different types of adult squirrels. Use her data to complete the blanks, make histograms to represent the data, and answer the questions.

Eastern Gray Squirrels' Weights (grams)

423, 434, 448, 465, 466,
472, 477, 478, 478, 486,
486, 491, 492, 493, 494,
497, 509, 517, 518, 518,
524, 528, 528, 544, 562

Minimum: _______________

Maximum: _______________

Range: _______________

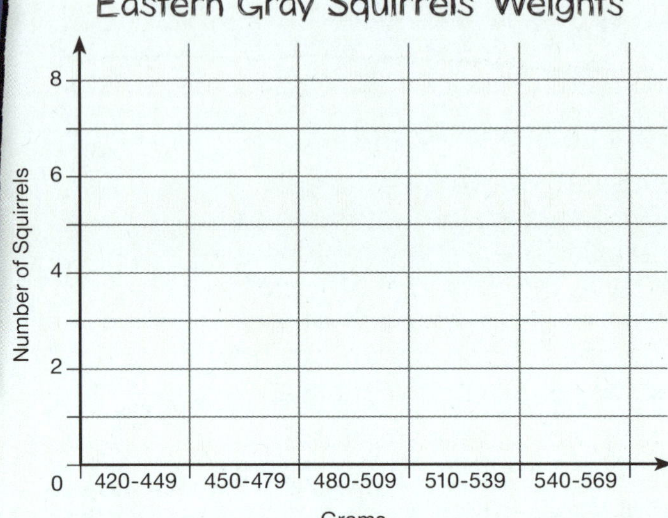

American Red Squirrels' Weights (grams)

203, 205, 213, 215, 217,
218, 219, 220, 221, 224,
225, 227, 228, 230, 232,
234, 235, 236, 238, 239,
240, 242, 243, 245, 249

Minimum: _______________

Maximum: _______________

Range: _______________

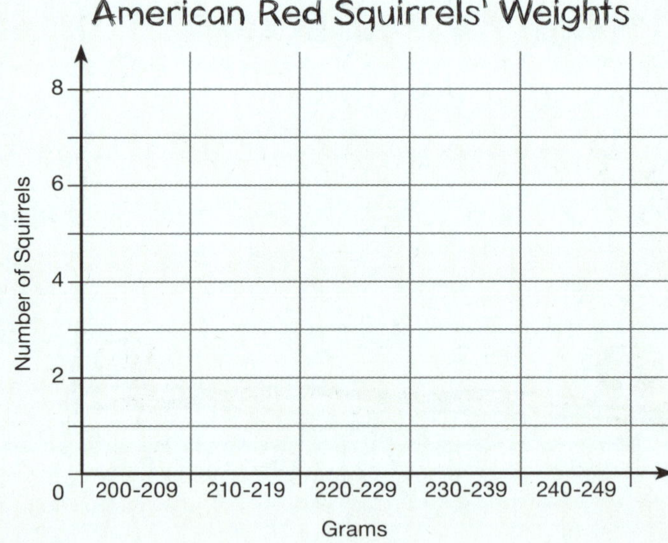

Which type of squirrel is usually lighter?

Which type of squirrel has a wider range of weights?

Review

Find how far each number is from –2. Use the number line to help.

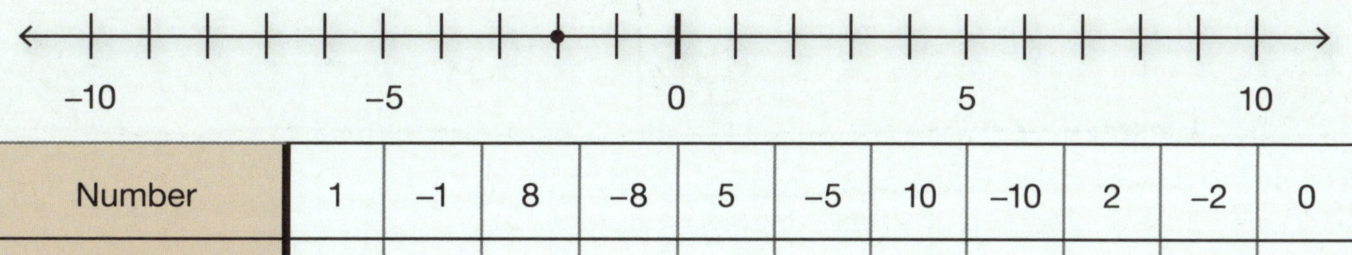

Number	1	–1	8	–8	5	–5	10	–10	2	–2	0
Distance from –2	3	1									

Move the decimal point to find the product, quotient, or percentage.

0.531 × 10 = _____________   36 × 1,000 = _____________   10% of 192 = _____________

0.531 ÷ 10 = _____________   36 ÷ 1,000 = _____________   10% of 13.48 = _____________

Micah's family is planning a spring holiday dinner. Use the information to help them plan the menu. Write the equations you use.

The lamb roast weighs $6\frac{1}{2}$ lb. If each person eats $\frac{1}{2}$ lb. of meat, how many people will the roast serve?

The potato recipe calls for $1\frac{3}{4}$ lb. of potatoes. Micah's family wants to make $2\frac{1}{2}$ times the recipe. How many pounds of potatoes do they need?

Micah's family expects to have 10 people at the dinner. If each person eats $\frac{1}{4}$ lb. of green beans, how many pounds of green beans should they buy?

Micah makes $7\frac{1}{2}$ c. of punch. He wants to divide the punch evenly into 10 glasses. How much punch should he pour into each glass?

Lesson Activities 

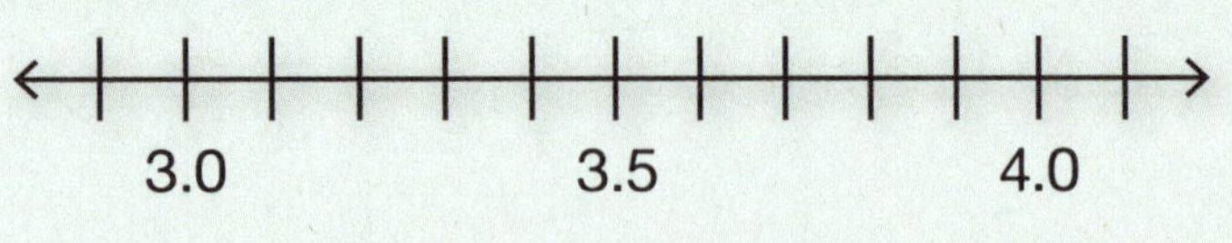

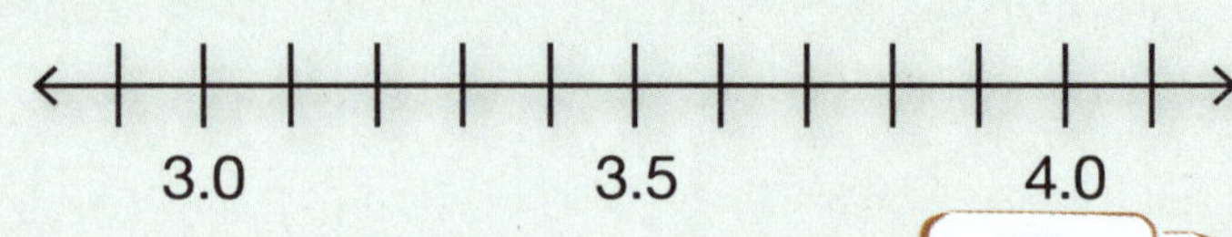

3.0   3.5   4.0   3.0   3.5   4.0

B

Mean Absolute Deviation

The mean absolute deviation measures how far the values in the data set deviate (or vary) from the mean.

1. Find the mean.
2. Find how far each value is from the mean.
3. Find the mean of these distances.

Ex. Find the mean absolute deviation for Pierre's croissants. Write your answer with 2 decimal digits.

$$\frac{3.4 + 3.0 + 3.6 + 3.1 + 3.9 + 2.9 + 4.1 + 3.2}{8} = 3.4 \ \text{mean}$$

Weight	3.4	3.0	3.6	3.1	3.9	2.9	4.1	3.2
Distance from 3.4	0	0.4	0.2	0.3	0.5	0.5	0.7	0.2

$$\frac{0 + 0.4 + 0.2 + 0.3 + 0.5 + 0.5 + 0.7 + 0.2}{8} = \mathbf{0.35}$$

 What is the mean weight of Jacques's croissants?

Weight	Distance from Mean
3.9	
3.5	
3.6	
3.2	
3.7	
3.6	
3.5	
3.4	

What is the mean absolute deviation for Jacques's croissants?

Whose croissants have a more consistent weight, Pierre's or Jacques's?

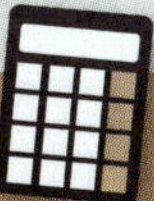

Practice

Myla and Jasmine are on a basketball team and keep track of how many points they score. Use their data to make a dot plot for each player. Then, use a calculator to answer the questions and complete the charts. Write your answers with 2 decimal digits.

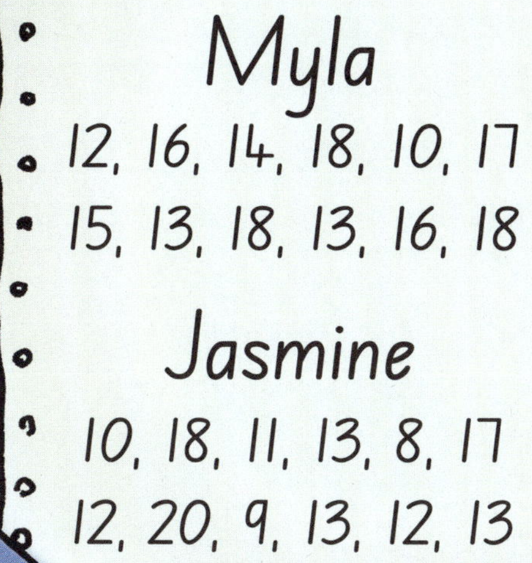

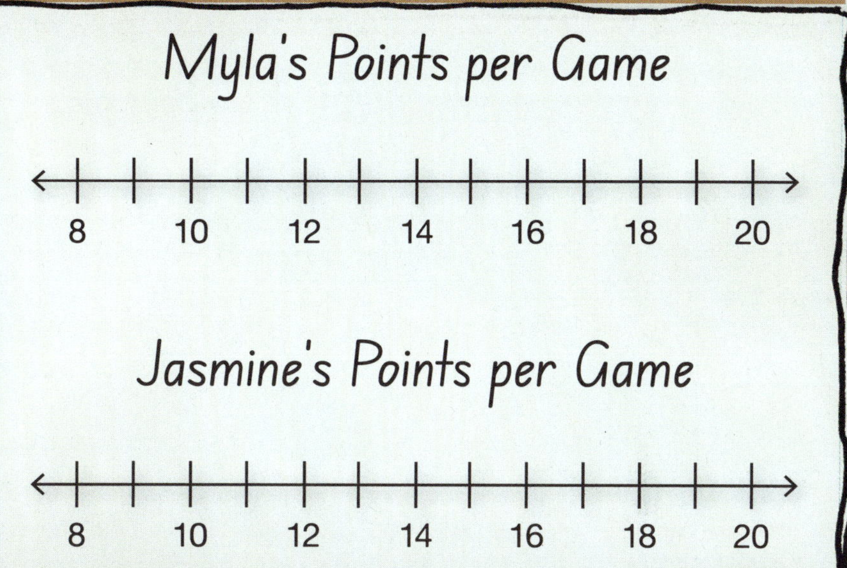

Myla

12, 16, 14, 18, 10, 17
15, 13, 18, 13, 16, 18

Jasmine

10, 18, 11, 13, 8, 17
12, 20, 9, 13, 12, 13

Myla's Points per Game

Jasmine's Points per Game

What is the mean number of points that Myla scores per game?

What is the mean number of points that Jasmine scores per game?

On average, which player scores more points per game?

Myla's points	12	16	14	18	10	17	15	13	18	13	16	18
Distance from Myla's mean												

Jasmine's points	10	18	11	13	8	17	12	20	9	13	12	13
Distance from Jasmine's mean												

What is the mean absolute deviation for Myla's points?

What is the mean absolute deviation for Jasmine's points?

Which player scores a more consistent number of points in each game?

Review   Find the product or quotient.

$0.6 \times 0.4 =$ _______	$0.5 \times 0.5 =$ _______	$8 \times 0.6 =$ _______
$0.07 \times 0.7 =$ _______	$0.09 \times 0.04 =$ _______	$7 \times 0.04 =$ _______
$0.9 \div 0.3 =$ _______	$0.63 \div 0.07 =$ _______	$2.00 \div 0.25 =$ _______
$1.8 \div 0.2 =$ _______	$3.0 \div 0.5 =$ _______	$0.3 \div 0.05 =$ _______

Use the net to find the surface area. Write the equations you use.

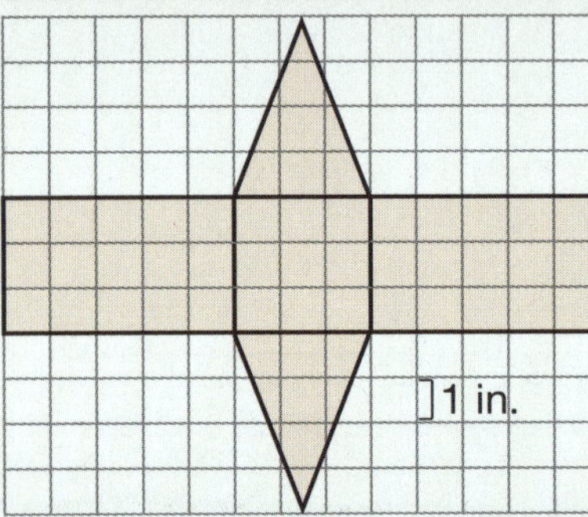

Surface area: _______________________________

Answer the questions.

The movie poster is 30 in. long and 24 in. wide. What is the ratio of its length to its width?

At the concession stand, $\frac{2}{3}$ of the customers buy popcorn, and $\frac{1}{3}$ do not. What is the ratio of customers who buy popcorn to customers who do not buy popcorn?

The ratio of adults to children at the movie is 2:3. If there are 38 adults, how many children are there?

The ratio of adults to children at the movie is 2:3. What fraction of the movie-goers are adults? What fraction of the movie-goers are children?

Lesson Activities

Chemistry Project Scores

Ali - 35	Marcus - 46
Julie - 49	Maeve - 32
Caeden - 27	David - 38
Kristin - 23	Winnie - 41

A Write the science fair scores in order from least to greatest. Then, draw lines to separate the scores into 4 equal groups.

Award level	Honorable Mention (bottom 25%)	Bronze (next 25%)	Silver (next 25%)	Gold (top 25%)
Student winners				

Quartiles

Quartiles are numbers that split a data set as equally as possible into 4 groups.

1. Write the values in order.

2. Draw a line that splits the values in half. Then, draw lines that split the lower half and upper half of the data set in half. Your lines may go through a number or between two numbers.

3. Use the lines to find the numbers that split the data set into these groups. If the line goes through a number, that number is the quartile. If the line is between two numbers, the quartile is the median of these two numbers.

B

 **Ex.** Find the quartiles for these engineering project scores.

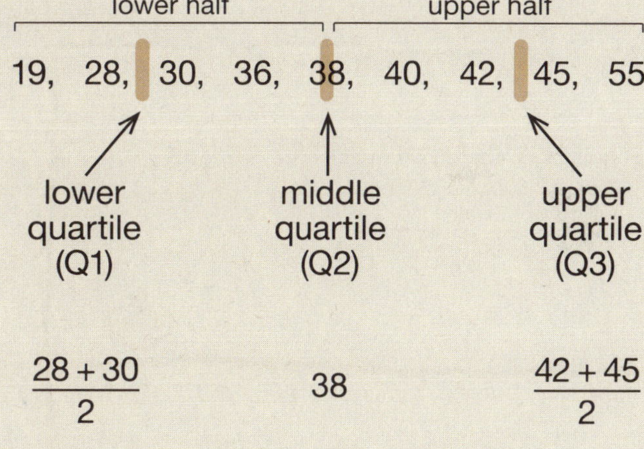

$$\frac{28 + 30}{2} \qquad 38 \qquad \frac{42 + 45}{2}$$

Q1: **29**   Q2: **38**   Q3: **43.5**

C

Chihuahua Weights (lb.)

2, 3, 3, 3, 4, 4, 4, 4, 4, 5, 5, 5, 6, 6

Q1: _______   Q2: _______   Q3: _______

Golden Retriever Weights (lb.)

56, 58, 61, 62, 64, 67, 69, 70, 74

Q1: _______   Q2: _______   Q3: _______

Practice

Find the quartiles for each set of science project scores.

Robotics

30, 31, 35, 36, 36, 39, 39, 41, 43, 47, 48

Q1: _________ Q2: _________ Q3: _________

Environmental Science

15, 17, 18, 18, 20, 21, 23, 24, 24, 29

Q1: _________ Q2: _________ Q3: _________

Animal Science

42, 43, 43, 44, 44, 45, 45, 45, 45, 46, 46, 47

Q1: _________ Q2: _________ Q3: _________

Plant Science

4, 4, 5, 7, 8, 8, 8, 9, 10, 11, 11, 12, 12

Q1: _________ Q2: _________ Q3: _________

Jayden compared two types of tomato plants for his science project. He grew 10 of each type of plant and counted how many tomatoes each plant produced. Use his data to complete the blanks and answer the questions.

Number of Tomatoes (Type A)

19, 20, 22, 24, 25, 26, 28, 29, 32, 35

Minimum: _________ Q1: _________

Maximum: _________ Q2: _________

Range: _________ Q3: _________

Number of Tomatoes (Type B)

22, 22, 23, 24, 25, 26, 27, 27, 28, 30

Minimum: _________ Q1: _________

Maximum: _________ Q2: _________

Range: _________ Q3: _________

Which type of plant has the higher median number of tomatoes?

Which type of plant has a greater range?

Which type of plant produces a more consistent number of tomatoes?

Review

Use mental math to find the percentages.

10% of 60 = __________   50% of 22 = __________   10% of 9 = __________

20% of 60 = __________   100% of 22 = __________   20% of 9 = __________

30% of 60 = __________   150% of 22 = __________   30% of 9 = __________

**A biologist measured the heights of the trees in the park.
Use his histogram to answer the questions.**

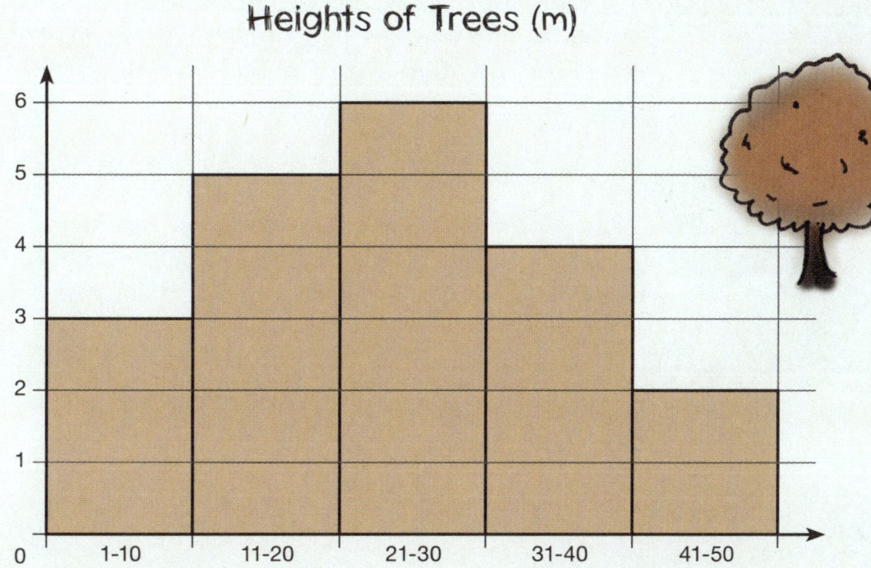

How many trees are less than 11 m tall?

How many trees are greater than 40 m tall?

Solve. Write the equations you use.

The basketball hoop's regular price is $349.99. Today, the basketball hoop is on sale for 30% off the regular price. What is the sale price? Write your answer with 2 decimal digits.

The drink dispenser holds 15.4 L of sports drink. One serving of sports drink is 0.8 L. How many servings are in the dispenser? Write your answer with 1 decimal digit.

Lesson Activities 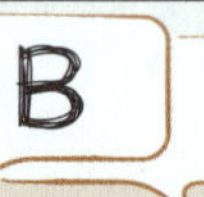

Beginning-of-Class Swim Test Scores

0, 1, 2, 2, 3, 3, 4, 5, 5, 5, 6, 8

Minimum: __________   Q1: ____________

Maximum: __________   Q2: ____________

Q3: ____________

Five-Number Summary

The five-number summary for a data set includes the minimum, Q1, Q2, Q3, and maximum. These five numbers give a rough idea of how the data is distributed.

Ex. The swimming instructor recorded her students' scores on the end-of-class swim test. Find the five-number summary for the data set.

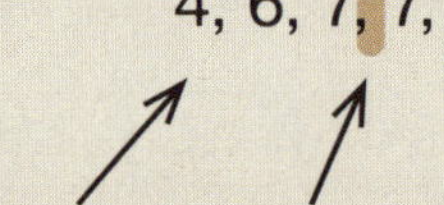

4, 6, 7, 7, 8, 8, 8, 9, 9, 9, 10, 10

min.: **4**   Q1: **7**   Q2: **8**   Q3: **9**   max.: **10**

Interquartile Range

The interquartile range (IQR) is the difference between the upper quartile and lower quartile. It tells the range for the middle 50% of the values.

$$Q3 - Q1 = IQR$$

Ex. Find the interquartile range for the scores.

middle half of the data

4, 6, 7, 7, 8, 8, 8, 9, 9, 9, 10, 10

IQR: $9 - 7 =$ **2**

IQR War (2-Player Game)

Player 1	Player 2

Q1: __________   Q3: __________   IQR: __________   Q1: __________   Q3: __________   IQR: __________

Q1: __________   Q3: __________   IQR: __________   Q1: __________   Q3: __________   IQR: __________

Q1: __________   Q3: __________   IQR: __________   Q1: __________   Q3: __________   IQR: __________

Practice

Joseph asked four different groups of people how many times they exercised last week. Complete the chart for each data set. Then, answer the questions.

Number of Exercise Sessions Last Week

Track Team Members
4, 5, 5, 5, 6, 6, 6, 6, 6, 6, 7, 7, 7

Min.	Q1	Q2	Q3	Max.	IQR	Range

Chess Club Members
0, 0, 1, 1, 1, 2, 2, 3, 4, 4, 6

Min.	Q1	Q2	Q3	Max.	IQR	Range

Art Club Members
0, 1, 1, 2, 2, 2, 3, 4, 6, 7

Min.	Q1	Q2	Q3	Max.	IQR	Range

Soccer Team Members
3, 3, 3, 3, 4, 4, 4, 4, 5, 5, 6, 6, 7

Min.	Q1	Q2	Q3	Max.	IQR	Range

Which group has the highest median?

Which group has the highest IQR?

Which group has the highest range?

Which group has the lowest median?

Which group has the lowest IQR?

Which group has the lowest range?

Which group's members varied the least in how much they exercised last week?

Which group's members varied the most in how much they exercised last week?

Review — Circle the best estimate for each product or quotient.

4.9 × 2.17	0.87 × 9.856	23.84 × 0.9967
5 10 15	10 15 20	18 24 30

1.96 ÷ 2	1.96 ÷ 0.2	1.96 ÷ 0.02
1 10 100	1 10 100	1 10 100

Complete the charts.

c	$c + 6$
0	
	24
40	
	80

d	$3d$
1	
100	
	24
	90

e	f	$e + 2f + 1$
5	6	
6	5	
10		51
	100	210

Solve. Write the equations you use. Write your answers with 1 decimal point.

A marathon is 26.2 miles long. Allison's goal is to run her first marathon in 5 hours. At what speed does she need to run (in miles per hour) to reach her goal?

The world record time for completing a marathon is approximately 2 hours. How fast do you have to run (in miles per hour) to complete a marathon in 2 hours?

Lesson Activities

Box Plots

A box plot is a graph that shows how the data in a data set is distributed. Each box and whisker in the box plot represents about 25% of the data.

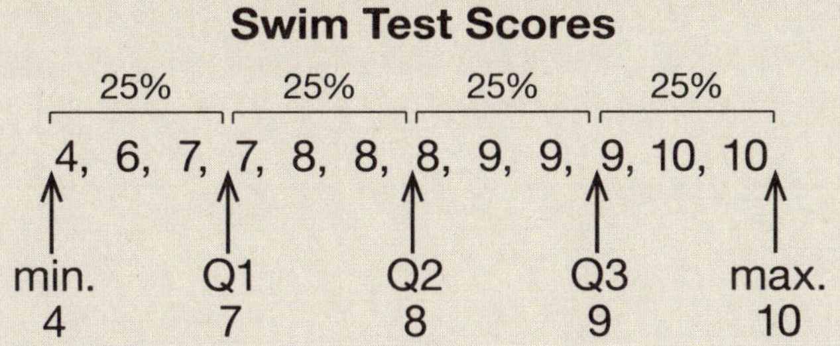

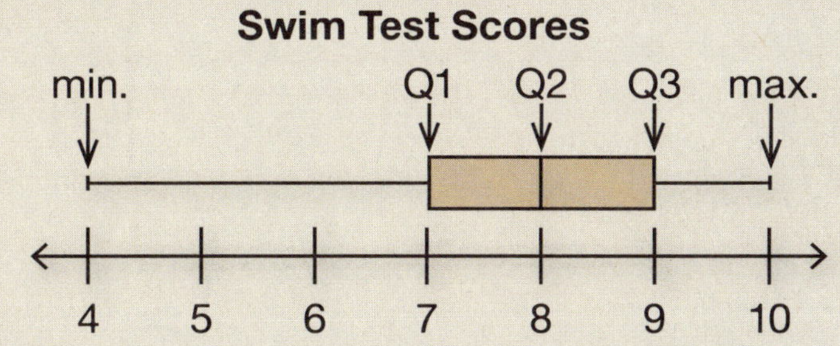

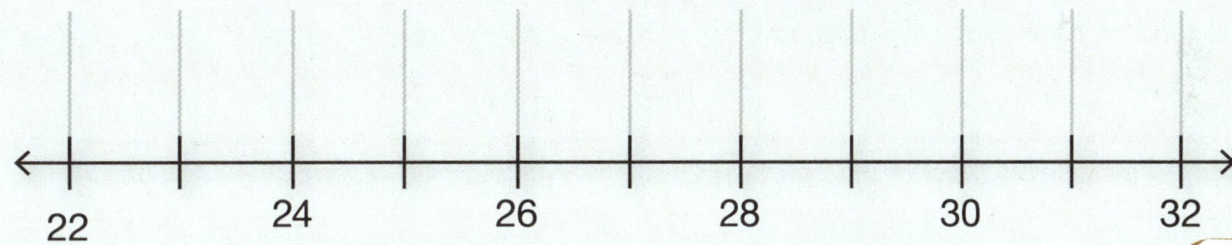

Minimum: __________ Q1: __________ Q2: __________ Q3: __________ Maximum: __________

Sit-to-Stand Results (Age 11-13)

Sit-to-Stand Results by Age

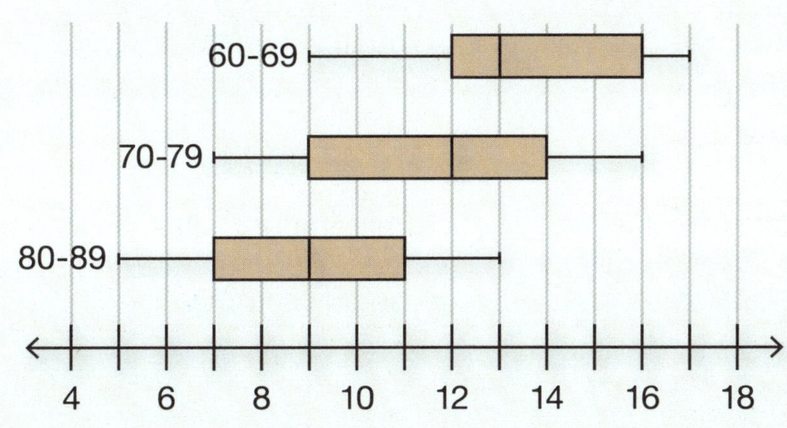

Age	60–69	70–79	80–89
Min.			
Q1			
Q2			
Q3			
Max.			

Practice

Use the data to complete the five-number summary. Then, create a box plot to match.

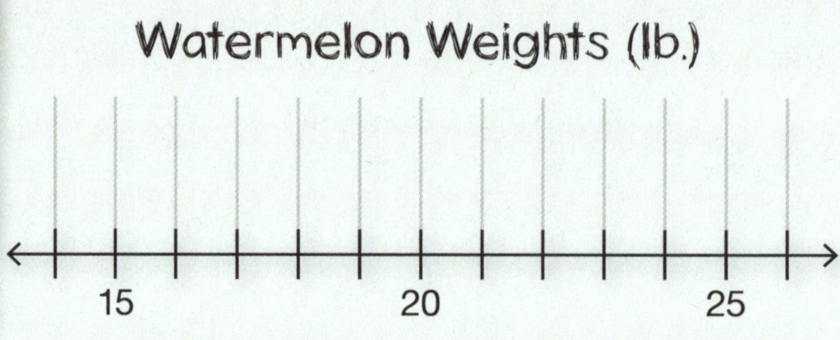

Watermelon Weights (lb.)

15   20   25

Minimum: _________ Q1: _________ Q2: _________ Q3: _________ Maximum: _________

Use the box plot to complete the chart and answer the questions.

Annual Rainfall (in.)

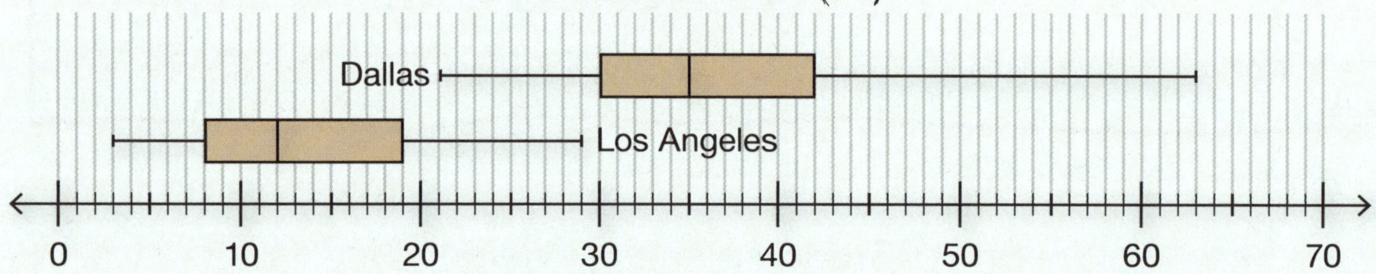

City	Min.	Q1	Q2	Q3	Max.	IQR	Range
Dallas							
Los Angeles							

Which city has a higher median rainfall?

How much greater is Dallas's range than Los Angeles's range?

Is the data for Los Angeles right-skewed, left-skewed, or roughly symmetric?

Which city has a higher maximum rainfall?

How much greater is Dallas's IQR than Los Angeles's IQR?

Is the data for Dallas right-skewed, left-skewed, or roughly symmetric?

Review

Find the product or quotient.
Write your answers with the given number of decimal digits.

3.8 × 0.76 = ___________

3 decimal digits

15.84 ÷ 6 = ___________

2 decimal digits

0.7 ÷ 0.03 = ___________

1 decimal digit

Use bar models to complete the ratios and answer the questions.
Write the ratios in simplest form.

The volunteers plant marigolds and geraniums at the park. The ratio of marigolds to geraniums is 3 to 1. They plant a total of 200 flowers.

How many marigolds do they plant?

How many geraniums do they plant?

Geraniums : Marigolds

___________ : ___________

Geraniums : Total flowers

___________ : ___________

Marigolds : Total flowers

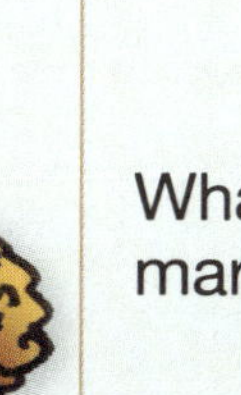

___________ : ___________

What fraction of the flowers are geraniums?

What fraction of the flowers are marigolds?

Unit Wrap-Up

Use the words in the word bank to complete the blanks.

The most frequently occurring value	The middle value	The sum of the values, divided by the number of values
______________	______________	______________
A distribution with two sides that roughly mirror each other	A distribution with a tail on its left side	A distribution with a tail on its right side
______________	______________	______________

Left-skewed

Mean

Median

Mode

Right-skewed

Symmetric

Bennett and Eli kept track of how many minutes they exercised each day. Use a calculator to complete the blanks and answer the questions.

Bennett

15, 20, 30, 35, 30, 45, 35, 20, 20, 30

Mean: 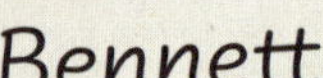 ______________

Eli

0, 45, 60, 0, 50, 60, 80, 0, 55, 0

Mean: ______________

Bennett's data	15	20	30	35	30	45	35	20	20	30
Distance from Bennett's mean										

Eli's data	0	45	60	0	50	60	80	0	55	0
Distance from Eli's mean										

What is the mean absolute deviation for Bennett's data?

What is the mean absolute deviation for Eli's data?

On average, did Bennett or Eli exercise more?

Did Bennett or Eli vary more in how much they exercised each day?

Unit Wrap-Up

Find the five-number summary for each data set, and make a box plot to match. Then, answer the questions.

Heights of players on the 1992 U.S. Olympic men's basketball team (in.)

73, 78, 78, 79, 79, 80,
81, 81, 81, 83, 84, 85

Heights of players on the 2024 U.S. Olympic men's basketball team (in.)

74, 75, 76, 76, 77, 77,
80, 81, 81, 82, 82, 84

Q1: _____________   Minimum: __________

Q2: _____________   Maximum: __________

Q3: _____________

Q1: _____________   Minimum: __________

Q2: _____________   Maximum: __________

Q3: _____________

1992 Players' Heights (in.)

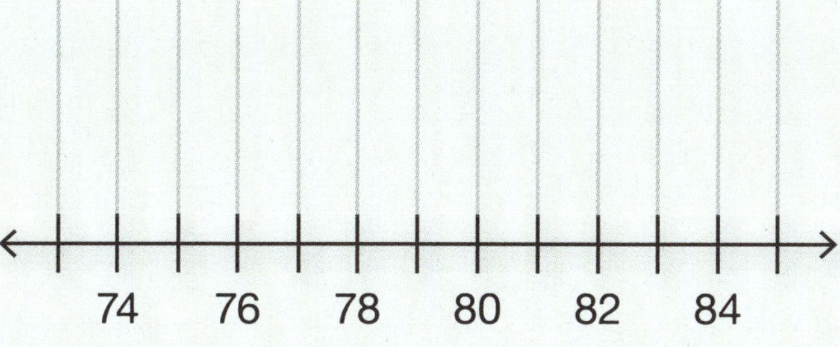

74   76   78   80   82   84

2024 Players' Heights (in.)

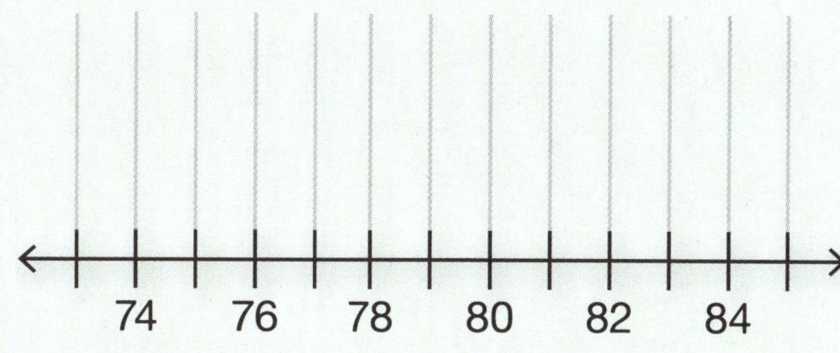

74   76   78   80   82   84

What is the range for the 1992 team?

What is the range for the 2024 team?

Which team had a greater median height?

What is the interquartile range for the 1992 team?

What is the interquartile range for the 2024 team?

Overall, which team was taller?

Lesson Activities

A

Fraction		$\frac{3}{100}$			$1\frac{23}{100}$	
Decimal	0.48			1.19		
Percentage			99%			201%

B

Five in a Row (2-Player Game)

25%	$\frac{3}{5}$	$\frac{7}{10}$	2.0	0.1	0.2
0.7	1	0.4	$\frac{3}{4}$	0.8	50%
$\frac{1}{10}$	0.3	$\frac{1}{5}$	90%	60%	1.5
0.9	0.25	1.0	200%	0.5	30%
20%	$\frac{4}{5}$	40%	10%	100%	$\frac{2}{5}$
2	$\frac{1}{2}$	$\frac{9}{10}$	$1\frac{1}{2}$	70%	0.75
75%	150%	$\frac{3}{10}$	0.6	$\frac{1}{4}$	80%

Practice

Solve. Write your answers as mixed numbers in simplest form.
Then, find the blanks that match each answer.
Write the matching letters in the blanks to solve the riddle.

T $\dfrac{3}{4} + \dfrac{7}{8} + \dfrac{1}{8} =$

W $\dfrac{5}{12} + \dfrac{5}{6} - \dfrac{2}{3} =$

O $\dfrac{4}{5} - \dfrac{1}{2} - \dfrac{1}{10} =$

I $\dfrac{2}{5} \times \dfrac{15}{24} =$

G $\dfrac{3}{4} \times \dfrac{8}{9} \times \dfrac{1}{2} =$

Y $\dfrac{2}{3} \times \dfrac{8}{7} \times \dfrac{7}{8} =$

H $4 \times \dfrac{5}{8} =$

S $3\dfrac{1}{4} \times \dfrac{2}{5} =$

E $1\dfrac{1}{3} \times 3\dfrac{3}{5} =$

A $1\dfrac{5}{6} \div \dfrac{1}{2} =$

N $\dfrac{3}{8} \div \dfrac{1}{2} =$

M $5 \div 1\dfrac{1}{3} =$

Why did the boy get upset when his friend called him average?

$\dfrac{1}{4}$ $\quad$ $1\dfrac{3}{4}$ $\quad$ $\dfrac{7}{12}$ $\quad$ $3\dfrac{2}{3}$ $\quad$ $1\dfrac{3}{10}$ $\quad$ $3\dfrac{2}{3}$ $\quad$ $3\dfrac{3}{4}$ $\quad$ $4\dfrac{4}{5}$ $\quad$ $3\dfrac{2}{3}$ $\quad$ $\dfrac{3}{4}$

$1\dfrac{3}{4}$ $\quad$ $2\dfrac{1}{2}$ $\quad$ $\dfrac{1}{4}$ $\quad$ $\dfrac{3}{4}$ $\quad$ $\dfrac{1}{3}$ $\quad$ $1\dfrac{3}{4}$ $\quad$ $\dfrac{1}{5}$ $\quad$ $1\dfrac{3}{10}$ $\quad$ $3\dfrac{2}{3}$ $\quad$ $\dfrac{2}{3}$

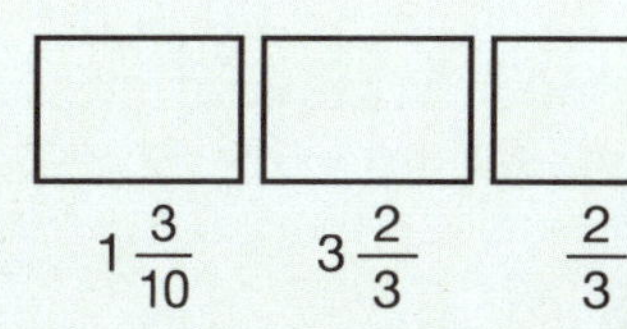

Review

Write whether each dot plot is right-skewed, left-skewed, or symmetric.

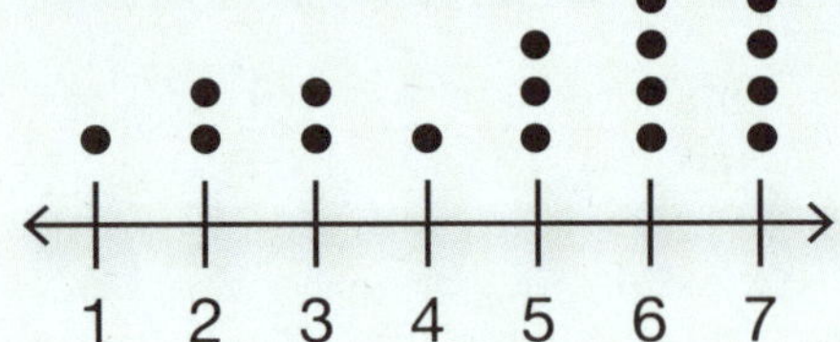

1 2 3 4 5 6 7

____

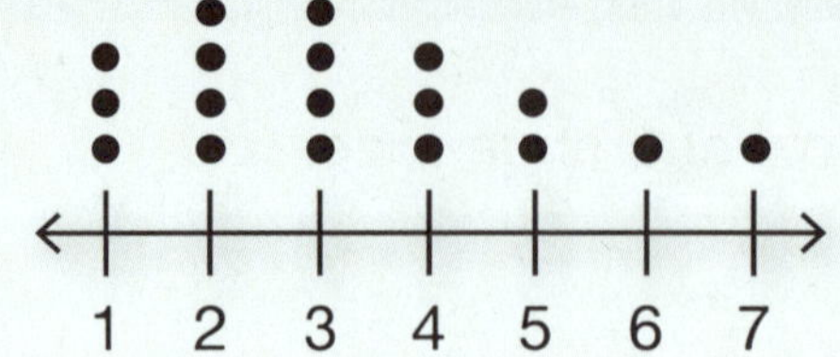

1 2 3 4 5 6 7

____

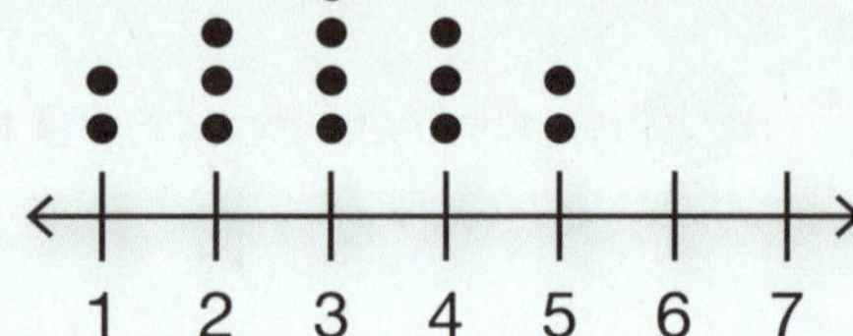

1 2 3 4 5 6 7

____

Evaluate.

$7 \cdot 9 + 1$

$20 - 15 + 5$

$8 + 6 \cdot 5 - 4$

$7 \cdot (9 + 1)$

$20 - (15 + 5)$

$8 + 6 \cdot (5 - 4)$

Use the bar models to complete.

8

?

20% of __________ = 8

?

200

75% of 200 = __________

25

75

__________ % of 75 = 25

Solve. Write the equations you use.

The bottle of shampoo holds 13 fluid ounces of shampoo. Sabrina uses 0.4 fluid ounces each day. How many days will the bottle of shampoo last?

The bottle of lotion costs $6.98 and holds 8 fluid ounces. What is the unit price per ounce? Write your answer with 2 decimal digits.

Lesson Activities 👥

___________________ mixes ___________________ fl. oz.
GIRL'S NAME · MULTIPLE OF 3
of pineapple juice with 9 fl. oz. of orange juice.

Write the ratio of pineapple juice to orange juice in simplest form.

She decides to make a batch with the same ratio. If she uses 21 fl. oz. of orange juice, how much pineapple juice should she use?

___________________ baked a total of
BOY'S NAME
___________________ cookies. The ratio of
MULTIPLE OF 4
___________________ cookies to
COOKIE TYPE A
___________________ cookies was 1:3.
COOKIE TYPE B

How many of each type of cookie did he bake?

___________________ rode her ___________________ at
GIRL'S NAME · SOMETHING YOU RIDE
a speed of ___________________ kilometers per hour
MULTIPLE OF 6
for 2 hours. Then, she traveled the same distance
home. It took her 4 hours to travel home.

How far did she travel in all?

What was her speed for the return trip?

Practice

**Use the chart to answer the questions.
Write the ratios and fractions in simplest form.**

Green beans .... 15 lb.

Carrots .... 10 lb.

Total .... 25 lb.

Green beans : Carrots	Carrots : Green beans
_______ : _______	_______ : _______
Green beans : Total	Carrots : Total
_______ : _______	_______ : _______
What fraction of the total harvest was green beans?	What fraction of the total harvest was carrots?

Use ratio tables to solve.

The television's length-to-width ratio is 16 : 9. If the television has a width of 27 in., what is its length?

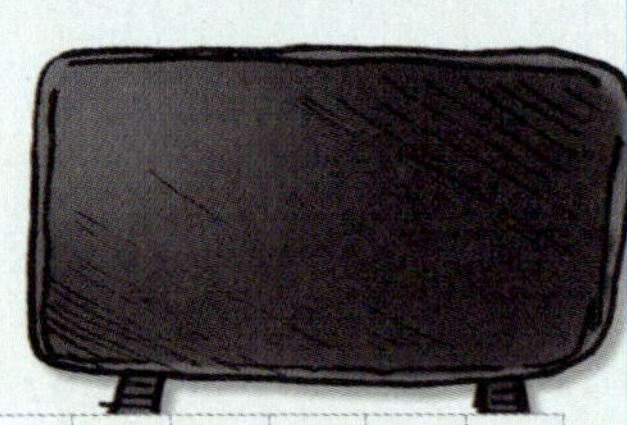

length	
width	

Two computer monitors have the same length-to-width ratio. The smaller monitor has a length of 24 in. and a width of 18 in. The larger monitor has a length of 36 in. What is the larger monitor's width?

length	
width	

Complete the chart. Use mental math or write your equations in the work space.

Type of transportation	Speed (miles per hour)	Time (hours)	Distance (miles)
Airplane	500	8	
Train		4	200
Car	70		210
Canoe	2		4
Scooter		$\frac{1}{4}$	2
Bike		3	36

Review   Evaluate.

$1^2 =$ ________	$6^2 =$ ________	$1^3 =$ ________
$2^2 =$ ________	$7^2 =$ ________	$2^3 =$ ________
$3^2 =$ ________	$8^2 =$ ________	$3^3 =$ ________
$4^2 =$ ________	$9^2 =$ ________	$4^3 =$ ________
$5^2 =$ ________	$10^2 =$ ________	$5^3 =$ ________

Use mental math or fraction multiplication to find the percentage.

80% of 35	30% of 140	75% of 120

Omari kept track of how many eggs his family's chickens laid each day. Create a dot plot for his data. Then, use a calculator to complete the blanks and answer the questions.

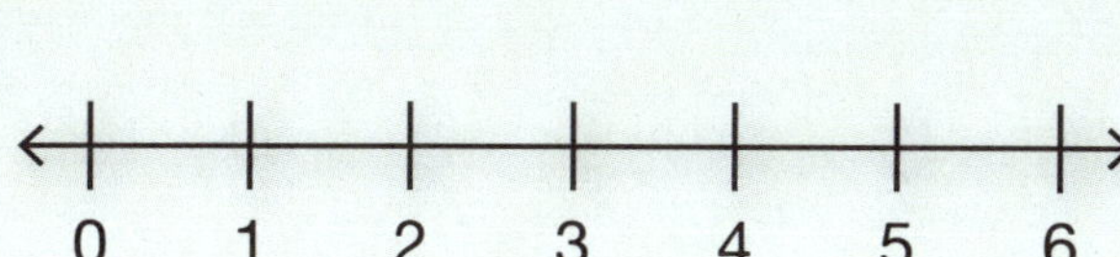

Number of eggs	2	3	3	3	4	4	4	4	5	6	6
Distance from the mean											

Minimum: ________   Mean: ________

Maximum: ________   Median: ________

Range: ________   Mode: ________

What is the mean absolute deviation for the data? Write your answer with 2 decimal digits.

Lesson Activities 👥

A

$n + 4$	$3n$	$2n + 5$	$n^2 - 1$	$4(n + 1)$	$\dfrac{3n}{2}$

n		n		n	
1	7	1	1.5	1	3
2	9	2	3	2	6
3	11	3	4.5	3	9
4	13	4	6	4	12
5	15	5	7.5	5	15

n		n		n	
1	8	1	0	1	5
2	12	2	3	2	6
3	16	3	8	3	7
4	20	4	15	4	8
5	24	5	24	5	9

B

What was your favorite math activity this year?

What math topic was most interesting to you this year?

What math skill did you work hardest to learn this year?

What do you hope to learn in math next year?

Practice

Find the volume and surface area of the box. Write the equations you use in the work space.

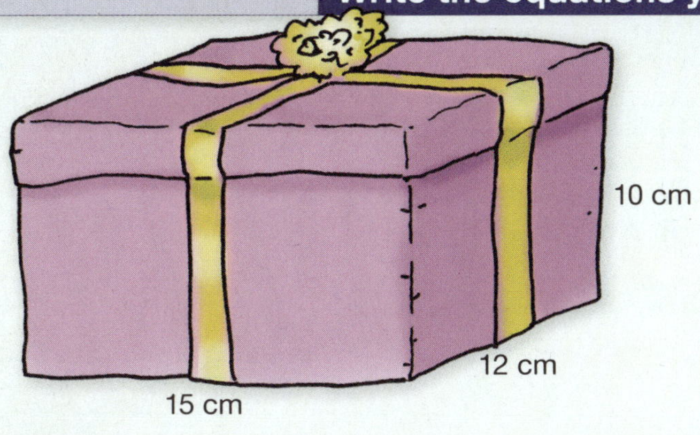

Volume: _______________________

Surface area: _______________________

Graph the points and connect them to create a triangle. Then, find the area of the triangle.

(−5,−2)	(−1,−2)	(2,3)

What is the area of the triangle?

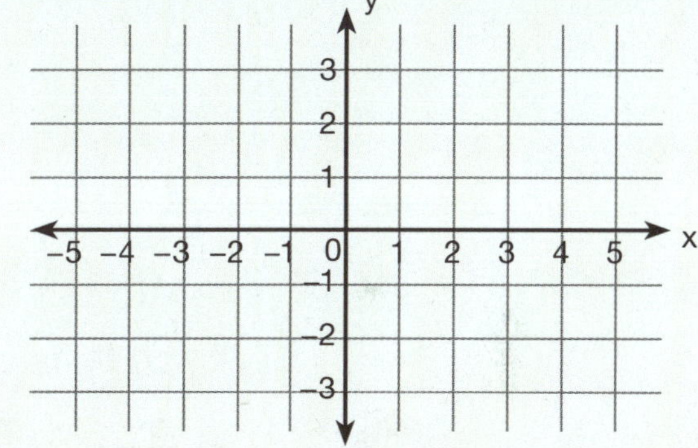

Kiara and Jack had a lemonade stand. They kept track of how much they earned each day. Use their data to complete the five-number summary. Then, create a box plot to match.

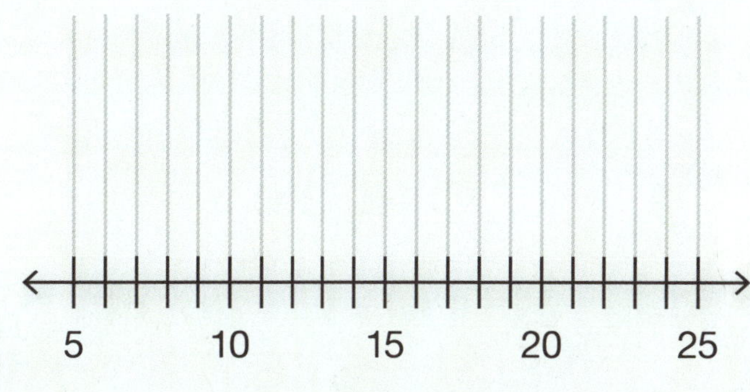

Minimum: _________   Q1: _________   Q2: _________   Q3: _________   Maximum: _________

CONGRATULATIONS!

Presented to

____

for successfully completing

Sixth Grade Math
with Confidence

_____________________   _____________________
Date   Signature

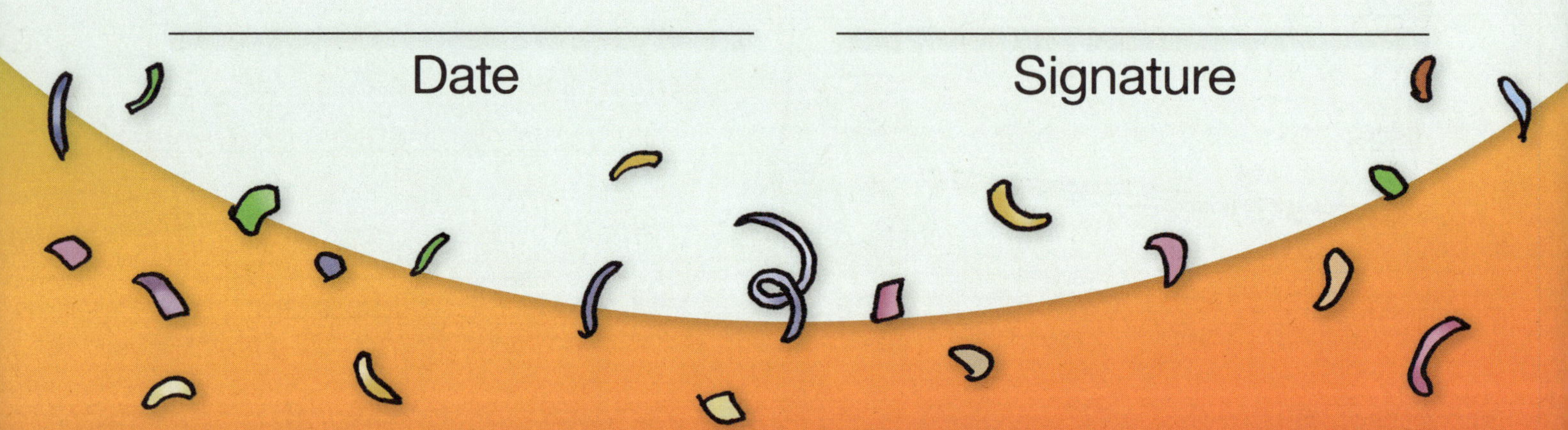

Variables and Expressions

A **variable** is a letter that stands for a number. We use variables to represent numbers that can vary or change.

An **expression** is part of a number sentence without an equals sign. When we write an expression with a variable, the expression tells what to do to the variable.

To write an expression with a variable, use words to describe what to do to the variable. Then, translate the words into mathematical symbols.

Ex. The hexagon has 6 equal sides. Write an expression that tells the perimeter of the hexagon. Use s to stand for the length of each side.

9.1

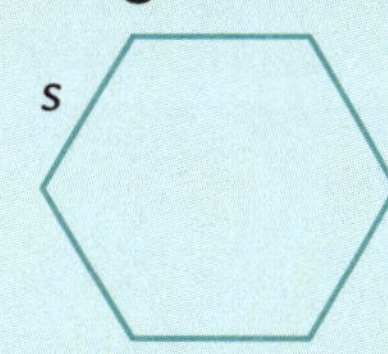

Multiply 6 times the length of each side.

$6 \cdot s$

Ex. Evaluate the expression for $s = 10$. If each side is 10 cm long, what is the hexagon's perimeter?

$6 \cdot s$

$6 \cdot 10 = $ **60 cm**

Coefficients

When we multiply a number by a variable, the number is called the variable's coefficient.

We don't usually use the times sign ($\times$) when we write coefficients, because it might get confused with the letter x. Instead, we use the multiplication dot or write the coefficient directly in front of the variable. All of these expressions mean "5 times g."

$5 \times g \qquad 5 \cdot g \qquad 5g$

Ex. What is the coefficient of h in this expression?

9.2

$4h + 1$

coefficient   variable

Ex. Evaluate the expression for $h = 6$.

$4h + 1$

$4 \cdot 6 + 1$

$24 + 1$

25

Terms and Constants

The **terms** of an expression are the parts that are added or subtracted together.

Terms without variables are called **constants**, because they stay constant and don't change.

Like terms are terms that are like each other.

- Terms with the same variable are like terms.

- Constants are like terms.

Ex. How many terms are in this expression? How many constants?

9.3

$2m + 3 + m + 1$
4 terms

$2m + 3 + m + 1$
2 constants

Ex. Identify the like terms in this expression.

$2m + 3 + m + 1$

$2m$ and m both have the same variable, so they are like terms.

3 and 1 are both constants, so they are like terms.

Combine Like Terms

To simplify expressions, combine the like terms.

If two terms have the same variable, add or subtract their coefficients. (If a variable doesn't have a coefficient, we think of its coefficient as 1.)

If two terms are constants, add or subtract the constants.

Ex. Simplify the expression.

9.3

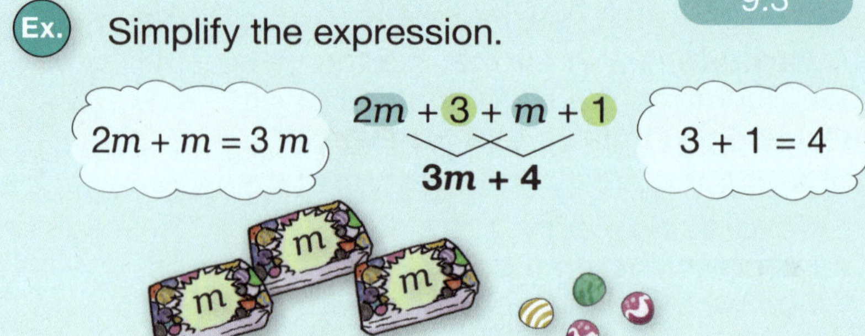

Use Multiplication Properties to Simplify Expressions

9.4

When we multiply a number by an expression in parentheses, we sometimes write the number directly in front of the parentheses. To simplify an expression with parentheses, remove the parentheses and write it in the simplest way possible.

Ex. Use the distributive property to simplify $3(n + 4)$.

$$3(n + 4)$$
$$3n + 3 \cdot 4$$
$$3n + 12$$

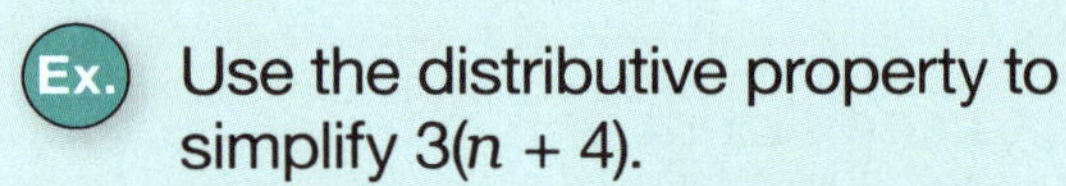

Ex. Use the associative property to simplify $3(2z)$.

We can multiply in any order without changing the product. So, we can multiply $3 \cdot 2$ first.

$$3(2z)$$

$$6z$$

Expressions with Two Variables

If there is more than one variable in an expression, we use a different letter for each variable.

Terms with the same variable are like terms. To simplify expressions with more than one variable, we combine like terms.

9.5

Ex. Write an expression for the perimeter of a rectangle with length l and width w.

$$l + w + l + w$$
$$2l + 2w$$

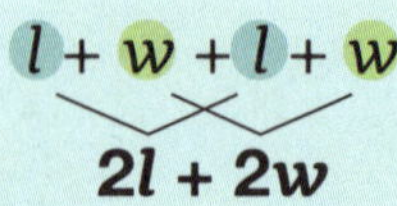

Percentages

Percent means "out of 100." We use a percentage to represent part of a whole, just like a fraction or decimal.

 **Ex.** Write 61% as a fraction.

Percent means "out of 100," so we write the percentage as the numerator and 100 as the denominator.

$$61\% = \frac{61}{100}$$

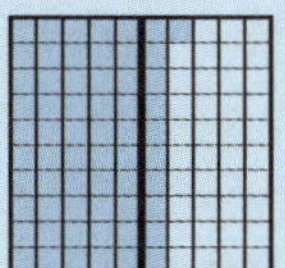

 **Ex.** Write 25% as a decimal.

We use fractions as a bridge between percentages and decimals.

$$25\% = \frac{25}{100} = 0.25$$

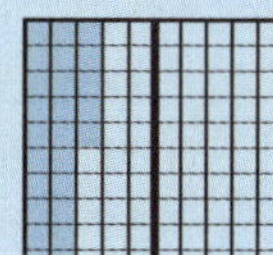

 **Ex.** Write $\frac{99}{100}$ as a percentage.

$$\frac{99}{100} = 99\%$$

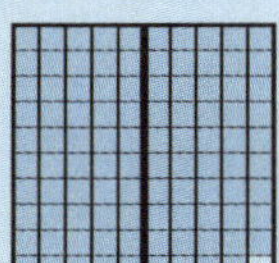

 **Ex.** Write 0.03 as a percentage.

$$0.03 = \frac{3}{100} = 3\%$$

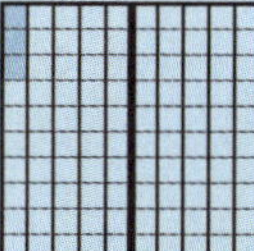

Write Fractions as Percentages

To write a fraction as a percentage, write an equivalent fraction with 100 as the denominator. Then, write the matching percentage.

To write a percentage as a fraction, write the percentage as a fraction with 100 as the denominator. Then, simplify the fraction.

 **Ex.** $\frac{2}{5}$ of the children in the orchestra play the violin. What percentage of the children play the violin?

$$\overset{\times\,20}{\frac{2}{5}} = \underset{\times\,20}{\frac{40}{100}} = 40\%$$

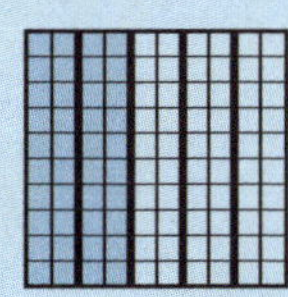

 **Ex.** 8% of the children in the orchestra play the string bass. What fraction of the children play the string bass?

$$8\% = \overset{\div\,4}{\underset{\div\,4}{\frac{8}{100}}} = \frac{2}{25}$$

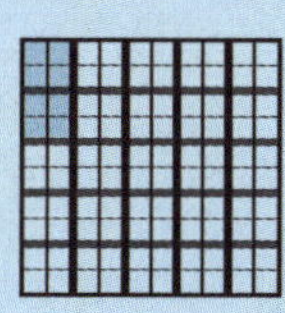

Unit 10 Reference Page

Find a Percentage of a Number

In math, "of" often means multiply. We can use fractions to find a percentage of a number.

1. Convert the percentage to a fraction. Use the simplest fraction possible.

2. Multiply the fraction by the number. Or, use mental math to find the fraction of the number.

Caitlin tried to make 36 baskets. She made 75% of her baskets. How many baskets did she make?

$75\% = \dfrac{3}{4}$, so we want to find $\dfrac{3}{4}$ of 36.

Mental Math

$36 \div 4 = 9$

$9 \times 3 = 27$

$\dfrac{3}{4}$ of 36 = **27 baskets**

Fraction Multiplication

$\dfrac{3}{\cancel{4}_{1}} \times \cancel{36}^{9} = \textbf{27 baskets}$

Use 10% to Mentally Find Other Percentages

Ex. Dinner at the restaurant cost \$80. Taylor's mom wants to leave a 20% tip. How much money should she leave as a tip?

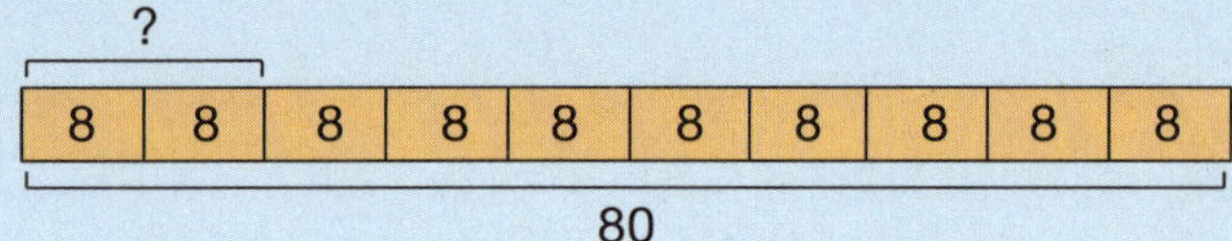

$\dfrac{1}{10}$ of 80 = 8 → 10% of 80 = 8

$2 \times 8 = 16$ → 20% of 80 = **\$16**

Ex. Lunch at the restaurant cost \$40. Brendan's dad wants to leave a 15% tip. How much money should he leave as a tip?

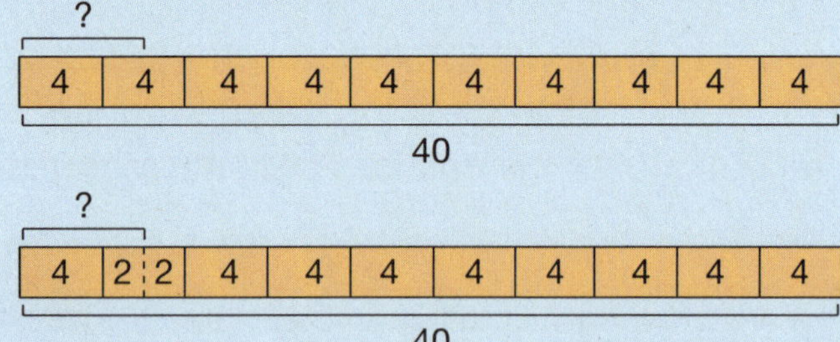

$\dfrac{1}{10}$ of 40 = 4 → 10% of 40 = 4

$\dfrac{1}{2}$ of 4 = 2 → 5% of 40 = 2

$4 + 2 = 6$ → 15% of 40 = **\$6**

Use a Percentage to Find the Total Amount

Ex. Brynn scored 12 points at the basketball game. She scored 30% of her team's points. How many points did her team score in all?

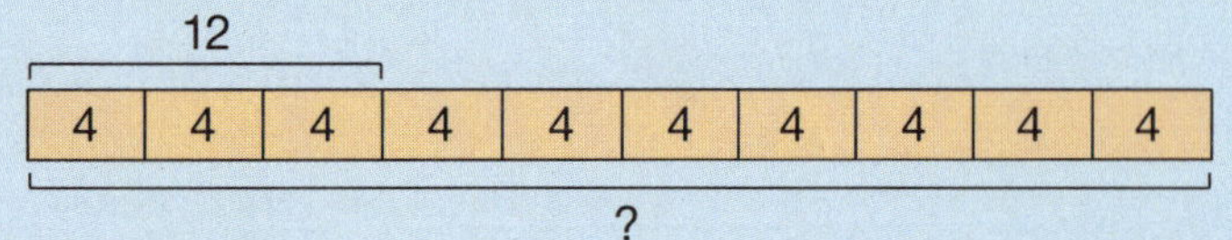

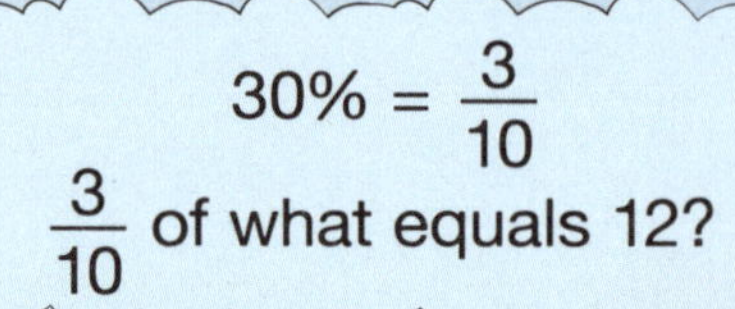

$30\% = \dfrac{3}{10}$

$\dfrac{3}{10}$ of what equals 12?

$12 \div 3 = 4$

$4 \times 10 = \textbf{40 points}$

Percentages Greater Than 100%

We use percentages greater than 100% to stand for more than a whole amount.

 **Ex.** Write 150% as a whole number or mixed number.

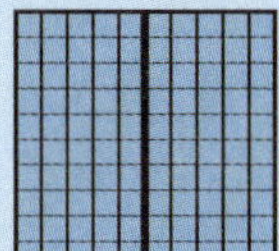

100% = 1 whole $50\% = \dfrac{1}{2}$

100% + 50% = 150%

$1 + \dfrac{1}{2} = 1\dfrac{1}{2}$

 **Ex.** Write 200% as a whole number or mixed number.

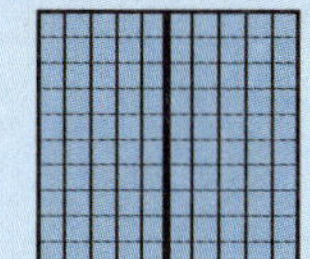 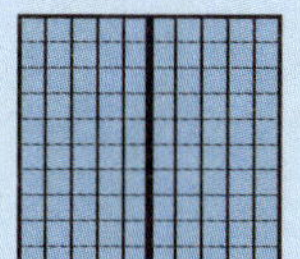

100% = 1 whole   100% = 1 whole

100% + 100% = 200%

$1 + 1 = 2$

Percentages Greater Than 100%

 **Ex.** Marc set a goal of raising $40 for the charity fundraiser. He ended up raising 150% of his goal. How much money did he raise?

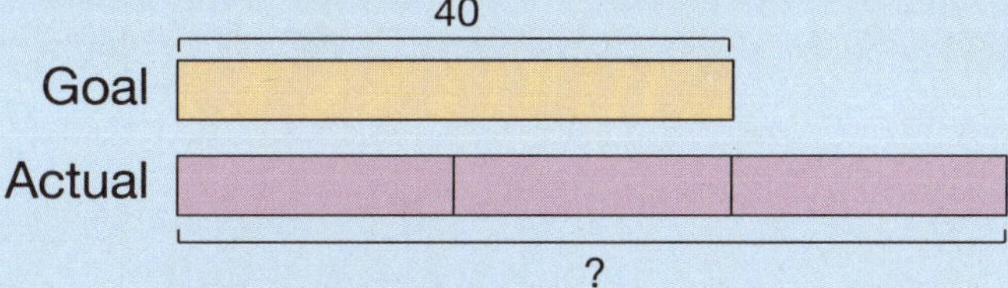

Mental Math

100% of 40 equals 40.

50% of 40 equals 20.

40 + 20 = 60, so Marc raised **$60**.

Fraction Multiplication

150% of 40 → $1\dfrac{1}{2} \times 40$

$\dfrac{3}{2} \times \overset{20}{\cancel{40}} = \dfrac{60}{1} = \mathbf{\$60}$

Increase and Decrease Problems

1. Use the percentage to find the amount of the increase or decrease.

2. If the problem involves an increase, add the increase to the original amount.

3. If the problem involves a decrease, subtract the decrease from the original amount.

 **Ex.** The sweater's regular price is $40. Today, the sweater is on sale for 25% off the regular price. How much does it cost?

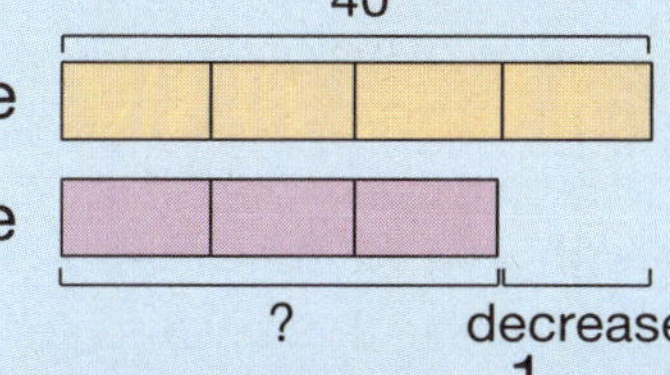

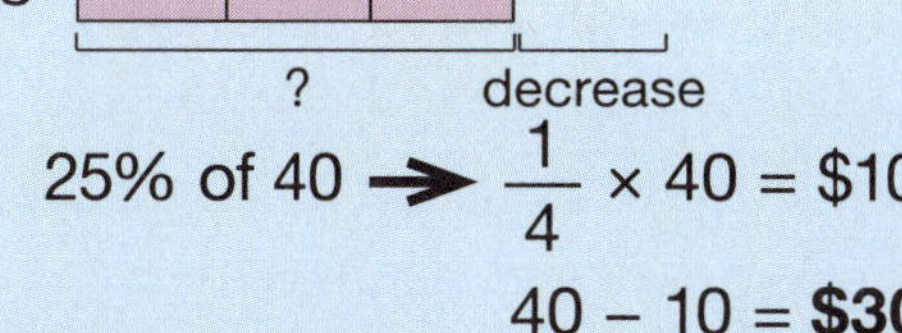

$25\% = \dfrac{1}{4}$ 25% of 40 → $\dfrac{1}{4} \times 40 = \$10$

$40 - 10 = \mathbf{\$30}$

Inequalities

11.1

Inequalities are mathematical statements that compare unequal quantities. We can use variables in inequalities.

$$a < 6 \qquad b > -2 \qquad c \geq 1 \qquad d \leq 0$$

a is less than 6.

b is greater than −2.

c is greater than or equal to 1.

d is less than or equal to 0.

Ex. The bag of candy weighs more than 2 lb. (Use *w* to stand for the weight.)

$$w > 2$$

Any number greater than 2 is a possible value for *w*.

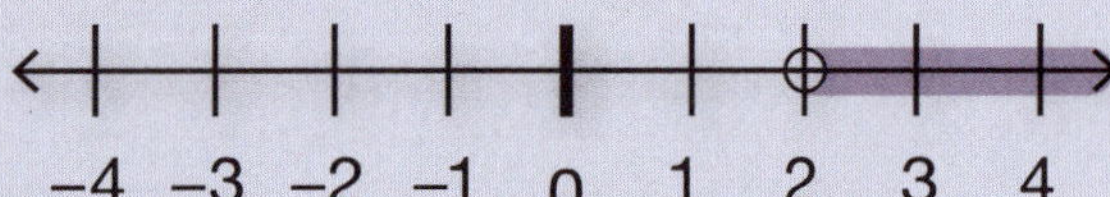

The open circle means that 2 is not included in the graph.

Ex. The temperature is less than or equal to −1°. (Use *t* to stand for the temperature.)

$$t \leq -1$$

Any number less than −1 is a possible value for *t*. −1 is also a possible value for *t*.

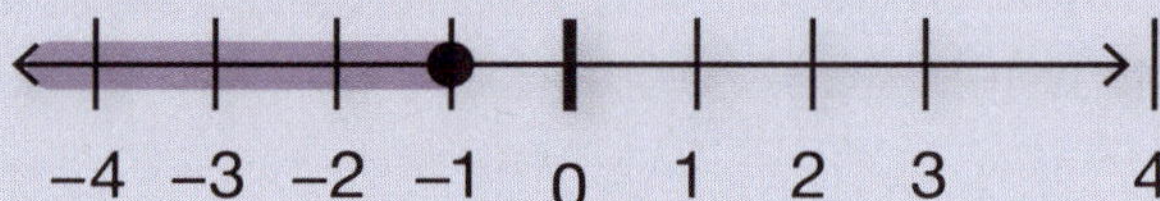

The closed circle means that −1 is included in the graph.

Equations

11.2

An equation is a mathematical statement with an equals sign. The two sides of the equation are like the two sides of a scale. The equals sign tells that the two sides equal each other and are in balance.

A solution to an equation is a value for the variable that makes the equation true. To check whether a number is a solution to an equation, substitute the number into the equation. Evaluate both sides and check whether the two sides are equal.

Ex. Is $a = 4$ a solution to this equation?

$$6 = 2a$$
$$6 \stackrel{?}{=} 2 \cdot 4$$
$$6 \neq 8 \qquad \textbf{No.}$$

Ex. Is $b = 3$ a solution to this equation?

$$2b + 1 = 7$$
$$2 \cdot 3 + 1 \stackrel{?}{=} 7$$
$$6 + 1 \stackrel{?}{=} 7$$
$$7 = 7 \qquad \textbf{Yes.}$$

Solve Equations, Part 1

11.3

To solve an equation, we change both sides until we have the variable by itself on one side of the equation.

The two sides of an equation are like the two sides of a scale. If you change one side of the equation, you must change the other side in the same way.

1. Identify what happens to the variable in the equation. Do the opposite operation to both sides of the equation.
2. Simplify both sides.
3. Substitute the solution into the equation to check your answer.

Ex. Solve: $x + 18 = 27$

In this equation, 18 is added to x. So, we subtract 18 from both sides to get x by itself on one side of the equation.

$$\begin{array}{rcr} x + 18 &=& 27 \\ -18 & & -18 \\ \hline x &=& 9 \end{array}$$

Check:
$$9 + 18 \stackrel{?}{=} 27$$
$$27 = 27 \checkmark$$

Solve Equations, Part 2

11.4

We solve multiplication equations with the same steps we use to solve addition equations. We change both sides in the same way until we have the variable by itself on one side of the equation.

1. Identify what happens to the variable in the equation. Do the opposite operation to both sides of the equation.
2. Simplify both sides.
3. Substitute the solution into the equation to check your answer.

Ex. Solve: $3z = 21$

In this equation, z is multiplied by 3. So, we divide both sides by 3 to get z by itself on one side of the equation.

$$3z = 21$$
$$\frac{3z}{3} = \frac{21}{3}$$
$$z = 7$$

Check:
$$3 \cdot 7 \stackrel{?}{=} 21$$
$$21 = 21 \checkmark$$

Equations with Two Variables

11.5

Some equations express the relationship between two variables. To write an expression with two variables, describe what you do to one variable to get the other variable. Then, translate the words into mathematical symbols.

Ex. Write an equation that tells the relationship between the number of times a cricket chirps in 15 seconds and the temperature. Use n to stand for the number of chirps and t to stand for the temperature.

The number of chirps plus 40 equals the temperature.  $n + 40 = t$

Ex. If the cricket chirps 25 times, what is the temperature?
$$n + 40 = t$$
$$25 + 40 = t$$
$$65 = t$$

The temperature is **65° F.**

Unit 12 Reference Page

Review Volume

A rectangular prism is a three-dimensional shape with 6 rectangular faces. We use these formulas to find the volume (V) of a rectangular prism.

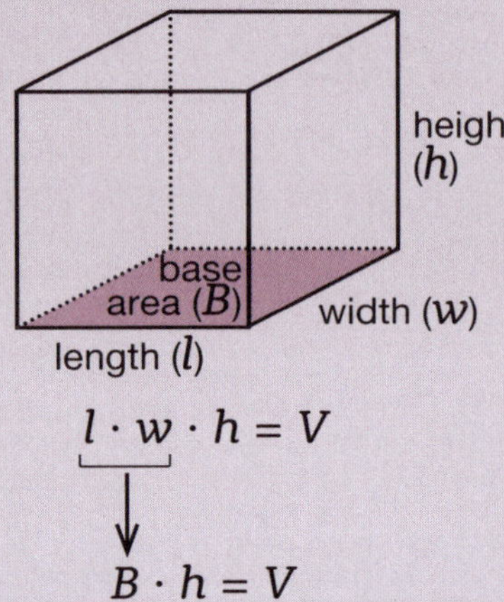

$$l \cdot w \cdot h = V$$

$$B \cdot h = V$$

We can choose any face to be the base, as long as we measure the height perpendicular to the chosen base.

Ex. The jewelry box is 25 cm long, 10 cm wide, and 10 cm tall. What is its volume?

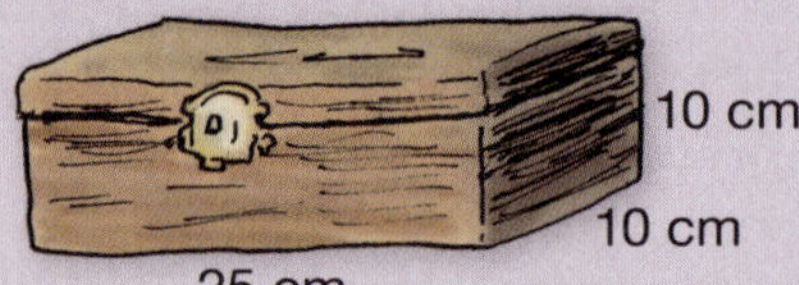

$$l \cdot w \cdot h = V$$

$$25 \text{ cm} \cdot 10 \text{ cm} \cdot 10 \text{ cm} = \textbf{2,500 cm}^3$$

Ex. The wardrobe sticks out 2 ft. from the wall. The back of the wardrobe covers 60 ft.² of the wall. What is the volume of the wardrobe?

$$B \cdot h = V$$

$$60 \text{ ft.}^2 \cdot 2 \text{ ft.} = \textbf{120 ft.}^3$$

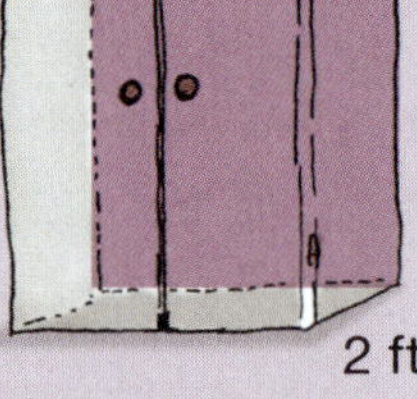

2 ft.

12.1

Divide to Find Base Area or Height

If you know the volume of a rectangular prism and its height, you can divide the volume by the height to find the area of the base.

$$V = B \cdot h \;\Rightarrow\; \frac{V}{h} = B$$

If you know the volume of a rectangular prism and the area of its base, you can divide the volume by the area of the base to find the height.

$$V = B \cdot h \;\Rightarrow\; \frac{V}{B} = h$$

Ex. At the aquarium, the jellyfish tank is 4 ft. tall. It has a volume of 48 ft.³. What is the area of the bottom of the jellyfish tank?

$$\frac{48 \text{ ft.}^3}{4 \text{ ft.}} = \frac{48 \text{ ft.} \cdot \text{ft.} \cdot \cancel{\text{ft.}}}{4 \cancel{\text{ft.}}} = \textbf{12 ft.}^2$$

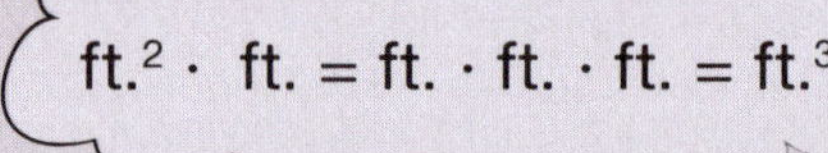

Ex. The tropical fish tank covers an area of 3 m². It has a volume of 3 m³. What is its height?

$$\frac{3 \text{ m}^3}{3 \text{ m}^2} = \frac{3 \text{ m} \cdot \cancel{\text{m}} \cdot \cancel{\text{m}}}{3 \cancel{\text{m}} \cdot \cancel{\text{m}}} = \textbf{1 m}$$

12.2

Use Fractions to Find Volume

12.3

Ex. The foam dice company cuts foam into cubes to make foam dice. What is the volume of a foam die that is $\frac{1}{2}$ ft. long on each side?

$$\frac{1}{2} \text{ ft.} \times \frac{1}{2} \text{ ft.} \times \frac{1}{2} \text{ ft.} = \frac{1}{8}\textbf{ ft.}^3$$

Ex. How many $\frac{1}{2}$-foot dice can the company cut from a foam cube that is 1 ft. long on each side?

$$2 \times 2 \times 2 = \textbf{8 dice}$$

Use Fractions and Mixed Numbers to Find Volume

12.4

Ex. What is the volume of this box?

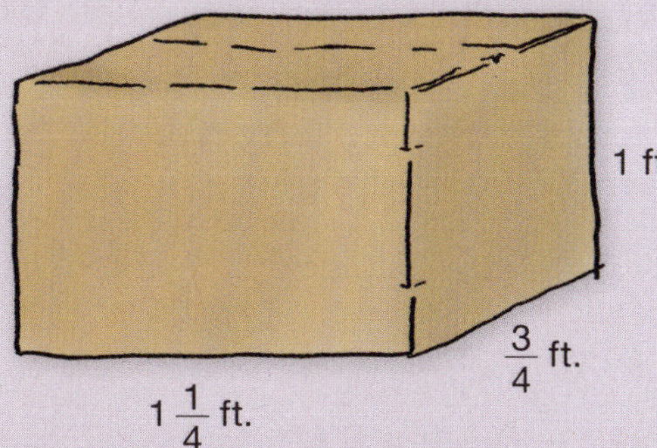

$$l \cdot w \cdot h = V$$

$$1\frac{1}{4} \text{ ft.} \times \frac{3}{4} \text{ ft.} \times 1 \text{ ft.}$$

$$\frac{5}{4} \text{ ft.} \times \frac{3}{4} \text{ ft.} \times \frac{1}{1} \text{ ft.} = \frac{15}{16}\textbf{ ft.}^3$$

Convert Measurement Units to Find Volume

12.5

When we multiply measurements to find volume, the measurements must have the same unit.

If the measurements have different units, first convert them all to the same unit. Then, solve like usual.

Ex. What is the volume of this gift box?

$$1\frac{1}{2} \text{ ft.} \times 1 \text{ ft.} \times 3 \text{ in.}$$

$$\frac{3}{2} \text{ ft.} \times \frac{1}{1} \text{ ft.} \times \frac{1}{4} \text{ ft.} = \frac{3}{8}\textbf{ ft.}^3$$

3-D Solids and Nets

Three-dimensional solids are solid shapes that take up space. Each flat surface of the solid is called a face.

Nets are flat, two-dimensional shapes that show what a 3-D solid looks like when it's unfolded.

Ex. If you fold this net, what shape do you create? How many faces does it have?

13.1

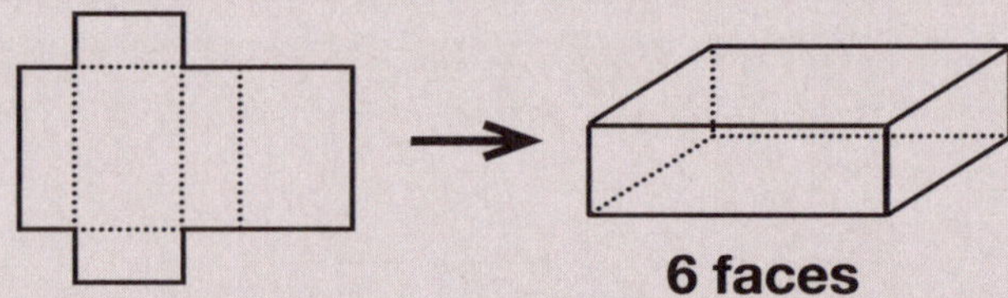

6 faces

Rectangular Prism	**Cube**	**Triangular Prism**	**Pyramid**

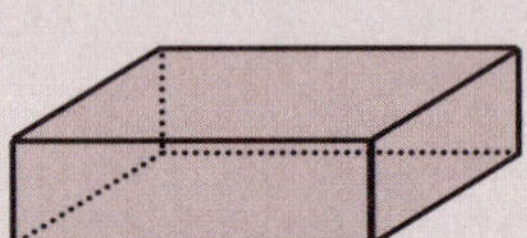 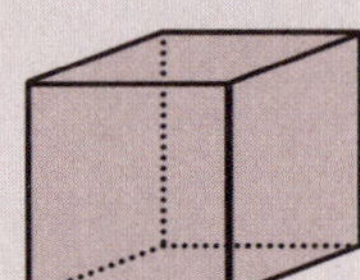 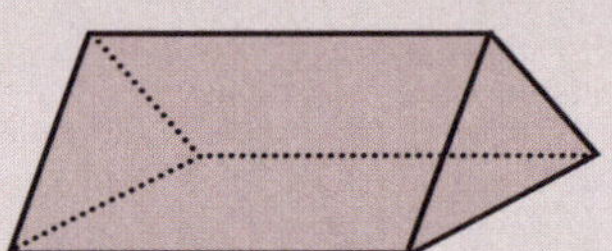 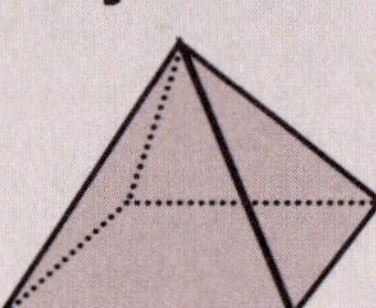

6 rectangular faces
3 pairs of parallel faces

6 square faces
3 pairs of parallel faces

1 pair of parallel triangular faces, connected by 3 rectangular faces

1 flat face, connected to a triangular face along each side

Surface Area of Rectangular Prisms and Cubes

13.2

The surface area of a 3-D solid is the total area of all its faces.
To find surface area, we find the area of each face and then add the areas.

Ex. What is the surface area of the box?

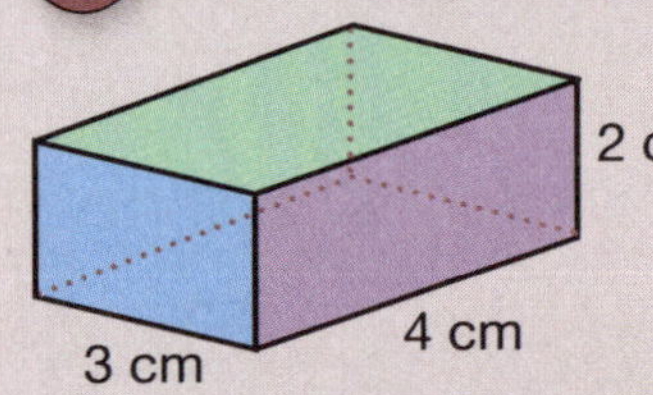

Area of each green face: 4 cm × 3 cm = 12 cm^2

Area of each blue face: 2 cm × 3 cm = 6 cm^2

Area of each purple face: 4 cm × 2 cm = 8 cm^2

12 cm^2 + 12 cm^2 + 6 cm^2 + 6 cm^2 + 8 cm^2 + 8 cm^2 = **52 cm^2**

Surface Area of Triangular Prisms and Pyramids

13.5

Ex. What is the surface area of the chocolate bar's box? (All measurements are in centimeters.)

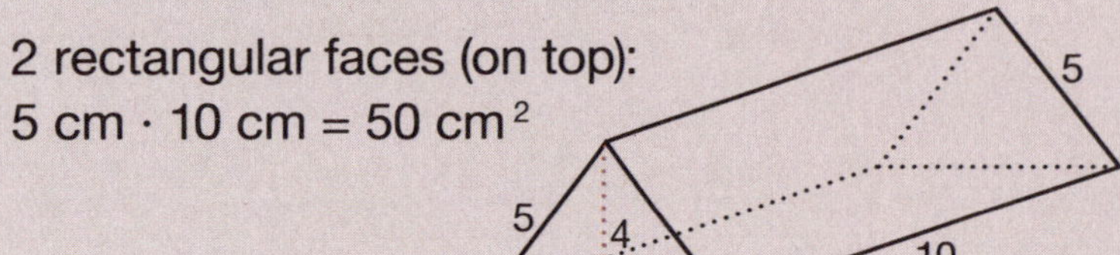

2 rectangular faces (on top):
5 cm · 10 cm = 50 cm^2

2 triangular faces:
$\frac{1}{2}$ · 6 cm · 4 cm = 12 cm^2

Rectangular face (on bottom):
6 cm · 10 cm = 60 cm^2

2 · 50 cm^2 + 2 · 12 cm^2 + 60 cm^2
100 cm^2 + 24 cm^2 + 60 cm^2
184 cm^2

Rate

A rate is a special type of ratio that compares two quantities with different units. We write rates with the word "per," a fraction bar, or a slash. Per means "for each."

 **Ex.** The cow's heart beats 50 times in 1 minute.

50 beats per min.

50 beats/min.

$$50 \; \frac{\textbf{beats}}{\textbf{min.}}$$

Unit Rate

A unit rate compares a certain number of units of one quantity to one unit of the other quantity.

To find a unit rate, use a fraction bar to divide one quantity by the other. Use the quantities' units to decide which quantity to write above the fraction bar and which quantity to write below the fraction bar.

 **Ex.** The whale's heart beats 35 times in 5 minutes. What is its heart rate in beats per minute?

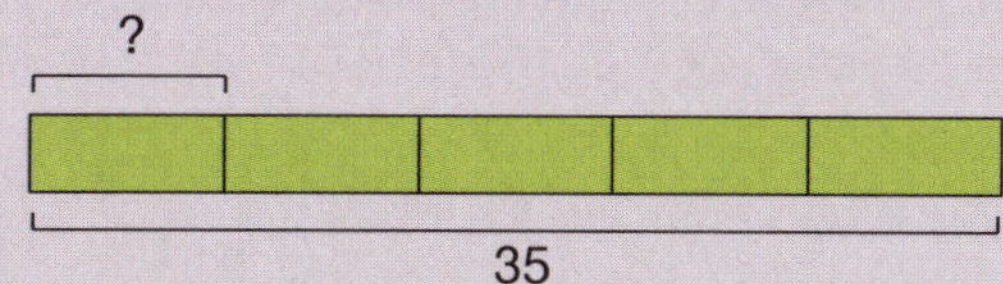

We want to express the heart rate in beats per minute. So, we write the number of beats above the fraction bar and the number of minutes below the fraction bar.

$$\frac{35 \text{ beats}}{5 \text{ min.}} = 7 \; \frac{\textbf{beats}}{\textbf{min.}} \qquad 7 \text{ beats per min.}$$

Solve Rate Problems

 **Ex.** Callie types at a rate of 40 words per minute. How many words can she type in 5 minutes?

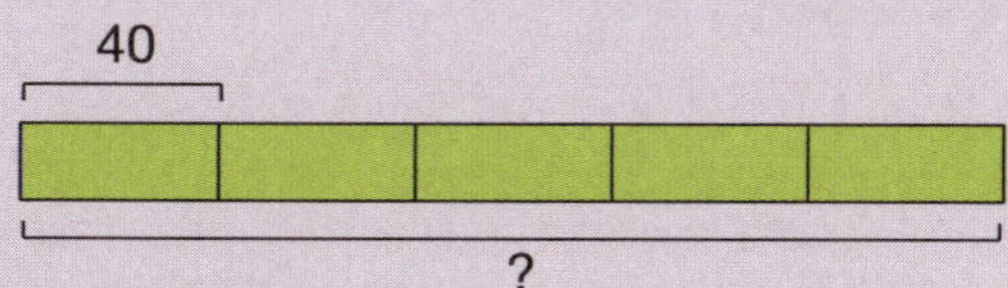

$$40 \; \frac{\text{words}}{\text{min.}} \times 5 \text{ min.} = \textbf{200 words}$$

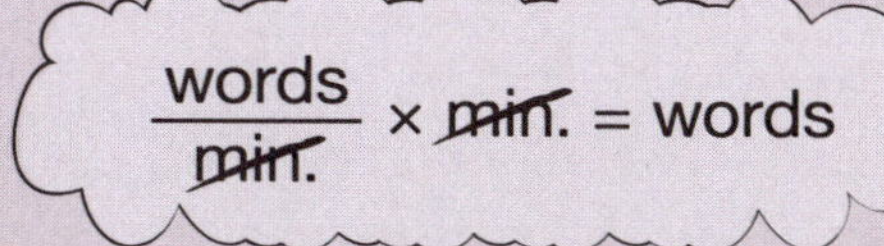

 **Ex.** Callie types at a rate of 40 words per minute. How long does it take her to type 320 words?

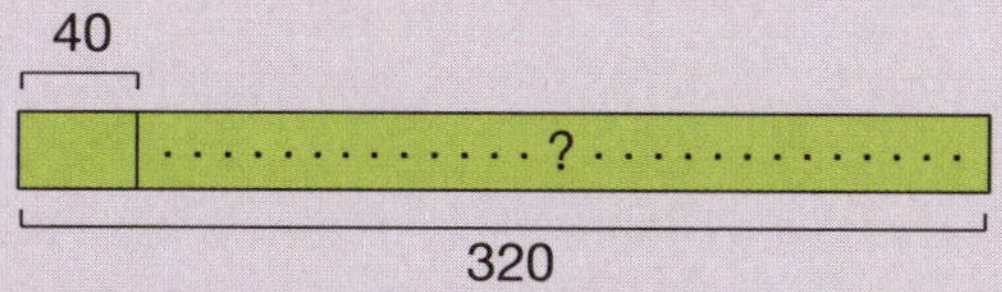

$$320 \text{ words} \div 40 \; \frac{\text{words}}{\text{min.}} = \textbf{8 minutes}$$

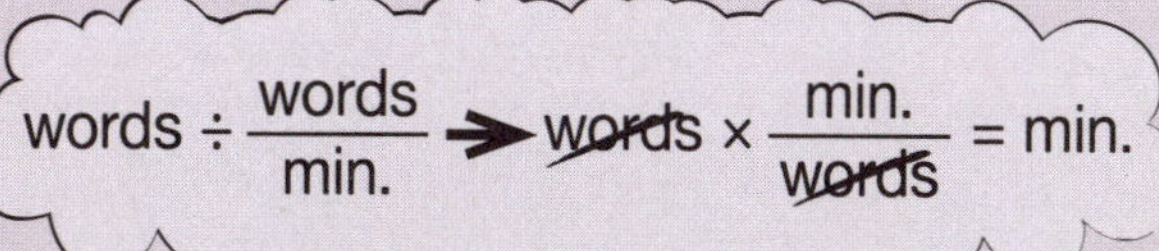

Speed

Speed is a special type of unit rate that compares distance to one unit of time.

$$\frac{\text{distance}}{\text{time}} = \text{speed}$$

Measurement units for speed always include both a distance unit and a time unit. We sometimes use p to stand for "per" in measurement units for speed.

miles per hour

miles/hour

mph

Ex. James is training for a marathon. On Sunday, he ran 12 miles. It took him 2 hours. What was his speed (in miles per hour)?

14.4

$$\frac{12 \text{ miles}}{2 \text{ hours}} = \textbf{6 miles per hour}$$

Ex. On Monday, James ran 10 miles. It took him $1\frac{1}{2}$ hours. What was his speed (in miles per hour)?

$$\frac{10 \text{ miles}}{1\frac{1}{2} \text{ hours}} \longrightarrow 10 \div 1\frac{1}{2}$$

$$\frac{10}{1} \div \frac{3}{2} \longrightarrow \frac{10}{1} \times \frac{2}{3} = \frac{20}{3} = 6\frac{2}{3} \text{ mph}$$

Ex. The airplane travels at a speed of 600 miles per hour. If the plane flies for $1\frac{1}{2}$ hours, how many miles does the plane travel?

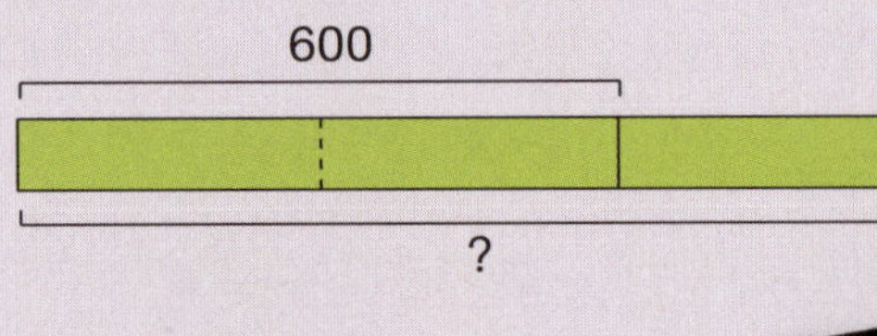

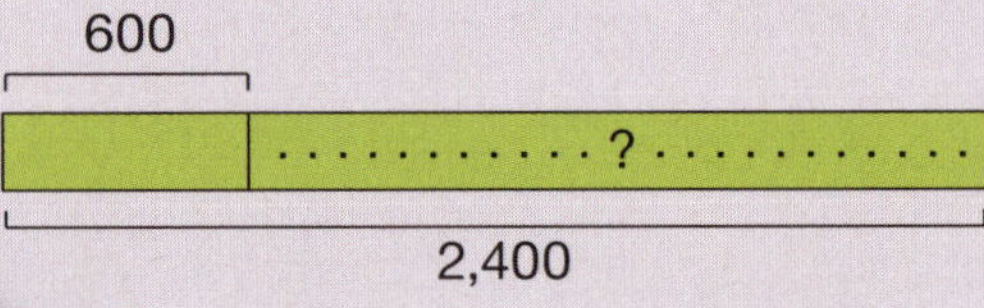

$$600 \frac{\text{miles}}{\text{hour}} \times 1\frac{1}{2} \text{ hours}$$

$$\overset{300}{\cancel{600}} \frac{\text{miles}}{\text{hour}} \times \frac{3}{\underset{1}{\cancel{2}}} \text{ hours} = \textbf{900 miles}$$

speed × time = distance

Ex. The airplane travels at a speed of 600 miles per hour. How long does it take the plane to travel 2,400 miles?

14.5

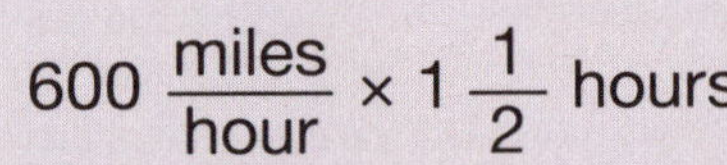

$$2{,}400 \text{ miles} \div 600 \frac{\text{miles}}{\text{hour}} = \textbf{4 hours}$$

distance ÷ speed = time

Solve Speed Word Problems

 **Ex.** Thomas runs for $\frac{1}{2}$ hour at a speed of 6 miles per hour. Then, he walks the same distance home at a speed of 3 miles per hour. How long does it take him to walk home?

First, find the one-way distance Thomas runs.

$$6 \frac{\text{miles}}{\text{hour}} \times \frac{1}{2} \text{ hour} = 3 \text{ miles}$$

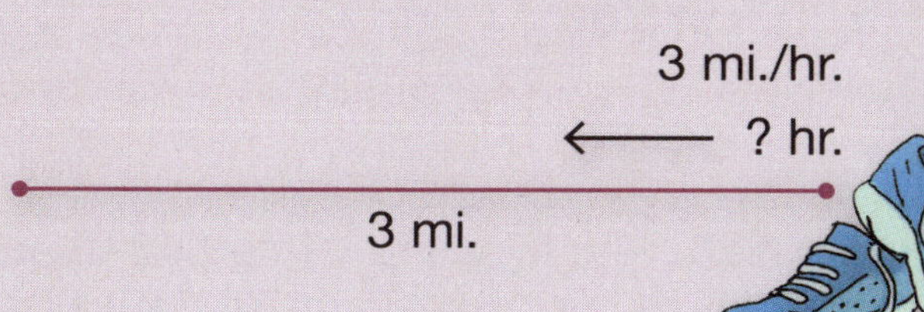

Then, use the one-way distance to find how long it takes him to walk home.

$$3 \text{ miles} \div 3 \frac{\text{miles}}{\text{hour}} = \textbf{1 hour}$$

Use 10% to Find Percentages of Decimals

15.1

Ex. The cowboy hat originally cost $95.00. Today, it's on sale for 20% off. What is the sale price?

10% of $95.00 = $9.50

$9.50 × 2 = $19.00 → 20% of $95.00 = $19.00

$95.00 − $19.00 = **$76.00**

Use Decimal Multiplication to Find Percentages

In math, "of" often means multiply. We can use decimals to find a percentage of a number.

1. Convert the percentage to a decimal.
2. Multiply the decimal by the number.

15.2

Ex. Faith buys a board game for $38. She lives in a state that charges 6% sales tax. How much is the sales tax on the board game?

What is 6% of 38?

6% = 0.06

$$\begin{array}{r} 4 \\ 38 \\ \times 0.06 \\ \hline \$2.28 \end{array}$$

Decimal digits

$$\begin{array}{r} 0 \\ +2 \\ \hline 2 \end{array}$$

Ex. What is the total cost of the game?

$38.00 + $2.28 = **$40.28**

Multiply Decimals by Decimals with Mental Math

1. Multiply the non-zero digits. Ignore the decimal point and any leading zeros.
2. Find the total number of decimal digits in the factors.
3. Write a decimal point so the product has the same number of decimal digits as the factors.

15.3

Ex. The poster is 0.3 meters wide and 0.5 meters long. What is its area?

0.3 × 0.5 = **0.15**

Decimal digits
1 + 1 = 2

The poster has an area of 0.15 m².

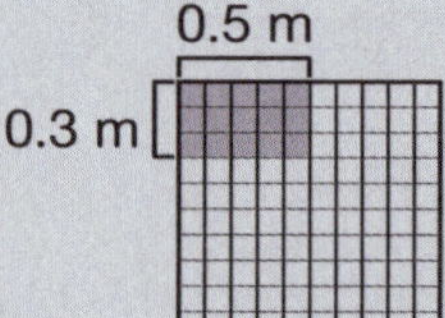

$$\frac{3}{10} \times \frac{5}{10} = \frac{15}{100}$$

Multiply Decimals by Decimals

15.4

1. Multiply like usual. Ignore the decimal point and any leading zeros.
2. Find the total number of decimal digits in the factors.
3. Write a decimal point so the product has the same number of decimal digits as the factors.

 **Ex.** Green beans cost $2.19 per pound. How much do 1.2 pounds cost? Write your answer with 2 decimal digits.

$$
\begin{array}{r}
1 \\
2.19 \\
\times\ \ 1.2 \\
\hline
438 \\
+\ 2190 \\
\hline
2.628
\end{array}
$$

Decimal digits

$$
\begin{array}{r}
2 \\
+1 \\
\hline
3
\end{array}
$$

2.6<u>2</u>8 ≈ **$2.63**

Use Decimal Multiplication to Find Percentages

15.5

 **Ex.** Luis wants to buy a ukulele that costs $68.50. He lives in a state that charges 5% sales tax. How much is the sales tax on the ukulele? Write your answer with 2 decimal digits.

What is 5% of $68.50?

5% = 0.05

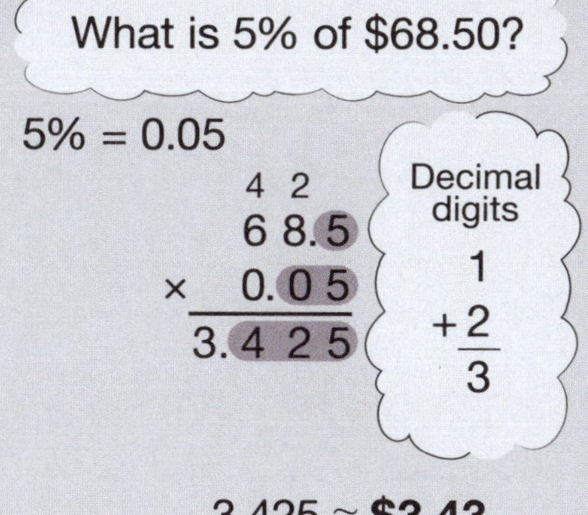

$$
\begin{array}{r}
4\ \ 2 \\
68.5 \\
\times\ \ 0.05 \\
\hline
3.425
\end{array}
$$

Decimal digits

$$
\begin{array}{r}
1 \\
+2 \\
\hline
3
\end{array}
$$

3.4<u>2</u>5 ≈ **$3.43**

Ex. A guitar costs 40% more than the ukulele. How much does the guitar cost?

What is 140% of $68.50?

140% = 1.4

$$
\begin{array}{r}
68.5 \\
\times\ \ 1.4 \\
\hline
2740 \\
+\ 6850 \\
\hline
95.90
\end{array}
$$

Decimal digits

$$
\begin{array}{r}
1 \\
+1 \\
\hline
2
\end{array}
$$

$95.90

Use Place-Value Thinking to Divide Decimals by Decimals

15.7

Ex. Chris has a board that is 0.6 m long. He cuts the board into pieces that are each 0.2 m long. How many pieces does he make?

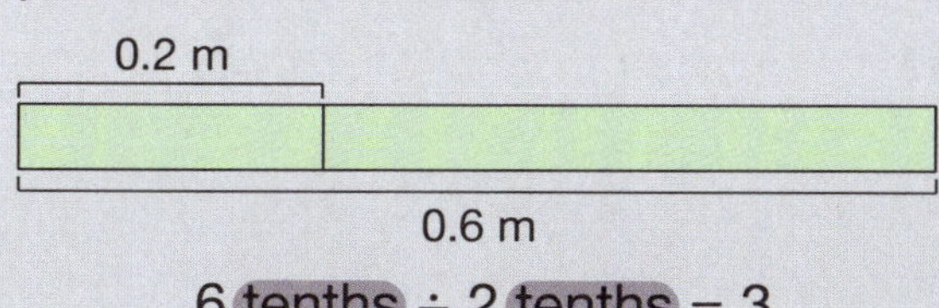

6 tenths ÷ 2 tenths = 3

0.6 ÷ 0.2 = **3**

 **Ex.** Sienna has a piece of wire that is 0.3 m long. She cuts the wire into pieces that are each 0.05 m long. How many pieces does she make?

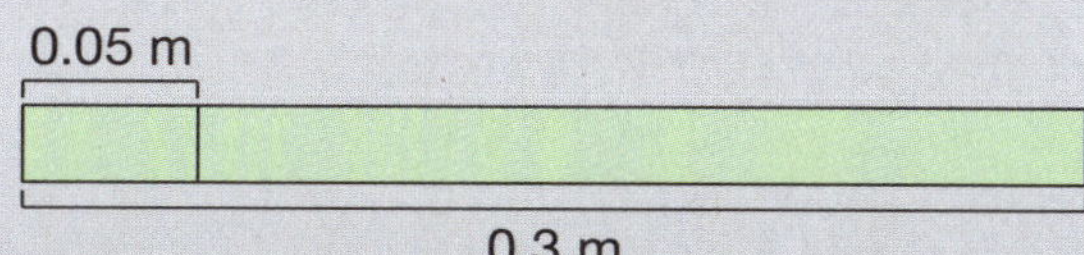

30 hundredths ÷ 5 hundredths = 6

0.3 ÷ 0.05 = **6**

Divide Decimals by Decimals with Long Division

1. Move the divisor's decimal point to the right. Move the decimal point as many places as you need to make the divisor a whole number. Mark the new position with a caret (^).

2. Move the dividend's decimal point the same number of places to the right. Mark the new position with a caret (^).

3. Divide like usual. Ignore any leading zeros.

4. Place the decimal point in the quotient directly above its new place in the dividend.

Ex. Alexandra has 4.2 cubic feet of potting soil. Each flower pot holds 0.3 cubic feet of soil. How many flower pots can she fill?

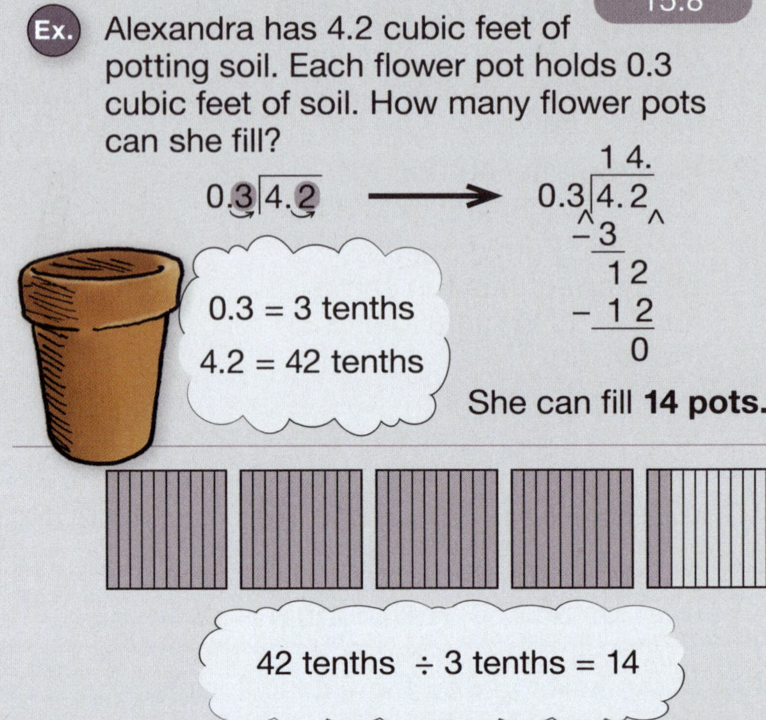

Tack on Zeros to Divide Decimals 15.9

Sometimes, you need to fill in zeros as you move the decimal point.
After you move the decimal point, tack on trailing zeros in the dividend to match the number of decimal digits you want in the answer.

Ex. Prue has 1.1 kg of sugar. She needs 0.25 kg for each batch of brownies. How many batches of brownies can she make? Write your answer with 1 decimal digit.

4.4 batches

0.25 ⟌ 1.10 → 0.25 ⟌ 1.100
− 100
100
− 100
0

Ex. Paul has 1.74 kg of flour. He needs 0.4 kg for each batch of cookies. How many batches of cookies can he make? Write your answer with 2 decimal digits.

4.35

0.4 ⟌ 1.74 → 0.4 ⟌ 1.740
− 16
14
− 12
20
− 20
0

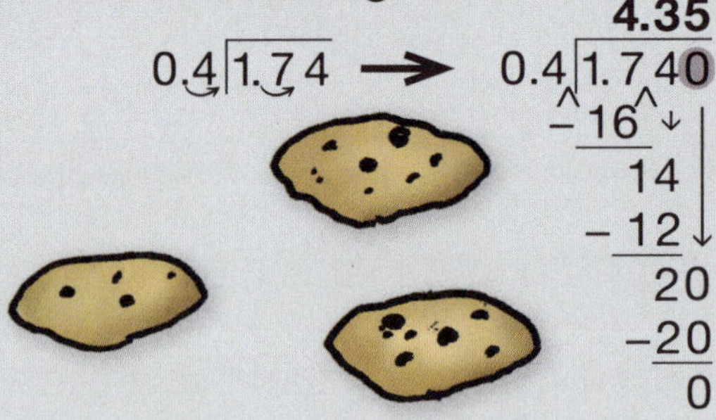

Round Quotients to a Given Number of Decimal Digits

15.10

Ex. The bag of chips weighs 6.3 ounces. Each serving is 0.8 ounces. How many servings are in the bag? Write your answer with 1 decimal digit.

1. Set up the problem and move the decimal point. Tack on trailing zeros to match the number of decimal digits you want in the answer.

2. Follow the long division steps.

3. If there is a remainder, tack on 1 more zero and follow the long division steps again. Round your answer to the correct number of decimal digits.

$$0.8\overline{)6.30}$$

$\longrightarrow$

$$\begin{array}{r} 7.8 \\ 0.8\overline{)6.30} \\ -5\,6 \\ \hline 70 \\ -64 \\ \hline 6 \end{array}$$

$\longrightarrow$

$$\begin{array}{r} 7.87 \\ 0.8\overline{)6.300} \\ -5\,6 \\ \hline 70 \\ -64 \\ \hline 60 \end{array}$$

7.87 ≈ **7.9 servings**

Use a Calculator to Solve Unit Price Problems

15.11

Ex. Chicken costs $7.99 per pound. How much do 1.34 pounds of chicken cost? Write your answer with 2 decimal digits.

$7.99/lb. × 1.34 lb. $\longrightarrow$ `10.7066`

10.7066 ≈ **$10.71**

Ex. Miriam pays $12.85 for a package of chicken. How many pounds of chicken does she buy? Write your answer with 2 decimal digits.

$12.85 ÷ $7.99/lb. $\longrightarrow$ `1.6082...`

1.6082... ≈ **1.61 lb.**

Dot Plots

A dot plot is a graph made from dots and part of the number line. The number of dots above each number tells how many times that number occurred in the data set.

Ex. Lee rolled a die 16 times. Make a dot plot to show his results.

16.1

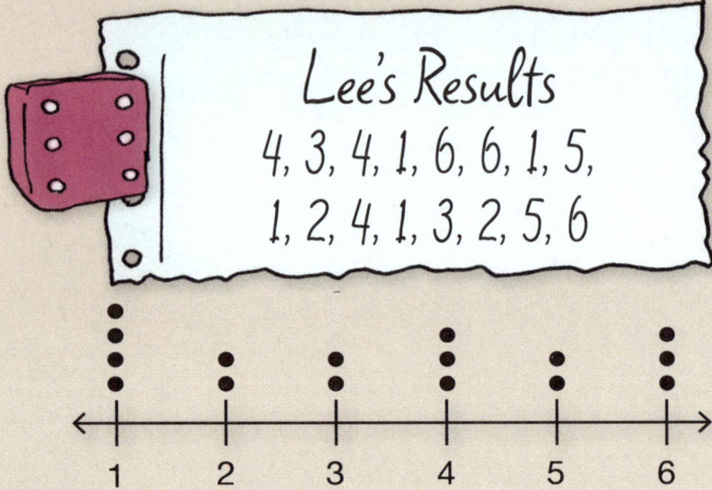

Mean, Median, and Mode

Mean, median, and mode are three different ways to describe the center of a data set:

- The mean is the sum of the values divided by the number of values.
- The median is the value in the middle when you put the values in order.
- The mode is the value that occurs the most frequently.

Ex. Find the mean, median, and mode of Lee's results.

Mean: The sum of Lee's results is 54. $54 \div 16 = \mathbf{3.375}$

Median: 1, 1, 1, 1, 2, 2, 3, 3, 4, 4, 4, 5, 5, 6, 6, 6

The two numbers in the middle are 3 and 4. The mean of 3 and 4 is 3.5, so the median is **3.5**.

Mode: The number that occurs the most often is **1**.

Ways to Describe the Shape of a Distribution

16.2

A **symmetric distribution** has two sides that roughly mirror each other.

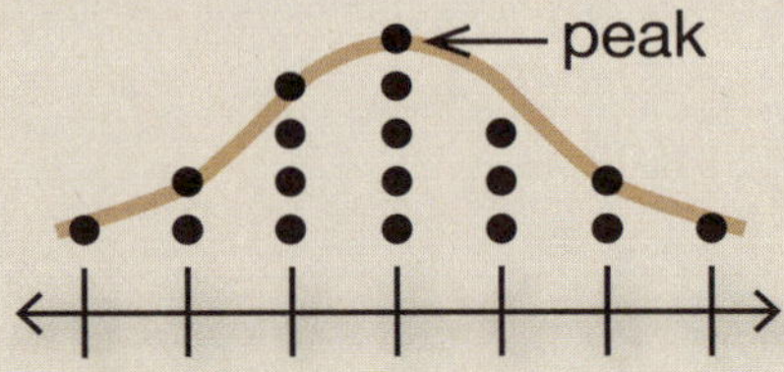

A **peak** is a value that occurs more frequently than the values around it.

A **left-skewed distribution** has a tail on its left side.

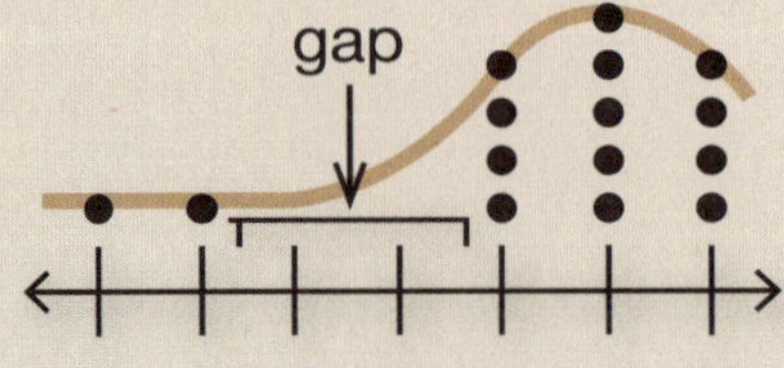

A **gap** is an interval where there are no values.

A **right-skewed distribution** has a tail on its right side.

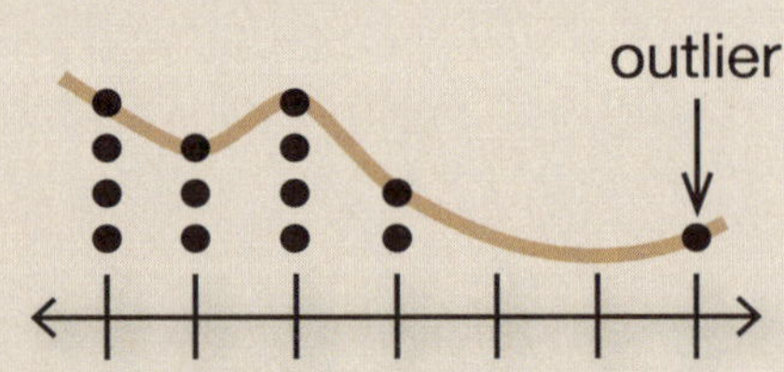

An **outlier** is a value that is very different from the other values in the data set.

Histograms and Range

A histogram is like a bar graph that groups data into intervals on the number line. (The intervals must have the same length, and the bars must touch each other.) The height of each bar shows how many values are in the interval.

The range of a data set is the difference between the highest value and the lowest value.

16.3

Ex.

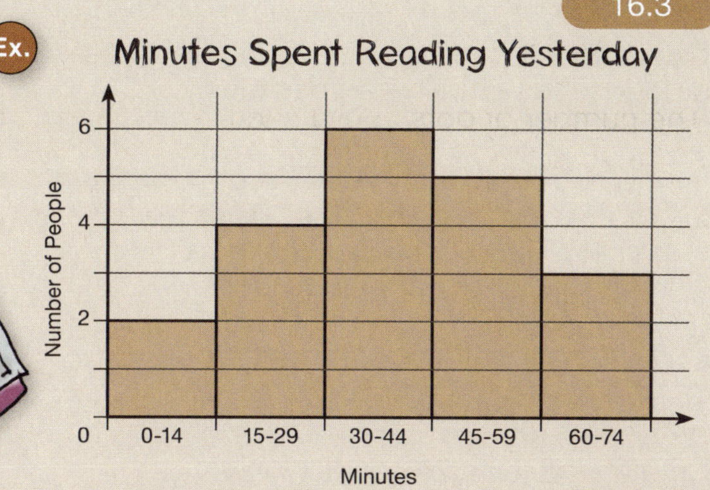

Mean Absolute Deviation

The mean absolute deviation measures how far the values in the data set deviate (or vary) from the mean.

1. Find the mean.
2. Find how far each value is from the mean.
3. Find the mean of these distances.

16.4

Ex. Find the mean absolute deviation for Pierre's croissants. Write your answer with 2 decimal digits.

$$\frac{3.4 + 3.0 + 3.6 + 3.1 + 3.9 + 2.9 + 4.1 + 3.2}{8} = 3.4$$

mean

Weight	3.4	3.0	3.6	3.1	3.9	2.9	4.1	3.2
Distance from 3.4	0	0.4	0.2	0.3	0.5	0.5	0.7	0.2

$$\frac{0 + 0.4 + 0.2 + 0.3 + 0.5 + 0.5 + 0.7 + 0.2}{8} = \mathbf{0.35}$$

Quartiles

Quartiles are numbers that split a data set as equally as possible into 4 groups.

1. Write the values in order.

2. Draw a line that splits the values in half. Then, draw lines that split the lower half and upper half of the data set in half. Your lines may go through a number or between two numbers.

3. Use the lines to find the numbers that split the data set into these groups. If the line goes through a number, that number is the quartile. If the line is between two numbers, the quartile is the median of these two numbers.

Ex. Find the quartiles for these engineering project scores.

16.5

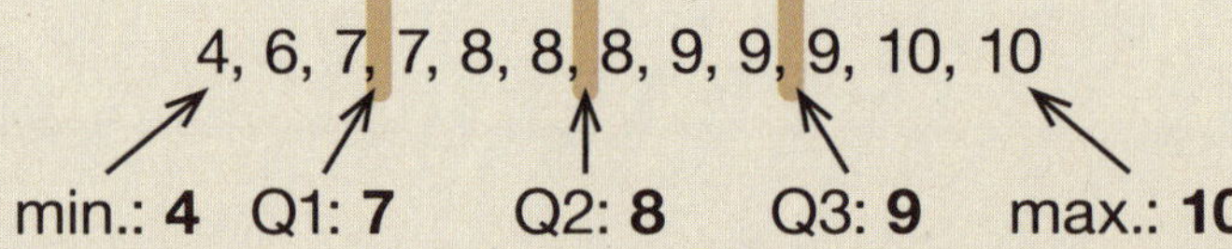

$$\frac{28 + 30}{2} \qquad 38 \qquad \frac{42 + 45}{2}$$

Q1: **29**   Q2: **38**   Q3: **43.5**

Five-Number Summary

The five-number summary for a data set includes the minimum, Q1, Q2, Q3, and maximum. These five numbers give a rough idea of how the data is distributed.

Ex. The swimming instructor recorded her students' scores on the end-of-class swim test. Find the five-number summary for the data set.

16.6

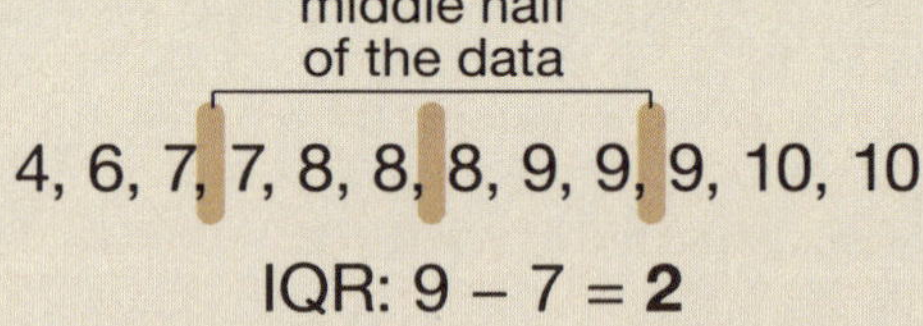

Interquartile Range

The interquartile range (IQR) is the difference between the upper quartile and lower quartile. It tells the range for the middle 50% of the values.

$$Q3 - Q1 = IQR$$

Ex. Find the interquartile range for the scores.

middle half of the data

4, 6, 7, 7, 8, 8, 8, 9, 9, 9, 10, 10

IQR: $9 - 7 = $ **2**

Box Plots

16.7

A box plot is a graph that shows how the data in a data set is distributed. Each box and whisker in the box plot represents about 25% of the data.

Swim Test Scores

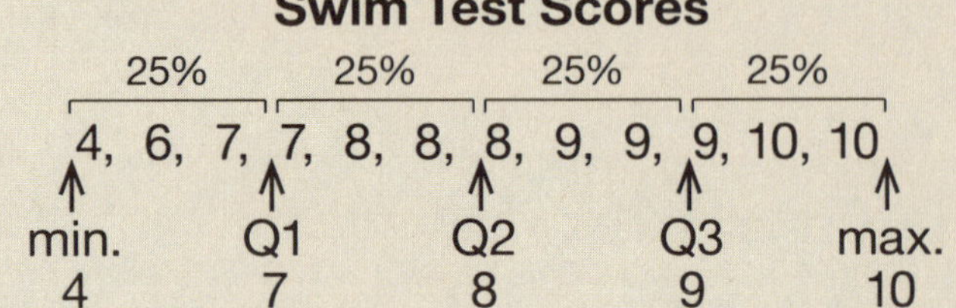

Swim Test Scores

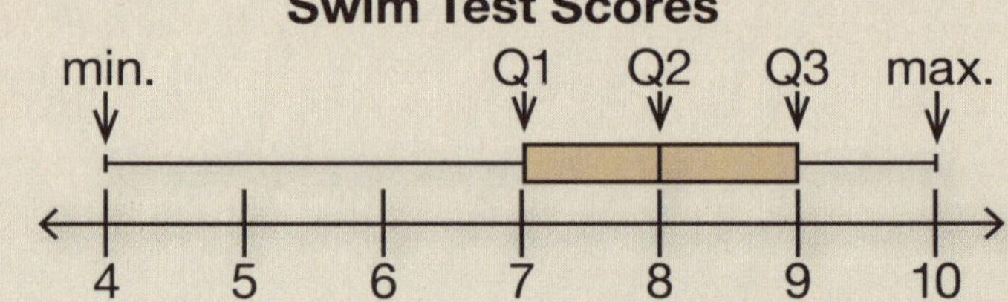